Helping *Parents* Help Their *Children*

Helping *Parents* Help

BRUNNER/MAZEL, Publishers • New York

Their *Children*

Edited by

L. Eugene Arnold, M. Ed., M. D.

Associate Professor of Psychiatry and Pediatrics
Ohio State University

THIRD PRINTING

Copyright © 1978 by L. Eugene Arnold

Published by

BRUNNER/MAZEL, INC.

19 Union Square West, New York, N.Y. 10003

Library of Congress Cataloging in Publication Data

Main entry under title:
Helping parents help their children.

    Includes bibliographies and index.
    1.   Family psychotherapy.   2. Children—Management.   I.   Arnold,
L. Eugene, 1936-
RC488.5.H44   618.9'28'915   77-24520
ISBN 0-87630-146-4

To My Favorite Parent
BILLIE MARIE,
Mother of Our Five
Children

Preface

Parent guidance might be defined as the offering to parents of information, clarification, advice, support, counsel, directives, supportive psychotherapy, or other interaction with a professional helper, with the intention of indirectly helping the child. It recognizes the profound influence that parents have on their children's development and mental health, an influence far greater than that which any professional could exert even with intensive intervention. It presupposes a cooperative working alliance between the parent and the helping professional, both of whom are interested in the welfare of the child.

For decades parent guidance has been recognized as an important constituent of a comprehensive approach to child mental health work. Most of the important schools of thought within psychiatry, clinical psychology, social work and other mental health disciplines have implicitly recognized its importance. Most major child-oriented works in these fields touch on it in some way. Even more impressive has been the voluminous popular literature produced for consumption by parents, in an effort to "administer" parent guidance in a cheap, popular, mass-production fashion. Unfortunately, most such works have fallen short of their high aspirations, possibly because of the problem of individual variability in parents, in children, and in the parent-child "fit" from one family to another.

There still remains a compelling need for professional involvement in parent guidance at a personal, face-to-face level. In this light, it seems strange that to the best of my knowledge there has not yet appeared any volume written for the professional, devoted to intensive, comprehensive consideration of this most important issue. This book attempts to fill part of that gap, to provide both a textbook for the beginning professional and a review or reference book for the established practitioner.

With this in mind, the book treats parent guidance in five dimensions:

1. General principles are first explicated.

2. The insights of various schools of clinical thought and their special contributions to effective parent guidance are elucidated by experts of those schools.

3. The special considerations pertaining to guidance of parents whose children suffer various types of problems are dealt with in appropriately titled chapters.

4. Special considerations in guiding special kinds of parents are discussed.

5. Finally come descriptions of parent guidance by professionals who are not ordinarily considered mental health specialists but who are often called on by parents for advice and counsel.

Some chapters serve double purposes. For example, Adams' chapter 18 discusses both guidance of parents of neurotic children and guidance for parents whose children are in psychotherapy, and Prugh and Eckhardt's chapter 29 presents a child development approach to parent guidance and discusses guidance by physicians, nurses, and other health personnel. Wherever possible, the dual focus of such chapters is expressed in the title, such as "Guiding Parents of 'Neurotic' Children," and "Guidance by Physicians and Nurses: A Developmental Approach."

Though authors were chosen for their expertise in particular topics without any effort at quota representation for the various disciplines involved in parent guidance, I was pleased to note after the dust settled that the book includes contributions from psychiatry, psychology, social work, education, pediatrics, law, and religion. The result, I believe, is a feast of practical guidance ideas that the professional can sample, savor, shun, or select from. Perhaps there are some pearls in the oysters. Bon appétit!

L. Eugene Arnold, M.Ed., M.D.

Contributors

PAUL L. ADAMS, M.D.

Professor of Psychiatry; Vice Chairman, Department of Psychiatry and Behavioral Sciences, University of Louisville.

E. JAMES ANTHONY, M.D.

Blanche F. Ittleson Professor of Child Psychiatry; Director, Eliot Division of Child Psychiatry, Washington University, St. Louis, Missouri.

ALAN S. APPELBAUM, Ph.D.

Assistant Professor, Division of Child and Adolescent Psychiatry, University of Texas Medical Branch, Galveston.

L. EUGENE ARNOLD, M.Ed., M.D.

Associate Professor of Psychiatry and Pediatrics; Director, Division of Child Psychiatry, Ohio State University.

NORMA BARNEBEY, Ph.D.

Clinical Assistant Professor of Psychiatry, Ohio State University.

ELISSA P. BENEDEK, M.D.

Director of Training, Center for Forensic Psychiatry, Ypsilanti, Michigan; Clinical Associate Professor of Psychiatry, University of Michigan, Ann Arbor.

RICHARD S. BENEDEK, J.D.

Washtenaw County Friend of the Court, Ann Arbor, Michigan.

SAUL L. BROWN, M.D.

Director, Department of Psychiatry, Cedars-Sinai Medical Center; Clinical Professor of Psychiatry, University of California at Los Angeles, Neuropsychiatric Institute.

STELLA CHESS, M.D.

Professor of Child Psychiatry, New York University Medical Center.

MORTON CHETHIK, M.S.W.

Associate Professor of Psychiatry; Lecturer in Psychology, University of Michigan.

KATHARINE DIXON COLLEY, M.D.

Assistant Professor of Psychiatry and Pediatrics, Ohio State University.

LLOYD O. ECKHARDT, M.D.

Assistant Professor of Psychiatry and Pediatrics, University of Colorado.

ALBERT ELLIS, Ph.D.

Executive Director, Institute for Advanced Study in Rational Psychotherapy, New York.

IRENE FAST, Ph.D.

Professor of Psychology, University of Michigan.

JULIAN B. FERHOLT, M.D.

Assistant Professor of Pediatrics and Psychiatry, Yale University Child Study Center.

VINCENT J. FONTANA, M.D.

Medical Director and Pediatrician-in-Chief, New York Foundling Hospital Center for Parent and Child Development; Professor of Clinical Pediatrics, New York University College of Medicine.

RICHARD A. GARDNER, M.D.

Associate Clinical Professor of Child Psychiatry, Columbia University; faculty of the William A. White Psychoanalytic Institute.

WILLIAM GLASSER, M.D.

Founder and President of the Institute for Reality Therapy.

WILLIAM HETZNECKER, M.D.

Professor of Psychiatry, Associate Professor of Pediatrics, Temple University, Child Psychiatry Center at St. Christopher's Hospital for Children; member A.P.A. Task Force on School Consultation.

LAWRENCE G. HORNSBY, M.D.

Professor of Psychiatry and Pediatrics, Chief of Child and Adolescent Psychiatry, University of Texas Medical Branch, Galveston.

ENRIQUE HUERTA, M.D.

Assistant Professor of Psychiatry and Pediatrics, Ohio State University.

JOHN JAMES, M.A.

Co-Director, James & James Transactional Analysis Institute.

MURIEL JAMES, Ed.D.

Co-Director, James & James Transactional Analysis Institute, Lafayette, California; co-author of *Born to Win*.

ELISABETH KUBLER-ROSS, M.D.

International consultant in the care of dying patients and their families; author of *On Death and Dying, Death: The Final State of Growth,* and *Questions and Answers on Death and Dying*.

MYRTLE L. LEBOW, M.D.

Director, Centinela Child Guidance Clinic; Assistant Clinical Professor of Child Psychiatry, University of Southern California; Director, Child Therapy Training Program of Los Angeles.

OGDEN LINDSLEY, Ph.D.

Professor of Education, University of Kansas.

MANON McGINNIS, A.C.S.W.

Lecturer in Social Work, Washington University School of Medicine, St. Louis.

THOMAS McGUINESS, M.S.Ed.

Assistant Director of Educator Training Center, Institute for Reality Therapy, Los Angeles.

JOSEPH PACHECO, M.Div.

Pontifical College Josephenum, Columbus, Ohio.

ARLENE PHILLIPS, M.A.

Certified teacher; Director, E.S.E.A. Title III Project "Improving Classroom Climate."

DANE G. PRUGH, M.D.

Professor of Psychiatry and Pediatrics, University of Colorado, Denver.

MARJORIE ROWE, Ph.D.

Assistant Professor of Psychiatry, Ohio State University.

ELIZABETH RUPPERT, M.D.

Professor of Pediatrics, Ohio State University.

ROBERT M. RUSSELL, B.A., B.D.

Pastor, Northminster United Presbyterian Church, Columbus, Ohio.

DANIEL J. SAFER, M.D.

Assistant Professor of Child Psychiatry, Johns Hopkins University; Regional Director of Youth Services, Eastern Community Mental Health Center, Baltimore County, Maryland.

CECILIA SCHNEIDER, M.S.W.

Executive Director of The New York Foundling Hospital.

ERIC SCHOPLER, Ph.D.

Editor, *Journal of Autism and Childhood Schizophrenia*; Director, Division TEACCH, Department of Psychiatry, University of North Carolina at Chapel Hill.

ALBERT J. SOLNIT, M.D.

Sterling Professor of Pediatrics and Psychiatry; Director, Yale University Child Study Center.

ALEXANDER THOMAS, M.D.

Professor of Psychiatry, New York University Medical Center.

HERMAN A. TOLBERT, M.D.

Clinical Instructor in Psychiatry, Ohio State University.

KENNETH W. WATSON, M.S.W.

Assistant Director, Chicago Child Care Society.

Contents

PART III

HELPING PARENTS COPE WITH SPECIFIC PROBLEMS OF CHILDREN

PART IV
GUIDING PARENTS WHO HAVE SPECIFIC PROBLEMS

PART V
GUIDANCE BY PROFESSIONALS OUTSIDE THE
MENTAL HEALTH FIELD

Helping *Parents*
Help Their *Children*

Part I

General Principles of Parent Guidance

Chapter 1

Strategies and Tactics
of Parent Guidance

L. Eugene Arnold

This chapter will outline some general principles of parent guidance preparatory to the more specific chapters and will discuss a few specific issues not important enough to warrant special chapters, but too important to leave out of the book.

APPRECIATING THE PARENTS' POSITION

Since Kanner found it necessary to write *In Defense of Mothers,* we have hopefully progressed beyond a simplistic blaming of parents for children's problems. It may now seem trite to include a reminder of the need to identify with the parents' situation, empathize with their feelings, and assume a cooperative alliance. Nevertheless, it is easy for professionals who care about children to be carried away by their zeal for promoting the child's welfare and forget such practical considerations as:

3

1. The parents have been attempting to improve the child's situation for longer than the professional has.

2. There is usually some reason for the parents' doing whatever they did, no matter how ill-advised it may at first appear.

3. Any successful intervention will require the parents' cooperation.

4. Before the parents can cooperate, they need to understand and accept what is recommended.

5. It is unlikely that any recommendations will be understandable or acceptable if the professional making them does not first understand empathically "where the parent is coming from."

6. Failure to reconnoiter the parents' predicament from the parents' viewpoint will impair the professional's ability to tailor interventions to the specific needs of that family and will expose him as an impractical dispenser of canned advice.

CHOICE OF INTERVENTION

Parent guidance may be seen as a continuum from simple information-giving or education on one end through clarification, permission, advice, persuasion, facilitation, and channeling or manipulation of feelings, to psychotherapeutic tactics. The appropriate choice of intervention for a given situation depends on the problem, circumstances, parents' personality and strengths, what the parents want to "buy," and the particular obstacle to effective parenting. For example, if the main obstacle to effective parenting is lack of information, education may be the best approach. If the lack of information is compounded by erroneous counterproductive beliefs that are not neurotically determined, persuasion may be indicated. (See Chapter 8 for elaborate persuasive techniques.) If the obstacle seems to be interference of friends or relatives in the parents' carrying out what they intuitively see needs to be done, the best intervention may be directive advice, which the parents can use as a buffer between themselves and the criticism. If the parents are overwhelmed by counterproductive feelings, those feelings may need to be manipulated or channeled into a more productive direction. If a parent demonstrates a neurotic conflict interfering with effective parenting, psychotherapeutic tactics may be necessary.

Escalation

When parents present a mixture of types of obstacles to effective parenting and it is not immediately obvious which is the dominant problem, it often makes sense to assume at first the simplest and easiest problem. Any inadequacy of intervention based on this assumption will soon become obvious and the professional can escalate to the next level of complexity. For example, if the professional assumes that the problem is largely ignorance or confusion and begins offering information or clarification, it may soon become obvious verbally or nonverbally that the parent already knows and understands. At this point one might assume that the parent needs directive permission to act, hence the professional gives advice. If the advice does not seem wholeheartedly accepted (judging from both verbal and nonverbal cues), one might then explore the parents' reservations and attempt persuasion. If the parent seems intractable to rational explanation and persuasion, one might be forced to the conclusion that there are parental neurotic conflicts interfering with parental openness to accepting and executing what he needs to do for his child, and the professional would then proceed to psychotherapeutic tactics or exploration. If the problem seems deeper than can be handled by superficial or supportive psychotherapeutic techniques, a psychotherapy contract or referral could then be offered.

Directive Versus Nondirective Guidance

This is actually an artificial dichotomy: Guidance is distinguished from most "therapy" by a more directive, educational emphasis, and within a given case effective guidance tends to utilize both directive and nondirective techniques. However, there is a subgroup of parents seeking guidance who have been exposed to accurate and correct information, sense in some way that they ought to do, and possess the practical resources to implement it, but feel unable to proceed because of some confusion or uncertainty in their own minds that they would like to work out with the help of a professional who is willing to act as a sounding board, reflector, or clarifier. For such parents an approach similar to nondirective therapy can be very helpful. Some might argue that this actually constitutes supportive psychotherapy under the guise of parent guidance. The main distinction is that in guidance the focus is on the parents' difficulty with the children rather than on interpersonal or intrapsychic problems in general.

Even with parents who have other needs, it is possible to take a more or less directive approach. Information can either be flatly stated, allowing parents to draw their own conclusions, or the implications can be spelled out. Advice can be stated 1) in the imperative, or 2) as a request:

"Would you consider . . . ," or 3) as a subjunctive contingency: "If you wished to stop his tantrums, it would be necessary to stop giving in to him each time he has one." The degree of directiveness should be largely dictated by the preference of the parents: Some parents wish merely to get some ideas and then make their own decisions, while other parents feel a desperate need for specific, well-structured direction. Tailoring the style, as well as choice, of intervention to the parents' needs and wishes relates to the idea of guidance as nurture, developed in Chapter 14.

The Child as Ticket of Admission

Some parents bring their children to a mental health professional as a way of getting such help for themselves when they would be embarrassed to seek it directly. Such parents will often indicate their true wish during the first interview by some statement such as, "Sometimes I think it's mostly my problem," or "Do you think it's me?" or "I think I need somebody to talk with myself." Such statements need to be explored more fully without jumping to a conclusion prematurely that psychotherapy is indicated for the parent. Sometimes such statements are merely reflections of the popular misconception that if a child is having a problem, his parent must be disturbed, or at least mismanaging him. When it turns out that the parent does indeed wish and need psychotherapy or marital counseling, this statement can usually be elicited from the parent, who can then be offered assistance in finding an appropriate resource if such therapy cannot be offered by the professional doing the current interview.

THE PROFESSIONAL AS A CONSULTANT TO THE PARENT

In many situations the guidance relationship closely resembles a consultative relationship such as might occur between two professionals, one of whom seeks consultation on a difficult problem from another professional with special expertise. *An effective parent is a child's most important "therapist."* By sheer length and frequency of contact, an effective parent gives his child more noncontingent approval than Carl Rogers could, does more interpreting, confronting and clarifying than Freud could, antithesizes more games than Muriel James could, corrects more internal sentences than Albert Ellis could, and assists with more reality planning than William Glasser could. The therapeutic role of the parent has even been recognized and legitimized in the filial therapy approach (Chapter 11). In many ways, therefore, the professional involved in parent guidance can see himself as a consultant and employ many of the same techniques and tactics employed in other consulting relationships. Among these, of course, are clarification, goal definition, prioritization, support, permission giving, endorsement, cautioning, presenting alternatives, and advising.

Theme-Interference Reduction

Caplan's (1964) theme-interference-reduction technique of client-centered case consultation seems particularly applicable to parent guidance. It is suitable for situations where the consultee's (parent's) ability to function effectively in the best interest of his client or patient (child) is impaired by some recurring theme or "hangup" from the consultee's (parent's) own past. This often involves a fallacious conscious or unconscious premise, such as "masturbating will cause one's mother to die." The latter could arise from a temporal coincidence in the consultee's life which resulted in his erroneously feeling guilty that he had caused his mother's death by masturbating. This theme then interferes with the consultee's ability to deal objectively with masturbation by his client (child). The consultant helps the consultee to resolve the theme by focusing on the situation with the consultee's client or child rather than on the consultee's own intrapsychic problem. If successful, the consultee is psychologically free to deal more effectively with similar problems in the future, even though he has not been directly engaged in psychotherapy.

Unlabeled examples of the application of such a technique appear in Chapter 28 as applied to very disturbed parents. The technique can also be appropriate for less disturbed parents, particularly where they come into the guidance situation with a contract to get help only in dealing with their children's problems, not with their own. In some situations, of course, it may be appropriate to identify the interfering theme from the parent's past and deal with it directly. This could occur where there is an implicit contract for occasional brief psychotherapy of the parent, where the parent would be agreeable to negotiating a contract for psychotherapy of specific problems that come to light, or where there is a contract to treat the parent-child relationship.

A DERMATOLOGICAL AXIOM OF GUIDANCE

As applied to parent guidance, the dermatological axiom "If it is dry, wet it; if it is wet, dry it; if it itches, irritate it; if it is irritated, soothe it," might also be summarized as "Swim against the current." Chapter 4 describes well the importance of a balanced, middle-of-the-road parental stance. The dermatological axiom assumes the parents who need help in managing their children may be deviating from the golden mean in some way. It is then up to the professional to help the parents identify in what way they are deviating and redirect them towards a balanced approach—for that individual child. For example, the overprotective, smothering parent could be directed to nurture the child's autonomy and self-confidence; the aloof, distant parent who is afraid of spoiling the child can be instructed to give hugs and kisses for good performance. The harsh, punitive parent can be advised, "You can lead a horse to water, but you can't make him drink," while the overpermissive, vacillating parent can be advised, "Spare the rod and spoil the child."

This axiom appears deceptively simple and obvious, but its execution can be complicated and taxing. If the parents could easily respond to simple direct prescriptions like, "Be firm," they might not be in the professional's office, for such advice abounds at the neighborhood coffee klatch, lunch counter, or beauty shop. Of course, some parents are merely looking for permission to do what they already want to do but need authoritative approval for, and some others will act on advice from an authoritative professional after rejecting the same advice from peers, or will act on advice they are paying for after rejecting the same advice when it was too "cheap." In most cases, though, the challenge for the professional is to find a way of tactfully making the recommendations egosyntonic, or at least acceptable.

Making Recommendations Egosyntonic

If the professional is to formulate recommendations that are palatable and feasible for the parent, he needs to *identify with the parents'* situation, feelings, and previous efforts at managing the problem. In this process he will discover with most parents areas of parenting strength that can be used as a basis for explaining the new ideas. These new ideas need to be worded as much as possible in the *coinage learned from the parents* in the interview. Often the new recommendations can be formulated as *expansions or elaborations of the preexisting parental tendencies,* including even tendencies which, as originally presented to the professional, appear destructive or ill-advised. Here are three examples, facetiously overstated to make the point:

1. To an overprotective, overdirective, smothering parent one might say, "I've noticed that you have a great devotion to your child and have spared no expense of time or energy to do a good job of making

sure he receives adequate care and supervision. I am glad to see that you're such dedicated parents, because he is now moving into a stage of his development where you will need to do some additional things for him. You will now need to *make sure that he learns to do things by himself.* For example, now that he is 12 years old, you need to see to it that he dresses himself without any assistance from you. You need to shut the door and not do anything at all to help him until he finishes dressing and comes out."

In cases where it is doubtful the parents will be able to leave the door shut without doing anything, they can be given diversionary assignments that do not impinge on the child's breathing space, such as, "While he is dressing, I have an important job for you. I would like you to time how long it takes him to get dressed by himself and make a graph charting his increased speed from day to day. It is important that you don't tell him about this graph or about how long it took him, but bring it to me at your next appointment." (Note that this charting of progress has a different function from a behavior modification chart, which should be done with the child.)

2. To a harsh, angry, punitive parent one may say: "I can see that you have taken your parental responsibility seriously and have gone the extra mile in attempting to stop your child's misbehavior. You have demonstrated heroic feats of punishment. It seems obvious that you have done your part. No one at this point could blame you if you gave up attempting to discipline this ungrateful wretch who refuses to respond to your punishment. There is really no point in you continuing to waste your valuable energy and time punishing him. Let him take the consequences for his own behavior at school and with the other kids, and with the police if necessary. He will have to learn the hard way."

3. To a perfectionistic, overcoercive parent one might say, "I can see that you're working really hard to do as good a job as possible of raising your child. You obviously want the best for him and are willing to do anything to help him become a success. In order for him to be a success as an adult, one of his needs at this point in his development is for some goof-off time, at least an hour a day on weekdays and a half-day on weekends. This needs to be time he can waste or kill or have some kind of fun with friends. You will need to make sure that he does not plan any work for this time or undertake projects that will be very demanding or stressful in terms of achievement or success. He himself may not understand the importance of having such goof-off time, so it will be up to you as his parent to *make sure that he does goof off.*

REDEFINING THE PROBLEM

Parents who come for help usually do so because they have defined a problem which they feel unable to deal with. Part of the professional's job is to help the parents redefine the problem in terms that they can feel less helpless about, can live better with, or can feel more compatible with the child about. For example, the parent can be helped to see that the child's stealing or vandalism is really an acting out of depression secondary to the death of his beloved grandparent or the moving away of his best friend. Such a redefinition clarifies the potentials for effective action. Rather than seeing the child's problems as a moral failure requiring a stern disciplinary approach and reflecting on the parent's adequacy, the parent can support and empathize with the child while setting firm limits on the acting out. Another example of redefinition can be found in Chapter 17.

The Parent as an Innocent Bystander

One productive interface between individual therapy with the child and parent guidance is the judicious use of knowledge of the child's psychodynamics to give the parent insight that he is not wholly responsible for all the child's problems. Many parents are burdened with the assumption that any problems manifested by the child are a result of some parental mishandling or are seen as such by the child. Such a parent may have a hard time realizing, without professional assistance, that the child's autonomous mental life can occasionally manifest problems that have nothing to do with the parent. The child may even engage in activity apparently hostile towards the parent as a convenient means of acting out or resolving a problem that basically has little or nothing to do with the parent and is not accompanied by any real hostility for the parent. It is important to help parents realize at such times that there is "nothing personal" in the child's attitude or behavior. This can then free the parent to be more objectively empathic and helpful to the child. Two examples of this approach are mentioned in the case illustration in Chapter 25. Those particular examples pertain to a stepparent, but the same thing can happen with a natural parent.

Confidentiality

Such sharing with the parents of information gained individually with the child carries the risk of impairing the child's confidence and trust in the therapist and requires careful preparation. Some therapists, such as Gardner, claim that there is no confidentiality from parents with children below the age of 10 and invite the parent to sit in on psychotherapy. However, for the majority of therapists there is some assumption of confidentiality, and it needs to be explained carefully to the child ahead of time what would be shared with the parents and why. A good way to handle such sharing of information would be to encourage the child to tell the parents himself in a conjoint session.

TREATING THE PARENT-CHILD RELATIONSHIP

Chethick (1976) advocates selective use with parents of a *form of sector psychotherapy,* which he calls treatment of the parent-child relationship. This is clearly psychotherapy within the guidance context. It is insight-oriented and deals with unconscious conflict of the parent or unconscious unions between parent and child. It is restricted in scope and distinguished from total treatment by recurring intrusion of the question, "How has this material (e.g., the struggle you had with your mother) influenced what goes on between you and your child now?" Interpretations are always related to the effect that the parents' unconscious conflicts have had on the relationship with the child. This approach assumes a rather intense involvement of the parent with a mental health professional and is invoked only as the need arises—with problems that cannot be dealt with by the advice-information approach. It is only practical for parents with enough psychological strength to benefit from limited insight therapy.

Debunking Myths

The professional is often called on to dispel some popular notions which may be burdening the parent-child relationship and distorting the parents' otherwise reasonable efforts to help their children. One of the foremost of these is that all children in the family should be treated the same. Not only is this impossible to achieve in most cases, but even if it were possible, it would not be good. The best development of the child's individual personality and potential can be facilitated by a parent's recognizing and valuing the individual, different assets of each child.

Other popular notions or unconscious assumptions the professional may need to correct include: 1) There's one bad egg in every nest—or black sheep in every family, or bad apple in every barrel—that needs to be discarded. 2) Children are all alike at birth—or boys are all alike, or girls are all alike. 3) When children are small, they tramp on your toes; when they grow up, they tramp on your heart. 4) All adolescents rebel violently or destructively. 5) Any adolescent who rebels is abnormal. 6) Children should not get angry with their parents. 7) Parents should not get angry with their children. 8) Children should approve of the way their parents are raising them. Some of these assumptions would fit the definition of irrational beliefs in Chapter 8.

THE EXPENDABLE PROFESSIONAL

As distasteful as it may seem, the professional assisting a family is expendable in the long-term welfare of both parents and children. It is the parents' relationship with the child that is essential for the child's mental health, not the professional's relationship with the child, or even the professional's relationship with the parents. Consequently, an effective professional may at times need to let himself be "used" in ways which may at first appear to constitute a failure of the guidance or therapy effort, but which on closer examination show a good result for the parent-child relationship.

For example, parent or child may at times project a problem onto the therapist and then abruptly terminate therapy. The crucial question is not whether the professional has been scapegoated, but whether there is a lasting benefit from the process. A more common application of the professional's expendability is the decision about what parents should be told in the child's presence.

What to Tell Parents in Front of the Child

The concept of professional expendability as compared to parental permanence has some practical implications for the timing and situation of advice-giving. The strategy is to make the parents look as good or as blameless to the child as possible in order to promote a more harmonious parent-child relationship and to facilitate the ease of the parents' functioning effectively with the child. To this end, I have found the following twofold axiom helpful:

> 1. *Be the Heavy.* When advising the parents to do something the child will probably not like, such as being firmer, stricter, or tougher, inflicting a punishment, or depriving the child of something pleasant but harmful (such as excessive television time or too much junk food), *tell them in front of the child to crack down.*
> This lets them off the hook in one way and hooks them into carrying out the recommendations in another way. It allows them to avoid much of the negative reaction of the child by letting the professional "play the heavy," making them do what the child finds unpleasant. This makes it much easier for the parent, particularly an ambivalent or guilt-ridden one, to carry out things with which

he agrees but which he would find very difficult if he had to shoulder the complete responsibility in facing the child over the issue. At the same time, when it is explained that cracking down is necessary for the child's welfare and that the parent will need to do it if he really cares about the child, the parent is put in a therapeutic bind: He cannot escape unpleasantness by ignoring the unpleasant recommendation. If he does not carry out the unpleasant recommendation, he will still be left with the unpleasant realization that he has failed to carry out something which his child knows he was supposed to have done for the child's benefit.

2. *Be Santa's Secret Helper.* When advising the parents to do *something that the child will probably find pleasant,* such as relaxing restrictions, spending more time with him, or getting him some desired object that seems necessary for peer acceptance, *tell them privately, out of the child's hearing.*

This will allow the parents to take full credit for the pleasant changes and does not reflect adversely on them for neglecting to carry out one or another "positive" recommendations. There is no need for the child to know about the recommendations not acted on, but only about the positive moves that the parents made. If they had been given these recommendations in front of the child, the child would be inclined to hold them accountable in such a way that the changes would not really be an indication of their love but something they had to do, and any recommendations not carried out would be a source of additional friction in the parent-child relationship.

An exception to this axiom would be the case of a disturbed parent who is so unreasonable that it is necessary for the reality testing of the child to hear that another adult thinks his parents' strictures are unreasonable and unusual. For more about special considerations in dealing with very disturbed parents, see Chapter 22.

GIVING PERMISSION FOR MORE EFFECTIVE PARENTING

Parents who seek professional help sometimes know what they should do and want in some way to do it, but are paralyzed by internal or external inhibitions. External inhibitions may include conflicting advice or pressure from relatives, friends, or neighbors. Internal inhibitions can arise from trying too hard, identifying too strongly with the child, or having feelings of guilt or anxiety. Such feelings can be triggered by the thought of doing things that either seem unfair or may elicit from the child a negative reaction, possibly including accusations that the parent does not love the child. Such parents need permission to exercise their own good judgment.

For the more severely inhibited parents, effective permission from the professional may paradoxically need to take the form of imperative directiveness. The imperative acts as an antidote or neutralizer for the inhibiting counter-imperative, thereby freeing the parent to act independently. Thus, the mother who is afraid to say "no" to a three-year-old tyrant because she would be criticized by the doting grandmother can now quote the professional's "orders" that she has to do so. Furthermore, in her own mind, she has the professional's fantasied disapproval for failing to say "no" counterbalancing the grandmother's disapproval for saying it. If she is afraid to say "no" because she would feel guilty or threatened if the child throws tantrums in response, she can now assuage her guilt with the thought that she is merely carrying out the orders of an expert. Furthermore, she has the threat of guilt for saying "no" counterbalanced by a threat of guilt for failing to say no after having been directed to.

Manipulating and Channeling Parental Feelings

In the preceding example an inhibiting or paralyzing feeling of the parent was neutralized or mitigated by professional intervention. In addition, the opportunity sometimes arises to channel apparently destructive feelings into a more constructive direction. Guilt is one of the most common feelings presenting this kind of opportunity. For example, if the mother who found it hard to say "no" to her three-year-old tyrant because of her own guilty feelings could not respond to an effort at simple neutralization of the guilt, the guilt might be redirected. Thus: "Your child needs for you to set limits on him at this time. He has a right to that. It is your parental duty and responsibility. If you continue to give in to him, you will warp his personality and rob him of the chance for normal psychological development." An example of an attempt to rechannel the rage of a punitive parent is given above under "Making Recommendations Egosyntonic." Another example of attempting to rechannel guilt can be found in Chapter 20.

MODELING THE PARENTAL ROLE

At times the professional needs to model appropriate interpersonal adult-child and parent-child behavior. This may be particularly important where the parent has not been exposed to appropriate adult models in his own childhood. When the professional has occasion to deal directly with the child in the presence of the parent, he will have an opportunity to model such things as respect for the child's feelings and autonomy, kind but firm limit setting, positive reinforcement, accentuating the positive, and expectation of improvement and cooperation. Even where the professional does not directly contact the child in the parents' presence, there is still an opportunity to model appropriate parental behavior because for many parents the professional-parent relationship recapitulates emotionally the parent-child relationship. Though we might wish for and attempt a more collaborative relationship, some parents wish for the child-to-parent paradigm in their relationship with the professional, and this may be the most productive relationship they are capable of at that point in their development. The professional can make this experience most useful for the parent by modeling in his relations with the parent the kind of caring, respect, understanding, and, if necessary, limit setting he would wish the parent to show to the child.

Billiard Ball Limit Setting

Limit setting is one of the foremost problem areas for modern parents. Some parents need only permission to proceed or absolution from guilt for proceeding. Others need more directive support, such as exemplified under "Channeling of Feelings."

For some parents, their inability to set limits on children is a manifestation of their inability to set limits on themselves and their own mpulses, whch may be related to lack of exposure in their own rearing to limits that they could internalize. In such cases, setting limits on the parents (e.g., in such matters as keeping appointment times, carrying out of "homework" assignments between appointments, or giving proper doses of medication) may result in an improved ability of the parents to set limits on their children. This situation is analogous to the impact being transmitted to the last billiard ball in a line when the first one is struck. This is not a novel idea in dealing with children's mental health problems: Many clinicians have observed that a depressed child of a depressed parent will "spontaneously" improve when the parent's depression is effectively treated, even if the child himself is not directly treated.

Loaning an Ego

One reason a parent may find such limit setting by a professional helpful is similar to one of the reasons children find parental limit setting helpful: It provides some structure, certainty, and security. This kind of "loaning" ego structure can also be helpful to disorganized or impulsive parents in matters other than limit setting. Examples would be helping them stop and consider alternatives before acting, helping them clarify and foresee consequences of a proposed change in the child's school, and helping them define what other resources they need to call on. Such concrete, specific assistance is especially important for the very disturbed or abusing parent, and more elaborate discussion can be found in Chapters 22 and 28, including the concept of being a parent to the parent.

MAKING PARENTS EXPERT PUNISHERS

Punishment has had a bad press, but any professional who attempts to deny its existence or occasional necessity is simply out of touch with the realities confronting the parents in the trenches. There are several things the professional can do to help parents develop the most humane and effective behavioral management:

Clarifying the Purpose of Punishment

Surprisingly, many parents are not really sure why they are punishing. They may have some vague sense of righteousness or that they should punish for given infractions in order to be a good parent, or that they should not "let the child get away with it." Such fuzziness often leads to a situation where the parent becomes intent on seeing evidence that the child is hurt, such as crying or looking unhappy. Most parents are willing, when it is explained to them, to accept that the goal of punishment is to prevent the child from repeating the same misbehavior. This can free them to use an operational criterion for the effectiveness of punishment—whether it prevents a recurrence of the behavior—without the need to worry about whether the punishment was "hard enough." They can then allow the child to put on a brave front and refuse to cry or otherwise assert face-saving autonomy.

Efficiency of Punishment

It is essential that the parent not waste his valuable child-raising energy on inefficient approaches to behavioral management. Accordingly, he needs to know:

    1. Though punishment is usually effective in curbing undesired behavior, it is usually rather inefficient, even ineffective, for eliciting desired behavior. Positive reinforcement (see Chapter 7) is usually much more effective to elicit desired behavior. "You can lead a

horse to water and stop him from drinking but you can't make him drink; he has to want to drink." Positive reinforcement fosters the desire to drink.

2. Punishment, especially corporal punishment, tends to lose its effectiveness when repeated. Therefore, punishment should be treated as a valuable commodity, spent sparingly for objectives deemed worth the price.

Save the Big Guns for the Big Game

Most parents will agree on the need for prioritization of misbehaviors to be stamped out. Further, they will usually agree that the top of the list should include issues of health, safety, and rights of others, including destruction of property. Ordinarily, corporal punishment should be reserved for these "big three"—although even these three can be dealt with by noncorporal punishment in many cases.

Finding What Works

Punishment, like any other aspect of child raising, needs to be individualized to the child's needs. Some children may respond only to corporal punishment, whereas other children may respond well to a mild scolding (and may not respond at all to corporal punishment!). Finding the right punishment for an individual child is even more important than finding the right reinforcer for a positive reinforcement paradigm. A positive reinforcement paradigm without an effective reinforcer tends to collapse of its own weight, doing little harm even though it also did no good. However, a punishment paradigm with an ineffective punishment tends to continue lurching along, possibly even gaining momentum, with destructive consequences. This is what makes the following question so important.

Popping the Unfair Question

An elementary but loaded question shat should be asked every parent who seems to be engaging in a lot of punishment is, "Is it working?" If he answers "yes," he should then be asked why he needs to do it so often if it is really working. When he admits that it is not working, he should be asked, "Then why do you keep doing it if it is not working?" Only after the parent has been nudged out of the punishment rut can he begin to consider other options.

Enriching the Variety of Punishment

Many parents equate punishment with corporal punishment (although occasionally a parent will use "punishment" to mean any noncorporal punishment, making whipping or spanking a special category). Many parents are quite willing to try other punishments once they have been apprised of them: deprivation, restriction of activity, sending the child to his room or otherwise banishing him from adult company, fining him part of his allowance, or an "active" punishment such as paying for what he destroyed or doing something nice for a person that he hit or kicked. Having a variety of punishments at the parents' disposal helps to prevent development of "tolerance" and escalation of doses. It also tends to facilitate the parent's giving more thought to the punishment and the need for it rather than reflexively dispensing the same timeworn punishment repeatedly.

Keeping It Safe

Parents who find it necessary to resort to corporal punishment need to be apprised of some elementary safety facts: 1) a rigid object such as a hard paddle carries the risk of fat embolism, with some cases of death reported. 2) Shaking the child, even though it may appear more humane than whipping, is actually more dangerous, carrying the risk of subdural hematomata. 3) The head is off limits for any corporal punishment. Even an innocuous-appearing slap on the cheek may land by mistake on the ear and rupture the tympanic membrane.

Enlisting the Child's Cooperation in the Punishment

Surprisingly few parents seem to think of the very effective ploy with older children of asking them to *choose a punishment* that will help them remember not to repeat the offense, or of offering them a *choice between two punishments*. Perhaps they feel it is "not right" to ask the child to turn on himself by cooperating with the punishment or cannot believe that the child would do it.

Actually, most children, at least those with some basic health in the parent-child relationship, welcome the opportunity to exert some control over their own fate, and are sometimes harder on themselves than the parents would be. Even when they choose an apparently milder punishment, it tends to be more effective than a more severe one unilaterally imposed by the parent: The child at this point has a vested interest in making sure that the punishment is "effective," defined as preventing a recurrence of the offense. The success of this approach naturally depends on the parent's having accepted the premise that the sole objective of punishment is to prevent recurrence of the misbehavior, not to dispense justice, hurt the child, or take revenge.

A variant of offering the child two choices would be to offer him an alternate means of *"working off"* *the punishment.* For example, if his punishment is not being allowed to ride his bicycle for a week, he could have that time reduced by one day for each time he goes to bed or does the dishes without being reminded. Again, this gives the child a feeling of some control over his fate, diminishing his negative reaction to the punishment, and gives him a vested interest in demonstrating to the parent that this approach is more effective than unmitigated punishment. Some parents may object to letting the child off so easy or may fear that reducing the punishment would be a form of inconsistency. They can be reminded that even hardened criminals get "time off for good behavior."

THROWING THE BOOK AT THEM

The glut of books advising parents how to handle their children, some with divergent or conflicting messages, reminds one of the adage that when there is more than one treatment of a disorder, none of them is 100% effective. One of the problems with parents getting help from the kind of canned advice that is feasible to put into books arises from a diabolical synergism of these facts: 1) No two parents or two children are exactly alike; hence the guidance needs of no two families are identical. 2) For each child there is a golden mean of balanced parenting. Deviations that an author might wish to modulate can be in either direction, excess or deficit, on many variables. 3) An author must write for the whole spectrum of potential readers. Anticipating the readership of overcoercive, punitive parents, he may appeal for respecting the child's personality and autonomy, while in another place he exhorts the vacillating overpermissive, oversubmissive parent to be firm and consistent. 4) People tend to hear, see, and remember selectively in line with their preexisting prejudices.

Therefore, the punitive, overdirective parent will tend to remember the part about being firm and consistent (translated "harsh and rigid") and forget the part about respecting the child's autonomy and personality, while the overpermissive, oversubmissive parent will tend to remember the part about respecting the child's personality (translated "let him do what he wants") and forget the part about being firm and consistent. Thus, *any parental pathology* that may be present *can be reinforced* by reading objectively valid books that were written with good intentions *unless there is an opportunity for discussion* with another person.

Notwithstanding these drawbacks of solitary parental reading, it sometimes is useful as an economy measure to ask a parent to read something in preparation for the next guidance session, when there will be an opportunity to correct any misinterpretations, restate the overlooked points, and tone down the exaggerated conclusions. It would be irresponsible to recommend a book or article to a parent without setting up another appointment to discuss it. The discussion might be in a group or individually.

One way in which the professional can model appropriate parental behavior is to demonstrate a recognition of the limits of his own abilities and of the contract he has with the parent. Part of the professional's job is to refer the parent to appropriate resources for services which he himself may not be able to offer: financial assistance, education, legal help, temporary placement of children, moral guidance, psychotherapy, etc.

Recommending Therapy for the Parent

One of the most difficult referrals to make (or contracts to renegotiate) is when it becomes obvious that a parent needs psychotherapy in addition to guidance. Though some parents may request psychotherapy, others may volunteer resistance to the idea. Some preliminary work will then be necessary to prepare the parent for the recommendation of psychotherapy.

It is important to find some point of common agreement that provides a rationale for the recommendation. For example, a parent, while focusing on the child's problems, may complain, "He gets on my nerves." The professional can empathize with this predicament and use it as a basis to suggest that the parent may understandably by this time be so frazzled from the wear and tear of this difficult child that he deserves some help in repairing his frazzled nerves and strengthening them to withstand the child's abuse. Another point of agreement could be the desire to help the child. One could point out how much better the parent will be able to meet the child's needs after he has done something for his own depression or anxiety. This allows the parent to use the rationale that he is doing it for the child rather than because he really needs it himself. This ploy could backfire if the parent is so resentful of the trouble caused by the child that he sees this suggestion as one more imposition on him by the child. For such a parent, it may be more helpful to emphasize the parent's own right to have something for himself, including therapy, rather than devoting all resources to the child.

Gradualism Guiding the Quest

Sometimes the problem is not convincing parents to accept another service, but rather restraining an impatient or desperate quest, perhaps in hopes of a quick cure.

One of the hardest ideas to sell many parents is the expectation that *improvement will come in small increments* and perhaps erratically, two steps forward and one back, but with definite improvement over a long period of time. It may help to point out to them that a normal child takes nearly two decades to develop into a normally functioning adult with good impulse control, mature judgment, adequate social skills, and respect for the rights of others. Therefore, they should not get discouraged if a deviant child takes several years to show increased maturity in these areas. There are two aspects to this issue: 1) It is not fair to compare a six-year-old's behavior, judgment, and considerateness to adult standards. 2) It is not fair to expect a six-year-old who is functioning like a four-year-old to accomplish in two days what it took two years for the normal six-year-old to accomplish. Childhood is a disorder that is not easily or quickly cured, but time is on the side of those who can rejoice in small gains.

REFERENCES

CAPLAN, G.: *Principles of Preventive Psychiatry.* New York: Basic Books, 1964.
CHETHICK, M.: Work with parents: Treatment of the parent-child relationship. *J. Amer. Acad. Child Psychiatry,* 15:453-463, 1976.
KANNER, L.: *In Defense of Mothers.* Springfield, Illinois: Charles C Thomas, 1941.

Chapter 2

Functions, Tasks, and Stresses of Parenting: Implications for Guidance

Saul L. Brown

WHY EMPHASIZE THE "STRESSES" OF PARENTING?

Far too frequently this most fundamental of all humanizing experience begins in casual and even callow ways. The entire parenting process, so intricate and so much in need of profound and careful reflection, is largely taken for granted. Politicians, leading citizens, religious leaders, physicians, philosophers, economists and even most educators need to be prodded to acknowledge its importance—as if they have not themselves experienced the stresses of raising or having been children. A certain naïveté and magical thinking underlie our societal assumption that a reasonable and humanistic society of adults can evolve in the absence of a massive social commitment to helping parents rear their children. Far too many marriages become depleted of positive feelings, and far too many children become troubled and even disturbed because parents are going it alone. The more directly we face the realization that parenting is stressful, the greater the likelihood of achieving a humanistic society.

Another reason for dwelling on stresses of parenting has to do with the attitudes of some professionals who in their work with children must also deal with parents. Hopefully, clinicians who are in a position to help guide parents have themselves experienced at least some phases of parenthood, or have lived very close to friends or relatives who are struggling with that role. At the risk of offending some professional colleagues, I would assert that guiding parents without having been a parent oneself is a little like coaching swimmers without having ever been in the water. It's possible, but stresses need to have been experienced in some reasonably close approximation if one is genuinely to empathize with the stress others experience. I have heard too often the ring of criticism and judgment and sometimes derision in the voices of beginning clinicians when discussing the parents of a child who is under their treatment. Frequently I have felt compelled to remind trainees just how stressful parenting is. I have learned that it usually requires about two years of tactful but firm reminding for genuine tolerance to evolve. Of course, trainees learn best if their mentors practice what they preach!

PARENTING IN THE DEVELOPMENTAL CYCLE OF FAMILIES

In order to give depth to understanding the functions of parenting, the notion of developmental cycles of families is essential. One needs to keep in mind several people all at once, each going through some kind of developmental change. It is tempting to pretend to one's clinical self when working with a single child that the various members of the family, namely the parents and grandparents and the siblings, are all in some kind of steady state, unchanging and stable, while the child we are treating or observing is independently moving along through a succession of developmental phases. Keeping track of developmental changes in several people all at once and in the family group as an entity becomes a very challenging task.

Comprehending individual psychic functions within the family group is possible and even exciting if one can work in an oscillating fashion, shifting focus back and forth between the group process and the reactions of each individual. Adding historical and development dimensions to this fills out the notion of a *developmental cycle of families* and brings us closer to comprehending the need as well as the stresses both of parents and of children. Because of the transactional and interactional frame of reference inherent in the notion of a developmental cycle of families, one then becomes accustomed to thinking in multicausal and reciprocal terms about what happens to *all* the people in a family.

Conceptualizing a Family Developmental Task Cycle

In order to think about a developmental cycle of families, it seems easiest to define a series of phases, each with a major developmental task. This follows the model established by Erikson, who defined a sequence of psychosocial tasks necessary for integrated individual development (Erikson, 1950). Based on the work of Pollak (1965), Winnicott (1969), Benedek and Anthony (1970), and Brown (1973), I have found the following family developmental phases useful to consider:

1. Establishing Basic Commitment.
2. Creating a System for Mutual Nurturance.
3. Defining Mechanisms for Mutual Encouragement of Individuation and Autonomy.
4. Facilitating Ego Mastery.

(For a discussion of intrapsychic development of parents from their own childhood, see Chapter 28.)

TASK 1: ESTABLISHING BASIC COMMITMENT

This developmental task requires a relative disconnection by both partners from their families of origin. Also, it requires a buffering by both partners of various engrossing involvements with careers, old friendships, and recreational activities. Unless there is a crystallization of commitment to each other which is relatively exclusive of various other interpersonal commitments and which takes some precedence over other activities, the newly formed marital dyad will not be able to provide consistently integrative parenthood in the next phase. Instead, a great potential for divisiveness, schisms, misalliances, splitting, and distortion of the oedipal experience will occur as the children are born, grow and introduce new and ever more complex emotional vectors into the family system. Clearly, this first developmental task has meaning only when two people intend to have a family together. In those situations where fathers are transients or where a communal environment provides several potential fathering persons, this first phase can only be a symbolic one. What the absence of a stable marital dyad does to the psychic organization of children is a subject beyond the limits of this chapter.

TASK 2: CREATING A SYSTEM FOR MUTUAL NURTURANCE

That families need to nurture children biologically is obvious. Beyond that, however, the family system needs to be one in which everyone provides *emotional* nurturance to everyone else. I believe this occurs best when, in the preceding phase, a vital and genuine commitment to the marriage has occurred. Almost of necessity, a successful basic commitment includes early interpersonal and emotional structures for mutual nurturing of each spouse by the other. Flowing out of this is an environment that invites nurturing attitudes *from* each child as well as providing these *to* each child. This is a spiral phenomenon (see Chapter 5). As each receives nurturance from the other, each develops greater capacity for providing nurturance. Mutual support and emotional warmth prevail. What is of core importance in the preceding formulation is the issue of *mutuality* and *reciprocity*. Infants warm the hearts of parents. Older children do so in ever more subtle ways. Siblings can be warm and supportive to each other when parents expect them to be and when parents do not play them off against each other or have favorites, or establish alliances with one or another child in order to fight each other.

The stresses upon parents around establishing and sustaining a mutually nurturing environment are often formidable: physical fatigue, money problems, physical ill health, emotional conflicts within one or the other parent, unresolved conflicts with in-laws (grandparents), marital conflicts between the parents, neighborhood or environmental problems, problems with aloneness or social isolation, feelings of uncertainty in responding to children's needs, and so forth. When any of these is occurring in a powerful way, the system for mutual nurturance is subject to disruption; once such disruption occurs, there is a strong tendency for interpersonal tension to reverberate throughout the family system and for the disruption to escalate. Maintaining integration of positive nurturing attitudes in the face of complex and conflictful feelings is a primary functional responsibility of parenthood.

Repairing the Nurturing System

When disruptions of the mutual nurturing system occur, we need to help each person in the family realize and express angry, anixous, guilty, or sad feelings so that positive nurturing attitudes can reemerge. I do not view myself or other professionals as fueling machines feeding positive feelings into a family; rather I believe we need to be facilitators, who help the family members experience and express their nurturing, positive feeling attachments *to each other*. Naturally, our own emotional warmth helps, but we cannot transpose quanta of nurturance into a family.

Nevertheless, there are some strong implications for clinical practice. Unless clinicians comprehend the functional need of families along the lines I have defined, the clinical response to parental stress early in the family cycle tends to be atomistic. That is, one or another of the family members may become involved in a therapeutic program when what is needed *first* is a mobilization of the intrafamilial mutual nurturance system. Clinical help provided in the sequence that I am suggesting requires considerable clinician flexibility, comprehension of interpersonal and systems phenomonology, a sensitivity to individual psychodynamics, and a strong degree of empathy for people called parents.

TASK 3: DEFINING MECHANISMS FOR MUTUAL ENCOURAGEMENT OF
INDIVIDUATION AND AUTONOMY

Margaret Mahler (1975) has clarified the developmental tasks faced *jointly* by mother and infant in facilitating an infant's evolving autonomy. Her focus is upon mother with infant or toddler. I will place that dyadic process into the intrafamilial context, emphasizing interweaving factors which make for the vitality of parenting.

Given reasonably positive outside environmental circumstances and assuming a fairly successful resolution of the first two developmental phases, the intrafamilial environment is ripe for encouragement of genuine emotional autonomy in each of the family members. If *mutual* nurturance has become a prevailing intrafamilial attitude, and mechanisms for implementing it exist in the family, warm encouragement of each person's individuation may very well follow. This does not occur automatically, however, since encouraging individuation in each other requires complex intrapsychic and interpersonal processes.

Inevitably, each person's exploration of independence produces stress upon other members of a group. Each new self-assertion dislocates comfortable group equilibrium to some degree. The phenomenon of *resistance to developmental change* in a family is ever present as individuation proceeds in husband, wife, child no. 1, child no. 2, child no. 3, and so on. Small interactional crises occur, sometimes from day to day, as the complexity of the family's life grows. However, if there is a basic commitment to each other in the marriage, each partner develops ever more responsive internal mechanisms for maintaining deep emotional connection to the other even as each maintains appropriate degrees of independence and defines "ego boundaries."

Cultural systems that are tradition-bound simplify this process although there are penalties to be paid. Rigid rules about what each can do and cannot do in a marriage reduce uncertainty, especially if both partners understand the rules and stick to them. A viable basic commitment may occur but it may be somewhat constricting, especially if it is authoritarian in nature. When that occurs, autonomy becomes a scarce commodity, allocated to some family members but not to others.

The looser and more open-ended style of present-day mating complicates the process of establishing and maintaining marital attachment enormously. The rules keep shifting as social and marital roles undergo major redefinition. Powerful social forces like Women's Liberation, women's search for careers outside the home, frank sexuality, and prominently displayed nonconventional life-styles all require couples to reevaluate the nature of their commitment to each other. Some are learning to renegotiate this commitment while continuing the marriage. Stressful as such a process is, a potential reward lies in the resulting respect that each gains for the other and in the possibility that this attitude of respect for the genuineness of each other's feelings can generalize into a *style of response* in the family life. What evolves is a marital and family system that encourages individual initiative and grants the freedom to explore, experiment, and initiate something new without fear of being shamed, teased, or scorned should failure occur.

Clinical Significance of Parents' "Task 3"

What clinical implications derive from the foregoing? Mainly, there is the realization that we can be of profound help to parents when we can speak directly to them about what they need to do in their family life if they want their children to grow as genuine and distinct persons. Many parents may require individual psychotherapy in order to overcome intrapsychic conflicts that are interfering with their ability to parent effectively. But I believe there are crucial first clinical steps to be taken before individual therapy gets underway. The first of these is a study of the family as a group, carried out in an openly sharing fashion in which we clarify our purpose as we go. Our basic message to all family members needs to be that we want to help them recognize how they may be impeding each other's psychological growth.

Both generations learn more if we find ways to share our discoveries about them with them in fairly concrete ways. Thus, if the children are very young, play therapy of an appropriate kind carried out with the parents present and even participating in the play provides excellent revelations to everyone, if we comment directly to the parents about their own respective roles in the play. I have found that the timely introduction of an art therapist into a family session can help everyone become self-observing. It also may provide data to refer back to in subsequent discussions with parents. Video playback, family psychodrama, and family self-observation through one-way windows provide ways to mobilize a family toward self-observation and respect for each other's individuality and sense of self without fear of being controlled by the other. If we can show troubled parents, using concrete illustrations, how one member of the family cancels out or negates the individuality of another by verbal or nonverbal means, and how this leads to underground revenge behavior or other kinds of passive aggressive reactions, then creative remedies for the family's malady begin to emerge.

TASK 4: FACILITATING EGO MASTERY

The work of Lois Barclay Murphy (Murphy and Moriarty, 1976) has awakened us more clearly than ever to the need to differentiate defensive mechanisms from coping mechanisms when we offer help to parents and children. While our traditional focus upon psychodynamics and upon internalized intrapsychic conflicts provides crucial depth to our clinical work, it is equally essential that we understand what interpersonal experiences are necessary in order that humans can progress from relatively asocial to relatively social levels of function. While the socialization process necessary for children seems almost self-evident to most intelligent and educated people, effective day-to-day implementation and facilitation of the process seem woefully lacking in family after family coming for clinical help.

Erikson (1950) pointed out how the Sioux Indians of past decades carefully taught their young how to master their dangerous world. He described how this educational process was carried out in small increments with new experiences carefully timed and then reinforced (see Chapter 7). The qualities of patience and forebearance he alluded to in that long ago society seem enviable in our far more chaotic world. We know that, in the gross sense, children can grow up under any number of adverse circumstances. But the risks for becoming dehumanized in the ghetto may be only somewhat more obvious than the potential for growing up dehumanized in middle-class environments where superego values are diffuse and where children are so distant from the basics of survival that they feel peculiarly detached from the cause and effect phenomena in the world around them (see Chapter 13 on drug abuse).

The stresses and tasks of parenting converge dramatically in that phase of the family developmental cycle in which relatively young parents are barely finding their place in the adult world while simultaneously trying to clarify the nature of the real world for their young children. Just as they themselves feel most vulnerable, they are faced with the task of helping their children to feel safe and to achieve mastery. Thus, while father and mother are trying to stabilize their work identities and their economic resources, they are also needing to define their family as a viable and stable social unit—i.e., a family in a neighborhood where there are other families to whom their children and they themselves can relate.

By now they may have passed through some of the earlier stresses in discovering themselves in the roles of "mommy" and "daddy." Presumably they have become used to their relative lack of personal freedom and to the boundaries set for them by parenthood. But what they still need to learn more and more about are very basic instrumental behaviors that provide family life with vitality and color and a sense of direction. These mechanisms include the ability to plan projects that are of meaning to everyone in the family and to carry them out so that there is a prevailing feeling of growth and progress, and a deep sense of how to set goals and achieve them. For this to occur the positive aspects of the first three developmental phases should now be operating at full tilt. All too frequently, they are not!

Very fundamental interpersonal phenomena need to be mastered and practiced:

> *Communication:* speaking out one's thoughts clearly to others in the family and listening to each other with genuine interest;
>
> *Observation:* looking at the world around with pleasure and interest and sharing what each has observed;
>
> *Reacting emotionally:* experiencing real events with feeling while simultaneously learning to monitor those very same feelings and to to talk about feelings in a genuine way;
>
> *Resolving interpersonal conflicts:* demonstrating in the everyday interactions of the family that conflicts of feeling may be expressed without all-or-none victory or defeat; that the expression of differ-

ing feelings does not require trampling on the self-esteem of others; and that acknowledging "I was wrong" does not require that one feel a loss of control;

Participating in community: contributing to constructive human causes outside the immediate family circle;

Relating to authority: finding ways to get along on the outside with diverse authority figures such as employers, school principals, teachers, police, neighborhood bullies (adult and child), bureaucrats, etc., without being hypocritical or non-genuine;

Enjoying the human body: experiencing one's body without shame and without fear of depreciation from family attitudes;

Sharing emotional and physical intimacy: finding security and pleasure in touching and being touched and in talking about one's inner feelings and fantasies with others.

Clinical Implications of Parents' "Task 4"

I need to emphasize once again the *interpersonal* and *transactional* aspects of the preceding and to underline my belief that our clinical role should include activation and reinforcing of the various family functions that are essential if people are to be and feel human. When individual adults come for psychotherapy because of "feelings of emptiness," it is often because they failed to experience these kinds of interchanges in their families of origin. Many of the hyperactive, excitable, and stimulus-hungry children and adolescents clinicians see are the products of families where patterns for mutual gratification through a well ordered progression of socializing experiences barely exist.

It is important for clinicians to provide a model to parents of how to be direct and authoritative with children of all ages without being punitive or depreciating. This kind of modeling can be particularly important in relation to adolescent patients. We ourselves may need to insist that they relate meaningfully to us in the presence of their parents, thereby providing an example of clear and responsible communication. At the same time we can urge the parents to do the same thing with each other and with their adolescents. It is my bias that if we deeply understand the functions of parenting, we as clinicians may be required to stand up to the adolescent and insist he or she relate in meaningful ways to the parents while at the same time insisting of the parents that they do the same with each other and with their adolescent (s). It is somewhat easier to do this in the earlier phases of the family cycle. When children are smaller and less effectively blustering than adolescents, parents can be guided to take firm stands and carry out their functional role without waffling when we take time to teach them what the interpersonal phenomena of family life are and how mutual respect for each person's individuality gets established. I use the word "teaching" advisedly. I believe skillful clinicians can work with psychodynamics and also teach patients and their parents certain essential behaviors.

CLINICAL WISDOM FOR SPECIFIC STRESSES AND PITFALLS

If something is happening right now in an interpersonal context we cannot afford to be diverted from it and to preoccupy ourselves with speculations about "underlying dynamics" or "organic deficits" or "genetic predispositions" or "traumatic histories." While each of those phenomena certainly exists, the here and now of parental needs must be recognized and attended to first:

Parental Ambivalence: Our clinical wisdom needs to encompass the fact that becoming a parent creates disequilibrium in father and in mother. A new father very soon discovers his most personal needs being pushed aside and placed in second priority. A new mother soon realizes that her body is no longer her own, her moment-to-moment movements are no longer private, and her space and her psyche have become invaded! I believe most young parents are at least somewhat ambivalent about what has happened to their lives with the arrival of a baby. Clinicians need openly and freely to identify with parents in these new experiences and help them verbalize their ambivalent feelings. Our task is to recognize the strong potential for mutual projection that exists in this early phase of family life. Our remedy is to teach parents how to share their ambivalent feelings with each other, instead of becoming alienated from each other.

Aloneness: Young parents not only feel invaded and controlled by their babies, with a loss of their former individual freedom, but they may also experience an unexpected aloneness. Especially for the mother, the hours may pass very slowly between feedings, clothes washing, baths, etc. Telephone conversations with friends or parents become precious diversions for a new mother. Neighbors formerly avoided suddenly become sought after companions. The alcoholic lady across the way suddenly sounds like a philosopher and sage. It helps parents enormously if the reality of their aloneness can be verbalized openly between them. Unfortunately, many husbands experience such verbalizations from their wives as accusations (sometimes they are!). If we help parents address their newly realized aloneness as a real phenomenon that merits mutual sympathy, we help them sustain and reinforce a nurturing environment in this early phase of the family life.

Self-Doubt: In the absence of smoothly functioning extended family systems where experienced aunts or grandparents can help with a new infant, young couples may begin parenthood with severe self-doubt. A downward spiral of dispiriting defeat and of mutual projection of failure can easily become established. The great American emphasis upon competence makes it difficult for many young parents to acknowledge their self-doubts. Once again, encouraging an open sharing of anxieties in the marriage is a most important contribution.

Competitiveness and Envy: Parents have always compared their children with others. Competitive feelings are not pleasant ones. Envious feelings are even more unacceptable. But they are real and inevitable. A sister's or brother's infant crawls sooner or talks sooner or is bigger or more petite or has more charm. New parents need to be helped to talk over those subjective reactions with each other and to support one another instead of leaving them unspoken or putting each other down when they are verbalized.

Alliances and Split Loyalties: A great danger that arises soon in a new family is the tendency for pairing off—a mother and child excluding dad or dad responding to an urge to buddy-up with his toddler and push mom to the side. Sometimes Oedipus and Electra dominate the scene. In pathologic families we have learned that intrafamilial schisms can develop which soon are almost beyond repair. Such parents need careful and delicate reminding that if the basic commitment and unity in the marital relationship become lost, fragmentation of the family will follow. Splitting of feelings and role behaviors occurs, with labeling: the "good one" and the "bad one."

Finding One's Self in One's Children: Why not? Certainly the gratification available to parents through identifying with their children's attractiveness, competence, and achievement is an essential reward for parenthood. However, the danger of imbalance is ever present. The need is very great indeed for us to help parents define and redefine appropriate boundaries so that they do not sacrifice their own individuality and the marital relationship to fantasies about their "perfect" children.

Projecting Judgments: Some parents are peculiarly vulnerable to the phenomenon of placing into their children the power to make them, the parents, feel good or bad. This may be a by-product of early failure in the marriage. The opportunity missed early to become supportive friends to one another leaves each parent overly sensitive to judgments made by their children and unable to keep their children's views of them in appropriate perspective.

Ever-Present Separation Pain: Parents can never be entirely free of the peculiar kind of emotional distress that separation engenders. Genuine commitment to another person brings with it an inevitable vulnerability to the loss of that person. The complex process of individuation beginning as soon as an infant can crawl evokes separation anxieties in mothers and in many fathers. Each new developmental milestone carries with it the potential for separateness. Under average circumstances this rarely becomes a powerful stress for parents until adolescence arrives. But for some parents, separations are felt to be extremely painful almost from the beginning. How two people in a marriage manage togetherness and separateness from one another is a strong determinant of how they will do so with their children. Some families create massive cover-ups of feelings so separation won't be experienced consciously. Other families cling together for similar reasons. In the context of our present society, with the isolation of families and individuals that occurs in urban life, the process of separation and connection between individuals is a subject of profound importance. At each developmental phase, both individual and familial, the process of separation and individuation is the primary phenomenon operating between the family members. Whether it is felt as opportunity or whether it is felt as stress is a function of the totality of the interpersonal relationships in the family and of each person's intrapsychic organization.

Parents as Authorities: Recent research carried out by Baumrind (1976) emphasizes all over again what some have been asserting for many years, namely that *authoritative* parenting, as distinguished from *authoritarian* parenting, produces children with vitality, optimism, and competence. However, in clinical work with families we repeatedly see parents who have difficulty distinguishing authoritarianism from authoritativeness. They have not learned ways to be authoritatively clear, definitive, helpful, but also limiting and structuring, without being restrictively and punitively authoritarian. Minuchin's clinical studies of families emphasize the profound importance of helping families to structure appropriate intergenerational boundaries (Minuchin, 1974). In order to achieve this, parents need to be helped to be firmly authoritative. This can only occur if they learn how to establish effective interpersonal processes within the everyday life of the family. The mere presence of parental warmth is not enough—instrumental guidance is essential.

FINAL COMMENTARY

The process of encouraging ego mastery and instrumental competence within the family life is an outgrowth of the earlier developmental phases of the family. If two parents have become able to provide emotional nurturance to each other, and this has become generalized in the family, and if the parents have learned how to encourage each other's autonomous growth, the basis is present for ever increasing ego mastery in all family members. A family may have a great potential for healing itself with a clinician's guidance. But the clinician needs to comprehend what the family as a whole needs before he can guide. He can do this only if he deeply understands and empathizes with both the stresses and the tasks of parenting.

REFERENCES

BAUMRIND, D.: The contribution of the family to the development of competence in children. *The Schizophrenic Bulletin*, No. 14. U.S. Department of Health, Education and Welfare, Public Health Service, Alcohol, Drug Abuse and Mental Health Administration, 1976.

BENEDEK, T. & ANTHONY, E. J. (eds.): *Parenthood: Its Psychology and Psychopathology* (by 29 authors). Boston: Little, Brown, 1970.

BROWN, S. L.: Family experience and change. In R. Friedman (Ed.), *Family Roots of Learning and Behavior Disorders*. Springfield: Charles C Thomas, 1973, pp. 5-43.

ERIKSON, E.: *Childhood and Society*. New York: Norton, 1950.

MAHLER, M.: *The Psychological Birth of the Human Infant: Symbiosis and Individuation*. New York: Basic Books, 1975.

MINUCHIN, S.: *Families and Family Therapy*. Cambridge, Mass.: Harvard University Press, 1974.

MURPHY, L. B. & MORIARTY, A. E.: *Vulnerability, Coping and Growth from Infancy to Adolescence*. New Haven and London: Yale University Press, 1976.

POLLAK, O.: Sociological and psychoanalytic concepts in family diagnosis. In B. L. Green (Ed.), *The Psychotherapies of Marital Disharmonies*. New York: The Free Press, 1965, pp. 15-25.

WINNICOTT, D. W.: *The Child, the Family, and the Outside World*. Baltimore, Md.: Penguin Books, 1969.

Part II

Conceptual Options in Parent Guidance

Chapter 3

Psychoanalytic Insights for Parent Guidance

Marjorie Rowe

Some of the subtle variables which can contribute to the quality and the effectiveness of the parent-counselor relationship are to be considered in this chapter.

THE PARENTS' FEELINGS AND BACKGROUND

It may be very difficult for some parents to make an appointment with a mental health worker to obtain help or advice about a worrying, puzzling child. They may have needed months or years before they were able to seek help. Even then, they may not have been sure that they were acting wisely. How often we have heard parents say, "We thought that he would outgrow it, that it was just a phase that he was going through." These parents, who find it so difficult to ask for help, have probably agonized with guilt and doubts about their adequacy as parents, as well as suffering through periods when they attempted to blame the school or each other. Undoubtedly they at times felt not only angry and frustrated, but also helpless in attempting to cope with their child's problems. Behind their attempts to deny the problem, conflicted by the nagging superego and the inner awareness that nothing is getting better, often lies fear of stigma. The severity of their belief that a stigma attaches to people who need psychiatric help may even be projected onto their neighbors or the community.

Too little recognition is given to this dramatic, *initial step—seeking help*. Although it may seem tentative and small, it is a step with many positive messages for the professional who is listening. It may imply that the parent is taking responsibility, doing something about his child's problems and his family's unhappiness. He has hope that someone can help his child even if he cannot. He may be painfully giving up his omnipotence and recognizing himself as an ordinary human being, unable to change some things; this can sometimes cause depression. Yet the parent may also experience relief.

Parents' Personal Problems

Often parents who bring their child may have problems of their own that contribute to their feelings of guilt and responsibility for their child's unhappiness. They may be suffering marital stress; they may have other emotional problems or illnesses within the family. A parent may be struggling to manage without the emotional support of a marital partner (see Chapter 24). Parents are often rejected or ostracized by neighbors because of their child's behavior, or they may feel harassed or persecuted by the school. A case in point was a mother who had to bring her three-year-old psychotic daughter to the clinic by bus. On one occasion the girl started to hallucinate and scrambled, shrieking, underneath the bus seat. While the mother attempted to quiet and retrieve the shrieking child, the other passengers verbally attacked her for "mistreating" the girl, and even threatened to report her to the police.

Some parents may stress that the child is the patient in order to deny their own emotional problems. Occasionally a distraught parent will use the child as a "ticket of admission," hoping for help for himself. Others are really looking for an arbitrator in family squabbles.

Transference by Parents

Transference is the unconscious and ubiquitous phenomenon in which the parent may relate to the professional with feelings carried over from earlier intense emotional relationships. The parent may displace onto the professional feelings he still carries for important figures in his childhood. Thus, some parents may see the professional as a parent, and attempt to take on the role of dependent child, wanting specific instructions in how to handle their offspring. Sometimes it is necessary to comply with that wish. Others may attempt to please or placate the professional. Or they may come with an unconsciously rebellious or hostile attitude that is really felt for their own parents. This may be most germane to the child's problem; the child may be acting out the parent's unconscious rebellion.

GUIDANCE VARIABLES

The Professionals' Feelings

The professional doing parent guidance, whether a social worker, psychiatrist, psychologist, pediatrician, nurse, guidance counselor, pastor, or other, should have come to terms with his own problems so that he is aware of his sensitivities or prejudices and is able to keep them separate from those of the parent. The fact that he is a professional does not invalidate his human qualities, which, like the parents', have arisen from earlier emotional relationships. He has fantasies, conscious and unconscious, of which he must be constantly aware. Some of these are omnipotent-rescue fantasies in which the worker unconsciously denies his own professional limitations and attempts to cope with problems which are beyond his capabilities (see the Rescue Game in Chapter 6).

Countertransference is a delusion similar to transference. In it the professional displaces onto client-parents feelings he really holds for important figures from his own past. This can keep him from seeing the parents' (and child's) problems objectively, or can entice him to take sides or to become morally critical.

The most effective counselors seem to be those who have come to terms with their own personal problems, who are comfortable in their own inner worlds, and who can *use themselves in listening* to the parents' problems without becoming emotionally entangled (see, also, Chapter 23).

The Setting and Its Message

Highly competent people have done excellent parent guidance under deplorable conditions which compelled them to share office space, use empty classrooms, or even see parents in storage closets. The parents ordinarily understood these difficulties, often identified with the counselors, and appreciated their willingness to tolerate such conditions in order to help them.

However, those who have appropriate office space should attend to the manner in which the office is furnished, since furnishings can offer messages which are quickly perceived by the parents and may trigger fantasies that can interfere with the counselor's work. For instance, the opulent, expensively furnished office may cause the parents to feel uncomfortable and possibly resentful of the counselor's fees, or may leave them wondering how the counselor could possibly understand their "everyday" problems. On the other hand, some workers feel that an opulent appearance of success encourages the parents to have confidence in them. The sterile office which provides only straight-back chairs, a telephone that interrupts intermittently, a desk covered with papers, and a wall covered with diplomas offers little feeling of privacy, warmth, or the counselor's undivided attention. It may suggest that he is in a hurry, is too busy, or has other things on his mind.

In general, the setting should be comfortable, conducive to privacy, and free from interruptions by secretaries or telephone calls.

Starting Appointments on Time

The worker who keeps the parents waiting could be giving the message that he is neither aware of nor concerned about their anxiety. It is difficult for parents who have already gone through indecision and lengthy debate about obtaining help to have to wait beyond the appointed hour. They have made their decision and may feel that they are about to expose their inadequacies as parents. Being on time helps them avoid further pain and anxiety.

Reassurance

Simple reassurance is usually not helpful and may arouse further anxiety. It may offer the message that the counselor is not hearing what the parents are saying, but rather is denying the pain and apprehension that they are experiencing. The parents have probably heard time and again such clichés as "everything is going to be all right," or "you have nothing to worry about," from friends and relatives. On the contrary, the parents may feel within themselves that things are not going to be all right or may wonder if changes can be made. They will be more comfortable if the counselor hears and *accepts their feelings.*

Loss and Mourning

It is important to understand the psychodynamics of loss and the mourning process because a large proportion of parents and children seeking help are either suffering losses at the time of referral or have suffered them in the past without working them through. Losses can include marital partners, siblings, the idealized self—even the loss of limbs, capacities, or social position—or loss of the expected normal child (see Chapter 14 for mourning as related to birth of a defective child). It is what the individual does with his losses that determines his mental health. Thus, knowledge of the stages of mourning and recognition of the inability to mourn or of pathological mourning often help the counselor to decide whether he is able to cope with the parent's problems or should refer for more intensive treatment.

UNCONSCIOUS SPRINGS THAT FEED THE CHILD-PARENT RELATIONSHIP

Following the separating-out process in which the infant discovers the difference between "me" and "not me" (Winnicott, 1958), ambivalence becomes a part of all relationships. These are not "mixed feelings," but rather feelings that coexist. We would not know about one feeling if we were not acquainted with the other. For instance, we could not know about independence if we had not experienced dependence; nor could we know about hate if we had not experienced love. We have to assume that somewhere behind each feeling lies its opposite.

Mothering the Normal Infant

Klein (1960) was one of the first to recognize the mother's role in accepting her infant's projections. The mother allows the infant to project his loving or hating feelings onto her and then to take them back into himself. In so doing, he gradually gains some form of awareness with emotional growth that his anger or his love is his own and has not destroyed her. A mother is aware of the intensity of her infant's greedy love for her which can quickly change to angry feelings so that he tries to hit or bite. The ordinary mother accepts such shifts in mood because she is sufficiently, though unconsciously, in touch with her own infantile feelings so that she understands this as a part of being a baby.

Thus the parent, in particular the mother, acts as a container for both the good and the bad projections of the growing infant. He gradually becomes aware that the feelings he projects are really his own. They have not destroyed the other and, indeed, are not all that powerful. Each time the reintrojections occur, they are reintegrated into further ego development with concomitant reduction in the child's feelings of omnipotence. The parent's role seems simply to be able to survive and to enjoy. (For more on normal parenting, see Chapters 2 and 28.)

What Can Go Wrong?

1. The mother suffering severe marital *stress, depression, or physical or mental illness* may be incapable of responding to her infant's needs and hence unable to accept his loving or hating feelings or his messiness. The result may be that her mothering is chaotic or so rejecting that the infant cannot use her to distinguish his feelings as his own.

2. Other mothers may have had such *inadequate mothering themselves* that they have few resources in their own inner worlds to help them to get in touch with their infant's needs. (See Chapters 22 and 28 for more on inadequate past mothering of the mother.)

3. It occasionally occurs that it is the *infant who rejects* his mother's overtures, who is not comfortable with bodily contact, and who is not the kind of satisfying baby who helps the mother feel good about herself and adequate as a mother (See Chapter 12). This could put an unbearable strain on the relationship.

Growth Through Conflict

These three examples of broken or damaged mother-infant relationships seem to lead to a *neurotic* chain linking one generation with another. However, even when there has been a good beginning with adequate parenting, lesser conflicts are still part of the *ordinary* developmental process which is composed of the child's and adolescent's growing attempts to establish autonomy. The adolescent's basic ambivalence and increasing swings between love and hate are difficult for parents to cope with and to understand. This is particularly so because during his recent latency he has generally regarded his parents, particularly the father, as omnipotent and omniscient. Identification was strong, and although there were sorties into independent behavior, his security and emotional ties remained steadfastly bound to the home and the family. However, at adolescence, with increasing growth, experience, and shifting of identification to the peer group, his fantasies about his parents as omnipotent, omniscient figures become more unconscious. On the conscious level he begins to see the parents as ordinary human beings with all their vulnerabilities, weaknesses and inconsistencies. The struggle for autonomy thus becomes more open.

All of these stages of growth in the adolescent contribute to mixed and fluctuating feelings on the part of the parents, who must maintain emotional support, steady limits, and the readiness to be there when the adolescent suddenly gets into trouble or regresses to dependent behavior for brief periods. Such regression may be necessary to facilitate consolidation of his gains.

It is necessary that the professional have a thorough understanding of child development and a consistent theoretical framework on which to hang it—be it humanistic, experiential, eclectic, learning theory, or psychoanalytic. It is only by knowing the ordinary physical and emotional developmental patterns that one is able to help parents discern those deviations that may be sufficiently pathological to necessitate further consultation or referral.

MISREADING THE CHILD'S SENSITIVITY

The commonly used expression, "What the child doesn't know won't hurt him," can be used as a rationalization by parents to avoid telling the child unpleasant facts which the child may need to know. *Silence can become overstimulation.* What the child doesn't know, he will fill in with his fantasies. What he knows, he will embellish with his fantasies. It is usually better to let him have the facts to revolve his fantasies around than for him to have to create his own distortions and then embellish them further. The destructive power of too little information is shown in the case of Tom:

> Five-year-old Tom was referred because of cutting himself, suicidal threats, feelings of worthlessness, and debilitating anxiety. His father had killed himself with a shotgun while Tom was asleep upstairs. Tom was awakened by the sound of the gun. He heard the emergency squad's siren as well as the commotion downstairs, which was followed by his father's disappearance. His mother insisted that he should not be told what had hapened. She subsequently lived with another man for several months and then suddenly broke off with him. In Tom's eyes, he, too, disappeared. Since his mother offered no explanation and did not respond to his questions, he had only his fantasies to fall back upon to account for these hap-

penings. At this age he naturally had omnipotent destructive fantasies as part of his oedipal fantasies. Fearing that these had somehow been acted out, he felt guilty. He began to construct further fantasies about his own guilt and worthlessness. He became terrified that he, too, would disappear. He needed psychotherapy and his mother needed help in order to become comfortable enough to talk about the painful facts at Tom's level of understanding.

The parent's inability or refusal to tell the child simple facts may be a sincere effort to protect the child from disturbing knowledge; it also may be an indication of the parent's own anxiety and intrapsychic conflicts about the information. Withholding of information is facilitated by the parent's denial or lack of awareness of the child's sensitivity to parental moods, hushed talk, or covert signals to the other parent or other adults. This insensitivity may arise out of the parents' repression of how sensitive they were as children. Such repression would naturally interfere with their appreciation of their child's level of awareness.

In contrast to such overstimulation by silence, *parents can also overstimulate by giving too much information* to their child. A child asks simple questions and is usually satisfied with simple answers that do not go beyond his request for information. He will asks when he needs more.

Fantasy Stimulators

Other parental behaviors which seem to deny the child's sensitivity and arouse his fantasies are: 1) talking about him in his presence as though we were an object; 2) going around in the nude; 3) using the child as an ally in marital conflicts; 4) using the child as a contraceptive by encouraging him to share mother's bed (especially destructive to the male child); 5) telling the child in the single parent family that he is to fulfill the role of the absent parent; and 6) prohibiting expressions of feeling within the family.

The child often copes with the parental behaviors by creating fantasies about himself and the situation. These are ordinarily primitive, omnipotent, and sexual. The child may become so preoccupied with them that his school work deteriorates. He may also show indications of poor sexual identification, difficulties with peer relations, or withdrawal into a more satisfactory world which he has created for himself.

THE PARENT'S STRENGTH

Such parental attitudes and behaviors towards the child do not arise from perversity. One can assume that they result from the parent's own parents' attitudes and relationships with him. (See Chapter 6 for more about internalized parents.) The parent is aware of this somewhere within himself. Yet he knows no other way of behaving. Parents often feel guilty and pained about what is going on between them and their child. They want to be "good" parents and they want to have a better relationship with their child. This is evidenced by their seeking help.

Almost all parents have a healthy part of themselves with which it is necessary to get in touch in order to develop a therapeutic alliance. Not only can this healthy part develop an alliance with the professional, but it can also become the observing part of the self used by the parent to recognize and help change his own inappropriate or destructive behavior. It is this collaboration between the counselor and the parent's healthy part that provides the consistent support for the changing relationship between parents and child. Often, as the result of having gained an understanding of their relationship with one child, parents find themselves more comfortable and better equipped to help their other children through the vicissitudes of childhood and adolescence.

REFERENCES

CARR, H. & LEARED, J.: The effect on a child of a mother who though physically present was emotionally unavailable. *J. Child Psychotherapy*, 4:61-79, 1975.

FRAIBERG, S., ADELSON, E., & SHAPIRO, V.: Ghosts in the nursery. *J. Amer. Acad. Child Psychiatr.*, 14:387-421, 1975.

ISAACS, S.: The nature and function of phantasy. In J. Riviere (Ed.), *Developments in Psycho-Analysis*. London: The Hogarth Press, 1952, pp. 67-121.

KLEIN, M.: *Our Adult World and Its Roots in Infancy*. London: Tavistock Publications, 1960.

WINNICOTT, D. W.: Aggression in relation to emotional development. In: *Collected Papers through Paediatrics to Psycho-Analysis*. London: Tavistock Publications,, 1956, pp. 204-218.

Chapter 4

Growing Up Together:
The Mutual Respect Balance

Katharine Dixon Colley

Missildine's (1962) "mutual respect balance"* approach to parenting recognizes that it is essential for both parent and child to grow in an atmosphere which highly values positive self-regard and does not allow infringement on the rights of either parent or child. Each child has rights and responsibilities as an individual as well as phase-specific developmental needs. At the same time, the parent has not only rights and responsibilities as a parent, but also phase-specific needs as an adult (see also Chapter 2). Respecting these needs, rights, and responsibilities of parent and child and limiting any infringement on the rights of each other result in a mutual respect balance.

* Dr. Hugh Missildine, Clinical Professor of Psychiatry, Ohio State University, developed the mutual respect approach to parent guidance during many years as a clinician and teacher. Dr. Katharine Colley was one of his students. He graciously reviewed the manuscript of this chapter in its formative stages and approved it as a summary of his ideas.

THE MIDDLE GROUND

A mutual respect balance involves neither overcontrol nor undercontrol, neither overpermissiveness nor rigidity, neither intrusiveness nor neglect. It is the middle ground. It recognizes the rights of individuals, whether parents or children, to grow in an atmosphere where neither parents nor children are expected to cater to the whim of the other. Rules, limits, rights, and responsibilities are explicit and parental responses are consistent rather than random. Parents need to provide enough structure for the child so that he may have guidelines while developing, yet possess enough flexibiilty and awareness of phase-specific characteristics and needs that the child will not be stifled.

Occasionally, a mutual respect imbalance may occur as a transitory response to stress, hardship, or loss of a parent or sibling. In fertile ground, a transitory imbalance may become a vicious cycle which crystallizes into a chronically disordered parent-child realtionship. More often, the imbalance has been longstanding; a family homeostasis exists about which family members loudly complain, but which they seem unwilling to change, even if they are victims of such a system. (See Chapter 5 for more about vicious cycles and homeostasis.)

The professional needs also to choose the middle ground concerning the value and application of the mutual respect aproach, neither neglecting it entirely nor using it exclusively. Like other parent guidance approaches, it is not a cut-and-dried technique intended to offer instant diagnosis and cure. It needs to be creatively tailored to each family. However, it does offer a beginning counselor a framework for working with parents. With experience it can then become part of a larger guidance armamentarium.

Parents seeking help for their child or themselves are often confused about the cause and remedy of their difficulties. Their confusion may take the form of denial, self-blame, projection of blame onto others, hostility in the counseling situation, or indifference.

PARENTING STYLES AND CHILD REACTIONS

It is not unusual to observe parents treating their child in a manner which reflects how they feel about themselves or to see that they are projecting culturally reinforced roles and expectations onto the child. People tend to treat themselves and their children as their parents treated them in the past. (For corroboration, see Chapters 2, 6, 22, and 28.) Identification of pathological parental styles ("parental pathogens") will therefore give direction to the process of restoring the mutual respect balance.

Overcoercion

The overcoercive parent excessively directs and redirects the child's activities without respecting the child's rights to initiate and govern his own daily living. The child may respond as a) an outlaw whose defiance is needed to maintain his individuality; b) a puppet who loses his individuality while gaining parental approval; or c) a dawdler who tries both to retain parental approval and maintain individuality through passive resistance.

Oversubmission

The oversubmissive parent capitulates to the child's demands and wishes without regard to the parent's own rights. The reason for this attitude may be self-belittling by the parents, a chronically ill child (see Chapter 15), an adopted child (see Chapter 27), a last or only child, or a parent's feeling that confuses submission to a child with giving him "love and security." The children of oversubmissive parents tend to be impulsive, demanding, inconsiderate, and subject to temper tantrums, fears, and somatic complaints. A vicious cycle is often set up in which the child makes demands, the parent has his rights infringed upon, the parent feels irritation, the parent feels guilt over the irritation towards the child he is supposed to be loving, and the parent becomes more submissive, thus reinforcing the child's demanding behavior.

Perfectionism

The perfectionistic parent withholds acceptance until the child's performance is more mature than that with which the child is comfortable at his present level of development. The child's resultant self-belittling thoughts and disappointments in his own performance interfere with his ability to achieve, thus insuring more non-acceptance from the parent.

Punitiveness

The punitive parent may be using the child as a target for his own personal aggressions, or may be responding to a cultural value which says that a child must be hurt to be reared adequately. These parents launch a verbal or physical assault on the child, often in the name of discipline. Their children may react with fear, self-belittling, a tendency to place themselves in punitive situations, or a longing to retaliate which may or may not be expressed.

Neglect

The neglectful parent has often been so scarred in his own childhood that he has little emotional support left for the child or any model on which to base nurturant parenting (see Chapters 6, 22, and 28). The child may have trouble forming close relationships or getting satisfaction from them. He may show a lack of self-control, be impulsive and clinging, and have learning difficulties.

Rejection

The rejecting parent withholds acceptance from the child altogether, usually unconsciously and covertly. Overt, frank, admitted rejection is one of the most destructive situations that can be encountered in parent guidance; it often suggests consideration of other living arrangements for the child. The rejected child will likely be bitter, hostile, and isolated, actively keeping people at a distance.

Hypochondriasis

The hypochondriacal parent will repeatedly inquire about and express overanxious concern for the child's health and body functions. The child, in turn, becomes anxiously preoccupied about his own health.

Overindulgence

The overindulgent parent showers the child with goods and services without regard to the child's needs. The overindulged child tends to be bored, blasé, and lacking in initiative and persistence.

Overprotection

The overprotective parent attemps to shelter the child from the threats and demands of the world in anticipation that they will exceed the child's capacity to cope. This parental style can interfere with the development of the child's natural abilities to tolerate frustration, handle stress and master new situations.

Seduction

The parent who is overtly or covertly seductive with a child stimulates an early preoccupation with sexual matters. In addition, this often blurs the boundaries of the parent's and child's roles in the family. This parental pathogen has implications for future sexual adjustment and behavior.

Excessive Responsibility

The parent who imposes excessive responsibility on the child tends to rear a child who lacks the ability to play and to enjoy mutually nurturing relations with others. [TA (Chapter 6) might say that the adult is hypertrophied at the expense of an underdeveloped nurturing Parent and playful Child. In fact, it could be interesting to go through each of the parental styles and conceptualize the child's response in TA terms. Missildine's ideas, though preceding TA, seem very compatible with it; he even entitled one of his books *Your Inner Child of the Past.*—Ed.].

It is not unusual to see a parent who combines several pathological styles of parenting. Overcoercive and perfectionistic attitudes are a frequent and maybe even culturally acceptable combination. The rarer, but lethal, punitive-neglectful-rejecting parents fill our institutions and prisons with their damaged children.

IMPORTANCE OF FAMILY HISTORY

No adequate substitute exists for a thorough history and evaluation of the child-parent relationship. With the increasing demand for delivery of mental health services, it becomes tempting (sometimes necessary) to shortcut the diagnostic process. A careful family history, an area often sacrificed in a shortened intake, can provide enlightening information regarding the contribution of the parents' parenting to the current situation. The following case illustrates this:

> As the parents and their adopted three-and-a-half-year-old boy entered the office, the mother gave a clue to her parenting style: She nudged the child and said, "Go on in," even though he appeared to be proceeding well on his own. During the session she admonished him: "Don't chew your fingers," and "Sit back down." Many aspects of the child's behavior about which the parent complained seemed normal for a three-year-old. However, the mother's belittling admonitions had a scripted role in a transgenerational

tragedy. She related that both sets of grandparents had been "strict" and although she wanted to "modernize" her parenting, she did not know how to go about doing it.

RESTORING THE MUTUAL RESPECT BALANCE

Identifying the parenting style diplomatically to the parents will open the door for further discussion on both sides. For instance, it can be explained to oversubmissive parents that in some ways they are "too good' as parents, but that their catering to the child is not helping him to learn the necessary self-controls that he will need in school and with his relationships with other people. The counselor's openness to the parents' ideas about their parenting will enhance the parents' feeling of involvement in the process of helping their child. As the parents gain some understanding about how their behavior and attitudes help shape their child's behavior and attitudes about himself, they will want to talk about ways in which changes may be effected.

Mutual Respect Guidelines

Changes will occur by the parents practicing different attitudes and behavior.

1. *Offer the child time* without the child having to ask for attention with negative behavior.

2. *Limits are to be clearly defined* rather than implied or ambiguous. The parent should intervene before the behavior escalates out of control, yet should avoid admonishing in anticipation.

3. *Set firm and consistent limits.* Send the child to his room temporarily when his demands, complaints, temper, or disrespect are infringing on the rights of others. When a parent must enforce a limit, it is to be done *without lecturing, moralizing, scolding, or belittling.*

   Shaming or comparison among siblings is not a useful way to shape the child's behavior. Spanking as a method of enforcing limits should be used only with the young child, and in instances which involve potential danger such as playing with matches or running into the road. Rarely, spanking may be used with the older child to clear the air between parent and child.

   Enforcing limits with adolescents can be especially difficult if there has been a longstanding history of permissiveness or inconsistency in limit setting. At times, the only levers a parent may have with an adolescent are: a) isolating oneself from the infringing adolescent temporarily; b) giving him money only for work completed; and c) calling on law enforcement officers when laws are broken.

4. When an uproar occurs, there should be *simultaneous isolation* of the children involved until the roaring stops. Isolation should continue until they think they are able to come around more peacefully. If they come out continuing the uproar, they must be sent back to their rooms for a longer time.

5. There should be *restitution* by the child for anything broken, stolen, marred, or lost. Restitution may be made by extra work or deduction from allowance.

6. *Chores* should be *in one time period* so that the child is not on constant call. Elementary school age children may have two chore times, e.g., a time after school to help a parent and some time at night preparing for the next day (bath, clothes, etc.). There should be no distinction between male and female chores, but consideration should be given to the age of the child. [Depending on sexual politics, some experts would disagree with this prohibition against sex distinctions in chores.—Ed.]

7. Beginning about the third grade, there should be a *study time* with the radio and television off. The overcoerced child needs to be left alone, while the oversubmitted-to child needs the work checked to insure that he has given it a reasonable try.

8. The child is to be *left alone on things that are his.* He is to be free of his parents' overintrusiveness and anxious admonitions, urging, scolding, lectures, and criticism.

9. *No catering* should occur, especially after the preschool years.

10. *Training in self-respect* should be done by setting limits on the child's self-belittling. The parent should insist with an "I want it stopped," and the child should be sent to his room if he continues to run himself down.

11. The *parents need a time* for adult fun away from children.

Applying the Guidelines

Homework assignments for parents emphasize that they are expected to practice the new attitudes and behaviors outside of the counseling sessions. For example, specific suggestions can help overcoercive parents relinquish their directing and redirecting of the child's activities, while limit-setting suggestions to oversubmissive parents can help them draw in the reins. The counselor's recognition of the parents' strengths and limitations can help him set the proper pace in his work with the parents.

Control over one's impulses, achieving a sense of the individual self, and resolving feelings toward family members and important others are developmental tasks throughout all phases of development from early childhood through parenthood. Early intervention can modify a potentially habitual maladaptation. However, families with a long-standing imbalance often find themselves invested in maintaining this imbalance and therefore unable to follow guidelines consistently, even after some initial success. Often they find an excuse for not following through with the counselor's suggestions even though they agreed to them in the previous session. They may hope the counselor has some magical powers to resolve their difficulties. Some parents wish not to work to modify their own attitudes, but only for their child, the identified patient, to cease being a nuisance.

A parent who is self-belittling or lacking in his own self-control must come to grips with the "inner child" that continues to live within him. This is the part of him that continues to treat himself in the same ways that his parents did. [TA (Chapter 6) would call this the inner "Parent."—Ed.] The mutual respect imbalance that exists between the adult parent and his "inner child" often hinders the process of restoring a balance within his current family. How can a parent expect his child to control his temper when he flies into rages himself? At times, a parent has been so damaged in childhood that he needs more intensive treatment than parent guidance to help him become a nurturing, respecting, and self-respecting parent with his children. In such instances, parent guidance would be an adjunctive treatment.

The enmeshed, overprotective family of a child with a psychosomatic or chronic illness can be helped to recognize and respect greater individual autonomy and responsibility (see Chapters 15 and 16). The parents of a hyperkinetic child can be helped to provide the structure he needs, while guarding against their taking over his life in their efforts to control his incessant activity. Parents of the impulse-ridden child are often deficient in self-respect, so that they feel guilty each time they have to set limits; they can be helped to set limits despite their discomfort (see Chapter 1), and eventually develop more comfort with less guilt as they see their increasing competence as parents. Parents of a neurotic child can learn with help to reduce their overanxious concerns and intrusiveness that often aggravate the child's symptoms (see, also, Chapter 18).

REFERENCES

MISSILDINE, W. H.: The mutual respect approach to child guidance. *Amer. J. Dis. Child.*, 104.116-121, August, 1962.

MISSILDINE, W. H.: *Your Inner Child of the Past.* New York: Simon and Schuster, 1963.

Chapter 5

Helping Parents Beat the System

L. Eugene Arnold

The application of *general systems theory* to parent guidance might be called the comprehensive approach. It conceptualizes the parent-child relationship as a dynamic system with many component subsystems, both homeostatic and deviation-amplifying, with input from other such complex systems as the neighborhood and community, society, the economy, and the school system. Input from any of these other systems or intervention within the parent-child system by doing or saying something to the parents tends to have far-reaching reverberations throughout the parent-child system and other affiliated systems. Systems guidance makes use of this understanding by choosing points of intervention that are most likely to initiate constructive reverberation and by keeping in mind the likelihood of other components affecting the component being considered.

HOMEOSTASIS

Homeostasis, or maintenance of a steady state, is ordinarily considered desirable because of its necessity for biological functioning. However, it can also be undesirable when it preserves an undesirable state or discourages desirable change or growth. An example would be a parent maintaining a child in a chronic state of mild anxiety by relieving stress when the child shows severe anxiety and imposing unreasonably stressful demands when he seems relaxed and secure. Another example would be maintaining a ten-year-old at a level of dependency appropriate for a five-year-old by disapproving behavior whenever the child shows either four-year-old dependence or six-year-old independence.

Homeostatic Bugs

In addition to such undesirable homeostasis, there can be problems even with homeostatic systems that are desirable in themselves but are malfunctioning. The popular analogy of the homeostatic feedback between a furnace and its thermostat is often cited to illustrate the smooth functioning of a system maintaining a desirable steady state. This analogy can illustrate four common problems with homeostasis:

1. *Insensitivity* of the thermostat may require too great deviations in temperature to activate it. For example, the temperature for turning on the furnace may be 40° and the temperature for turning it off 85°. The sensitivity of the thermostat may have to be "tuned." Similarly, a professional may need to "tune" the parent-child homeostasis by helping the parents be more sensitive to the child's needs. Perhaps a father does not set limits on his daughter's exuberance until it escalates to intolerable misbehavior. Then he launches into a binge of harsh suppression that continues heedless of her obvious signs of repentance and does not cease until she withdraws into mute isolation. He needs to be taught how to monitor her behavior more sensitively.

2. *Oversensitivity* can also be a problem. If the furnace turns on at 68.25° and off at 68.26°, the frequency of switching will soon wear out both furnace and thermostat. Some parents wear out themselves and their children by constant monitoring and too frequent adjustments. A typical vignette might be: "Relax; don't be so tense ... sit up straight; don't slouch. Don't yell so loud ... speak up; say what you think ... watch your language..." This kind of system needs to have some "tolerance" developed in it.

3. *Inconsistency* results from the thermostat turning on at different temperatures on successive trials. Dirt fouling the thermostat may account for such erratic performance. Parents who ignore gross misbehavior one day and "turn on" severe punishment for minor infractions the next day may have anxiety or guilt fouling their "behaviorstat." Techniques for cleaning it out may be found in Chapter 1 and throughout this book.

4. Even a steady, smooth homeostasis may be maintained at an *undesirable level*, such as when a thermostat-furnace system maintains room temperature between 96° and 98°. Sometimes parents maintain a smothering level of protection by turning on an overprotective attitude or intervention in response to any potential or fantasied danger for the child. The parents' "protectionstat" can be reset by correcting misinformation or setting the "guilt button" for a higher threshold. Some protectiveness is desirable from a parent as some heat is from a furnace; the only problem is regulating the intensity and amount.

The preceding examples illustrate one advantage of a systems conceptualization of family problems: It helps the professional see the normal salvageable component of even the most pathological appearing system, to recognize when it is necessary not to dismantle or scrap the furnace, but merely to adjust the thermostat.

VICIOUS AND VIRTUOUS CYCLES

No less important than homeostasis in the parent-child system is *deviation-amplifying feedback*. When the deviation being amplified is undesirable, the result is a vicious cycle; when the deviation is desirable, the result is a virtuous cycle. Though ubiquitous, such cycles are most commonly recognized in such economic phenomena as inflation (vicious cycle) and the accumulation of capital (virtuous cycle?).

Normal Development from Virtuous Cycles

Virtuous cycles characterize the normal parent-child interaction that nurtures normal development. For example, a normal infant, when fed and tended, manifests satisfaction by gurgling, cooing, squealing, and smiling. This behavior provides reinforcing feedback to the mother that she is doing an adequate job. The infant's confirmation of her maternal adequacy endears him to her, ensuring her further efforts to care for him and, incidentally, to provide social stimulation, such as talking, cuddling, and stroking. The infant responds to this by further and more explicit signs of satisfaction, pleasure, and happiness, eliciting more positive interaction from the mother and winning father's favorable attenion, with development of a second social virtuous cycle with the father.

As the infant's social vocalizations begin to sound like words, the parents react with heightened interest and vocalize back to him. This parental reinforcement increases the frequency of such early verbalization and elicits more parental attention and pride in the infant's new skill. Similar virtuous cycles operate in other areas of the child's development. A clinical example of a virtuous cycle can be found in the first case in Chapter 11.

Reinforcement as Feedback

Much of the feedback in virtuous cycles could be redefined as positive reinforcement. In fact, most virtuous cycles could be stated in behavioral terms, and one of the goals of most behavior modification programs is to initiate virtuous cycles of behavioral change that are eventually self-perpetuating.

Expectation

A special kind of feedback is the behavioral expectation that one person in the system has for another. In the example of the infant beginning to talk, the parents will begin to expect after the first few words that the child will begin to ask for what he wants, rather than pointing, and will communicate this in many ways. For example, they may tend to listen and look at his mouth instead of looking at his hands. If they tend to respond to his newly developed verbalizations more quickly than to his obsolete gesturing and pointing, the child may soon develop the expectation of a quicker parental response to words than to gesture. This expectation will tend to develop a preference in the child for the modality with a quicker payoff, thus confirming the parents' expectations that he will ask verbally. Thus, positive expectations, as well as positive reinforcement, are essential parts of normal, healthy, deviation-amplifying feedback.

When the System Goes Wrong

Occasionally, an otherwise normal mother-infant interaction is detoured into a vicious cycle such as "colic": The mother perceives some

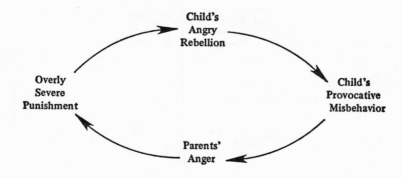

Figure 1. A simple parent-child vicious cycle

minimal distress of the infant and reacts anxiously to it. Her anxiety further upsets the infant, who reacts with more dramatic signs of distress, making the mother anxious. The mother's increased anxiety upsets the infant further, ad infinitum. A well-established technique of disrupting this vicious cycle is to have a calmer, more objective person hold the infant long enough to demonstrate to the mother that the infant is not "really" as distressed as she thought. Once the mother's anxiety is thus allayed, she is able to resume the virtuous cycle of maternal soothing and infant contentment.

Vicious cycles of parent-child interaction are among the most common problems encountered in guidance. Sometimes the vicious cycle is a fairly simple and straightforward one, such as Figure 1: An angry parent punishes a child who rebels against the punishment by further misbehavior, which elicits more frequent and severe punishments from the determined parent, thereby eliciting more rebellion and acting out from the child, with an escalating battle of wills. Often, though, the vicious cycle is very complex, with subsystems extending to different geographical and social situations, such as school. An example of such complexity is the psychosocial-educational vicious cycle initiated by minimal brain dysfunction (Figure 2). A cursory look at Figure 2 will confirm that the parents' feelings about the child's problems and the child's reaction to the parents' feelings affect and are affected by the child's school behavior and achievement, as part of an overall complex system. More about this particular vicious cycle can be found in Chapter 17.

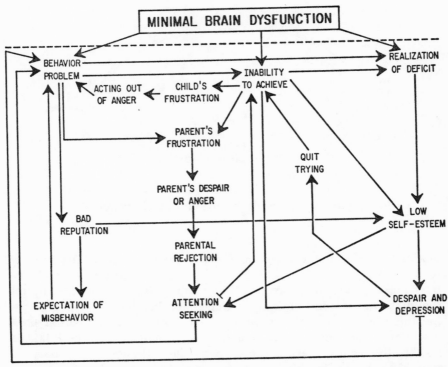

FIGURE 2. A complex psychosocial-educational vicious cycle initiated by minimal brain dysfunction. The self-perpetuating cycle can continue long after the initiating cause ceases. (Reprinted by permission from *Clinical Pediatrics*, 12:35-41, 1973.)

A VOLCANIC DOUBLE WHAMMY

The homegrown volcano is a combination of vicious cycle and unhealthy homeostasis. A mother may mistakenly believe that good parents never get angry or impatient with their children; she therefore suppresses and represses any feeling of anger or irritation and puts on a calm front of patient understanding, with enough permissiveness to prove to herself and to the world that she is not a mean, angry mother. The child, as might be expected, responds to permissiveness and lack of negative feedback by further misbehavior. He may be testing limits or looking for controls. In some cases, he may even be acting out anxious or depressive conflicts that arise when he senses the negative feelings that the mother thinks she is covering up. The child's misbehavior engenders more negative feelings in the mother, about which she then feels guilty and has to disprove by an even more patiently permissive posture, which invites further misbehavior from the child. Thus far is the vicious cycle.

The homeostatic mechanism in this case appears no less destructive than the vicious cycle. When the pent-up pressures of repressed and suppressed anger and irritation eventually overwhelm the mother's inhibitory resources, she may explode against the child, possibly even with child abuse. This may temporarily shape the child's behavior into a more acceptable direction (or the child may merely be disorganized by the apparent unpredictability of the outburst). In any event, the mother's subsequent guilt and sense of failure usually induce her to redouble her efforts at patient permissiveness, setting the stage for a repeat vicious cycle escalating to another explosion.

The length of cycles between homeostatic maternal outbursts varies with the durability and inhibitory resources of the parent and the energy and wisdom of the child. A very smart, manipulative child may be able to work the situation for all he can get and always stop short of the parents' boiling point, with only occasional miscalculations resulting in a parental explosion. Even without such conscious manipulation by the child, cycles may be several years long. On the other extreme, they may be as short as a few hours. Probably the latter situation, with more frequent outbursts, is actually healthier because it provides some sort of "consistent inconsistency" rather than exposing the child to an occasional very traumatically unpredictable outburst. It also gives the child a sporting chance to figure out the connection between his previous limit testing and the current eruption.

Cooling the Volcano

The relative desirability of more frequent, less intense eruptions provides the strategy for one of the interventions into this destructive system. The strategy is to turn an unhealthy destructive homeostasis with intervening vicious cycles into a healthier form of homeostasis which prevents the development of a vicious cycle. Even relatively unsophisticated parents are able to understand the principle of a "safety valve" and accept the necessity for "letting off some steam" before the pressure builds up to the explosion point.

The analogy with the volcano, with the implication of natural forces, helps many parents feel less defensive, guilty and anxious. The fact that the process can be analyzed and understood helps them to feel more control over the situation. One can compare the guilt after an eruption to the cooled rock that plugs a volcano and holds back the pressure until it builds up to another explosion. This can help parents see that their guilt-motivated attempts to "keep the lid on" actually lead to the destructive eruptions that they are trying to avoid.

Even without the current emphasis on energy conversation, it makes sense to try to harness volcanic pressure. Parents can learn to channel their "anger energy" into manageable quanta to use for such things as enforcing limits, providing appropriate negative feedback, and protecting the child from his own impulses.

TAMPERING WITH THE SYSTEM

What are the general guidance implications? How can the professional help parents beat the system?

Accentuate the Positive, Eliminate
the Negative, Modify the Modulation

It seems trite and obvious to say that the *underlying strategy* is to initiate virtuous cycles that will amplify anything positive within the family, to disrupt undesirable homeostasis and vicious cycles of negative interaction, and to reset appropriate areas of family homeostasis at a more desirable level of modulation.

1. State the Obvious. What may be obvious to an objective observer, especially to a sophisticated professional, may not be equally obvious to the parent caught up in the system. Therefore, one can sometimes contribute to breaking up a vicious cycle by a simple observation such as, "Now let's see—from what you said, it sounds like the more things he destroys the more you punish him, and the more you punish him the more things he destroys. That sounds like inflation. Have you figured out how to beat that system?" Of course, this statement carries the risk that the parent may see it as a statement of hopelessness or helplessness, since individuals are not able to do much about inflation. Sometimes a parent may need to be encouraged to think a little bit about what options he actually does have in this situation. Knowledge is power, at least in a small system where one person constitutes a significant component. This brings us to the next tactic.

2. Parents as Systems Analysts. Some intelligent, sophisticated parents may profit from basic education in the concepts in this chapter. I have even given parents a reprint of Wender's (1968) article on deviation-amplifying feedback and the perpetuation of behavior. As with any other reading assignment for parents, the parents need to have adequate opportunity for discussion afterwards, and should not be merely left to carry out the implications of the printed message. One advantage of parents as systems analysts is that this approach helps defuse negative parent-child interactions by redefining them as curious scientific phenomena rather than blame-worthy moral failings, as vicious cycles rather than vicious people. With older children and teenagers, it can even provide a medium for constructive parent-child cooperation: They can work together analyzing the system, how they are caught up in it, and what they can do to control the system rather than being controlled by it.

3. *Develop Positive Expectations.* Many psychosocial systems run on expectation. A boy whose parents expect him to pick on his siblings because that has been his previous pattern and who continues to pick on them because his parents expect it will find it easier to quit picking if his parents can develop an expectation that he has now outgrown that kind of behavior. Parents who a) expect a three-year-old's tantrums to be uncontrollable, b) therefore give in to them, and c) thereby reinforce their frequency and intensity, which d) confirms their expectation that the trantrums are uncontrollable, usually find a rather pleasant surprise once they become truly convinced that the tantrums can be controlled. This simple change of expectation can turn a vicious cycle into a virtuous cycle. Accomplishing this change of expectation is the challenge. Sometimes this can be done merely by explanation, for example, that tantrums are normal at this age and can be safely ignored. Persuasive facts may need to be cited (for example, that the parent is five times the size of the toddler and could easily win in any physical endurance struggle). Occasionally an outright pep talk is needed.

Pep talks are held in low regard because of the relative ineffectiveness of general "keep your chin up" reassurance approaches. However, the kind of pep talk we are considering here is a logical system intervention by altering a specific expectation believed to be crucial to the perpetuation of a vicious cycle. The pep talk is frequently most effective when coming from another parent who has been through a similar situation (see Chapter 10).

4. *Prepare for Change.* Preparing the parent to capitalize on positive things as they happen is in one sense a way of setting up positive expectations: The parent who is prepared to act on positive changes will be

looking for them. But its importance goes beyond that. It also programs the parent to initiate a virtuous cycle to replace a vicious cycle. Families abhor systems vacuums; they will fill any available time with some sort of system, either homeostasis, vicious cycle, or virtuous cycle. (See the functions of pastimes, games, and scripts described in Chapter 6.) Therefore, one of the best ways to get rid of a vicious cycle is to substitute for it a virtuous cycle—"change the sign" to positive rather than negative. An example will be found in Chapter 17.

REFERENCE

WENDER, P.: Vicious and virtuous cycles: The role of deviation-amplifying feedback in the origin and perpetuation of behavior. *Psychiatry*, 31:4, Nov., 1968.

Games Parents Play

Muriel James and John James

Muriel James and John James

STUUCTURAL ANALYSIS AND PARENT GUIDANCE

Transactional Analysis (TA) designed by Eric Berne, is based on the concept that everyone's personality has three ego states: Parent, Adult, and Child, diagrammed with three vertical circles. An ego state is a "consistent pattern of feeling and experience related to a corresponding consistent pattern of behavior" (Berne, 1966). When people feel and act as their parents once did, they are likely to be in the Parent state. When they are dealing with current reality, gathering facts and analyzing objectively, they are likely to be in the Adult state. When they are feeling and acting as they did when they were children, they are likely to be in the Child state.

Asking parents and literate children to fill in the diagram in Figure 1

Dr. Muriel James is the author of *TA for Moms and Dads.*

Figure 1

The crisis or problem is _____

Mom would say _____   Dad would say _____
and do _____   and do _____
and feel _____   and feel _____

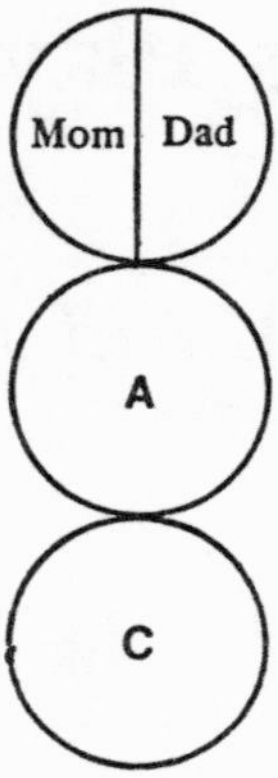

Facts I already have: Facts I need to get:
_____   _____
_____   _____

My basic uncensored feelings   The feelings I learned to have
about this are: _____   about things like this are:
_____   _____
_____   _____

My hunch is: _____
_____

often crystallizes the kind of guidance needed for a particular problem (M. James, 1974a). When applicable, the names of substitute parent figures are used instead of "Mom" and "Dad."

Telling Where You Are Now

The sense of self can be experienced in any of the ego states. Knowing which ego state is active and therefore feeling like the self may involve four kinds of diagnosis.

Behavioral diagnosis is related to words, body posture, facial expression, gestures, etc. Both parents and children can become aware of how specific behavior comes from each of their ego states. One technique for this is an ego state portrait: a quick sketch of the three circles showing the amount of psychic energy that seems to be in each ego state in particular situations (Figure 2).

Social diagnosis involves an awareness of other people's response. For

Figure 2

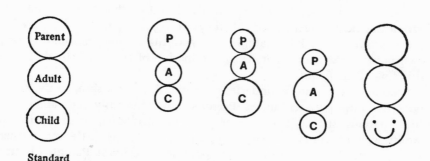

Standard
Ego State Diagram

Typical Ego State Portraits

example, a compliant or rebellious Child response in others suggests that one is acting like a critical or nurturing Parent.

Historical diagnosis flows from information about parents and childhood. Diagnosis of the Child state can come from questions like: "How did you usually feel when things went wrong when you were little?" "What did you do with your feelings?" "Now, how do you currently feel when things go wrong?" When parents become aware of how they "collect" their familiar childhood feelings as though collecting stamps, they can give up blaming games of "she or he makes me feel so ......" They begin to own their feelings.

Historical diagnosis of the Parent state involves questions such as: "What words would describe your parent figures as you perceived them when you were little?" "What mottos or saying did they use?" "Was their own behavior consistent with their words?" "What were some of the things they said or did that you liked or didn't like?" "Do you ever do some of these things?" These kinds of questions guide clients into an evaluation of their parenting practices.

Phenomenological diagnosis is the emotional reexperiencing of an earlier situation, a "working through." It can happen spontaneously or be encouraged by the therapist.

Ego State Boundary Problems

Ego state boundaries can be thought of as semipermeable membranes which separate the ego states and through which psychic energy needs to flow.

One common problem is when a person's Adult thinking is contaminated by archaic elements from the Child or the Parent or both. In such cases people feel and think they are right when actually they lack the necessary facts. For example, exaggerating or underestimating one's own power or that of others is contamination of the Adult by delusional thinking of the Child.

Sometimes ego state boundaries are rigid, like thick skin, so the energy does not flow between states. Persons may constantly feel and act as their parents once did, or as they did in childhood, or as computing adults who continually analyze situations but show little involvement with people. Thus, a person can respond as a Constant Parent, Constant Adult, or Constant Child. Rigid ego boundaries of both parents and children tend to relax and become more permeable in a non-threatening environment, where the professional only confronts when they are ready to profit from it. [Contrast this with the more aggressive approach in Chapter 8. See, also, Anthony's plea in Chapter 28 for gradualism and patience with psychotic parents.—Ed.]

GUIDANCE FOR STROKES AND TRANSACTIONS

A stroke is any form of recognition, verbal or nonverbal, *positive or negative*. For example, sarcasm is a negative stroke; smiles are positive strokes. Strokes can be unconditional, such as "I love you," or conditional such as "I accept you if you . . ." Children need both kinds. Unconditional strokes are affirming at the deepest levels. Conditional strokes are motivating at the action level.

Many parents stroke each other and their children with threats, such as "If you don't change I'll leave you (beat you, get sick, etc.)." Teenagers often intimidate their parents with similar words and actions. Younger children, though feeling less powerful, may use the same kinds of statements and actions.

The giving and getting of strokes are directly related to individual needs. Maslow's hierarchy of needs is easily drawn and explained so that parents can become aware of their family's needs and how to care for them (Figure 3).

The experience of these needs changes from time to time and from person to person. For example, a stepparent may have difficulty becoming part of the total family and therefore have a belonging need (see, also,

Figure 3

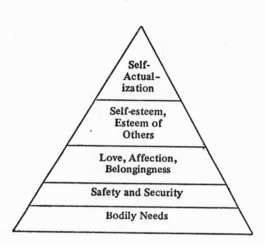

Chapter 25). A parent with a demanding job who also keeps house and cares for a family may be continually fatigued and have a physiological need for rest. A single parent who does the same may, in addition, feel lowered self-esteem because of being single.

Parents can be guided to recognize the children's levels of needs. When death, desertion, or serious illness occur, children are likely to feel threatened at the safety level (see Chapters 23 and 24). If a family moves away from people with whom they have strong friendship ties, those involved may lose their feelings of belongingness and esteem.

Target Stroking

Selective stroking reinforces the preceding behavior. Parents who want to enhance their children's nurturing capacities can learn to compliment their children for nurturing actions and statements. Those who want their children to think clearly can stroke (recognize and give feedback to) the children's Adult. Those who want to stimulate obedience can note how their children have been adapted—positively or negatively—in specific areas and give strokes to the Child ego state for the wanted behavior. (See Chapter 7 for more on teaching parents to modify their children's behavior.)

Figure 4

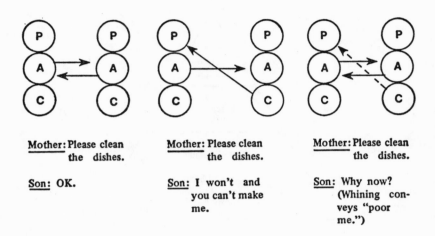

Mother: Please clean
        the dishes.

Son: OK.

Mother: Please clean
        the dishes.

Son: I won't and
    you can't make
    me.

Mother: Please clean
        the dishes.

Son: Why now?
    (Whining con-
    veys "poor
    me.")

Transactions are exchanges of two or more strokes. When a stimulus stroke receives the expected response stroke, it is complementary. When it receives an unexpected response, it is crossed. When there is a double message involved, it is ulterior. Transactions can be diagrammed, as the transaction between a mother and son is shown in Figure 4. Some children openly cross their parents. Others are more subtle; they send ulterior messages of rebellion, compliance, or resignation. Procrastination (passive aggression) is often rebellion or despair thinly disguised. The simple question, "How will your children respond if you say ...... from your ...... ego state?" can help a parent prevent problems by exploring other options. The children can be taught the same skill.

GAMES FAMILIES PLAY

Every family has its own repetitive pattern of fighting, arguing, manipulating, or withdrawing to solve or to avoid solving problems. These habitual ways of dealing with problems are often psychological "games." A game is a predictable series of transactions with an ulterior message. It concludes when at least one person gets a negative feeling, colloquially called a "trading stamp" because the feelings are "saved up" and "cashed in."

First-degree games involve small collections of stamps, cashed in for small prizes such as weeping, making a mistake, having a temper tantrum, or getting drunk. Second-degree game players have more invested in their feelings and in justification of their behavior. They save larger collections for a "quit" prize such as quitting school, a marriage, or a job. Third-degree game players "go for broke" for the big prizes—homicide or suicide.

Showing parents 1) how to identify games, 2) how to deescalate "hard" games into "soft" games that are less destructive, and 3) how to give them up in favor of authenticity and intimacy, is part of parent guidance.

Drama Roles

One way to recognize games is to learn how to observe family interactions in terms of three roles: Persecutor, Rescuer, and Victim (Karpman, 1968). These can be authentic or can be game roles. A "real" persecutor is chosen or paid to fulfill this role (i.e., a judge), whereas a "game" Persecutor chooses the role out of frustration, revenge, jealousy, or anger, and persecutes others with a sense of vindictiveness or self-righteousness. A real rescuer effects necessary rescues and encourages independence in others (e.g., a lifeguard); a game Rescuer spends a lot of time helping others, even when they don't want help. A real victim hurts because of a specific unavoidable crisis (e.g., recent death of a friend); a game Victim *often* feels hurt, sad, scared, confused, misunderstood, or ignored. Game players often play the same games over and over, as seen in the following family game (from James and Jongeward, 1971):

Son:
(as Persecutor yelling angrily at Mother)

You know I hate blue. Here you went and bought me another blue shirt!

Mother:
(as Victim)

I never do anything right as far as you're concerned.

Father:
(rescues mother, persecutes son)

Don't you dare yell at your mother like that, young man. Go to your room and no dinner!

Son:
(now as Victim, sulking in his room)

They tell me to be honest, and when I tell them what I don't like, they put me down. How can you satisfy people like that?

Mother: (now Rescuer, sneaks him a tray of food)	Now don't tell your father. We shouldn't get so upset over a shirt.
Mother: (as Persecutor, returning to father)	John, you're so tough with our son. I'll bet he's sitting in his room right now hating you.
Father: (as Victim)	Gee, honey, I was only trying to help you, and you kick me where it hurts the most.
Son: (calling out as Rescuer)	Hey, Mom, lay off, will ya? Dad's just tired.

The switch in roles adds an element of melodrama to the game. Often family members perceive themselves in one role while others see them differently. In the previous example, the son sees himself as a Victim, yet Persecutes his mother and Rescues his father. Both parents also play the three roles, unaware of the games they play. Family members can often decrease the intensity of their games as they come to recognize these three roles and choose not to play them.

Professionals also play games, even when giving parental guidance. A common game is Courtroom, initiated by couples who want to get out of a marriage or get even with each other.

> When they come for counseling, often related to an issue involving their children, each acts like a Victim and insists that the spouse is a Prosecutor. Each hopes to be rescued and hopes that his spouse will be persecuted by the therapist. In this game, as they explain the situation from a Victim position, they also make persecuting statements to or about their spouse. If one spouse acts upset, the other may switch and become a Rescuer with a remark such as, "Well, it really isn't that bad" (M. James, 1973).

The professional who joins the game as a Rescuer may also play the other roles, persecuting the couple with criticism, then feeling like a Victim when they reject the "advice." Games can be played internally, like a game of solitaire, as well as between people. Three-handed games occur when parents feel they have to referee between siblings or between a child and the other parent. Children also set up three-handed games by getting parents angry at each other. Grandparents increase the possible number of hands. Parents can avoid three-handed games by contracting not to intervene unless necessary and to eschew ineffective rescues. Effective rescues lead to resolutions of conflicts rather than just truces between battles.

Discounts

Another way to break up family games is for parents to stop the "discounts" (Schiff and Schiff, 1971). Parents often discount their children by assuming they are unable to think for themselves. Or children discount parents by treating the parents as if they were Bosses, and not people with feelings. In each case, the importance of someone's feelings, thoughts, or problem-solving abilities are discounted and made to seem unimportant (or sometimes overly important). When families exaggerate each others' strengths or weaknesses, they discount each other, leading to games and bad feelings. As parents learn to recognize discounts, they can begin to give positive strokes instead.

The Game Plan

Parents can be taught to recognize games easily by looking for the "Game Plan" (J. James, 1973). As in a football game where certain plays are planned, families often act out predictable patterns. These can be recognized by asking the following questions:

> What keeps happening over and over again?
> What happens first?
> What happens next?
> What happens next?
> How does it end?
> How does each person feel in the end?

One family came because the parents could not get along with their 16-year-old son. They recognized the following game plan:

> Son asks to borrow the car.
> *Ma:* No.
> *Son:* Why not?
> *Ma:* Because . . .
> Son argues each point, begins yelling.
> Ma yells back, bringing up other past errors of the son.
> Son leaves the house, slamming the door.
> Ma goes and cries to Pa.
> Son feels misunderstood; Ma feels inadequate.

Figure 5

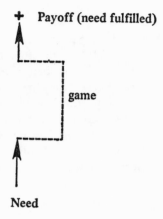

When the parents recognized this pattern, they decided that they would not raise their voices when talking with the son. Later they decided to give their reasons only once and not to bring up his past misdeeds each time he asked for something. As a result, they sounded more sure of themselves and less angry. Within a short time, the son began to stop his yelling and talk reasonably. They then began to set mutually agreeable standards for behavior which would allow him to use the car.

Positive Payoffs After Games

Parents who are concerned about their children's welfare usually ask, "Why do we play these games?" The answer is: because everyone needs attention and excitement and if these needs are not met directly, people play games—indirect routes—to get what they need (Figure 5).

For example, a son may want his father's attention. If Dad spends time with the boy, then all is well. But if Dad is "too tired" from a busy day at the office, the son may do something (fight with his sister, stub his toe, or kick the dog) to evoke Dad's attention. The attention the son thus elicits is his "positive payoff," satisfying the underlying need (J. James, 1976b).

Parents can be taught to discover the positive payoffs for games by asking a few key questions:

> After things go wrong, how do you (or your children) get rid of your negative feeling?

> Who comes to your (their) rescue? How do you (they) rescue yourself (themselves)?

The positive payoff is a "rescue" from the negative feelings. Common payoffs are: time alone or time with someone else, attention and tenderness, excitement and stimulation.

Parents experience relief as they learn to recognize the positive payoffs, the "real" reason for playing games. "In recognizing the positive payoffs for games, people become aware that their *needs and struggles have an OK aspect* to them. The need for games diminishes and games are discarded in favor of Adult-chosen means of taking care of needs directly" (J. James, 1976a).

SCRIPTS AS LIFE PLANS

A psychological script can be briefly defined as a life plan, much like a dramatic stage production, that an individual feels compelled to act out.

Scripts are unknowingly selected in childhood, strongly affected by the transactions between parents and children, even by names and nicknames. Script themes are suggested by parents who may say: "He's a chip off the old block." "She's just like her mother." "There's always a black sheep in our family."

Stage instructions on how to act are then given by mottos such as: "Children should be seen and not heard." "You are the laziest person I've ever met." "Don't trust men (women)."

All parents give children scripting messages. If they ask their children, "Why do you do such stupid things" the children hear the underlying message "you're stupid," and are likely to continue acting in stupid ways. If children are complimented for being creative, they will probably enjoy their creativity and feel confident in being creative more often. Parental programming helps develop scripts which are constructive, destructive, or banal.

Destructive life scripts are often chosen by children who are beaten, abused, or frequently told they'll never amount to anything. Such children when they grow up are likely to act scared and passive or hostile and abusive like their parents.

Banal, "going nowhere" scripts often are chosen by children whose parents live dull, boring lives, or who are unsure of themselves and do not show their children how different life can be.

Children are likely to have constructive, winners' scripts if they have parents who are happy, who enjoy other people, and who believe in and support the strengths of their children. Such parents encourage their children also to enjoy life and to achieve their goals. [Contrast this relative emphasis on parental determinism with Ellis' (Chapter 8) aggressive exoneration of parental responsibility. Note, however, that both approaches offer parents hope for changing and helping their children improve.—Ed.]

Parents can learn to recognize how their children are scripted by asking the questions:

> If they go on as they now are, where are they likely to be in 5, 10, or 20 years?
>
> What kind of friends do they have and what do they do with their time? How will these kinds of friends and these ways of spending time help or hinder them when they're 20, 30, or 40 years old?
>
> What models of being a man or a woman have we shown them? What marriage model have we lived which they're likely to copy? What about our patterns of solving problems, having friends, keeping a job or enjoying working, getting an education, handling money matters? Are those patterns we've shown our children destructive, non-productive or constructive?

Being on Stage

The home is the primary stage on which children learn about people and the scripted parts they play. They learn what to do to get the spotlight. They may discover roles like the Tragedy Queen, the Sad Sack, the Joke-happy Clown, the Helpless Waif, the Superman, or the Hovering Nurse. They experiment with these roles when playing games such as "House," "Cops and Robbers," "School," or "King of the Mountain." They learn how a change of voice, action, costume, or scenery affects the drama. They are leading characters and supporting characters acting out fairy tales and children's stories that feel "right" to them because they identify with the characters.

In guiding parents, a series of theatrical stages can be drawn. Stick figures can be drawn on the stage to show the prominence of various family members at different times. Some stages seem overcrowded, some despairingly empty.

Figure 6

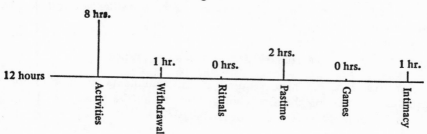

In some families, one or both of the parents are center stage and the children merely supporting figures. In other families it may be reversed. In any case, learning how to share the stage and learning how to enhance the drama by changing actions and dialogue are forms of guidance that both parents and children find useful (M. James, 1973).

ANALYSIS OF TIME STRUCTURING

The way families spend time can be used as a thermometer of their satisfaction or dissatisfaction. Do they spend time away from home or always at home? Do children seem to want all their parents' time, or do they feel forced to spend time with their little brothers or sisters, or do they spend most of their time in front of the television set? Do adolescents come home on time? Do parents feel they have enough time for themselves, their marriage, or their friends?

There are six ways to spend time: activities (work and hobbies); psychological withdrawal into fantasy; ritual stereotyped transactions; superficial pastimes; games; and genuine intimacy.

Parents can be asked to make a Time-O-Gram (M. James, 1974a) and graph how they spent the last 24 hours, as individuals or as a family. For example, a mother who spends two hours talking with a friend about vacations, two hours shopping, four hours parenting, two hours cooking and cleaning up, one hour reading, and one hour relaxing with her husband, would draw her Time-O-Gram as in Figure 6. With this picture, she can evaluate her time structuring and set new goals.

However, it is not the quantity of time families spend with each other, as much as the quality, that enhances family life. Some families do not save "prime time," quality time, for each other (M. James and Savary,

1976). They give each other "left over time." Complaints may arise, "But you never have time for me," or "When we are together you're too tired to enjoy it."

Effective T.A. guidance requires giving parents permission to solve problems, protecting them psychologically during the process, and being potent when faced with treatment challenges.

Permission

Many messages parents give their children are unnecessarily inhibiting and difficult to modify. "Permissions," on the other hand, encourage free choice and responsible independent thinking. They are permits, like fishing licenses. Particularly important are permissions to love, to change, and to do things well (Berne, 1972).

Parents give permissions to their children verbally with statements such as, "It's OK with me if you do it," and with questions such as "What do you think?" They also give permissions nonverbally by laughing joyously, speaking honestly, acting considerately, etc.

Professionals can give parents permission verbally by saying, "It's OK with me if you . . ." or "I think you have a great idea that will be to your benefit." They can also model permissions by talking about feelings and by raising questions about options, about time structuring, and about "antidependence" versus independence. Also, by listening carefully and avoiding games, they *model behavior* which can be new and revitalizing to parents.

Protection

Potent professionals, able to give permission, often need to provide protection simultaneously. Protection means the professional uses his or her clinical skills and personal resources to support parents as they change. The professional's interventions are timed to reinforce constructive change and prevent nonproductive or destructive changes. In some situations professionals need to be both tender and strong to be protective (M. James, 1976b).

They can also give protection by refusing to gossip about other family members who are absent from the therapy session and by direct statements such as, "If you make these changes, expect your children to test your new limits. They may be resistant at first, but eventually they'll probably cooperate."

When parents and children are making important script changes, their dreams may become more vivid, perhaps frightening. Forewarning them that this is common can protect them.

Protection is also provided with the use of therapeutic prescriptions such as, "It's not good to hit your children. Experiment for a few minutes when you're alone yelling or hitting a pillow or banging a tennis ball. Allow yourself to direct your anger into less destructive directions and outlets."

Professionals also give protection by sharing information with parents, often about children in general: "It's normal for children at three years not to clean their room. It's developmentally too early to expect them to do that. How does that affect your current situation?"

Potency

Potency comes with the professional's own confidence, positive regard for others, and willingness to risk, to grow, and to enjoy life. (See Chapter 14 for more about the professional's feelings.) These qualities get transmitted to the parent in myriads of obvious and subtle ways. Since these transactions are the basis of successful living, parents get a continual image or model of health and encouragement.

Potent professionals have sufficient training and experience to understand the needs of families in crisis. They use crisp, clear statements. They are willing to take a stand on their values, e.g., it is not OK to beat children; excessive drinking is always destructive to families; everyone deserves the right to express his feelings if done in considerate and nondestructive ways; children need the consistent care and affection of their parents; children can think and be responsible, etc. Potent professionals confront destructive behavior and encourage clear thinking with the Adult rather than overindulging the Parent or Child ego states.

Some well meaning parents (and professionals) lack potency in their Parent ego state because their own parents were inadequate in some way. They may have been overcritical, overnurturing, indifferent, superorganized, conflicted, wishy-washy, or emotionally over-needy. Such people need self-reparenting (M. James, 1976).

SELF-REPARENTING

The first step is to recognize this need by making long lists of the positive and negative characteristics of one's parent figures. Next comes an agreement deliberately to use more of the positive qualities one already has in the Parent state and to develop new positive parenting attributes to balance the old negative ones. The professional guides the parents to read books about parenting and observe other parents in their caretaking practices. Such observation can occur in supermarkets, nursery schools, or playgrounds. This observation is followed by discussion to strengthen the Adult ego state and help the decontamination process.

The next step is for the parents to have a fantasized dialogue between their inner Child and Adult. The Adult questions the Child: "What do you need? What do you want?" and listens to the inner Child's requests. If the requests are reasonable, the Adult contracts to act as a new substitute parent, meeting the appropriate needs and desires of the Child. During this dialogic process, the professional may use regressive techniques, such as holding the parent for a few minutes if he or she experiences deep grief or anger. (Cf., the surrogate mother to the mother in Chapter 22.) Of course, the regression techniques are discussed and the purpose for using them is made clear.

After the parent practices having his Adult take care of his inner Child for a considerable period of time, the caring becomes automatic. It shifts into the Parent ego state to become a New Parent with the positive attributes that are needed for the particular person.

CONTRACTS

Permission and protection are accelerated by contracts. Contracts are plans of action to which a person is committed. They contain details of what, when, where, how, and with whom. They can be made with oneself or with others (M. James, 1976a, b). A contract is an agreement to do something about something, such as to spend one hour each day talking or playing with the children, or to ask other family members for their appreciations in addition to their resentments, or to confront a child for being continually late, or to take time out for a vacation.

There are three types of contract: 1) to change behavior (e.g., to respond promptly to the child's request); 2) to change feelings (to stop feeling like a Victim when criticized); 3) to decrease psychosomatic symptoms (such as being overweight or having high blood pressure).

The establishment of a goal comes first, dealing with these questions:

1. What do I want that would enhance my life?
2. What would I need to change so that I could reach my goal?
3. What would I be willing to do to make the change happen?

4. How would others know when I have effected the change?
5. How might I sabotage or undermine myself so that I would not achieve my goals?

At times, family members will agree that they have a problem between them which they would like to resolve. When people are willing to work together to improve their relationship, an "Interpersonal Contact," using the following questions, can be useful (M. James and Savary, 1977).

1. What goals do we have for our relationship?
2. How would each of us describe the goals?
3. In what ways are our goals compatible? Incompatible? Or a compromise?
4. How would achieving our goal benefit us? Other family members? The total family unit?
5. In the process of working on the goals, how might changes affect each family member?
6. What are each of us willing to do or change to achieve our goal?
7. How will we know when we've reached our goal? How will others be able to tell (in specific observable behaviors) when we've achieved our goal?
8. How could each of us sabotage our goal? How might other family members sabotage our efforts?

When making Interpersonal Contracts, it is essential that each question be discussed at length. Parents or children who are overly busy and say they "don't have enough time," or who are indifferent and say, "I don't care," or who are hopeless and say, "It's no use," or who are passive and say, "You do it," are sabotaging themselves and their family's health.

Wishing and wanting without deciding and acting often sabotage a contract. A good TA therapist teaches parents and children how to act and decide.

REFERENCES

BERNE, E.: *Principles of Group Treatment.* New York: Grove Press, 1966, pp. 358, 364.

BERNE, E.: *What Do You Do After You Say Hello?* New York: Grove Press, 1972, pp. 123, 125.

JAMES, J.: The game plan. *Transactional Analysis Journal,* 3:4, pp. 14-17, Oct. 1973.

JAMES, J.: Positive payoffs after games. *Transactional Analysis Journal,* 6:2, July, 1976 (a).

JAMES, J.: Family therapy with TA. *Techniques in TA for Psychotherapists and Counselors.* Reading, Mass.: Addison-Wesley, 1976 (b).

JAMES, M.: *Born to Love: Transactional Analysis in the Church.* Reading, Mass.: Addison-Wesley, 1973, pp. 108-109, 134ff, 170f.

JAMES, M.: *Transactional Analysis for Moms and Dads*. Reading, Mass.: Addison-Wesley, 1974, p. 70; Chapter 6 (a).

JAMES, M.: Self-reparenting: Theory and process. *Transactional Analysis Journal*, 4:3, 32-39, July, 1974 (b)

JAMES, M.: *Techniques in TA for Psychotherapists and Counselors*. Reading, Mass.: Addison-Wesley, 1976.

JAMES, M. & JONGEWARD, D.: *Born to Win: Transactional Analysis with Gestalt Experiments*. Reading, Mass.: Addison-Wesley, 1971, p. 91.

JAMES, M. & SAVARY, L.: *The Heart of Friendship*. New York: Harper & Row, 1976, pp. 140-142.

JAMES, M. & SAVARY, L.: *A New Self: Self Therapy with Transactional Analysis*. Reading, Mass.: Addison-Wesley, 1977.

KARPMAN, S.: Fairy tales and script drama analysis. *Transactional Analysis Bulletin*, 7:26, 39-43, April, 1968.

SCHIFF, A. & SCHIFF, J.: Passivity. *Transactional Analysis Journal*, 1:1, 73, Jan., 1971.

Chapter 7

Teaching Parents to Modify Their Children's Behavior

Ogden Lindsley

This chapter summarizes experience from over a dozen classes teaching parents behavior modification. In some of the classes the teacher or advisor was an experienced nonprofessional with backup support from a professional. One class received its professional support by long-distance telephone after one face-to-face introduction to the concepts. Though parents can be taught behavior modification one-to-one, classes are more economically effective.

The concepts necessary for parents to know can be reduced to the simple principles—even slogans—described below.

DIFFERENT STROKES FOR DIFFERENT FOLKS

It has long been known that each person's behavior is more responsive to some consequences or reinforcers than to others. What is reinforcing to one child may not affect another. Furthermore, one child's positive reinforcer may even be another's punishment.

Most people's behavior can be accelerated with rewards. The trick is to find the best reward for each person. This need to individualize reward selection we call "different strokes for different folks."

Charting to Monitor Stroke Effects

Finding the right stroke for the right folk is easy once you believe it can be done, and you have the right measuring tool. We can custom-tailor rewards by watching daily frequency charts while trying different things as rewards.

Changing the immediate environment while watching for improvement in daily behavior is what behavior modification is all about. Behavioral frequency charts are watched by the behavior manager in the same way that heart and respiration frequency charts are watched by nurses and physicians as they adjust medication and dosage to the patient.

Skinner's three great contributions were:

1. Watch frequency of behavior—how often it happens in a minute or day.
2. Have behavers record and chart their own frequencies.
3. Custom-tailor the stimuli and rewards for each behaver.

For me, self-charting of behavior frequency was a major scientific contribution. It had already worked in the rest of natural science. Scientists made great leaps forward when they looked at the frequencies of light, sound, and electrical phenomena rather than their formal differences. Furthermore, it is economical, moral, and client-centered. I have long thought that the best science is humble and moral and interferes with the thing being studied as little as possible. (A good description of the differences within behavior modification over the issue of control and putting the power of the charts in the hands of the people can be found in Hilts, 1974, pp. 189-195.)

FROM THEORY TO PRACTICE

During my first five years at Kansas, I taught a four-course sequence of graduate education classes: 1) Functional Analysis of Human Behavior; 2) Classroom Applications of Free-Operant Conditioning; 3) Human Free-Operant Research Strategies; 4) Human Free-Operant Research Tactics. My plan, which looked good on paper, was: First we will teach how to describe behavior . . . how to talk like a free-operant conditioner. Then we will teach how to apply this information in the classroom. This would complete the teacher or Master's degree level. Later, Doctoral candidates would take the research courses.

However, I obligingly let some teachers take the second course, classroom applications, without having taken the functional analysis prerequisite. I compared the children's behavior improvement produced by the teachers who had not taken the "required" analysis course with the improvement produced by the teachers who had taken the course. The analysis course slightly *damaged* the teachers' management effectiveness at the .05 level of confidence!

Only after replicating these results twice did I abandon the functional analysis course. I converted it into a beginning classroom applications class, plunging the teachers immediately into behavior change. Functional analysis was taught later on to the Doctoral candidates in their research strategies class.

Therefore we simplified behavior modification for teachers and parents by discarding laboratory jargon and translating procedures into slogans, catch-phrases and plain English (Lindsley, 1972).

HOW TO MODIFY BEHAVIOR FOR FUN AND PROFIT

For teaching parents we simplified behavior modification into *four steps: 1) pinpoint, 2) chart, 3) change, and 4) try, try, again.* Each step has its own slogans, but two general slogans for the parents to remember throughout are:

"The child knows best"
"Care enough to chart"

1. Pinpoint

First parents need to pick a behavior to improve. There are four pinpointing requirements:

A) Parents must *pinpoint a complete cycle.* They know the behavior is over when the child is in position to do it again.

B) The pinpoint should *pass the dead-man's test.* If a dead man can do it, it is not behavior and one should not try to teach it. For example, not screaming at dinner is dead-man behavior. You should not try to accelerate silence! Rather you should pinpoint a behavior to accelerate—like appropriate conversation or using the napkin.

C) *Pinpoint action, not the child's word* for it. If parents pinpoint statements rather than action, they can easily produce lying.

The statements may accelerate from the rewards while the actions remain at a low frequency.

D) *Pinpoint a pair.* For every inappropriate behavior picked to decelerate one must accelerate a related appropriate behavior. This guarantees the accuracy of the parent's goal and is a way of saying with rewards, "Better this way!" Ann Duncan called these "fair pairs."

Some pinpointing slogans are:

"First things first, one at a time."
"Plan a behaver and manager success."
"Little steps for little feet."
"Make it harder to do but easier to learn."
"Move up the chart for more opportunities."

2. Chart

After counting and marking on the calendar seven daily frequencies for each behavior, the parent should chart them to project their course. From the charts the parents can see *how long it will take for counting alone to bring the behaviors to the aim (goal).* Charting is taught to parents who have a week's frequencies at the second or third class meeting. There are four charting requirements.

A) Chart on a *standard multiply-divide chart.** These charts are made so that any frequency that is doubling every week is parallel with a line from the lower left to the upper right corner. Any behavior that is dividing by two each week would be parallel with a line from the upper left to the lower right corner. Since behavior frequencies change by multiplying and dividing, they are best projected on a chart with a multiplication scale (Koenig, 1972).

B) *Chart ignored and no-chance days* so it is easy to see how much of the week was charted. In this way, weekly patterns and the effects of social factors can be readily seen on the charts.

C) Chart *record floors and ceilings* (e.g., 9:00 a.m. to 4:00 p.m.) to show how much of the behavior day was charted. This permits frequencies to be directly compared from chart to chart even though the behaviors were not counted for the same periods of time each day.

D) *Calendar synchronizing all charts* makes it easy for people to recognize the same dates on each other's charts. This increases excite-

---

*Standard Behavior Charts and a complete line of behavior counters and timers can be purchased from Behavior Research Co., Box 3351, Kansas City, Kansas, 66103.

ment and communication and the chance for discovery of unusual days. Further details of standard charting conventions can be found in Pennypacker, Koenig, and Lindsley, 1972.

3. Change

If the projected behavior courses from counting alone will not reach the parents' aims soon enough, then they must change the child's environment. The current environment is producing the charted behavior trend— so they must change something! Almost any change in the environment will change the frequency of the behavior. *Almost any change will work.* Children have dreamed up such interesting successful changes as: getting up and running around your chair every time your teacher throws a "tantrum," standing your Barbie doll in the corner for five minutes every time you whine, and sticking a cigarette in your ear for a minute rather than smoking it (Kansas City Star, 1968).

In a computerized collection of 12,000 behavior modification projects on 1,223 different behaviors, 1,046 different stimuli were programmed and 818 different consequences were arranged to modify the behavior (Lindsley, Koenig, Nichols, Kanter & Young, 1971). This dramatically demonstrates how wide the range of behavioral change agents is. Behavior is easy to change. What is hard to do is to start.

Some of the most notable change slogans are:

"Say, 'Better this way!' "
"Prime the pump."
"Sound signals leave the eyes at work."
"Back up and do it right."
"Repair or replace it."
"Announce before you arrange."
"Each time you do it, repeat it 20 times."
"Announce only what you can comfortably present."

4. Grandma's Law

I first heard, "*If at first you don't succeed, try, try again,*" from my grandmother, Mrs. James Ogden Lindsley.

"Try, Try, again" teaches parents the pragmatic, inductive approach. Discovery, search, and the reason for charting were built into this slogan.

Also, it prepares the parents for initial, and even secondary, failure. Consequently, the majority who have initial success are happy, while the minority (10 to 30%) who have to try again with another change tactic are not unhappy; they are merely expectant and eager to get on with their next change. Only five to 10% need to go on to their third try, and virtually all of these succeed. Therefore, *trying three different change procedures practically guarantees our parents success.*

But parents have to *be sure that each try is truly different,* and not just a different dosage of the first try. For example, "five minutes of television," "10 minutes of television," and "20 minutes of television" are not three different tries. They are just three different doses of the same try. The professional adviser should point this out and suggest something different for the second try, like, "a five-minute chore." It is usually best if the first try is suggested by the child, the second by one of the parents, and the third by the other parent or sibling. This involves the whole family in the planning, and takes the onus of being right off the adviser's shoulders.

HOW TO CONDUCT A PARENTS' CLASS

A parents' meeting should be light, positive, and humorous. All first names of both parents and children should be learned by the adviser by the second meeting. This is hard to do, but essential. The report of my first fathers' class (Lindsley, 1966) has been a good hand-out when someone demands something in print.

The "better, this way" teaching approach should be used. For example: "Hey, look at Ted's chart of Brent's shrieking and kind words!" "See how the kind words are going up faster and faster? When will they reach the aim?" . . . "An even better way to chart them might be on this multiply-chart. See how the kind words course is a straight path here?" . . .

All parents should have an opportunity to share how things are going with their child at every meeting. A way of insuring this is to give everyone three minutes at first, timing this with a reset bell timer which is passed around, and each parent sets his own timer. Though this sounds too structured, in practice it is fun and makes a lot of laughs. It's the only way I have found to guarantee that 30 parents will share their experiences since the last meeting and still have time left for a visiting testimonial, an answer to an involved question, and refreshments.

Strength in Numbers

You should start with a class large enough so that if attendance drops off, you will still have a group. Another tactic is to telephone parents the night before, often on the night of the meeting, asking if they have transportation or requesting them to bring some cookies or a six-pack. When tried, these meeting reminders produced perfect attendance. However, they did not increase the percent success. They got the folks out, but didn't make them try.

Troubleshooting

When parents report failure in their behavior modifying efforts, the trouble can usually be found in one of these pitfalls:

1. *Projecting stroke preference:* Just because a father enjoyed playing monopoly as a child, does not mean that the opportunity to play monopoly will be rewarding to his son. It may even be punishing! "The child knows best."

2. *Loopholes in the welfare system:* A child would have to be stupid to change his behavior to earn a cookie if he can raid the cookie jar any time he wishes regardless. Parents need to close all leaks in the system, including indulgent grandparents. If necessary, locks can be put on cupboard or refrigerator. The behavior manager (parent) needs to control the strokes.

3. *Reaching for the unreachable star* may be admirable philosophy but can be frustrating to a child and his parent. Behavior goals and the intermediate steps to be rewarded need to be realistic and attainable so the child and parent can experience success.

4. *Failing to grow with the child:* An initially challenging goal can become dull and aversive as the child masters it and girds for bigger and better goals. The behavior manager needs to keep pace with the child's progress.

5. *Trying too hard or wanting too much for the child:* The parent who continually reminds the child about the reward and what must be done to earn it is not allowing the behavior mod system to work. Among other things, such a parent is contaminating the reward with an aversive stimulus—nagging.

TREATMENT SUCCESS, CREDIBILITY, OR LETHARGY

We do not have a treatment success problem. People who try all four steps to success meet their modification goals from 95 to 100% of the time. We have either a treatment credibility or a parent lethargy problem, or —more realistically—a combination of both.

We know great lethargy exists, because very successful parents—even advisers to their own class—do not continue to use the methods after their class is over. Most, when faced with a severe behavior problem, will use the four steps, but they will not use them for minor problems, nor preventively. There is no credibility problem here, just lethargy and the same acceptance of sloppy behavior as they have for sloppy homes, offices, and clothes. Let's face it! Most of us are happy slobs. Why should we perfect behavior? Why should we work at it all the time?

If this logic be so, the follow-up question for parents' classes in behavior modification should not be, "How many are still doing it?" Rather, the questions should be, "Of those who took action for some behavior problem of their children, how many used behavior modification?"

LOVE, SCIENCE, AND CONDITIONS OF THE WARRANTY

You can guarantee parents and their children 100% success in meeting their behavioral goals if they learn to pinpoint, chart, change, and try, try again, and remember these slogans:

"Different strokes for different folks!"
"Care enough to chart!"
and
"The child knows best!"

If the child knows best, what does the parent know? The answer is "more than you, but less than the child."

If they both know more than you, then what can you teach them? The answer is: science. You can teach them to: Pinpoint, chart, change, and try, try again . . . and love them while they learn.

REFERENCES

A clear ear signals victory. *Kansas City Star,* Feb. 4, 1968.
GALLOWAY, C. & GALLOWAY, K. C.: Parent classes in precise behavior management. *Teaching Exceptional Children,* 3:120-128, 1971.
HILTS, P. J.: *Behavior Mod.* New York: Harpers Magazine Press, 1974.
LINDSLEY, O. R.: An experiment with parents handling behavior at home. *Johnstone Bulletin,* 9:27-36, 1966. Reprinted in: G. A. Fargo, C. Behrns, & P. Nolen (Eds.), *Behavior Modification in the Classroom.* Belmont, California: Wadsworth Publishing Co., 1970, pp. 310-316.
LINDSLEY, O. R.: Training parents and teachers to precisely manage children's behavior. *Special Education Colloquium Series.* Flint, Mich.: C. S. Mott Foundation, 1968.
LINDSLEY, O. R.: From Skinner to precision teaching: The child knows best. In: J. B. Jordan & L. S. Robbins (Eds.) , *Let's Try Doing Something Else Kind of Thing.* Arlington, Va.: Council for Exceptional Children, 1972, pp. 1-11.
LINDSLEY, O. R., KOENIG, C. H., NICHOLS, J. B., KANTER, D. B., & YOUNG, N. A.: *Handbook of Precise Behavior Facts.* Kansas City, KS 66103, Box 3222: Precision Media, 1971, 2 Vols.
PENNYPACKER, H. S., KOENIG, C. H., & LINDSLEY, O. R.: *Handbook of the Standard Behavior Chart* (Preliminary Ed.) . Kansas City, KS 66103: Precision Media, 1972.
SKINNER, B. F.: *Behavior of Organisms.* New York: Appleton- Century, 1938, p. 60.

Chapter 8

Rational-Emotive Guidance

Albert Ellis

Suppose that you want to help parents guide their children in accordance with rational-emotive principles. Let me briefly outline what you can do.

RET (rational-emotive therapy), although often viewed as a logical-persuasive method, actually has many dramatic-evocative and behavioral-activity components, including: unconditional positive regard (Rogers, 1961); rational-emotive imagery (Maultsby, 1975); rational encounter methods (Ellis, 1969); feeling-oriented exercises, such as shame-attacking exercises (Ellis and Harper, 1975); activity-oriented homework assignments, operant conditioning, behavioral rehearsal, assertion training, implosive therapy, and other deconditioning techniques.

RET does include, however, some uniquely cognitive components and takes a highly philosophic, psychoeducational outlook. It particularly shows people that they practically never get disturbed by external experiences, events, or conditions but that they *make themselves disturbed* by their own thoughts, attitudes, or interpretations *about* these conditions.

Alphabet Defined

In more technical, RET terms: when an *Activating Experience* or *Activating Event occurs at point A* and you feel a dysfunctional emotional *Consequence at point C,* A contributes to but does not directly cause C. B does. *B consists of your Belief System*: first, a *rational Belief (rB),* which creates an *appropriate Consequence (aC)*; and, second, an *irrational Belief (iB),* which creates an *inappropriate Consequence (iC).* In order to change or eliminate your *inappropriate Consequence (iC),* you go on to *D—Disputing* your *irrational Beliefs (iB's).* You then wind up with a new *cognitive Effect (cE),* as well as a new *emotional Effect (eE)* and *behavioral Effect (bE).*

To illustrate these ABC's of RET: Suppose that at point A I negatively appraise the system of parent guidance you now use and coldly reject you for using it. At point aC you feel sorry about my rejecting you and at point iC you feel depressed about it. You think—wrongly!—that my cold rejection (A) made you or caused you to feel depressed.

But, using RET, you now look for B—your Belief System about A. And you quickly find rB which goes something like: "I wish Dr. Ellis had not rejected me so coldly. How unfortunate that he takes that extremely negative attitude toward me! Let me see what I can do about getting him to ameliorate his opinions." This Belief seems rational because you want me to understand and accept you: It merely expresses the fact that you find my rejection of you undesirable and would like to change it. If you stick to this rB and do not go beyond it, you will tend to feel the aC (appropriate consequence) of disappointment, sorrow, regret, and frustration—negative feelings, admittedly, but feelings which help you go back to A and try to do something about it, change it for the better.

But since you did not only feel the aC of disappointment and frustration at C, but also felt the iC (inappropriate consequence) of depression, you now look for your iB (irrational Belief) that, according to RET theory, directly caused or created that feeling. And you soon turn up with iB's such as these: "I find it awful that Dr. Ellis has rejected me so coldly. I can't stand his rejection. I *should not* have acted so stupidly as to cause him to reject me, and since I did what I *should not* have done, I can only view myself as a rotten person, a no-goodnik, who will *always* do stupid things like this and therefore deserves to get coldly rejected!" If you look closely at what you have told yourself at B, you will see that these iB's and not your rB's have led to your iC of depression.

To go one important step further: You now use the logic-empirical method of science to Dispute (at point D) your iB's. You ask yourself such questions as: "What makes Dr. Ellis's rejection of me so awful? Why can't I stand it? What evidence exists that I should not, must not have acted so stupidly, how does that make me a totally rotten person, always doomed to do equally stupid things, and utterly deserving of constant rejection?"

If you really vigorously ask yourself these Disputing questions and think through the answers to them, you finally come up with a new cE (cognitive Effect) along these lines: "Nothing makes Ellis's rejection of me awful (since awful really means more than bad or 101% bad); it only remains highly inconvenient. I can definitely stand his rejection—though I probably will never like it. No reasons exist why I should not or must not act stupidly, for if such a law of the universe prevailed I could not violate it. It would prove much better if I don't act foolishly; but that never means that I have no right to do so. And even if I behave quite stupidly, I merely exist as a person who performed some senseless behavior and not as a totally senseless person. My trait or deed may have a low rating (because it fails to get me the goals I want in life), but it never makes me a low, rotten person."

As soon as you arrive at this new cE (cognitive Effect), says RET theory, you will almost immediately experience a new eE (emotional Effect)—you will tend to feel disappointed and sorry but *not* depressed and self-downing—and you will also experience a new behavioral Effect (bE)—you will tend to try to do something to rectify or live with my low opinion of you, instead of, say, withdrawing from me as you previously tended to do when you felt depressed about my criticism of you.

RET, then, states that humans largely create *their own* emotional problems, that they mainly do so with irrational Beliefs, that these Beliefs can quickly get brought to light and Disputed, and that if they clearly see and Dispute their own irrational, magical, absolutistic thinking, they can quickly, and ultimately permanently, think, emote, and behave differently.

ELIMINATING PARENTAL SELF-BLAMING

RET helps parents give up their self-blaming or self-damning in three main ways.

First, you can show parents that research demonstrates that *children have their own innate, biological tendencies to react* to external stimuli and environmental conditions in a unique, individualized manner (See Chapter 12 by Chess and Thomas). Therefore, parents can only legitimately assume, at most, partial responsibility for how their children turn out.

Secondly, you can show parents that even when they indubitably deal mistakenly and badly with their offspring—for example, unduly criticizing them—this mistaken parental behavior only provides the children with an obnoxious Activating Experience at point A. And this A does not directly cause the children's dysfunctional emotional or behavioral Consequences at C. If a hundred children receive similar blasting criticism from their parents, they hardly all display extreme self-downing or depression. Children, even at a fairly early age, have some ability to choose their own reactions to obnoxious stimuli. Those who choose to damn and depress themselves severely after their parents have wrongly excoriated them probably have some innate tendencies to do so. They do not *merely* pick these up from their parents. [Contrast this approach with Chess and Thomas' implication in Chapter 12 that parents have a responsibility to consider their children's innate response patterns.—Ed.]

Thirdly, RET theory *forgives poor parental behavior* even when it contributes significantly to childhood traumatization. You can say, for example, to a cruel or abusive parent, "Let's assume that you did significantly hurt your son by savage criticism. We need not condone your act or pretend that you had a good excuse for it. But no matter how wrong or bad your behavior, how does it make you a rotten person? Why do *you* rate as worthless because your child-rearing *practice* did so much harm? If you act kindly to your child, or sacrifice yourself for him, does that make you an angel—a thoroughly good individual? Of course not! Then how can the abuse you inflicted on him make you a worm?"

Rational-emotive guidance, in other words, holds parents responsible for most (not, of course, all) of their acts, but it never condemns them, labels them totally, or legislates an undeserving future for them when they have acted badly. It always accepts them as fallible, imperfect, and nonangelic. If you get this important message over to the parents you counsel, you can help them to stop damning themselves for their poor parental conduct—

and instead concentrate on how they can improve this conduct. [Cf. the philosophic similarities with reality therapy guidance, Chapter 9.—Ed.]

SHOWING PARENTS HOW TO OVERCOME THEIR ANGER

One of the main difficulties parents have consists of their angering and upsetting themselves about their children's poor behavior, especially when the children unfairly and exploitatively deal with the parents. Suppose a mother and father come to you because their daughter keeps stealing things from them and from others, and when they penalize her, she acts even worse, literally breaking valuable furniture in the home. Moreover, she forces them to spend much time talking to her teachers and principals, appearing in court, and having endless discussions about her with irate neighbors. They feel very angry about this and want to send her away.

In a case like this, you would first assume that the parents describe the situation correctly and that their daughter really does keep getting herself and them in needless, endless difficulties. Your dialogue with the parents might then go as follows:

Father: See! Even you admit that Josie's behavior stinks! Can you understand now why we feel so angry?

Counselor: Yes, I certainly understand it. Almost all parents in your situation would feel very angry. But that doesn't mean they act rightly.

Mother: You mean we're wrong when we feel like beating her up or putting her away. But you just said that almost all parents would feel like that!

Counselor: Yes, I think they would. But they're still wrong—at least as far as their anger is concerned.

Mother: But isn't anger right in such a case—when our daughter has unquestionably done, and keeps doing, such things?

Counselor: Of course not. Your *displeasure* is right; for who would feel pleased about your daughter's acts? But feeling very displeased and irritated about what she does isn't the same as hating her.

Father: I don't get it. What's the difference? Don't we always hate a person when her acts are that bad?

Counselor: Yes, we usually do. But we don't have to. For your daughter's acts, especially stealing and being disruptive, are only part of her. She doesn't always act badly, does she?

Mother: No, not always. But often!

Father: Yes, very often!

Counselor: But not always. But when you hate a person for her acts, that's what you usually mean: that she always tends to act badly; that her essence is badness; that she is practically doomed to act badly in the future; and that some law of the universe—some avenging angel—says that she must absolutely be damned, roasted in eternal hell, for acting that badly. Now is that what you really think—that your daughter's essence is bad; that she can't act better at any time in the future; and that she is so bad that she deserves to suffer eternal damnation?

Mother: Well, no. Not exactly that.

Father: No, I guess if she were that bad, totally bad, she really couldn't help herself at all. And I guess we couldn't very justly damn her for that.

Counselor: Right! I'm glad you see that contradiction. After dreaming up some kind of demoniacal force in her that dooms her to perpetual badness, you insist that she should be consigned to some kind of hell for being born and reared with that force. Don't forget: if she is essentially rotten, she must have got that way through heredity, environment, or both—right?

Mother: Yes, I guess so.

Father: Yes, I can think of no other ways she could have got that way.

Counselor: But she's certainly not responsible for her heredity, is she? She didn't *ask* to be born the way she was. And as for her environment, you, her school, her peers, her society in general largely created that —and she hardly created all of it herself! So if she has that rotten essence that you sometimes attribute to her, did she really bring it on herself?

Father: But are you saying that she has no will of her own, that she is completely dependent on the way she was born and raised, and therefore not responsible at all for what she does?

Counselor: No, not exactly. In RET, we take a *soft determinism* view: We hold that humans are not totally responsible for everything they do but that they are *partly or importantly responsible*: They do have choices. Your daughter, whatever her heredity and early environment, could now control and change her own behavior. So I'm not exonerating her and saying that she has to do what she now does. And I'm granting, along with you, that much of her behavior is abominable. I'm merely trying to show you that she isn't just her past and present behavior. She is a human—an ongoing process that has a future as well as a past and present. And she has thousands of different behaviors—all of which significantly change from time to time. You keep picking a few of her acts—which again I grant are execrable—and keep rating her, her totality, her ongoingness, her humanness by these few acts or traits. Now if I can get you to stop rating *her* and only to rate her *traits*, then I can get you back to the real issue: what you can do to help her change her traits, or at least to live more comfortably with them while they are unchanged.

Mother: So you want us to admit and to point out to her her rotten acts, but not to see her as a rotten person. Is that right?

Counselor: Yes, that's quite right. I would like you to stop making yourself angry at her and only to make yourself feel disappointed and annoyed with her acts. Stop consigning her to hell and work at teaching her to behave a little better—but never quite reach angelhood!

In this way, you can show parents, no matter what their child has unfairly done, that they don't have to identify the whole child with his or her crummy traits. If they can take the biblical attitude of forgiveness (to accept the sinner while clearly designating and trying to change his or her sins), they will 1) feel much better at a gut level, and 2) have a better chance of helping their child improve.

SHOWING PARENTS HOW TO OVERCOME THEIR INADEQUACY FEELINGS

Many parents condemn themselves and feel ashamed not only about the way they brought up their children in previous years but about the way they now act toward them. Further, the children now supposedly keep heaping shame and embarrassment on the parents' heads. For example, the two parents in the previous section could feel very inadequate because 1) they feel very angry toward their daughter, and 2) they can't face the teachers and neighbors when she gets into trouble—almost everyone blames them for her behavior. A typical dialogue with such parents might go:

Mother: I really see what you mean about my making myself angry at Josie. I realize that I'm wrong, especially when I keep screaming at her until I practically get hoarse. I know it's wrong, but I can't seem to stop it. And I hate myself later for having given in so childishly to my own temper tantrums.

Counselor: But do you see that you're merely compounding your wrongs here? First, you're wrongly making yourself furious at your daughter for acting badly. And second, you're castigating yourself for being

furious. Moreover, just as soon as you go into the second disturbance
—self-flagellation about your anger (anger at yourself for feeling
anger at your daughter)—you focus so much on that secondary symptom that you will find it almost impossible to work upon the primary
symptom: your original anger.

Father: You're right! Whenever my wife guiltily beats herself for getting
so angry at Josie, I notice that she does nothing whatever to make
herself less angry. In fact, her original anger seems to escalate.

Counselor: Correct. Let's see what you can do, rationally, to work this
out. First, let's start with your secondary symptom: your guilt or
shame about feeling so angry toward your daughter. What would
you say you keep telling yourself to create this feeling of guilt?

Mother: That I'm doing the wrong thing. That I'm hurting Josie by
yelling and screaming at her so hysterically.

Counselor: Right—but a little more than that. You're not only telling
yourself you're doing the wrong thing; what are you also telling
yourself about your doing that thing?

Mother: Oh, yes. I see. I'm saying, "I *shouldn't* get myself so angry at
Josie. I'm a bad mother for letting myself go that way."

Counselor: Good! you really hit it on the head that time. (Note positive
reinforcement.) At A, you're angry; and at C you're guilty about
your anger, "I shouldn't get myself so angry at Josie. I'm a bad
mother for letting myself get that way."

Father: But should she let herself go like that? Shouldn't she make
herself stop feeling so angry?

Counselor: No, you mean it would be better! But "It would be better!"
never equals "I therefore should or must!" Actually, she *must* yell
and scream at Josie in the sense that she *does.* For whatever we
have done, we must have done. So it's foolish for your wife to say,
"I should not, must not have done what I indubitably did!" *It
would have been preferable had she not, but she did!*

Mother: I see what you mean. I was wrong to make myself so angry at
Josie. But I have a right, as a human, to be wrong. All humans, at
times, act wrongly. So why shouldn't I?

Counselor: Precisely! (to husband): Do you see that she really has that
right, as a human, to do wrong, even very wrong things?

Father: Yes, I see what you mean now. Her yelling and screaming at
Josie are wrong. But that's the way humans frequently behave—
wrongly. Just like that's the way that Josie often behaves—wrongly.
And, I guess, she's human, too.

Counselor: Right! Josie, too, is human; and that's why she need not be condemned or damned, put into a *sub*human category, for her nonsense, her bad behavior. No human is anything but human—none of us is subhuman, and none of us is superhuman. That's why, even though you are wrong about your making yourself angry about Josie and her bad behavior, you are entitled to be wrong about that— and about anything else you happen to do wrongly—because you are human and will never be anything but human. Human means fallible, screwed up, wrong—and harmful, in some respects, to your own daughter. If we can get you to see that you are wrong to be angry at your daughter and accept yourself with that wrongness, then you can work on the wrongness itself, work on making yourself less angry at Josie and less harmful to her.

Father: But how about our feelings of shame over Josie's behavior? You indicated that we could also get rid of them. How?

Counselor: The same way, basically, that you can rid yourself of your anger and of downing yourself for being angry. For just as you have a right to act wrongly with Josie, so you have a right to have a daughter who acts badly with you and with other people. For isn't that what your shame is about—that you are the parents of this child who is acting so abominably?

Mother: It certainly is! I cringe when I have to go to school or to court about her stealing.

Father: And so do I! It makes us look like idiots, to have such a child. Maybe we're not, as you have been telling us, totally responsible for her immoral behavior. But what about the fact that everyone thinks we are, and blames us severely for raising a rotten child like Josie?

Mother: Yes, what about that?

Counselor: Well, what about it? Let's put it in our ABC model of human disturbance. At A, Josie keeps stealing and people blame you severely for having such a "bad" child. At C, both of you seem to feel quite guilty and ashamed. All right—what is B?

Father: That we shouldn't have such a rotten child.

Mother: And we should have raised her better.

Counselor: Right. Now, why *should* you, why *must* you have raised Josie better? Let's even suppose the worst: that you really could have raised Josie so that she'd practically never steal, and you lazily refused to do so and actually encouraged her to steal. Why should you not have behaved so badly as child-rearers?

Mother: Well, look at the results! And look how we're being blamed!

Counselor: Most unfortunate! But now you're merely giving reasons for
your *rational* Belief—that *it would have been better* had you raised
Josie more morally. Well, let's suppose it would have been. But why
must you do what would have been better? Why do you ever have
to act better when you could do so but actually don't.

Father: Oh, I see! There's no reason why we must—even though there
are many reasons why it would be preferable if we did. That god-
damned *must* again. We always seem to trap ourselves with it.

Counselor: Yes, you frequently do. That's what your shame—and virtually all your emotional disturbances comes from: *MUST-urbation.*
"We are responsible for Josie's stealing—and we must not feel so
much anger! We are blamed by others for Josie's bad behavior—and
we must not be blamed!" See! In every single case, look for the *must*
and you will quickly see the real cause of your upsetness: Not what
happens at A, but your *shoulds, oughts,* and *musts,* your absolutistic
and unrealistic commands to yourself and others, at B. Look at
those and you have the real reasons for disturbing yourself. Give up
those silly *musts* and you'll feel much better!

Other Rational-Emotive Methods

You can frequently use emotive methods of fully accepting the parents
themselves, no matter how poorly they have behaved. You can get them
to practice rational-emotive imagery (REI). You can give them various
kinds of emotive exercises to bring out their shame and anger, and then
to show them how to minimize these feelings. Behaviorally, you can
give them activity homework assignments—such as deliberately spending
more time with their children when they behave badly (constructive
self-punishment to replace the destructive self-flagellation) and making
steady attempts to teach the children the ABC's of RET. You can have
them use self-administered operant conditioning to reinforce their un-
conditionally accepting their children and to penalize their damning
them.

Lastly, I have a homework assignment for you: If you will make yourself conversant with RET principles, and if you will practice some of
them on yourself when you feel unduly anxious, guilty, depressed, self-
deprecating, or hostile, you will discover how to use them creatively in
parent guidance.

REFERENCES

ELLIS, A.: A weekend of rational encounter. In A. Burton (Ed.), *Encounter*. San Francisco: Jossey-Bass, 1969, pp. 112-127.

ELLIS, A. & HARPER, R. A.: *A New Guide to Rational Living*. Englewood Cliffs, N. J.: Prentice-Hall and Hollywood: Wilshire Books, 1975.

MAULTSBY, M. C., JR.: *Help Yourself to Happiness*. New York: Institute for Rational Living, 1975.

ROGERS, C. R.: *On Becoming a Person*. Boston: Houghton, Mifflin, 1961.

Chapter 9

Reality Guidance

Thomas McGuiness and

William Glasser

Although severe problems are best handled by a therapist who has had sufficient training in therapeutic techniques, parents can be taught to use Reality Therapy as a process for dealing with their children's discipline problems or to counsel them.

REALITY THERAPY AS THE BASIS OF REALITY GUIDANCE

Reality Therapy is a way of helping people look at, evaluate, and plan alternatives to any present behavior which is not allowing them to function well enough. The foundation upon which the technique is based is *involvement*—that is, establishing and maintaining a *positive, warm, caring atmosphere* between the person who needs the help and the person providing that help.

The underpinnings of Reality Therapy are *three basic beliefs* about

---

Dr. Glasser is author of *Reality Therapy* and *Schools Without Failure.*

people. The first is that *people are good*. The second is that there are two basic needs each person has—*love and worth*. Each of these needs is filled via a dual process. Not only does a person need to *be loved*, but that person must also *give love* for the love need to be completely satisfied. Likewise, each person must somehow see himself/herself as worthwhile and be seen by someone else as worthwhile. No person sees himself/herself as of great personal worth and value all the time, but for the basic human need to be fulfilled, each person must have an overall view of himself/herself that allows him/her to say "I am valuable."

The third basic belief is that *persons act in accordance with how they see themselves*. People who see themselves as good generally act in socially acceptable and personally satisfying ways. On the other hand, people who see themselves as bad often express themselves through delinquency, violence, or various forms of withdrawal or escape.

The task of Reality Therapy is to help someone who at present is behaving poorly develop new ways of acting which will allow him/her to meet his/her needs in socially acceptable ways according to the society he/she is trying to function successfully in—whether it be a child in school or at home, a person at work, an inmate in prison, or a parent at home. It does this through seven deceptively simple steps: 1) *personal involvement*; 2) *identifying present behavior*; 3) *value judgment*; 4) *planning*; 5) *commitment*; 6) *no excuses or punishment*; 7) *persistence*. These will be described more fully later in the chapter.

Parents as Reality Therapists

Parents trying to use Reality Therapy to help their children cope successfully have at once a blessing and a curse. The blessing is that they, above all others, are the most significant adults in their children's lives, and, because they often spend great amounts of time with their children, they can apply Reality Therapy almost as a way of life in their interaction with them. Unlike a therapist, who has limited time with a child and has continually to reestablish his/her involvement with the child each time they are together, parents can maintain a high positive involvement level in their home if they choose.

The curse comes from the fact that often family members—husbands with wives or parents with children—take for granted that the other people in the family know they are loved. And the simple truth is that *love cannot be assumed*. With very rare exception, people need to be assured and reassured of another's love. Children especially need a great deal of recognition and reaffirmation of their family's love for them.

So parents who often find themselves saying in wonderment, "Of course I love you, I'm your father," need to make their love more tangible. The testimony of love is not necessarily through gifts or toys or material things, but often more effectively through talking to or, better yet, listening to the children and finding ways to provide the humor, warmth, and affection, as well as the guidance and direction they need.

Emphasizing the "Reality" in Reality Therapy

Many parents are looking for a magic formula that somehow will transform their home into the motion picture set for the "Sound of Music," with laughter, song, and caring filling their homes and their lives. Of course, Reality Therapy is not that kind of magic; it can help facilitate the kind of family relationship they want, but it is just plain hard work getting there. As long as there are children living with parents, we will have young people pushing the limits and parents wondering how and when and where they went wrong. Children will always be searching for new boundaries, trying to broaden the borders of their personal world. And that's good—it's healthy. Reality Therapy will not completely stop children from fighting or acting out their fears and frustrations in violent or destructive ways, but it will provide a framework—a process to handle that behavior when it occurs.

When parents come to learn how to apply Reality Therapy at home, whether to support the work of their child's Reality Therapist or to prevent the need for a professional therapist, they come with some fears and misconceptions. First, it is necessary to get them over the scare word of "therapy." For some reason, parents are fearful that if they try to use Reality Therapy and do it wrong, they will do irreparable psychological damage to the child. They find it hard to accept the fact that parents can actively teach children how to act responsibly. Once parents review the steps of Reality Therapy and realize that there is no couch, no delving into the deep dark secrets of the child's soul and no psychological mumbo-jumbo involved, they begin to listen.

Parents, Self-Image, and Success

Many parents have poor self-images as parents. Rather than try to deal with all their self-judgments of inadequacy or to convince them that they can do it, it is best to postpone the issue and get them involved in learning the steps of Reality Therapy and how they are applied at home. The only effective way to convince parents they can use Reality Therapy effectively with their children is to help them experience success with it as soon as possible.

Using technical terms and trying to educate parents in clinical jargon just serve to confuse them or even confirm their suspicions of their personal inadequacy. It is necessary, however, to give parents some understanding of the formation of personal identity and the behavior indicative of identity so they can see to some degree how their children develop their views of themselves. In explaining the acquisition of a success identity and a positive self-image, one can talk to parents about how a child gains personal strength, the kind of strength the child needs to face and work through the difficulties and obstacles he/she will have to face in growing up and coping with what is expected. Helping parents identify the attitudes and behavior of a strong person is simple enough to do by having them identify strong people they know and then tell how they demonstrate their strength. Invariably they mention things like involvement with others, interest in and enthusiasm for many things, and dealing rationally with their lives. It is also useful to help parents identify and think about the regular pathways to a success identity: receiving and giving love, gaining worth and recognition, having fun, and becoming self-disciplined. The next obvious step, of course, is to help parents open up these pathways for the child by planning into their home lives opportunities for their children to gain strength.

Parents are also interested in how a child acquires a negative or failure identity and becomes a weak person whose personal world continuously diminishes and whose capacity to cope with the obstacles in life is weakened. Parents understand the concept of giving up; in many instances they have watched their child just give up in order to reduce the pain of trying to cope with something and failing time and time again. Often parents have lived with the obvious symptoms of a child in this process of trying to deny failure and reduce the pain. Reviewing symptoms like acting out, continuous emotional upset, bizarre behavior, and even psychosomatic illnesses often causes parents to nod their heads, affirming that they not only understand what is being said, but in some way they have watched it happen with their children and themselves. These simple lessons in identity formation usually help parents see a need of working with their child to reverse the process of drifting toward a failure identity.

After parents understand the basics of personal identity development, it is time to teach them the basic rudiments of Reality Therapy and how it is used to help the child gain and maintain a success identity. It is relatively simple to explain, but it takes a lot of time to break old habits in dealing with children.

INVOLVEMENT AS AN AUTHORITY BASE

Since Reality Therapy is based upon the *natural authority of personal involvement,* it is often necessary to help parents plan ways to create within their homes an atmosphere of warmth, harmony, and caring. It is difficult to build instant involvement just to use Reality Therapy. In some instances involvement may be more easily attained between therapist and child than between parent and child, because the therapist is starting at ground zero. If there has been much discord and mutual criticism in the parent-child relationship, the parent attempting Reality Therapy may be starting from a negative involvement point, far below zero. Many parents believe that a healthy, positive, harmonious pattern of family interaction just happens naturally—maybe because some people are naturally good at it. It is important to point out to them that the kind of involved atmosphere we are talking about can be *created.* It requires a willingness to try things that some parents and children may not always be comfortable with, but can be done.

Creating an atmosphere in the home that allows involvement to flourish does not mean that all of a sudden all parents must become overly affectionate or exciting conversationalists. It would take years for some parents to become open and affectionate with their children. But the parents who say, "I could never get involved with my kids, I'm just not like that," need to be challenged to change a little. They must find some ways to let the child know they care in a personal way.

The Involvement Trinity: CLC

Three basic conditions build the parent-child relationship: *courtesy, laughter,* and, most importantly, *communication.*

In the area of courtesy, a powerful recommendation to parents is to declare a moratorium on criticism, beginning with a short period of time and then extending it longer after the first period of success. As the days are added together, a mutually respectful relationship will develop. (See, also, the mutual respect balance in Chapter 4.) "No criticism" does not mean not correcting a child or letting him/her do as he/she pleases. "No criticism" means refraining from the little extra comments parents tend to make that seem to chip away at the person of the child rather than the behavior. Helping parents become aware of what they're saying to the child when problems arise lets them cut down on introductory comments like, "You're so inconsiderate!" "You don't care about anybody but yourself!" "How stupid can you be?" More subtle criticism can be conveyed by a mocking tone of voice. What criticism says to a child is, "You are not a very good person." This nudges him/her towards a failure identity.

It's hard to be angry or hostile when you're *laughing together*. The amount of laughter in a home is a pretty good barometer of the health of a parent-child relationship. Finding and creating laughter in the home are well worth the efforts for parents who want to re-involve themselves with their children.

Building Involvement Through Communication

Communication is partly teaching and partly sharing, partly verbal and partly nonverbal. For example, with a two-parent family, it's important to point out that the children are learning less from the parents' words than from the parents' lives. The children are watching their parents and their relationship with each other and acquiring attitudes and modeling behaviors they see the parents living. So *the most powerful teaching tool parents have is their relationship with one another*.

Sometimes parents need help in recognizing and capitalizing upon the everyday intimate moments with their children. Family meals can be a perfect time to build family involvement. A meal that begins with, "Pass the potatoes," and ends with an impatient dash for the door, with nothing happening in between, seems a foolish waste when you consider how that time could have been quality time. The problem often is that parents do not know how to get a discussion started with their kids or how to keep it going. Therefore, a simple but effective intervention is to help parents decide upon relevant family topics that would arouse the children's interest. The topics don't always have to be heavy, introspective, or problem-oriented. Simple, hassle-free topics work just as well to get parents and children sharing ideas. After parents learn how to develop topics, it is usually necessary to teach them how to ask thought-provoking questions to enable the children to experience the excitement of thinking. Parents often see their role as answerers rather than askers. Probable the single *most powerful involvement technique* parents can use is *listening*—and that means going beyond the word to discover the child who is speaking. Listening involves more than getting information; it involves an interest in and concern for the person speaking.

In addition to mealtime communal discussion, it is important for parents to build in some individual communication time. One good way is talking with the children *just before bed,* wrapping up the day, sharing the concerns or the fun of the day. Another way is finding *a few seconds here and there* to talk to the children—to tell them how much the parents care or to reflect to them the goodness or strength the parents see in them. It doesn't have to be a deep and profound exchange; just a simple coming together is enough. The parents can become a mirror for the children to see themselves through their parents' eyes of love. Getting parents to build in some *game time* is helpful. For some parents games seem awkward or artificial, but convincing them to act in spite of their awkwardness is important.

Parents who are experiencing real barriers between themselves and their children can expect to be rebuffed by their children when they try to get re-involved. But that doesn't excuse them; it just makes things harder. They'll have to plan small, realistic steps and be satisfied with tiny increments of success at first. They may even have to tolerate initial rejection by their children and say, "I knew it was going to happen but I'm going to persist." It is often necessary to have parents receiving some kind of encouragement and support from a counselor or from other parents.

SAUCE FOR THE GOOSE, GANDER, AND GOSLINGS

It is necessary to help parents apply the steps of Reality Therapy to themselves before they begin trying to use it with the child. More often than we like to believe, it is the parents' problem that needs to be dealt with, rather than or in addition to the child's.

It's important first of all to *help parents pinpoint exactly what the child's problem is.* Parents often have an I'm-going-to-work-hard-at-it-and-solve-it-overnight attitude, or they want something that will clear up all the problems at once. Holding them at bay and helping them to take one step at a time will give them a chance for success. Often parents will say they want to change the child's attitude or the way he thinks. They need to be apprised that that just won't work; it will be necessary to zero in on some specific behavior. Sometimes, of course, the problem behavior will actually be a specific grouping of behaviors, like picking on and constantly disturbing younger children, which could include bullying, taking things from them, and causing physical harm.

The *problem behavior should be* such that it is *potentially harmful* to the child or interferes in some way with the rights or needs of others. Conflicts in personal preferences always pose a problem in counseling parents. Long hair and sloppy clothes really are things to be talked out with parents. Reality Therapy is misused when it is intended to "force" a youngster into living according to the personal tastes of parents. Unless the behavior or condition is harmful to the youngster or is causing problems for others, it is questionable whether it needs to be changed.

Saucing the Goose and Gander

When the specific child behavior to be changed has been identified, the guided parent self-application of Reality Therapy actually begins with a simple question: "What do you usually do when the child behaves this way?" It is helpful to have them think about the most recent incidents of the behavior and then write down what they did on those last occasions, whether it involved screaming, slapping, ignoring, crying, begging the child to stop, or all of the above.

When they have listed their own behavioral reactions to the incidents, ask them if what they did worked. Obviously what they did had minimal effects, at least in terms of prevention, or else this behavior would not be a current problem. But it is important that the ineffectiveness of these methods be realized and acknowledged by the parents.

At this point simply ask the parents to stop doing what they've been doing. It should be clear to them by now that continuing an operation that is not working does not make any sense.

Effectively what you've done up to this point has been to take the parents through the first few steps of Reality Therapy. They have *identified their behaviors* when they face a particular problem with one of their children. They have made a *value judgment* about the worth of that behavior. They have entered into the first stage of a successful *plan*—to decide to stop doing what is not working or is causing problems. But for the planning process to be complete the parents must decide now what they can do to deal in a different way with their children when they display the undesirable behavior.

Saucing the Gosling

Next, ask the parents to consider doing something for the next several days that will allow them to become re-involved with the child. It doesn't have to be anything earth-shaking. Simply, what can they do in the next few days that will make the child's life a bit more pleasant? (This should be in addition to the general home-life family involvement plans already under way.) It's best if this little plan be kept personal, like special acts of kindness, spending time with the child, helping him/her do something each day, or preparing a special treat, rather than taking the child to a special place or buying him some expensive gift. Even something like getting up and eating breakfast with the child if he/she is not accustomed to it could be very helpful.

Several days will be necessary for the parents to develop the personal re-involvement with the child. Throughout the entire next sequence of activities, that atmosphere of involvement—concern, caring, friendliness— should be maintained. But this atmosphere *should not be confused with permissiveness.* The fact is that the behavior being demonstrated by the child must change and it is only through caring and persistence that the parent can help the child change the behavior.

STEPPING UP THE CHILD'S BEHAVIOR

After several days of intensifying the personal involvement, the next sequence of work begins. When the behavior in question is exhibited, the parent must stop what the child is doing and follow these *steps of Reality Therapy:*

1. Deal with Present Behavior

Ask the Child to State the Behavior. Questions like, "What are you doing?" "What's happening?" "What's going on?" should be used. The child must be aware of the behavior being questioned. Most good, healthy, red-blooded American kids will answer with something like, "Nothin'," but it's important that parents be persistent and repeat something like, "Something just happened a few minutes ago when you walked into the room—what was it?" Then we can expect comments like, "Well, he had it coming to him," or "Everybody else around here does it; why do you always have to bug me?" Parents must not be diverted by these kinds of comments. A simple, quiet reply like, "That's not the point here; what did you just do?" should be asked. Calm but unrelenting persistence is necessary. It's important that the behavior be out in the open; often people are unaware of what they're doing. Parents should not preach or practice history. Saying something like, "This is the 95th time you've done this . . . ," puts an intolerable burden on the child. He/she is having a hard enough time handling the fact that he has got himself in trouble right now. If children think they're expected to reform their entire past, they know they cannot do it and they just give up.

This step emphasizes *behavior*. Parents often want to get into feelings here. Sometimes, enthusiastic parents think that if they get into feelings, they are being like a real psychiatrist or a real psychologist. Though we realize that feelings are very important, the fact is that you cannot change them, so why deal with them here? [Contrast this with the rational-emotive (Chapter 8) emphasis on changing feelings by a rational decision.—Ed.] We're trying to help the child make decisions about his/her behavior and decisions should not be made on feelings, even though feelings are important in other contexts of the parent-child relationship.

2. Get a Value Judgment

After the child has identified what it is he/she is doing, it is necessary for the child to make a value judgment about it. *It is the child's value judgment that counts here, not the parents'*. Parents need to restrain the urge to preach. They should begin with simple questions like, "Is what you're doing helping you?" "Is it getting you anywhere?" "Is it good for your brothers and sisters?" "Is it good for us, your parents?" "Is it against the rules of the house?" This is a difficult step for the child and it is important to remind parents that patience and calmness are important. Shouting the questions just doesn't work. Silence is often evident in this step. Even though the child will generally respond with, "I don't know!" or with absolute silence, parents should not come back with a rapid fire barrage of questions. The child needs time to think and ponder. Sometimes the child will not answer at all and it may be necessary for the parent to say something like, "Well, it seems to me that what you're doing isn't really helping you." But that is the last resort. The value judgment stage must not be skipped and, needless to say, it is best if the child does the talking here.

3. Make a Plan

The child must learn that apologies, even with tears and genuine remorse, are not all that is needed. Somehow he/she must plan some kind of alternative to the behavior that is causing problems. The plan needs to be more than a mere, "I won't do it anymore." The question is, "What *will* you do?" The plan must not be viewed by the child or parents as a means of making the child pay back something; nor is it punishment. It is an attempt to replace an undesirable behavior with another behavior which will allow the child to meet his needs in ways that won't encroach upon the rights or needs of others.

Parents often assume that children know how to plan, but usually children do not. Through guiding questions, the child will usually be able to come up with something acceptable. Planning assistance is a teaching process. The parents must teach the child how to generate better alternatives than he/she has had in the past. The plan should be short-termed, accomplishable in light of the child's talents and capacities, and tangible enough in results that it can be acknowledged and reinforced when completed.

The plan has to have built into it some reasonable hope of success so that when the child completes it, he/she can begin to build a success base for future responsible behavior. And when the plan is completed, the parents have to be there to say, "Good!" or "See, you *can* do things well." Although positive reinforcement can be overdone, the child must be aware that his/her parents see him/her as responsible and successful.

4. Get a Commitment

There's nothing dramatic about the commitment; it simply seals the bargain. A very simple question like, "Now will you really do what you planned?" is usually sufficient. It's good to seal the agreement with a handshake or some other obvious acknowledgment, and sometimes it's good to get the agreement in writing and have the child sign it. Of course, the commitment is only as strong and meaningful to the child as the involvement between the child and the parents.

5. No Excuses

Without excuses many of us would really be in trouble, but for Reality Therapy to be effective, parents cannot settle for excuses. We're all good at excuses and we really like to accept them, but to accept excuses instead of results means that parents don't really care whether or not the child is responsible. To allow children to use excuses is providing them with a crutch that works against growth and responsibility. Even when the excuses are valid, it is best not to deal with them at all. Instead, parents should *recycle the child back into the planning stage* to get a new plan going.

6. No Punishment

It is difficult to help parents sort out all the differences between discipline and punishment. There have to be some consequences, of course, if the child refuses to make a plan, or refuses even to talk about what he/she has done. The only consequence in Reality Therapy that makes sense is some form of *isolation*. If the child is unwilling to take a good look at his behavior and solve it by acting in better or more reasonable ways, the parents should not hit, scream, or plead; they should just separate the child from the situation. Put him/her someplace; give him/her a time-out period alone somewhere and ask him/her to think about what has happened; have him/her sit on the couch for a while, or send him/her to a bedroom. Such isolation is recommended if the child refuses to plan or to keep the plan he/she has agreed to.

This separation time is not time for fun, nor is it merely punishment. It's time to think, to help the child realize that he/she cannot operate in a society as if his/her behavior did not make any difference. The child must learn that when a person is not willing to follow through on something, he/she loses the freedom to operate. How long should a child stay in his room? This time-out period should last until he/she is willing to work out a way to get along better. The child has to understand that this is serious, that there is a way to work things out, but that parents cannot continually accept unreasonable behavior.

Needless to say, starting this kind of approach with children when they are little will be most effective. With older children it will take more time, patience and parent support, but it can be made to work. Most children can learn from the parents to be responsible. They always have choices. They don't have to be isolated unless they choose to. There is always an alternative available—that is, working out a plan to act differently.

7. Never Give Up

This is perhaps the hardest step of all. But it is exactly what parents are trying to teach their children, not to give up. Giving up doesn't work. Learning to give up easily is a road to failure. Certainly parents don't want that for their children, so they cannot afford to give up on the children's behavior. By hanging in there, the parent is modeling an important behavior for the child.

Chapter 10

Parents' Groups

L. Eugene Arnold, Marjorie Rowe

and Herman A. Tolbert

The natural tendency of parents to discuss child-rearing problems with other parents can be channeled into a constructive process through group discussion facilitated by professional leadership and appropriate goals.

GUIDANCE OR GROUP THERAPY?

Some parents welcome direct treatment for themselves, and some parents groups successfully function with a therapeutic agreement similar to group psychotherapy. At the other extreme, some parents resist owning any problems or feelings themselves but accept information, education, advice, and persuasion about dealing with their children, and some groups successfully function with a "guidance" emphasis. (Even further to this extreme would be nonclinical educational groups, such as a group of expectant parents who are preparing for the birth and learning how to care for a baby, or parents who take a child development course to understand their children better.) Frequently, a parents' group functions surprisingly well in one of the ambiguous gradations between these extremes. Perhaps this is because some parents are accustomed to the idea that bringing their child for mental health assistance invites therapy for themselves. Consequently, they may tolerate much therapy under the aegis of guidance.

This is fortunate, because the distinction between group parent guidance and parent group therapy is not always as clean as one would like. Hopefully, the initial contract would specify in the case of parent group therapy that there would be emphasis on exploring the parents' feelings about their children, each other, themselves, and their own parents, and how these affect their relationship with the children, while group guidance would emphasize more the practical aspects of dealing with children. In practice, though, there tends to be a lot of overlap. Therapy groups tend at times to drift more into information-education-advice while guidance groups cannot afford to ignore entirely the feelings of the parents. A further complication is that parent group therapy at times verges on couples group therapy, especially when all the parents in the group are intact couples. However, the initial emphasis of parents' groups, even when composed of intact couples, is on the parents' relationship with their children rather than their relationship with each other.

The professional in charge of the group needs to monitor how far the group is drifting from its agreed task. Sometimes it is appropriate to let the group metamorphose if that is the common wish of all the members, but the professional needs to keep sight of group goals and cohesiveness. This emphasis on the group entrance contract is more important with parents' groups than with the usual group therapy, because the role of parents who bring a child for mental health services is much more ambiguous than either the role of a child in group therapy who is frankly acknowledged to be a patient or the role of an adult in group therapy who directly seeks help for himself and acknowledges himself as a patient. (See Adams' Chapter 18 comments about the parent as patient.)

Group Therapy vs. Group Guidance Continuum

The things that tend to make a parent group more like group therapy are: 1) a commitment from the group members to attend faithfully, 2) loose structure, 3) focusing on group processes, 4) focusing on parents' feelings, 5) focusing on the parents' past, including families of origin, 6) preference of the professional for anxiety-evoking techniques, 7) sharing of "here and now" feelings by the professional.

Things that tend to push a group more towards the guidance end of the spectrum are 1) open-ended group with short commitments of time from the members, 2) permission for members to attend the group ad lib without any commitment to consistency, 3) well-structured format and content, 4) information giving or information exchange, 5) advice giving or advice exchange, 6) intellectual explanations, 7) focusing on the child's behavior, 8) focusing on the efficiency or effectiveness of the parents' reaction to the child, 9) preference of professional for anxiety-reduction techniques, 10) sharing by professional of anecdotes derived from experience with other parents.

CORE ELEMENTS OF PARENTS GROUPS

Regardless of whether the main group emphasis is therapy or guidance, the following helpful elements can be appropriate in any parents group.

1. Peer Support

Group peer support can take several forms—empathy, alleviation of guilt, reassurance that one is not alone, encouragement to make some constructive change, encouragement to persist in a basically sound but not yet effectual action, or encouragement to look at one's own feelings.

2. Ventilation

An atmosphere of empathic peer support facilitates healthful ventilation. This can be especially helpful to parents who feel they have no right to certain feelings about their children. In this regard, reference to the amorality of feelings in Chapter 31 can be helpful. The professional needs to monitor the ventilation process to make sure it eventually facilitates rather than avoids constructive change and planning.

3. Vicarious Learning

Parents can modify their own strategies, reactions, or attitudes from hearing how another parent has succeeded or why he has failed, or perhaps merely hearing about a situation in which they can see their own problem caricatured in such a way that the solution is more obvious than it was before.

4. Mutual Help

Mutual help is often more effective than unilateral help from the professional. Many parents can accept empathy, insight, advice or confrontation from another parent, with whom they can feel better able to identify, than they could from a professional.

> Mrs. X., a rigid, obsessive-compulsive, divorced mother of two, leaned forward and intensely advised Mrs. Y. to let go of her 13-year-old daughter and allow her to grow up. She told how she had recently reacted with mixed anger and frustration to the knowledge that her 13-year-old son had become delinquent.
>
> Mrs. X. had previously left her children to care for themselves in a locked house while she pursued work and school. They were not allowed to admit anyone to the home or talk on the telephone except to answer her frequent check-up calls. The 13-year-old was not allowed any extracurricular activities at school so that he could be home for her close scrutiny.
>
> The group had helped Mrs. X. realize that her rigid controls only served to set up an atmosphere of continuous struggle and that part of the task of being a good parent was knowing when to let go. She was able to work through her anxiety about being a good parent and allow more freedom for her son. Mrs. X. expressed relief that she was also now free of a great burden.
>
> Both Mrs. X. and Mrs. Y. were intelligent, obsessive, hard working compulsive housecleaners who shared feelings of inadequacy in the mothering role. This identification allowed Mrs. Y. to adopt a more lenient approach even though similar advice from a psychiatrist had been rejected.

5. Dilution of Responsibility

The same phenomenon which can allow members of a mob to carry out atrocities which they would not have considered individually can operate in a constructive way with parents whose effectiveness is paralyzed by guilt. A parent who experiences unbearable guilt upon saying "No" to any request of his impulsive child may feel less guilty about limit setting if he can a) realize that other parents are being equally strict and b) feel a mandate from the group which he is merely carrying out without full responsibility. Of course, the professional needs to make sure the mandates the group gives individual members are reasonable and humane.

6. Mutual Imitation and Identification

Imitation and identification allow the parents to pool their resources. An oversubmissive parent can grow some backbone by partial identification with a very firm parent. A rigid, distant parent can develop some affective skills by identifying with a tender, sensitive, caring parent.

It is even possible for one parent's problem or weakness to be a source of strength to another. Thus, a stingy, depriving parent may move towards a more moderate position through imitation of an overindulgent one. Since many deficiencies in parenting are deviations from a golden mean, it should not be surprising that a heterogeneous group of parents would have someone deviating in each direction from the mean on many parameters. Exposing these deviants to each other tends to normalize both.

7. Reality Testing

Knowledge of the accepted community norm is often helpful. Some parents, without realizing it, are overly strict, oversubmissive or overindulgent because they have a distorted impression of what other parents are doing or allowing. Both the parent who allows a 12-year-old girl to date a 20-year-old man because the girl says that all of her friends are being allowed to do it and the parent who refuses to allow a 17-year-old girl to have any dates at all have something to learn from each other and from the other parents in the group.

8. Blessings by Comparison

Some parents experience great relief and comfort from learning that another parent's child has problems very similar to their own child's, or had them when he was the same age. In the latter case it is particularly helpful if the parent with the older child can report some improvement with time. When this is not possible, it still may be possible for the parent with the older child to acknowledge that the other parent is wise in seeking help this early, in order to prevent the complications that the older child has. The professional needs to monitor such exchanges closely enough to insure that the implications are understood constructively.

9. Blessings by Contrast

There is a peculiar phenomenon in parents groups which at first appears to be a one-way benefit, but can be mutually beneficial. Parents will frequently remark on the comparative severity of their children's problems. Some parents take heart and carry on successfully after learning that their child's problem, which they had thought was severe, is actually rather mild compared to the problems of some other children. Though one might expect that the parent whose child has the worst problems would conversely feel even more discouraged and helpless, this has not usually been the case in our experience. Such parents tend to feel supported by the group's recognition of the severity of the problem they are facing with their child.

10. Surrogate Parenting of a Parent

Some parents have trouble parenting because they did not receive adequate parenting themselves. (See Chapters 22 and 28 for more about this.) Their needs can sometimes be partially met through surrogate parenting by the other group members or by the professional leading the group. This interaction in the group setting is often helpful not only to the one who is receiving the surrogate parenting, but also to others who may identify either with the one being parented or with the person doing the surrogate parenting. Even the group member doing the parenting gains: Being able to help another increases one's self-esteem and sense of adequacy. Sometimes the whole group parents one member:

> Mrs. Q., a 54-year-old mother of six with a strong middle-class upbringing, attended group regularly. She presented difficulties in dealing with her 15-year-old who was often hostile, belligerent, selfish, and dyssocial. Mrs. Q. always tried hard to be seen as a "nice person" in all spheres of her life, including group, to the extent that she felt guilty about taking group time to discuss her problems. Her repressed anger came out in one session when she had accepted the group's focus to aid her in dealing with her elderly mother with a chronic brain syndrome. Mrs. Q. could no longer handle her mother's suspicions and accusations. She felt she had never been accepted and loved by her own mother even though she had always worked hard for mother's approval through suppression of her anger and the "nice" façade. She finally realized that in reality she was quite angry about this rejection: She had not had a warm, loving and accepting example of how to mother.
> The group was able to link her deprivation with her difficulties in mothering her daughter. The group then gave her warmth, support, and nurturing as a mother would. This allowed her to make a change in the relationship with her daughter.

11. Self-Esteem and Adequacy by Contributing

Not only by surrogate parenting, but also by contributing in other ways to the group and to individual members, parents can experience success in giving. Thus they develop confidence in their ability to help another person, a confidence that their experience with their children has not sufficiently confirmed.

12. Expectation and Hope

Misery loves company. A group of people with a common problem often feel more hopeful about the future than they could individually.

13. Testimonial

Testimonials can take several forms: the Alcoholics Anonymous type ("Here's where I made a mistake and this is what I have learned from it"); the pleased consumer type ("Dr. X. recommended Y and though I resisted it at first, I finally tried it, and much to my surprise, it worked"); or the historical type ("I had the same problem with George, but he seemed to outgrow it or get over it when he was just a little bit older than your John"). Such testimony may sound rather unsophisticated or unglamorous, but is often more effective in facilitating change in another parent than anything the professional could have done individually. Sometimes the professional can guide a testimonial in the most constructive direction.

14. Pep Talks

"You just have to put your foot down. You don't need to let him get away with that . . ." may seem at first like cheap advice, but can be useful if guided by the professional into a direction that constitutes a logical intervention in some vicious cycle (see Chapter 5).

GROUP TECHNIQUES AND THE PROFESSIONAL'S ROLE

In some groups, the professional's role is mainly that of facilitator, expeditor, and monitor of the constructive or therapeutic activity of the parents with each other. In other groups, the professional may assume more the role of an educator making use of a group as an efficient and congenial atmosphere for dissemination of information, facts, and advice. Even in the latter situation, the group should not necessarily be seen merely as a means of economy; even when most of the interaction is between the professional and individual parents rather than between the parents in the group, this may have an advantage. Some parents may find it easier to accept things from the professional as part of a group than if they feel they are singled out and different. One parent's resistance may be softened by the modeling of acceptance by another.

Often the professional needs to shift flexibly back and forth between the educational role and the group process facilitative role.

Facilitating

Standard group techniques useful with parents include:

1. *Introduction of group members* to each other or encouraging their introduction of themselves should include some mention of their child (at least age, sex, and school situation). Ordinarily, it is useful to encourage the parents to share a little bit about their child's problem when first joining the group, just as it is customary in other groups to encourage a new member to share some things about himself.

2. *Defining goals:* In some groups the goals are clearly understood ahead of time and need merely to be restated. In other groups, particularly in the formative stage, the group can be enlisted in clarifying the goals and what they particularly would like to get out of the experience. In contrast to most group therapies, it is acceptable for the members to include in their definition of goals the obtaining of appropriate kinds of information from the professional.

3. *Promoting group cohesion,* though not of as much value with the guidance group as with the frank therapy group, is still helpful. The professional can provide a model of sincere concern for the welfare, sensitivities, and problems of each of the parents in the group and subtly reinforce the same by the others.

4. *"Going around"* to elicit input from each member of the group about an important issue is useful not only in promoting group cohesion and peer support, but also in bringing useful ideas into the open.

5. *Inviting other viewpoints* is important not only in opening up alternative conceptualizations or action possibilities, but also in increasing the confidence and self-esteem of the parent offering an alternative. In this context it is permissible for the professional to make use of things he knows from outside the group, as long as he does not betray any

confidence. For example, one might say, "Mrs. Jones, I think you have another idea about that." Another way is to respond to nonverbal cues, such as, "Mr. Smith, you looked as if you didn't quite agree with something that Mr. Brown was saying. Would you share your thoughts with us?" Some professionals may prefer an open-ended question to interpreting the reaction of disagreement, but the latter has the advantage of implying that it is acceptable to disagree.

6. *Sharpening the focus* of the discussion, especially in the direction of some constructive action, helps to prevent the group from degenerating into an "ain't it awful" variant of the "PTA" game. For example, one might ask, "What could you do about this problem of the children fighting with each other? What things have people here in the group tried? What worked and what didn't work? Are there any other possibilities that haven't been tried?"

7. *Prevention of scapegoating* is important in any group. One might expect in a parents group a tendency to scapegoat the absent children, but this is usually not hard to avoid. Parents who would be most likely to scapegoat their children do not bother coming to the group, refusing to own any part of the problem. When it does occur, the professional must make a delicate judgment balancing the risks, on the one hand, of allowing the scapegoating to continue and, on the other hand, of possibly interfering with the parents' ability to engage in much-needed ventilation. Sometimes the scapegoating and blaming will extinguish merely by being ignored, with attention focused on more constructive areas. It may be helpful to remind the group that things can go wrong without anyone being to blame. One group found an unusual solution— driving out the scapegoat*er*:

> A 53-year-old unemployed businessman monopolized group time with lengthy complaints about his wife's laziness and incompetence, and his three adolescent children's failure to comply with house rules. When directly requested to express his feelings about these issues, he either denied having any or refused to acknowledge the questions, retreating into the continued litany of complaints. Over the course of a year the other group members continually confronted him with the catalytic role he played in the situation. They finally realized that he was using his absent wife and children as scapegoats in an effort to repress his anger and disappointment with them, and to deny his own contributions to the family's chaos. This was preventing others from using the group in a more constructive way. The group's solution was to expel him, since he had shown over a year's time his sabotage of the group process.

8. *Dealing with Transference.* Transference can occur within the guidance group, but does not necessarily require the same kind of interpretation as in group therapy. Positive transference can merely be allowed to do its work as a constructive mechanism in the group process. Negative transference can often be dealt with by a general realization that the parent is understandably irritated about all the problems he is having and that this irritation is spilling out against the leader or other members.

Educational Techniques

It is often appropriate for the professional to educate the parents in the group about such things as 1) the children's problems (particularly where the group consists of parents with children having the same type of problem), 2) normal child development (particularly when parents are classifying as pathology things which are within the wide normal limits of variability), 3) principles of human behavior, 4) defense mechanisms, 5) dealing with feelings, and 6) alternative methods of management, such as behavior modification. This education can be carried out in several ways:

1. *Socratic methods* are often feasible, and do not present as jarring a contrast to the more facilitative and therapeutic techniques as do some of the other educational techniques. For instance, one might ask, "What do you think is the reason Jane started wetting the bed again after the new baby was born?" "So you think it was because she wanted to be like a baby again herself. What are some of the advantages of being a baby that might appeal to Jane?"

2. *Mini-lectures* on some aspect of child development, defense mechanisms, feelings, or other topic may occasionally be appropriate, especially when the group seems unable to come up with useful ideas itself. For example, one might explain the homegrown volcano described in Chapter 5.

3. *"Chalk talks"* are occasionally appropriate with a parents group, especially when there is a topic of some complexity requiring the sharing of professional expertise with the parents.

4. *Straightforward answers* to questions by the professional, which are not usually favored in group therapy, may be appropriate in parent group guidance. However, the professional needs to be alert for a question that is really a disguised attack and try to help the parent ventilate the feelings of frustration, resentment, or guilt that are behind it.

DIFFERENT GROUPS FOR DIFFERENT TROOPS

Special parents groups have been formed to meet the needs of special parents.

Parents Anonymous

Parents Anonymous is designed mainly for child-abusing parents and is modeled on Alcoholics Anonymous in that the group members admit their problems to themselves and each other. They ask for help from the group and possibly from a higher power, because they realize they cannot overcome their problem by themselves. It differs from Alcoholics Anonymous in usually being sponsored by some agency of the "establishment" (such as a community mental health clinic) and in having a professional as the group leader.

Hyperkinetic Group

Groups for parents of children with similar problems are often helpful. A variation of this tried at the Ohio State University Child and Adolescent Psychiatry Clinic has been a combined group of parents and hyperkinetic children, which meets in common for five or ten minutes at the beginning and end of the hour, with the "filling" of the time sandwich being 30 or 40 minutes of separate groups for parents and children. The opportunity for the parents to see each other's children seems to provoke interest and discussion. In addition, the occasional presence of the children provides an opportunity for the professional to demonstrate techniques:

> An intelligent 30-year-old divorced mother and her bright but extremely impulsive, hyperkinetic seven-year-old son were in the group for about six months. The mother was overtly but mildly depressed, partly as a result of the divorce, but mostly because of the boy's behavior problems. Though extremely disruptive during the time of the combined parent-child group, he seemed eager to please the male group leader. The leader took the opportunity to demonstrate the efficacy and acceptability of physical restraint as a backup to limit setting. His mother, encouraged by the demonstration, began emulating it with success, and several other parents followed suit with their children. This mother found particularly helpful the support and empathy she needed for the embarrassing job of setting limits in public, and relished the professional's unabashed modeling of limit setting within the group.

Parents of Inpatients

In addition to required weekly family therapy for each patient in the adolescent inpatient program at Ohio State University, a supportive therapy group has been able to provide the "inpatient parents" peer support that is not possible with individual family therapy. The focus is on parents' feelings about having a son or daughter hospitalized, the consequent feelings of guilt and inadequacy, and the reaction to separation from the child. Grief reactions in the group concern both hospital separation and feelings about the adolescent growing up. To smooth continuity of outpatient-inpatient-outpatient care, parents are invited to the group prior to the adolescent's admission and for several sessions after discharge.

The natural scatter of admission and discharge dates in this open-end group insures at any time a mix of new and older members. The veterans tend to support the new members, and both gain from the experience. Thus, an individual's passage through the group tends to recapitulate normal development of parenting skills: Upon entering, the neonatal member with a failure self-image depends on and is nurtured by the group. He gradually develops trust, confidence, and the ability to contribute. By the end of his term in the group, he is effectively supporting and nurturing newer members, thereby experiencing surrogate success as a parent.

Therapy-Guidance Group

When there are sufficient resources, we have found it useful to provide parents with the option of a more sophisticated group that employs some techniques of group therapy and makes a fairly long commitment. Some of the vignettes earlier in this chapter were drawn from such a group.

Other Special Groups

Other specific groups are mentioned in the appropriate chapters (7, 11, 22, 24, 26). Group support systems for parents would also include Parent Effectiveness Training, a special structured approach that is usually taught in groups.

REFERENCE

YALOM, I. D.: *The Theory and Practice of Group Psychotherapy.* New York: Basic Books, 1970.

Chapter 11

Parents as Primary
Therapists: Filial Therapy

Lawrence G. Hornsby and

Alan S. Appelbaum

Filial therapy is a psychotherapeutic technique utilizing parents as therapeutic agents for their own children. It was developed and named by Guerney (1964). However, the prototype for this approach to the treatment of children was discussed by Freud (1909) in his "Analysis of a Phobia of a Five-Year-Old Boy"—or "Little Hans."

GUERNEY'S APPROACH

In the approach outlined by Guerney, *parents in groups* are taught to conduct play sessions with their own children in a very specific way, using *well-delineated guidelines and controls*. The groups consist of six to eight parents, about equally divided by sex, with spouses not included. The general approach and its rationale are first fully explained. Initially instructional techniques are used. *Demonstration play sessions* are conducted by the therapists, and, also, the *parents role-play* sessions with either another parent's child or their own. The therapist's and parents' observed sessions are discussed to enhance the group's understanding of the role and their mastery of it. After six to eight training sessions, the parents conduct play sessions in the home weekly. Parents continue to meet weekly with the therapist to discuss their interactions with the children and to draw conclusions and interpretations from the material gleaned from their sessions. There is an emphasis on *conclusions and inferences about the parents themselves* as well as about the children. Full attention is paid to the parents' feelings and reactions.

OUR APPROACH

We have elected to work with both parents and directly supervise play sessions with their own child. Initially the parents and child are thoroughly evaluated both individually and as a family unit (by means of psychiatric interviews and, when necessary, psychological testing). During this evaluation, the focus is on the individual dynamics of the family members and on the intrafamilial relationships. We attempt to make some assessment of the degree of parent-child conflict existing between the child and each of the parents.

The parent who appears to be less intensively or less pathologically in conflict with the child is designated as the "primary therapist." The technique is explained and all questions answered as thoroughly as possible. Every attempt is made to be supportive and to put the primary therapist at ease. Next, the primary therapist begins 30-minute play sessions in a well-equipped playroom on a weekly basis.

During these sessions the other parent and the professional are in an observation room viewing through a one-way mirror. The use of the *bug-in-the-ear* (a small, battery-operated hearing-aid-like device) makes direct communication between therapist and parent in the playroom possible. There are no wires and only the parent who places the device in his ear can hear the messages delivered through the professional's microphone in the observation room. Throughout the sessions the professional can make comments or suggestions at will and also give the other parent a running commentary on the interactions. While most children immediately leap into play with the parent and seem to disregard the fact that they are being observed, any question on their part is fully answered with no attempt at deception. At the option of the professional, the play sessions are simultaneously *videotaped*.

Following the session, the parents are seen by the professional for a half-hour *conjoint parental therapy* session. During this time the parents are asked to discuss their observations, conclusions and feelings as to the relationship and communication process between the primary therapist and the child, and the parents' reaction to the total process. While discussion of technique is always permitted, the parent shows less need for direct aid as time goes on. The emphasis shifts towards the exploration of his own feelings and problems in relationship to the child, especially if they are illustrated by his reactions and observations of his child within a play session.

In essence, this technique fosters the *re-creation of the typical or daily parent-child interaction* in a controlled setting. Underlying feelings and ineffective ways of responding on the parent's part are soon brought to light in a situation where they can be identified and modified. The parent is aided in dealing with his child on a reality basis with an emphasis on the quality of the relationship and increased empathy. We find that even under these artificial conditions parents are able to experience the most genuine of feelings.

CASE EXAMPLES·

A Borderline Psychotic Child

A five-year-old boy presented initially for evaluation of delayed speech development and stuttering, along with poor peer relations. The stuttering was more a problem of initial anxiety than of speech pathology. He was an anxious, shy, thin young boy thought to be relatively bright, but with blunted affect and resistant to engagement. His thought processes were disorganized, and he tended toward fantasies of omnipotent figures such as Ultra-Man, as a defense against feelings of impotence and isolation.

He was the product of an unwanted pregnancy and the parents had even considered an abortion. Neither mother nor father were able to accept the parental role and its consequent demands and responsibilities. Though the mother superficially appeared socially adept and confident, she had underlying ambivalence, chronic anxiety, feelings of inadequacy, and a great need for—but inability to accept—much affection and support. She dealt with her anger toward her needful child through reaction formation and greatly over-invested herself with him. The result was a double-binding, hostile-dependent, symbiotic relationship. The father, a quiet person with a casual approach to life and chronic feelings of inadequacy, had reacted to the demands of his husband and parent roles by slowly withdrawing from family life.

The therapeutic goals in this case were: 1) to aid the child to deal with his own inner conflicts in a supportive setting; 2) to help dissolve the hostile-dependent symbiotic aspect of the mother-son relationship; 3) to aid the father's reentry into the family and establishment of supportive relationships with his wife and son.

The almost classic "distant" father was chosen as the "primary therapist." In weekly filial therapy sessions the child was initially very withdrawn and would not involve his father in play. Through much support on the part of the therapist, the *father was encouraged not to react with reciprocal withdrawal, but to become gently intrusive* in the play and aid his son by initiating interaction. Soon the father began to see his son's capacity and genuine need for a closer father-son relationship. This direct reward encouraged the father to extend himself further and accelerate a mutually rewarding relationship. As the father and son literally discovered each other, it became evident that there was much carryover of the sessions' gains into their methods of relating at home.

While father and son were interacting in the play session, the professional was noting the *reactions and responses of the mother as she observed.* In this case the mother reacted with much criticism of the sessions, and became more anxious as she sensed the improving father-son relationship. This information was dealt with later in the conjoint parental therapy sessions.

As the parents became more comfortable about the technique and less defensive about their own feelings and conflicts, greater depth was introduced into the parental therapy session. The newly strengthened *father-son alliance continued in the play* sessions, allowing the son further support for separating from the mother. The increased support and gratification from her husband in the conjoint sessions aided the mother in directing clearer messages to her son, so that a dissolution of the symbiotic aspect of the mother-child relationship could occur. Once somewhat free of this tie, the child began to grow emotionally, reinforcing the parents' continued progress in their own development of healthier ways of relating to him. (This is a good example of the virtuous cycles discussed in Chapter 5). The identified patient is presently in the third grade at a private school and doing well socially and academically. Presently both parents take an active part in child rearing, while the mother is able to involve herself in more activities outside the home.

A Child in Active Conflict with a Parent

This six-year-old boy was referred for multiple behavioral difficulties both at home and in school. He resided with his divorced mother and twin sister. His behavior was characterized by immature negativism, with much whining and other behavior aimed at attracting sympathy. He was seemingly resistant to any punishment or limit setting. Peer relationships were poor. He seemed continually to "have a chip on his shoulder" and would act out his anger impulsively.

He seemed motivated by strong anger and resentment towards the combination of 1) an immature, rejecting, and inconsistent (irrationally punitive) mother, and 2) no contact at all with the father. Though manifesting strong needs for nurturance, he was unable to accept affection from his mother and seemed chronically to anticipate rejection.

After some initial individual therapy with the mother and child, filial therapy sessions were begun weekly. The initial sessions were difficult, with the boy behaving in his typical negativistic and hostile-teasing fashion, keeping much distance from the mother-therapist, oblivious to attempts at setting any limits. With support and guidance from the professional, the mother continued to act as the therapist until gradually the child's behavior began to change. He came to tolerate greater closeness (both physically and emotionally) and his unruly behavior all but ceased. At the professional's suggestion, the mother was soon able to engage him in reciprocal games, and he took great pleasure in sitting next to her while she read to him. Gentle probing by mother revealed much of the basis of her son's reactions to her. She was encouraged to show affection whenever possible and to avoid allowing his behavior to provoke her into becoming angry. The child was able to resolve his perception of his mother as a destructive, punitive person, and was able to work through his fantasy that the mother had driven his father away.

After approximately eight months of weekly filial therapy sessions, followed by half-hour counseling sessions with the mother, the child's behavior in the home and in social situations had improved. He had begun to establish a *more trusting relationship* with the mother— allowing her to gain control of his behavior by setting reasonable limitations that he could accept, thus reducing her frustration and anger and increasing her ability for affectionate interaction. The boy gradually resigned himself to the lack of a real father and began interaction and identification with those male models that were available.

The Handicapped Child

This eight-year-old boy was referred from a developmental clinic where a thorough diagnostic evaluation had been performed followed by several counseling sessions with the parents. The referring team felt that they had not reached the parents, who continued to have unrealistically high expectations of a child with limited ability. He was functioning overall in the borderline range of intelligence with a marked discrepancy between the Verbal (IQ = 79) and Performance (IQ = 96) abilities. He had great difficulty in the language area, with simplistic, concrete thinking, and lagged behind peers in social skills. Therefore he found academic and social situations difficult and frustrating. Yet, he could handle many performance tasks on an average level. He was being successfully medicated for minimal brain dysfunction.

The father, a rigid, compulsive, perfectionistic, architect, taught college. The mother, a junior high school counselor and teacher, appeared more passive than the father and was also somewhat rigid and lacking in warmth. Both parents worried endlessly about whether the child would ever be self-sufficient. Extremely anxious about the child's ability to learn, they were forever trying to improve what they referred to as his "reasoning ability." The father viewed every encounter as a teaching or learning experience. For example, he would drill the child on simple arithmetic problems at bedtime and first thing in the morning. When the child would respond incorrectly, the father became frustrated and angry—and on one occasion was reduced to tears. The child was becoming increasingly more moody, difficult to handle, and passive-aggressive.

Filial therapy sessions were begun bi-weekly because the parents lived at some distance. The father was designated primary therapist. In the playroom his manner was very much that of a teacher. His anger quickly escalated when the child was not able to follow his instructions or would handle motor tasks in a clumsy manner. When this was later pointed out to the father, he seemed genuinely amazed, apparently unaware of what he was doing. Gradually, the father became more flexible in his dealings with the child and more capable of expressing affection. Within four months both parents had made appreciable gains in their capacity to accept the child as he was and in their ability to emphasize things the boy could excel in, such as manual tasks, rather than language performance. As the parents decreased the pressure they had been putting on him, the child's temper tantrums, passive-aggressive behavior, and general moodiness and frustration vanished; he soon appeared affectionate and emotionally responsive. The parents agreed to his placement in a special education class where his performance was adequate and he began interacting more appropriately with peers.

WHEN TO USE FILIAL THERAPY?

From a series of some 60 cases we have been able to draw some empirical conclusions as to the types of cases that are most likely to respond favorably to this approach.

Those cases that respond consistently well and usually quite rapidly to this technique are the so-called *"adjustment reactions of childhood."* In most such cases we have found the parents to be reasonably *free of severe internal conflict* themselves and sincerely interested in their children and motivated to help them. Frequently, we have found that the parents simply lack basic knowledge and skills in good child rearing practices and consequently have tended to be quite inconsistent in their handling of the children and confused in their own expectations for them. It has been our experience that these parents quickly grasp the concepts of firmness and consistent limit setting once they are made legitimate by the professional. Then they are able to accept in themselves the empathy, warmth, and approval that have usually always been present but rarely or inconsistently expressed. The treatment of these cases is usually short-term (two to four months) and the results are usually excellent.

Another group of children in which we have found this particular technique quite successful are those who seem to continue in *active conflict* with one or both parents. These children have not yet internalized the parent-child conflict to a major degree. They are often given such diagnoses as hyperkinetic reaction of childhood, withdrawing reaction of childhood, or overanxious reaction of childhood (see also Chapter 17). In such cases there are usually many positive aspects to the parent-child relationship but there is usually some specific conflict in one or two areas. These areas of conflict usually become quickly apparent in the play therapy session and are therefore available to the parent for observation and discussion. The parent is then usually able to work through the conflict directly with the child, with the help and support of the professional. By having the child and parent work through the conflict directly rather than through a transferential process, the overall length of time necessary for resolution is considerably shortened.

In this particular group of patients we have found the concomitant use of videotape with a subsequent confrontation and discussion to be of great value. In most of these cases the parents are unaware of their nonverbal responses to the child in a conflictual area, and are frequently genuinely surprised to see their own actions and reactions on videotape.

In some cases we have found it very useful to "instant replay" a particularly meaningful segment of tape several times in order to further develop the import of the interaction and to help the parent deal with the emotionally-laden content often brought up by such confrontation. In several cases we have found that one particular tape with extremely emotionally meaningful interaction has proven to be quite dramatic as an impetus to rapid resolution of a specific parent-child conflict.

Somewhat astonishingly, the next group of patients who seem to respond well to this approach are the *borderline psychotic children* who have one reasonably healthy parent. In such cases there is usually a very severe conflict between the mother and child (although we have seen cases in which the primary conflict was between father and child). Usually such children seem to have the major conflict in the area of object relationships and seem to be arrested in the late stages of separation-individuation (Mahler, 1952). Even though these children are involved in an extremely conflictual relationship with the mother, they usually have a "latent" relationship with the father. By taking advantage of this latent relationship with the father and nurturing it through the use of filial therapy, these children often make dramatic and rapid gains. As the child is able to move out of the separation-individuation impasse, the mother too is able to grow emotionally and begin to relate to the child in a much more healthy manner.

Another indication for the use of this technique is where a child has *organic problems or borderline mental retardation,* and the parent or parents are not able fully to grasp the child's limitations (see, also, Chapters 14 and 15). In such cases the parents are often quite unreasonable in their expectations for academic achievement or social performance. By helping the parents look at these children realistically and develop a genuine appreciation of their capabilities as well as their handicaps, the therapist can help them to deal with the child on a much more appropriate basis.

Those cases in which we have found this technique *least effective* are children who appear to have *severe internalized conflicts,* particularly the more severely neurotic children. We have found that children with severe obsessive-compulsive features, such as are often seen in the encopretic child, generally do not do as well in this type of approach. We have also found that children with significant personality disorders and generally psychotic children do not respond particularly well to the filial therapy approach.

FRINGE BENEFITS

We feel that filial therapy has the advantage of tremendous carryover at home. Parents seem to like this approach very much as they feel they are genuinely involved in the psychotherapeutic process, and they feel very positive about the fact that they themselves have been instrumental in bringing about the changes they see in the child. This results in very positive attitudes about the professional, as opposed to the competitive, negative attitude often exhibited by parents of children in one-to-one psychotherapy (see Chapter 18 by Adams). In filial therapy the parents often develop a strong positive transference to the professional, seeing him in the role of a benign parent figure and teacher. This particular aspect of filial therapy makes it very rewarding to the professional.

REFERENCES

FREUD, S.: Analysis of a phobia in a five-year-old boy (1909). *The Standard Edition of the Complete Psychological Works of Sigmund Freud.* 10:5-149, London: Hogarth Press.
GUERNEY, B.: Filial therapy: Description and rationale. *Journal of Consulting Psychology,* 28:450-460, 1964.
MAHLER, M.: On child psychosis and schizophrenia: Autistic and symbiotic infantile psychosis. *The Psychoanalytic Study of the Child,* 7:286-305, 1952.

Chapter 12

Temperamental Traits
and Parent Guidance

Stella Chess and Alexander Thomas

Each child has an individual behavioral style of responding to and coping with environmental stimuli, expectations and demands. This individual style or temperament can be identified from early infancy onward.

Temperament in our usage contains no inference as to genetic, endocrine, somatologic, or environmental etiologies. It is a phenomenal term used to describe the characteristic tempo, energy expenditure, focus, mood, and rhythmicity typifying the behaviors of the individual child, independently of their contents.

Temperament may best be viewed as a general term referring to the *how* of behavior. It differs from ability, which is concerned with the *what* and *how well* of behavior, and from motivation, which accounts for *why* a person does what he is doing. Temperament concerns the way an individual behaves. Two children may dress themselves with

135

equal skillfulness or ride a bicycle with the same dexterity and have the same motives for engaging in these activities. Two adults may show the same intellectual interests or the same technical expertness in their work and have the same reason for devoting themselves to their jobs. Yet, these two children or adults may differ significantly with regard to the quickness with which they move, the ease with which they approach a new physical setting, social situation, or task, the intensity and character of their mood expression, and the effort required to distract them when they are absorbed in an activity.

Temperament, like any other psychological function, is not immutable. Consistency over time in temperament is sometimes striking, but in other instances modification or marked change may occur (Thomas and Chess, 1977).

We have defined *nine categories of temperament* through inductive analysis of behavioral data. These temperamental traits are: *activity level, rhythmicity, approach-withdrawal, adaptability, intensity of reaction, quality of mood, sensory threshold, distractibility,* and *persistence and attention span.*

TEMPERAMENTAL CONSTELLATIONS AND PARENTAL REACTIONS

Several temperamental constellations have been delineated from our longitudinal study.

The Difficult Child

A temperamental pattern with the greater risk of behavior problem development comprises the combination of irregularity in biological functions, predominantly negative (withdrawal) responses to new stimuli, nonadaptability or slow adaptability to change, frequent negative mood, and predominantly intense reactions. These are infants with irregular sleep and feeding patterns, slow acceptance of new foods, prolonged adjustment periods to new routines and frequent and loud periods of crying. Their laughter, too, is characteristically loud. Mothers find them difficult to care for and pediatricians frequently refer to them as the "difficult infants." They are not easy to feed, to put to sleep, to bathe, or to dress. New places, new activities, strange faces—all may produce initial responses of loud protest or crying. Frustration characteristically produces a violent tantrum. These children approximate 10% of the total study population but comprise a significantly higher proportion of the behavior problem group (Thomas, Chess and Birch, 1968). The stressful demands for these children are typically those of socialization, namely the demands for alteration of spontaneous responses and patterns to conform to the rules of living of the family, the school, or the peer group. Once they do adapt to the rules they function easily, consistently, and energetically.

We have found no evidence that the parents of the difficult infants are essentially different from the other parents. Nor do our studies suggest that the temperamental characteristics of the children are caused by the parents. The issue is rather that the care of these infants makes special requirements upon their parents for unusually firm, patient, consistent and tolerant handling. Such handling is necessary if the difficult infant is to learn to adapt to new demands with a minimum of stress. If the new demand is presented inconsistently, impatiently or punitively, effective change in behavior becomes stressful and even impossible. Negativism is a not infrequent outcome of such suboptimal parental functioning.

The problems of managing a difficult child not infrequently highlight a parent's individual reaction to stress. The same parents who are relaxed and consistent with an easy child may become resentful, guilty, or helpless with a difficult child, depending on their own personality structures. By contrast, other parents, who do not feel guilty or put-down by the child's behavior, may learn to enjoy the vigor, lustiness, and "stubbornness" of a difficult infant.

The Easy Child

At the opposite end of the temperamental spectrum from the difficult infant is the child who is regular, responds positively to new stimuli (approaches), adapts quickly and easily to change, and shows a predominantly positive mood of mild or moderate intensity. These are the infants who develop regular sleep and feeding schedules easily, take to most new foods at once, smile at strangers, adapt quickly to a new school, accept most frustrations with a minimum of fuss, and learn the rules of new games quickly. They are aptly called "easy babies" and are usually a joy to their parents, pediatricians, and teachers. In contrast to the difficult infant, the easy child adapts to the demands for socialization with little or no stress and confronts his parents with few if any problems in handling.

Naturally, these children as a group develop significantly fewer behavior problems proportionately than do the difficult infants. However, their very ease of adaptability may in certain circumstances be the basis for problem behavior development. Most typically, we have seen this occur where there is a severe *dissonance between the expectations and demands of the intra- and extrafamilial environments.* The child first adapts easily to deviant standards and behavioral expectations of the parent in the first few years of life. Stress and malfunctioning develop only when he moves actively into functional situations outside the home, such as peer play groups and school, where he finds the extrafamilial standards and demands in sharp conflict with the patterns learned in the home.

As a typical example, the parents of one such child admired individuality of expression and disapproved of any behavior or attitude in their child which they identified as stereotypical or lacking in imagination. Self-expression was encouraged and conformity and attentiveness to rules discouraged even when this resulted in ill manners and a disregard of the desires of others. As she grew older, she became increasingly isolated from her peer group because of continuous insistence on her own preferences. In school her progress was grossly unsatisfactory because of difficulty in listening to directions. The parents were advised to restructure their approach to place less emphasis on individuality and instead to teach her to be responsive to the needs of others and to conform constructively in class behavior and in activities with her peers. The parents, acutely aware of the child's growing social isolation and the potential seriousness of her educational problem, carried out this plan consistently. At follow-up six months later, the child had adapted to the new rules easily, the conflict between standards within and without the home had become minimal, she had become an active social member of a peer group, and had caught up to grade level in academic work.

The Slow-to-Warm-Up Child

Another important temperamental constellation comprises the combination of negative responses of mild intensity to new stimuli with slow adaptability after repeated contact. Children with this pattern differ from the difficult infants in that their withdrawal from the new is quiet rather than loud. They also usually do not have the irregularity of function, frequent negative mood expression, and intense reactions of the difficult infants. The mildly expressed withdrawal from the new is typically seen with the first encounter with the bath, a new person, a stranger, or a new place. With the first bath the child lies still and fusses mildly; with a new food he turns his head away quietly and lets it dribble out of his mouth; with a stranger who greets him loudly he clings to his mother. If given the opportunity to reexperience new situations without pressure, such a child gradually comes to show quiet and positive interests and involvement. This characteristic sequence of response has suggested the appellation *"slow-to-warm-up."*

A key issue in the development of slow-to warm-up children is whether parents and teachers allow them to make an adaptation to the new *at their own tempo* or insist on immediate positive involvement. If the adult recognizes that the slow adaptation to a new school, new peer group, or new academic subject reflects the child's normal temperamental style, patient encouragement is likely. If, on the contrary, the child's slow warm-up is interpreted as timidity or lack of interest, adult impatience and pressure on the child for quick adaptation may occur. The child's reaction to this stressful pressure is typically an intensification of his withdrawal tendency. If this increased holding-back in turn stimulates increased impatience and pressure on the part of the parent or teacher, a destructive child-environment vicious circle will be set in motion (see Chapter 5).

In other instances in our study population, nursery-school teachers have interpreted the child's slow initial adaptation as evidence of underlying anxiety. In one case an elementary school teacher estimated that a child's slow initial mastery of a new accelerated academic program indicated inadequate intellectual capacity. In these cases the longitudinal behavioral records documented a slow-to-warm-up temperamental style and made possible the recommendation that judgment be suspended until the child could have a longer period of contact with the new situation. The subsequent successful mastery of the demands of the new situation clarified the issue as one of temperamental style and not psychopathology or lack of intellectual capacity.

A contrast to the slow-to-warm-up child is the *very persistent child* who is most likely to develop stress not with his initial contact with a situation but during the course of his ongoing activity after the first positive adaptation has been made. His quality of persistence leads him to resist interference or attempts to divert him from an activity in which he is absorbed. If the adult interference is arbitrary and forcible, tension and frustration tend to mount quickly in these children and may reach explosive proportions.

The *distractible nonpersistent* child also creates maladaptive child-environment interactions in many instances. Parents and teachers may interpret this behavioral style as evidence of disinterest, lack of self-discipline, or laziness. The child's difficulty in carrying through a parental demand to completion without interruption may be interpreted as willful disobedience. The inability of the *high activity child* to sit still for long periods at mealtime, school periods, automobile rides, etc., may create exasperation and a punitive response in adults. The *low activity child* may be considered to be sluggish or even retarded (Thomas, Chess and Birch, 1968).

GOODNESS OF FIT

Goodness of fit (Henderson, 1913) results when the properties of the environment or its expectations and demands are in accord with the organism's own capacities, characteristics, and style of behaving. When this *consonance* between organisms and environment is present, optimal development in a progressive direction is possible. Conversely, poorness of fit involves discrepancies and *dissonance* between environmental opportunities and demands and the capacities and characteristics of the organisms, so that distorted development and maladaptive functioning occur.

Goodness of fit is *never an abstraction, but is always goodness of fit for specific certain end results* which may vary from society to society or from one socioeconomic group to another within any given society.

Goodness of fit does *not* imply an *absence of stress or conflict*. Quite the contrary, stress and conflict are inevitable concomitants of the developmental process, in which new expectations and demands for change and progressively higher levels of functioning occur continuously as the child grows older. Demands, stresses, and conflicts, when consonant with the child's developmental potentials and capacities for mastery, may be constructive in their consequences and should not be considered as an inevitable cause of behavioral disturbance. The issue involved in disturbed behavioral functioning is rather one of *excessive* stress resulting from poorness of fit, dissonance between environmental expectations and demands and the capacities of the child at any age-level of development. The goodness of fit concept, of course, does not apply only to temperamental attributes. Parental expectations and demands may be dissonant with a child's capacities in cognitive, perceptual, and motivational areas (see Chapter 14).

APPLICATION TO PARENT GUIDANCE

Parent guidance involves first the *identification of* those elements of *parental behavior* and overtly expressed attitudes that appear to be exerting a harmful influence on the child's development. This is followed by the formulation of a *program of altered parental functioning* which will modify or change the interactive pattern between child and parent in a healthy direction. In those instances in which clinical evaluation indicates the presence of a disorder in the child requiring special treatment or management procedures, parent guidance may still be helpful but not sufficient. Where the child's problem behavior or symptoms reflect a reactive disorder, alteration in parent functioning is not only helpful but usually sufficient.

Fit Rather Than Pathology

The rationale of the guidance program is explained to the parents in terms of the necessity of a goodness of fit between the child's characteristics and the parents' functioning. The specific area or areas of undesirable parent-child interaction are identified, the specific temperamental traits and other pertinent attributes of the child involved in this interaction are described, and the parental behaviors which are creating excessive stress are pointed out. Throughout this discussion, the parents are assured implicitly—and explicitly if necessary—that no judgment is being made that they are "bad parents," and that the same behavior with a child with different attributes might be positive instead of negative in its consequences. It is simultaneously emphasized that the child's disturbed responses to their benign intentions and efforts do not mean that he is "bad," "sick," or "willfully disobedient."

Illustrate Concretely

References to concrete incidents in the child's life are made to illustrate each suggestion. For example, the initial intense negative responses to new situations and slow adaptability of a difficult child are documented by details of the child's history with new foods, new people, new activities, new school situations, etc. These reactions are distinguished from anxiety or motivated negativism. Harmful parental attitudes, such as guilt, anxiety, and hostility, and undesirable management practices, such as impatience, inconsistency, and rigidity in unreasonable demands, are clarified, again with concrete illustrations. As another example, the restlessness and shifts in attention of a highly active and distractible youngster are distinguished from "laziness," willful inattention, and lack of interest. Parental demands that the child sit still on a long trip or concentrate for long periods without distraction on homework are identified, and their inappropriateness *for this child* and undesirable consequences explained.

Emphasize Specificity

This discussion of the parental attitudes and practices which are inimical to the child's healthy development focuses throughout on the specificity of the harmful effects for the particular temperamental constellation. Wherever possible, it is emphasized that the same parental functioning might be satisfactory for a child with different temperamental traits, with concrete illustrations. This helps to clarify the basic assumption that the necessity for change in attitude and behavior does not mean that the parents in some way want to wrong the child. The parents are then offered specific suggestions and advice for changing the identified undesirable attitudes and practices.

Follow-up

Even with parents who are eager and able to carry through the program of behavioral change recommended to them, more than one discussion is usually necessary for this to be fully implemented. Several sessions may be required for them to grasp adequately the concept of temperamental individuality and its influence on the child's ability to cope with parental and other environmental demands and expectations. It is important, at these follow-up discussions, to review the parents' behavior in a number of *specific incidents* which have occurred in the interim period. This review, which should be done in detail, is often required for the parents to become adept at identifying those situations in the child's daily life in which modification of their techniques of management are required.

Traits With Guidance Failure

The only correlation between the results of parent guidance and the child's temperamental pattern found in our longitudinal study was that guidance failed in all four cases in which the children were *distractible and nonpersistent.* For the parents in this middle and upper middle class group, great importance is attached to educational achievement for both sexes and to success in professional careers or business for the males. Characteristics of persistence and "stick-to-it-iveness" are highly valued. It was, therefore, hard for these parents to accept the fact that the characteristics of low persistence and distractibility were normal, and, more distressingly, could not be changed by pressure or persuasion. It is of interest that all four children in this group were boys, in whom the qualities of persistence and non-distractibility were especially prized.

All other temperamental patterns were much more acceptable to these parents. Thus, most of the parents were able to tolerate and be patient with the initial nonadaptive reactions of the difficult or slow-to-warm-up child in new situations, once they were convinced that with a change in their approach the child would finally achieve behavior congenial to their own standards. For the parents of these children, as for the easy, persistent, high, or low activity children, a change in their handling could bring the outcome they desired. For the parents of the distractible, nonpersistent children, however, a change in their handling could still leave the child functioning in a fashion uncongenial to them. We might speculate that with parents espousing different cultural values, parent guidance for such children could succeed better.

Some Management Considerations

In these parent guidance procedures no attempt is made to define or change any hypothetical underlying conflicts, anxieties, or defenses in the parent that may be presumed to be the cause of the noxious behavior or overtly expressed attitudes. Inevitably, the guidance sessions do reveal misconceptions, confusions, defensiveness, anxiety, or guilt in a number of parents which impede their ability to understand the issue and carry through the necessary changes in behavior. In such instances additional discussions are required for clarification of misconceptions and confusions or for explication of the inappropriateness of defensiveness, anxiety, or guilt. In some instances, psychopathology in the parents may be so severe as to prevent their making the necessary changes in behavior without psychotherapy.

An overall estimate from our experience is that two to three sessions of parent guidance, without direct treatment of the child, were markedly or moderately successful in approximately 50% of the children with behavior disorders. But its usefulness depends on the specificity with which undesirable areas of parent-child interaction are identified.

Parent guidance, as here formulated, presumes that parental dysfunction with a child is not necessarily the result of fixed parental psychopathology or family pathology. However, even in those cases where parental psychiatric disturbance or family disturbance is the prime cause of unhealthy influence on the child, parent guidance may sometimes be successful despite the absence of change in the parent's personality or family structure. Anna Freud (1960) has put it well. She "refuse (s) to believe that mothers need to change their personalities before they can change the handling of their child."

REFERENCES

FREUD, A.: The child guidance clinic as a center of prophylaxis and enlightenment. *Recent Developments in Psychoanalytic Child Therapy.* New York: International Universities Press, 1960.

HENDERSON, L. V.: *The Fitness of the Environment.* New York: Macmillan, 1913.

THOMAS, A., CHESS, S., & BIRCH, H. G.: *Temperament and Behavior Disorders in Children.* New York: New York University Press, 1968.

THOMAS, A. & CHESS, S.: *Temperament and Development.* New York. Brunner/Mazel, 1977.

Chapter 13

Parents, Prescriptions, Pills, and Pot

L. Eugene Arnold

This chapter deals with two issues which at first may appear to be only superficially related in that they both concern drugs—legitimate drug use and drug abuse. Many readers will undoubtedly feel that these two issues are sufficiently different to warrant two separate chapters. However, a little reflection will disclose many ties between the two types of drug use:

1. In both instances the drug may be seen by the user or by his parents (who may also be users) as either helpful or destructive, either as an escape from pain, disability, or other evil, or as an impairment of integrity.

2. In both instances a great deal of emotionality may cloud an objective appraisal of the situation.

3. In both instances there is a strong possibility of a parent-child conflict over use of the drug with one or the other resisting or

145

attacking its use and the other defending or urging it. Usually such drug-centered conflicts are symptomatic of deeper and broader disturbances in the parent-child relationship.

4. In both instances there is danger of a helping professional's being drawn into both the emotionality surrounding the drug use and into parent-child conflicts over it. This can occur either because the parent and/or child tries to enlist the professional as an ally in the struggle or because the professional shares certain emotional reactions to the thought of drug use.

5. Related to this is a strong tendency for cultural "prescriptions" and norms to influence both legal and illegal drug use.

6. Many experts believe that problems of drug abuse among youth are directly related to our drug-oriented, drug-dependent culture, with its cocktail parties, its beer, cigarette, coffee ("the think drink") and cola advertisements, and ubiquitous advertising of remedies for headaches, acid indigestion, insomnia, colds, allergies, etc.

Bearing these connections in mind we will nevertheless separate the two kinds of drug use for purposes of convenient discussion.

HELPING PARENTS MAXIMIZE PRESCRIPTION BENEFITS

Respecting the Family's Integrity

The prescribing physician must necessarily take a humble attitude towards compliance with the prescription. He cannot really "order" medication for an outpatient as he could for a hospitalized patient. Whether or not the child patient takes the medicine as prescribed depends not only on the child's interest and willingness, but probably to an even greater degree on the parents' judgment as to how important and how beneficial the medicine will be. This is probably appropriate, because the parent retains the legal, moral, and practical burden of insuring and guarding the child's welfare. The prescribing physician can only act as a consultant to the child and his parents (see Chapter 1).

Therefore, the physician needs to provide to the parents and child an adequate explanation of the reasons for the medicine, what it is, and what benefits and side effects might reasonably be expected. It may be advisable to preface the mention of side effects with a remark such as, "There are some possible side effects which I want to mention so that if they happen, you'll know what they are and not worry about them. Just call me about them and we can make adjustment in the dosage if necessary." Any questions the family may have should be answered fully in terms they can understand. This might also be called the process of "informed consent." In fact, they can often be asked, after adequate explanation, if they wish to have a prescription for the medicine. After all, no matter how strongly the physician feels the medicine is indicated, there is no point in giving them a prescription if they are sure they don't want it. This applies even to such obviously "indicated" drugs as antibiotics, but much more so to psychoactive drugs.

For example, part of adequate explanation in the case of stimulants for hyperkinetic children is the information that these drugs are listed by the federal government as "dangerous drugs" because of their addicting potential for adults. It can also be mentioned that of course addiction has not been found to be a problem for children who take these drugs for this purpose. This fortifies the parents for possible criticism by friends or relatives for "drugging" the child, assuming that they agree to it after being thus adequately informed. The physician's modeling of a rational, nondefensive attitude toward the medication helps to set a rational tone for the parents' decision.

As part of setting a rational tone, the physician needs to define the limitations of the medicine and emphasize the importance of other things that should be done to help the child, such as remedial education, behavior modification (see Chapter 7), structuring, and psychological support. Even in the case of such obviously medical problems as infection, the comprehensive physician will, in addition to prescribing an antibiotic, advise such supportive measures as rest, fluids, adequate diet or vitamins, heat, gargling, etc., to enhance the healing process and keep the patient comfortable. The same principles apply to psychopharmacological therapy.

PREVENT DRUGS FROM BEING WEAPONS

Some problems are more likely to arise with psychopharmacological therapy than with other forms of medication. One of the foremost of these is the involvement of medication-giving and medication-taking in a previously existing parent-child conflict. This is especially likely to happen if the medicine is seen by the family as an extension of parental control. In such a case, the child may see the medicine as an infringement on his autonomy. One means of preventing this and of dealing with the problem when it arises is to make a medication contract directly with the child, keeping the parent an interested observer who can be enlisted by the child and physician as an assistant in the process. Depending on the age, maturity, and responsibility of the child, the parent's assistance can consist of anything from merely purchasing the medicine, through providing unobtrusive reminders at appropriate times, to dispensing the medicine to the child at the appropriate time. As much as possible, coercion needs to be kept out of the transaction (on the part of either physician or parent). Rather, the assumption and expectation should be emphasized that the child will naturally wish to take the medicine because of the benefit he can expect from it (which has been explained). Sometimes one parent can successfully help the child with handling medication when the other cannot. When the child actively resists medication to the point of continuing hassles with both parents over the issue, there is a good deal of doubt as to whether the benefits of the medicine are worth the trouble. In such a situation the parents might be advised to abandon their coercive efforts and some sort of family therapy counseling should be offered to help deal with the basic parent-child conflict which is being focused on the medication. If the parent can "lay off," the child may after a week or two decide on his own that he is willing to try the medicine.

Parental Anxiety

An opposite problem may be parental withholding of medication even though the child is willing or desirous. This could be a subtle form of parental rejection, but a more common cause would be parental anxiety, relating either to the idea of the possible dangers of the drug or to ambivalence about having a "defective" child who needs medication. The physician needs to be alert to the anxieties of parents about various medicines and explore these. A nondefensive, frank willingness to discuss the actions, side effects, and other aspects of the various drugs is usually enough to dispel most of the parents' anxieties about dangers of the drug. In some cases, though, it may be judicious to offer delaying the medication until the parent has had a chance to think about it, if it is not an urgent situation. Sometimes it is helpful to point out that the physician is not willing to prescribe this medicine for every case, but that this particular problem seems to offer enough hope of benefitting from it that the physician is willing to prescribe it if the parent wants it. If the anxiety arises from ambivalence about the child's handicap or problem, an opportunity should be offered for discussing the diagnosis and prognosis and their implications. Several sessions may be needed for the parent to resolve his anxieties about this.

One final consideration for some parents, especially in economic hard times, is the *cost of the medicine*. The physician needs to be sensitive to this 1) in the choice of medication (a slightly less glamorous or effective medicine that is within the financial reach of the family may be a better prescription than a very expensive "first choice"), 2) in the dosage size chosen (a 10 mg pill is cheaper than two 5 mg pills), and 3) in apprising the family of possible sources of help to pay for the medication. In the latter regard, some druggists are cooperative and most major drug companies are willing to help out. Many families with children have financial pressures that may be contributing to the child's problems, and the physician should try to avoid augmenting these pressures unnecessarily.

ENHANCING PLACEBO EFFECT

Drugs are always an intervention in a complex system in which a child's disorder is overdetermined by feedback loops (see Chapter 5). For this reason most drugs usually have a placebo effect which is mediated by the effect of medicine-giving and medicine-taking on the expectations, attitudes, and other psychosocial sets within the various feedback loops. Though placebo effect is considered a nuisance in scientific investigation of the pharmacological effects of various drugs, it is actually a good thing in clinical practice, enhancing the benefits of any prescription. The patient has a right to enjoy the placebo effect in addition to any pharmacological benefit from a given drug, and it is the comprehensive physician's responsibility to enhance placebo benefit in any honest way possible. This involves an enthusiastic, optimistic, positive attitude about the expectations of benefit. Such an attitude by the physician is not incompatible with the previously explained obligation to describe side effects, define limitations of the medicine, and set a rational tone, as the following excerpt from "The Art of Medicating Hyperkinetic Children" (Arnold, 1973) illustrates:

> Enhancing the placebo effect of the unpredictable stimulants requires a little thought and planning until sufficient practice has made it second nature. One method begins by stating that there are many different medicines which are helpful to the kind of problem the child has, that one of these medicines may be better for one child and another better for another child, but there is no sure way of telling ahead of time which is best for a given child. Furthermore, the dose required is different for each child. Therefore, no

one should get discouraged if the dosage or even the type of medicine has to be changed several times in order to find the best dose of the best medicine for this particular child. This allows for the possibility that the first medicine tried may not be satisfactory, but couches it in terms of the optimistic assurance that another medicine might be better. Most people, on hearing this, will tend to pick up the optimistic, confident note rather than the implication of uncertainty.

Having built in these necessary disclaimers, the physician should explain in more detail the expected benefits: The child will probably find it easier to concentrate, to control himself (including his temper), to ignore distractions, and to do what he wants to do when he wants to do it. Medication will not make him be good but will make it possible for him to behave in the way in which he has always wanted to, but had difficulty doing until the present. Parents should expect to find that he learns better from experience, is easier to train, and is more even-tempered. They may find that where previously they had to whack him to get his attention, he may now break into tears if they raise their voices at him, requiring a more gentle approach. They should also expect him temporarily to lose his appetite, possibly become whiny and depressed, and possibly have trouble sleeping. Coupling the mention of side effects with the description of anticipated benefits tends to make them more acceptable. It also tends to make them reinforcers of the positive expectations. When the predicted side effects occur, they confirm the credibility of the doctor who also predicted the benefits: "The medicine is working just like the doctor said it would."

Teachers and other school personnel also need to be included in the placebo effort by similar specific predictions of improvement.

NONMEDICAL DRUG USE

It was difficult to decide whether to call this section "drug abuse," "illegal drug use," "recreational drug use," or "nonmedical drug use." The term "recreational" seemed objectionable because it implies something wholesome and does not encompass escapist use. Some drug use, though legal, could easily be classified as abuse on the basis of dependence (even addiction) with continued use despite self-destructive consequences. Obvious examples are alcoholism and nicotine addiction. Alcohol is obviously just as dangerous today as it was during prohibition when it was illegal. On the other hand, some illegal drug use (e.g., an occasional "joint" with the gang) may involve neither dependence nor significantly destructive consequences. In this light, legality and even classification as abuse become matters of rhetoric, politics, and majority whim.

Parents and the Politics of Drug Use

Parents, as authorities within their families, often find themselves in the same situation regarding their adolescent sons and daughters as government authorities find themselves in regarding popular drug use. No matter how much authorities feel responsible for protecting the population from various drugs, legal bans can only work as long as the vast majority take responsibility for abiding by them. Prohibition of alcohol was not successful because a significant proportion of the people continued to feel a need or desire for alcohol. Tobacco could not successfully be banned at present because too many people are unable or unwilling to give up their nicotine habit. Similarly, parents need to realize that they cannot unilaterally protect their children from drug use. They can only explain, encourage, argue, and set an example, but they cannot supervise a youngster 24 hours a day. Ultimately an adolescent, as an autonomous human being, must take some responsibility for himself. Therefore, a drug-using son or daughter does not prove parental negligence or failure.

Parents may be further consoled by the following idea if they can accept it: Drugs tend to be classified as bad, good, or neutrally innocuous and tend to be legalized or banned according to the belief of those who happen to have the power to legislate and enforce laws, rather than on scientific grounds. Sufficient popular sentiment can influence authorities to change both their beliefs and the laws, in either direction, as was seen with alcohol prohibition and subsequent legalization. Widespread enough use of any drug presently illegal could result in its being legalized. Since the legal status of a drug is more a matter of political chance than a scientific assessment of danger, parents need not worry that the illegality per se of the drugs their children use makes them any more dangerous than legal drugs. We are still left, of course, with the problem of drug use regardless of legality, which will be dealt with later.

Parents, like political authorities, tend to be conservative and view the established legal drugs as innocuous compared to the "dangerous" illegal drugs, which they tend to lump together indiscriminately. The danger of attempting to tar all illegal drugs with the same brush is that the youngster who discovers that marijuana is not as dangerous as had been represented may conclude that the danger of "hard" drugs is equally doubtful. A parent cannot individually do anything about the ill-advised rigidity of the authorities, but he can avoid falling into the same trap. Parents can avail themselves of a more flexible attitude about the relative dangers of various drugs. This, of course, does not negate parents' realistic concern that a youngster by using an illegal drug may run afoul of the law.

Generation Gap and Matristic Values

Distler (1970) has proposed that the conservative preference of parents for established legal drugs and the rebellious preference of adolescents for illegal drugs may mask the fact that they are both turning to drugs for the same reasons. There is often a common disillusionment with material values, achievement goals, and the Horatio Alger ethic, the kind of values that characterizes a patristic culture. The parents at their cocktail parties and the adolescents at their pot parties may both be searching for such matristic values and goals as sensitivity, communication of feelings, communion, caring, nurturance, and meaning. Paradoxically and tragically, they both seek psychological, philosophical, and spiritual goals by the use of a material chemical. This may explain the quasi-religious fervor with which each group defends its favorite drugs and attacks those of the other. Thus, the tool chosen to promote communion and communication becomes instead a source of divisiveness and misunderstanding. Parents who are able to understand and act on this knowledge have the opportunity to develop a meaningful relationship with their sons and daughters. This may obviate some of the need for drug use as they pursue their common quest for meaning.

WHAT PARENTS CAN DO

The following specific suggestions can be made to parents to help them prevent their children from using drugs nonmedically:

1. *Set an example* of abstinence or at least moderation in drug use. What's "sauce" for the goose and gander is also sauce for the goslings. It is difficult for a youngster to understand why he should abstain while his parent drinks or smokes heavily (or perhaps depends upon minor tranquilizers or sedatives). Such an adolescent may easily conclude that the parent does not view drug use very seriously: Actions speak louder than words, and example teaches more persuasively than exhortation. Unfortunately, parents will in many cases find it impossible to kick their own habits. In such instances it will be necessary to:

2. *Deflate the hypocrisy issue through frank admission* to the children of alcohol, nicotine, or caffeine dependence. Not only is

confession good for the soul, but it also puts the confessor in a morally unimpeachable position from which to give advice. It is much more compelling to say, "Look at the mistake I made and learn from it to save yourself," than to say, "What I am doing is really not so bad, but what you're doing (or about to do) is, so don't do it."

Many parents will find this concept hard to accept or else find the humbling admission hard to make in front of their adolescents. They will need much support, understanding, and encouragement.

3. *Respect the adolescent's psychological autonomy* and tolerate his differences of opinion in other areas. This should diminish his need to assert independence in the arena of drug use.

4. *Be concerned* for the adolescent's welfare *in ways unrelated to drug use.* This will fit the concerns about drug use into an appropriate context and demonstrate that it is not just a parental hangup. True concern for the adolescent's welfare includes the wish for the adolescent to enjoy some amusement. This demonstrates that parental cautions against drug use are not merely punitive interference with the adolescent's fun.

5. *Communicate with the adolescents* about: a) the numerous pressures in our society for use of drugs, such as advertisements on television and billboards and how these infringe on the individual's right to make decisions for himself about drug use; b) the gradations of gray rather than black and white in real life; c) philosophical issues such as the meaning of life. Such communications need to be discussions, not unilateral pronouncements or advice.

REFERENCES

ARNOLD, L. E.: The art of medicating hyperkinetic children. *Clinical Pediatrics,* 12: 35-41, 1973.
DISTLER, L. S.: The adolescent "hippie" and the emergence of a matristic culture. *Psychiatry,* 33:362-371, 1970.

Part III

Helping Parents Cope with

Specific Problems of Children

Chapter 14

Counseling Parents of Mentally Retarded and Learning Disordered Children

Julian B. Ferholt and

Albert J. Solnit

Children with intellectual handicaps have a wide range of problems which are very difficult for parents to understand and accept. Some of the children are retarded, and others, although not retarded, have difficulty with language, reading, arithmetic, or coordination. A significant number have associated emotional problems.

The challenge of counseling is to help parents cope with a painful situation in a way which is most constructive for their child. It should help them to understand their child, guide their use of resources, encourage active participation in remedial programs, and offer support for the care they give at home.

Professionals frequently underestimate the importance of social experiences when they plan to help a child with an intellectual problem, especially if the child is considered biologically impaired. Yet, no matter how limited a child's potential, his *level of intellectual achievement* will

157

almost always *depend on his experience as well as his equipment;* a child will become competent only insofar as he is helped to activate his potential, i.e., to develop the skills he is capable of acquiring. His sense of his own worth will result in large part from his family's attitude towards his problem. As with all children, the quality of a handicapped child's life largely depends on his experiences with his parents, whether or not there is a biological deficit. In fact, the biologically disadvantaged infant is most in need of optimal care to maximize his limited potential. Ironically, he is more often born into circumstances which interfere with good care, and more likely to behave in ways which are confusing or difficult for his parents.

Parent guidance is most effective when it *focuses attention on the child's resources* as well as his handicap, and intellectual remediation is only one of many important elements in the process of raising a handicapped child. Even highly specialized interventions are most effective when the emotional aspects of the child's experience are considered and when he is enabled to practice and enhance his strengths as well as cope with his deficits. Clinically, *motivations and personal relationships cannot be separated from cognitive behavior.*

The following example demonstrates the variety of challenges which a counselor takes on.

Mrs. Young, a pediatric nurse practitioner at our Birth Defects Clinic, was introduced to John's parents by the neurosurgeon when John was two days old, just before he was operated on for a defect in his back and spinal cord (meningomyelocele). Nine years later, he is retarded (trainable) and confined to a wheel chair with a urine bag, tight, weak muscles, arthritic joints, and a curved spine. Mrs. Young has met regularly with his parents for those nine years to help them care for him at home and to coordinate the many community resources involved.

Although John is learning to wash, eat, dress, and clean his urine bag himself, he is furious if he is not catered to. John refuses to touch the lower half of his body and he gags when he even accidentally touches his penis or the opening where his urine comes out. In addition he wonders, aloud, why he can't walk like other children. Mrs. Young tries to help John's parents to understand and assist him with his worries at the same time that she supports their efforts to curb his impulsive behavior.

From the beginning, Mrs. Young helped them deal with the shock of a serious congenital defect in their first child. Although she enabled them to know about the many problems ahead, she supported their decision to go ahead with the life-saving operation at two days. Supporting their participation in the baby's care during his first eight weeks in the hospital, she counseled the family during 12 subsequent surgical procedures by six different surgeons. She referred the parents to a Regional Center where John attends a special school and also receives occupational, physical, and speech therapy.

In counseling sessions, the parents have discussed many practical questions about home procedures like skin care, leg traction, the shunt valve, and exercises. They also have been helped to plan more time for themselves away from John and to make full use of financial and transportation assistance.

In addition, they discussed their marital tensions, an intrusive mother-in-law, and their concerns about having a second child. Mrs. Young helped the parents explain the pregnancy and prepare John for his sister.

Although John's retarded development had been apparent since his first year, his parents were repeatedly surprised and hurt by subsequent test results. At five years he could identify pictures at the four-year-old level and name objects at the three-year-old level. However, at nine years, his verbal behavior was only at a four-year-old level while his visual motor behavior was closer to the two-year-old level. Counseling has supported the parents' efforts while enabling them to cope with their disappointment.

(For more about parent guidance by nurses and other health personnel, see Chapter 28. For more regarding physical handicaps, see Chapter 15.)

THE COUNSELING PROCESS

Parent counseling is an educational process to help parents understand their child and themselves in a way which enables them to care for their child more effectively and with more self-fulfillment. A crucial goal of counseling is to help parents make sensible use of available resources.

Parents can avoid the double danger of rejecting the child or becoming overly involved only to the extent that they become aware of the needs of all members of their household, including their normal children. Each parent can then know more clearly how to take care of the family, how to use available time and energy, and how to maintain ongoing relationships with friends and relatives.

However, parents do have the right to give up their children. Appropriately, some parents use counseling to help them separate from their handicapped child. They may try to arrange the best possible care outside of their home or release their children for placement or adoption. The counselor may help them avoid feeling burdened with excessive guilt or humiliation. Unfortunately, our society offers few humane alternatives to the biological family and very few supports for parents in this predicament.

A child does best when his caregivers can provide experiences which protect his sensitivities, support his particular strengths, and encourage compensation for his weaknesses. Optimal care is tailored to fit the child's unique personality and then continuously altered for the circumstances of the moment. The parents of a child with an intellectual handicap can become more knowledgeable about their child, his handicap, and how the deficits are experienced by the child and other members of the family. These insights enable the adults to empathize with their child, expand their repertoire of parenting capacities, and feel more competent.

The impact of a parent's behavior on the child's development is determined in large part by details of their interaction with the child, such as timing, context, tone of voice, or facial expression. These details of care, in composite form, establish the emotional atmosphere of the home. They *cannot be prescribed* by a professional or self-consciously controlled by a parent. They depend on a sensitivity to the child based on affectionate acceptance of the kind of person he is. If the handicap is understood but not accepted, or if the parents are uncomfortable with their role, a family atmosphere dominated by anger, tension, or sadness is more likely to develop, and optimal care may be impossible.

Counseling as Facilitating

The counselor is more a facilitator of learning and problem-solving than a teacher of facts or an instructor in child-rearing effectiveness (Fried, 1975). Although a counselor should be a competent source of advice and information, specific child-rearing practices are rarely advised. It isn't necessary to pretend to be expert in all aspects of the child's problem. It is more constructive for the parents and the child to know that the counselor can help them find relevant information, clarify the issues, and reach a decision or plan that is compatible with their own value preferences and their life-style.

The *parents* ultimately *control what they talk about*. They decide, with advice, what is most relevant to them at the time, and they begin at their own level and proceed at their own pace. The counselor avoids too many specific directions, even when they appear to be helpful in the short run, because they dilute the process of enabling parents and child to be active on their own behalf. Optimally, the counselor helps with practical problems of child care by helping parents to be aware of alternatives from which they can choose what they prefer for their child and themselves.

Counselors support the gradual process of accepting and integrating new knowledge by stimulating discussions about the personal significance of what the parents learn. Talking about how it feels and what it means to be a parent of a child with a handicap can be very upsetting initially, but should gradually be relieving and liberating as parents and child move ahead step by step in a progressive manner. However, self-understanding and personality change are not the primary goal of the counseling process, as they are in some forms of psychotherapy.

A counselor needs to understand how the parents and child respond to new experiences and developmental changes. This includes parenthood as a significant phase of human development (see Chapter 2 for tasks and functions of parenting). The experienced counselor understands and respects the powerful, irritational aspect of these psychological and developmental reactions even in parents who are competent and resourceful.

Of course, the counselor should also understand retardation and other cognitive disorders and be familiar with community resources and relevant laws. A repertoire of practical child care suggestions and an ability to translate technical terms and concepts into useful communications for the parents and child are also important.

The Counselor's Feelings

Finally, counselors need to be sufficiently aware of their own feelings in order to use them constructively and in order to avoid imposing them on the parents. Counselors, like parents, experience strong feelings for different reasons, many of which may not be related to the intellectual problem at all. However, some counselors feel impotent in the face of retardation. Others find that they dislike or pity uneducated people. Some professionals become angry at parents who need to consider the possibility of placing their child. Others become intolerant of children with intellectual deficits.

Feelings about their role as parent counselor may also interfere. Counselors have to eschew the immediate sense of importance and power which appears to be associated with instruction or advising. Instead, they need to respect in themselves a nurturing approach which supports the parents' growth in directions which the parents choose for themselves. The counselor needs to have faith that parents will make sound choices (allowing for some mistakes along the way); when the counselor can no longer accept the parents' decisions, he should withdraw.

The success of counseling depends very much on the emotional atmosphere as well as the content of the discussions. Although the content of each interview will be unique, certain generalizations about the emphasis of the discussions can be offered. It is usually more useful to talk about the present than the past (see, also, Chapter 2 by Brown). The focus should be on conscious questions, impressions, and concerns. This includes fears, wishes, and other feelings of which parents are aware. If parents deliberately avoid certain topics or ideas, this should be respected. As the parents feel more accepted and trusting, they often do include these painful or conflicted concerns in working with their counselor. Parents' personal feelings toward the counselor often are exposed and can be evidence of a developing alliance. The counselor should be able to accept these personal feelings without "taking them personally." Although such impressions usually are not a major focus of the counseling process, in contrast to psychotherapy, they should not be avoided; such subjective reactions of the counselee can interfere with the counseling process if they are rejected or disallowed. If an error has been made, it should be acknowledged and rectified, perhaps with an apology. If no error has been made, and the parents misinterpreted an event, the situation should be clarified without necessarily exploring the source of the irrational feelings.

THE COGNITIVE DISORDERS

Children's cognitive disorders are heterogeneous, and experts disagree about their classification, etiology, and management; therefore, the situation is confusing for both parents and counselors.

Cognition refers to those psychological processes which allow us to use information in order to plan and carry out effective action. The ability to perceive, attend to, and store information is fundamental. Information currently perceived is classified and correlated with remembered information. Information is further organized around a hierarchy of desired goals in order to formulate plans for sequential actions. Movements are organized to achieve the realization of these plans, and finally the effects of each action are observed and evaluated in light of the original goals (Luria, 1973).

The clinical impression of intelligence depends upon both these cognitive processes and many non-cognitive qualities as well. The summary IQ score, although a relatively good predictor of academic performance, is by no means the definitive measure of intellectual potential in all children. IQ scores fail to reflect many problem-solving abilities which are crucial in non-academic situations. In addition, they have limited usefulness clinically when children are from lower socioeconomic classes or from different cultural backgrounds. However, test behaviors do provide a profile of achievements which allows us to make inferences in the light of other data.

Mental retardation, a generalized deficit in conceptual abilities, is really an operational—not an accurate behavioral—classification. The American Association of Mental Deficiency defines mental retardation as "significantly sub-average general intellectual functioning, existing concurrently with deficits in adaptive functioning and manifested during the developmental period." "Sub-average" generally means scoring at least two standard deviations below the mean on standard intelligence tests (below 84 on the WISC or below 83 on the Stanford-Binet). By including the criterion of "adaptive functioning," this definition of mental retardation intentionally excludes many individuals with IQ scores in the mildly retarded range who function adequately in society.

Although the profile of strengths and weaknesses of the individual child is always the basis for parent counseling, it is useful to separate retarded children into two groups: 1) the severely retarded (trainable with an IQ below 50) child, and 2) the mildly retarded (educable) child with an I.Q. above 50:

The Severely Retarded

Specific accomplishments like intellectual competence, social leadership, self-sufficiency, educational achievement, gainful employment, marriage, and parenthood may be a constructive standard for most people in our culture, but when the same standard is applied to a child with a *severe* cognitive handicap, failure becomes inevitable. Parents of children with significant intellectual handicaps need to help their children to accept goals which are less focused on achievement in general. They need values which give a high priority to social and emotional experience. For example, emphasis might be placed on the ability to derive meaning and fulfillment from worthwhile activities, whether or not they include gainful employment or special skills. Relationships involving mutual trust, understanding, and commitment over time are valuable whether or not they include marriage and parenthood. The ability to relate comfortably with friends may be achieved, and socially appropriate behavior with a range of people is possible, even if only in certain situations. A retarded child, self-sufficient or not, can and should feel worthwhile. Life can be experienced as interesting and meaningful although limited in achievement. No child can gain this perspective unless adults lead the way.

The Mildly Retarded

Mild retardation tends to be recognized primarily in the poor, especially adolescent boys living in urban slums. Many factors can help explain the link between poverty and mild retardation. Damage to the brain may result from poor parental care, maternal malnutrition, diseases of poverty and overcrowding, poor pediatric care, or infant malnutrition. The children are also deprived and traumatized by the experience of developing in families which are disorganized and isolated from the institutions which support good education, recreation, health, and occupational opportunities. Although the services which have been developed for the severely retarded child are also used by middle-class or upper-class children with mild retardation, the bulk of the mildly retarded individuals from low socioeconomic classes have received less attention. They not only need improved services, but also programs to combat racial prejudice, job discrimination, poverty and family disorganization.

COUNSELING APPROACHES

Even an abbreviated *assessment* should be broad enough to produce a profile of the child's strengths and weaknesses along with a formulation of their relationship to the disabilities. In addition, there should be a description of the child's environment, including the parents' fears and expectations. Data are obtained from talking with parents and perhaps other adults who know the child, as well as observations of the child in several settings. Intelligence tests yield not only quantified achievement scores which can be compared to norms, but also important information about the child's behavior with materials, interaction with adults, coping styles, and attitudes toward success and failure. An assessment of the child's physical functioning is important, but elaborate physiological studies or consultations with medical subspecialists are carried out only when they are indicated.

Understanding with Precision

The following example illustrates the importance of a careful, thorough evaluation which delineates the processes underlying a child's problems:

Sally, four years old, walked and talked late. She spoke only in short sentences, and her comprehension was uneven. The pediatrician thought she couldn't hear, and one audiologist agreed. However, a second audiologist used a special test which showed that her peripheral hearing was intact, although she acted as if she didn't hear; she didn't "cooperate" with standard testing. In addition, he noted several minor anatomical abnormalities and suggested to her college-educated parents that she was probably a "Mongol."

Sally's parents were terribly confused and upset with the doctors and each other. They told the consultant that Sally looked perplexed at times, and at other times seemed lazy or stubborn. Yet, she was affectionate and happy. Sally was "slow," they thought, but, on the other hand, she had excellent judgment about dangerous situations, and an excellent memory.

On our assessment, Sally had an IQ of 65. She failed two-year items that required verbal instructions, but solved several problems at a five-year-old level which did not require verbal instructions. She was functioning with a central language deficit which made it impossible for her to interpret long sequences of words, although she could understand single words or short phrases.

The parents were given an explanation of their previously puzzling experiences: Since Sally could not understand most sentences, she did not understand the audiologist's instructions or the standard hearing tests, nor the examiner's instructions on the intelligence tests. Her fantasy play and her relationship with the examiner in a non-test situation showed that stubborn behavior was not a significant problem. Studies of her chromosomes and her urine chemistries revealed no genetic or chromosomal abnormality.

With the counselor's help, Sally's parents worked out new ways to make themselves understood. The tension between them diminished as they could talk with their counselor about the terrible fears they had that Sally was retarded or genetically defective. Speech therapy was arranged to begin before her first school experience.

Etiologies and Parental Reactions

A cognitive disorder almost never results from a single cause: Formulating the etiology usually involves assigning relative importance to various biological factors, past events, and current experiences. Some intellectual functions such as early language development are quite sensitive to detrimental experiences. Other functions are relatively resistant to experience and more exclusively dependent on biological maturation, such as language syntax and the development of coordinated finger movements (Provence, 1975). As a result, certain patterns of cognitive deficit suggest a strong role of experience in their etiology, while others would be very difficult to understand without postulating a biological contribution. Such etiological issues are of great emotional concern to most parents.

The following example illustrates how knowledge of the pattern of a child's deficits can be useful to a counselor. It also illustrates how careless remarks by professionals can disturb parents who overhear them.

> When Brian was admitted to the hospital at 21 months of age with pneumonia, his pediatrician noted delayed development and suspected that it was due to poor maternal care. The nurses complained that Brian's unwed mother was always angry and rushed during her infrequent, short visits to the hospital. She was rude to one of her doctors. She wanted Brian discharged as soon as possible, and she would give very little information to anyone.
>
> A careful assessment of Brian's development revealed that he could pull to stand and walk holding on to the furniture. He had no pincer grasp, and he had great difficulty solving the formboard and the pegboards. He knew only two words but he imitated sounds and hand movements, and he communicated by pointing and grunting. He played pat-a-cake and peekaboo happily; however, he did not reach for a toy hidden behind a screen. This profile of delayed development suggested that he had been getting adequate care.
>
> With the help of a pediatric social worker, we learned that Brian had been cared for by an affectionate maternal grandmother since his mother began working full time. His mother began work when her boyfriend left her, shortly after her high school graduation a year ago. The worker also learned that Brian's mother had heard a doctor say that her son was a case of maternal deprivation. She became terribly afraid that the hospital would take him away from her and decided to get him home as fast as possible. With the help of a counselor, both Brian's mother and his grandmother were helped to understand his limitations, and they learned to maximize his learning experiences at home. A special preschool program was arranged for him a year later.

Beware of Hasty Labeling

Although the pattern of behavioral deficits is one clue to the etiology of higher central nervous system dysfunction, no single clue is sufficient. Even when there is known structural brain damage, it is not wise to assume that the brain damage is a complete explanation for the cognitive disability. On the other hand, even when we see abuse and neglect, we should not overlook the frequent finding that the child's experiences cannot fully account for the child's cognitive behavior.

Hasty formulations about etiology often result in inappropriate management. In this example, a counselor helped the parents to gradually understand the causes of their child's cognitive problem and its relationship to his emotional life:

A middle-class couple brought their four-year-old son, Ralph, to our clinic because of hyperactivity, impulsivity, and sleep disturbance, previously diagnosed as minimal brain dysfunction in neurology clinic. Sedative anticonvulsants had controlled the few seizures he had one-and-a-half years previously, but exacerbated his behavioral symptoms. These did not improve with stimulants over several months. Advice about firm discipline and structure had not been helpful, either.

We learned in our evaluation that Ralph's hyperactivity, awkwardness, short attention span, and impairment of synthetic ability were confined to times of anxiety. Even at his best, however, he had trouble with visual-motor integration. In addition, David didn't think before he acted on the test, and would persist in an unsuccessful approach. However, if the examiner asked him to scan the problem beforehand and helped him to approach a task in steps, he could solve most problems.

Along with these cognitive deficits, Ralph had severe anxiety, with night terrors. He could not tolerate frustration or failure, and he had a very low opinion of himself. He would procrastinate, demand the impossible, act impulsively, and have frequent temper tantrums with his parents and other adults. He was physically healthy except for his seizures. Ralph's father had had two seizures in adulthood and learning problems as a child.

Gradually, as they felt more involved, the parents explained that Ralph's unplanned birth came at a time of great marital conflict. As an infant, his mother could not comfort him, and she felt he was too active to nurse as she had her other children. (See Chapter 12 on temperamental traits.) From the beginning she associated his robust activity with dangerous, wild men she had known in her childhood. She unwittingly overstimulated him without offering enough consistency or organization. Ralph seemed impossible to manage even as a toddler.

Two younger siblings, a poorly planned move to a new house, continuous financial problems, and Ralph's seizures all placed additional stresses on Ralph's family. By the time of our evaluation, Ralph dominated the household from morning till night, and his parents considered him the source of all the family problems. His mother felt angry or guilty when she was with him.

A counselor helped the parents to accept psychiatric treatment for Ralph and regular parent counseling for themselves. They were helped to understand their family's predicament as a result of many factors, not only Ralph's "naughtiness." After certain shifts in the family's style, Ralph became much more comfortable at home; his school performance improved significantly; and special tutoring was arranged for his visual-motor problem. His anxiety, his disobedient behavior, insomnia, and night terrors improved considerably in treatment. He felt better about himself, and his parents could enjoy him and feel competent as parents.

Initial Interpretation of Findings

At the end of a diagnostic assessment, the parents should be informed of the results in a manner that is responsive to their questions and to their fears. The clinical inventory of the child should be presented first, emphasizing ways in which it agrees with, amends, or contrasts with their reports (see Chapter 19 regarding parents' accuracy in estimating their child's abilities). The child's strong points should be emphasized, along with his limitations, and the source of the problem discussed tactfully but candidly, including references to parental approaches which have been helpful and those which seemed not to have worked. The child's contribution to the problem should be presented without suggesting inappropriately that the problem was inevitable or that it cannot improve. If parents are rejecting a child as biologically damaged, the role of experience can be emphasized. On the other hand, for parents handicapped by excessive guilt, the child's contribution through biological endowment and current behavior can be given balancing emphasis. (See "the dermatological approach" in Chapter 1.) Genetic abnormalities need thorough explanation; physicians with special knowledge and skills in genetic counseling can be helpful as consultants or as counselors.

Although statements about the child's future can be hopeful, they should be strictly within the bounds of reality and avoid undue speculation, even when parents seem to demand it. (See Chapter 19 for more about parental expectations.) Accurate labels should not be avoided or replaced by euphemisms. However, they should only be verbalized after the balanced inventory of behavior is presented in an understandable manner. The pitfalls of misunderstanding the label should be reviewed and parents helped to communicate about the condition in their preferred ways to the child's siblings, grandparents, other relatives, and friends.

By the time of the evaluation, parents usually have their own theories about the problem, and they may already have experienced strong feelings of resentment, self-reproach, self-doubt, or even despair. After the assessment, parents are encouraged to express what they believe and what they fear, and to "guide" the counselor in presenting the findings and their interpretation. Their reaction to this explanation and the discussion of it varies according to many factors, including the nature of the handicap, the quality of the prediagnostic phase of adjustment, and the responses of other significant people. Of course, the unique personality of each parent and the nature of their relationship to their child are crucial in guiding the counselor in his explanations and interpretations and in how he listens.

As soon as parents are ready to participate actively, an initial management plan should be constructed. Parents have the right to further consultation, and the counselor should support this option, after offering to help them clarify their expectations and desires. In this way, the destructive aspects of shopping for help can be minimized.

Useful literature should be suggested. Task-oriented discussions with other parents who are in similar situations can be recommended as a useful supplement to parent counseling if the counselor is sure that they are well planned and implemented by skillful leaders.

Much of this practical planning and advice may need to be delayed when the parents' grief reaction seems overwhelming.

PARENTAL MOURNING

The mother of a defective newborn is especially vulnerable (Solnit & Stark, 1961). She is already emotionally and physically depleted. The quality of the parents' relationship to their new baby will depend in large part on the nature of the grief reaction and on how they are supportive to each other. (See "Mutual Nurturance" in Chapter 2.) All parents grieve when they learn that their child is defective or abnormal. There is numbness, shock, and disbelief before a tentative awareness of the reality emerges, and they begin to feel disappointed. Sadness, a sense of loss and despair, helplessness and guilt, rage, anxiety, and physical symptoms may occur repeatedly as denial gives way and returns again. In the process of reexperiencing memories, expectations, and painful events, a parent achieves varying degrees of emotional acceptance. The balance of denial and acceptance is dynamic and occurs on many levels. The reality of the events is accepted first, then the current feelings and short-range implications. However, the full significance of a serious handicap is often denied for a long time. Parents of severely handicapped children may experience "chronic sorrow" (Olshansky, 1962).

Intellectual handicaps are especially hard to deal with because they are often invisible, ambiguous, and unpredictable in the early years. The impact of the defect may only be evident later. In these instances, longer periods of denial may result, and parents often experience repeated episodes of loss and grief each time the defect becomes more apparent.

Two Abnormal Patterns of Attachment

Parents may become abnormally close to the child, with *overprotection*, overindulgence, and dedication to the point of overlooking their own needs and their responsibilities to other people. At the other extreme a parent may *reject* the child and deny the relationship. In addition, the two reactions can exist side-by-side in the same parent, resulting in unpredictable, inconsistent care, which is very destructive to the child and the family. As a result of the grief reaction, the handicapped child may be viewed as sick and encouraged to be more dependent than is desirable and necessary. He or she may be overprotected as an infant forever, or treated like a cute pet, an inhuman monster, or a cross to bear.

Helping with the Grief Work

It is a mistake to attempt to "cure" grief quickly. The counselor should be tolerant of a variety of normal parental reactions which occur over a significant period of time. For example, one couple may need to hear about their child's condition in all its detail and severity at a time when another couple would be overwhelmed. Some people will be handicapped by their denial of the child's condition. Others use denial adaptively. Some parents will be limited by their preoccupation with the reality of the child's problems. The counselor can heighten anxiety or depression if he does not respect parents' tolerance for how much they can cope with at any one time.

Discussion about the parents' feelings should be initiated tactfully while presenting the assessment. The counselor tries to communicate acceptance of the parents in the process of clarifying their feelings. It is often helpful to amplify or reword a parent's comments, but when parents are told how they feel before they discover it themselves, they may become insulted, thinking that the counselor has categorized them, losing sight of their individuality. However, a tentative comparison of the parent to other parents or to the counselor himself may help a parent to feel understood and to accept his own feelings with less guilt and shame. When parents present irrational fears, reassuring information should be offered in a way which does not curtail open discussion. Even when a parent is extremely upset, the counselor should resist the temptation to minimize the severity of the situation. The counselor should speak with *both parents together* and resist the temptation to deal first with the parent who is less upset. A marriage may be subtly weakened when parents are not seen together at the time of diagnosis and planning.

It is especially important that the parents of a newborn infant be informed tactfully of a serious concern about their child *before* the couple has begun to tell others that their child is all right. It is not useful to recommend early institutionalization of a newborn for severe retardation in order to prevent parental attachment and future pain, because a psychological attachment is present long before the baby is born. However, the counselor should be able to accept the parents' wish to be rid of a severely handicapped child. Only then can the parents be helped to explore the issue of placement, including the practical and emotional aspects of their reactions.

When a child's problem is recognized at a later age, the parents are usually more capable of coping, and the problem becomes apparent more gradually. The grief, which may follow a similar pattern as with a defective newborn, is less acute and less intense. Feelings of loss are often delayed, appearing gradually during the period of ongoing treatment and rehabilitation. Such grief is a challenge to the quality of the parent-child relationship, although not as powerfully.

Life or Death Decisions

When a child is born with a condition which is sure to result in profound retardation, a very difficult situation exists if the child also requires extensive medical management to sustain life through the newborn period. Some parents would prefer not to interfere with the natural death of their severely handicapped child. Others want to sustain life by every means possible. Immense suffering can result when well-meaning professionals impose their values on the parents at this time. Usually parents want professionals to help them understand the situation well enough so they can *share the decision* with the physician or be in a position to express their preference. The psychological, ethical, and legal implications of this dilemma are beyond the scope of this presentation. Usually, the infant's physician is in the best position to be the parents' counselor in such situations (Duff & Campbell, 1976).

A similar situation involves the *prenatal diagnosis of mental retardation*. Many genetic counselors feel that before amniocentesis is carried out, the complicated decision of abortion should be discussed or even decided by the parents based on the hypothetical possibilities of a defective fetus. However, when prospective parents who want a child decide to abort a defective fetus, they mourn intensely and they often feel guilty.

SHIFTING FAMILY EQUILIBRIUM

The family as a whole will attempt to adjust to a child's handicap without changing the existing family structure. However, family members may reach a point when ordinary social, economic, and personal expectations cannot continue to be met. First, they become dissatisfied in their relations with each other; for example, a mother may feel she cannot give enough to the children, or a sibling may feel he or she is not getting enough from mother. A role-organization crisis may crystallize in association with a high level of tension. In such a crisis, the delicately balanced family priorities may be altered with the possibility of shifts in roles and in the division of work and responsibility. Siblings are often expected to take over more adult responsibilities, and the father may need to become more involved in child rearing and household chores. The quality and frequency of recreational activities may also be changed. People who are not helpful may be avoided and reliable family and friends relied upon more. If family disequilibrium persists, there is the risk of a family break-up. Under such circumstances, the child may be extruded psychologically and/or physically by institutionalization or foster placement. A counselor can help prevent such undesirable crises by stimulating constructive changes gradually.

Follow-up

As a child grows up with a handicap, parents can use support in helping their child deal with his or her increasing awareness of the disability. Even a child with fairly severe retardation can perceive such deviance. At different stages of development, a child will attach different meanings to his handicap; for example, at different developmental periods the defect can be experienced as a stigma of unlovable qualities, a punishment for aggression, a weakness, or a lifelong limitation.

Parents usually need *ongoing counseling,* not just crisis intervention. The normal tasks of parents, such as weaning, toilet training, and discipline, can be anticipated and facilitated. These routine child-rearing tasks may be very difficult, but this is not inevitable. In addition, there are a number of fairly predictable challenges which occur in most families with a handicapped child. These include the child's separation reactions, first exposure to rejection by peers, the beginning of school, the problem of making friends as school progresses, the birth of a sibling, the problems of puberty and adolescent sexuality, problems of vocational planning and marriage, and legacy planning for the person who is not a self-sufficient adult.

Preventive Counseling

A working relationship that develops over the years facilitates the early reporting of difficulties; in addition, periodic appointments to gather an abbreviated profile of current data enable the counselor to be more useful on a continuing basis.

REFERENCES

DUFF, R. S. & CAMPBELL, A. G. M.: On deciding the care of severely handicapped or dying persons; with particular reference to infants. *Pediatrics,.* 57:487-493, 1976.

FRIED, R.: Thesis, Harvard Graduate School of Education, 1975.

LURIA, P. R.: *The Working Brain.* London: Penguin, 1973.

OLSHANSKY, S.: Chronic sorrow: A response to having a mentally defective child. *Child Social Casework,* XLIII, No. 4, April, 1962.

PROVENCE, S.: Unpublished communication, 1975.

SOLNIT, A. J. & STARK, M.: Mourning and the birth of a defective child. *The Psychoanalytic Study of the Child,* 16:523-537, 1961.

Chapter 15

Parents of Chronically Ill or Physically Handicapped Children

Norma Barnebey and

Elizabeth Ruppert

Parenting of chronically ill children is discussed in the same chapter with parenting of physically handicapped children because: 1) a chronic disease is a handicap in the broad sense; 2) a physical handicap is a dis-ease in the broad sense, and it is chronic; 3) the parenting problems arising from both conditions are similar. In fact, a physically handicapped child presents basically the same concerns to parents as a chronically ill child, except that, with a physically handicapped child, the stress on the family usually begins at the child's birth or shortly thereafter.

INITIAL REACTIONS VARY

Physical handicaps are disabilities of anatomy, function, or appearance that are usually apparent in infancy. Examples are cleft palate, cerebral palsy, myelomeningeocele, hydrocephaly, and congenital amputees. Usually the disability is manifested through gross motor development, but sometimes there are concomitant visual, auditory, and intellectual disabilities.

The initial disappointment of not having a perfect baby may evoke a series of parental reactions. Feelings of guilt ("What did I do wrong?"), shame, depression, and simply giving up are typical parental responses to their loss. (See Chapter 14 for more on the parents' need to mourn.) In an effort to relieve their distress, parents may express their guilt by punishing themselves or by projecting it onto professionals, blaming them for neglect during labor, delivery, or the neonatal period. Self-punishment may take the form of overprotectiveness and devotion of one's life (and the lives of others in the family) to caring for the child. Such smothering is eventually also punishing to the child, thereby embodying subtle rejection, which can also be manifested frankly.

An empathic attitude of nondefensive objectivity by health professionals can support the parents in resolving such feelings. Sometimes a frank discussion of how natural and understandable such reactions are can clear the air preparatory to a gentle nudge in the direction of realistic care for this special baby.

The Three Faces of Disease

Chronic illness in children can be divided into three major categories by effects of the disease process and its responsiveness to treatment:

1. *Fatal chronic diseases,* such as leukemia, some forms of cancer, and sickle cell anemia, can be definitely and accurately diagnosed and usually lead to death in the forseeable future. The child must experience both his disease and the anxieties and fears of those caring for him. The parents are presented with a harsh and painful reality contrary to what they had planned. Their temptation to deny death, especially the imminent death of their child, is reinforced by our modern cultural denial of death. (See Chapter 23 for more about "death-denying feats" and their consequences.)

2. *Persistent but treatment-responsive chronic disease* alters a child's way of life, and demands medications, treatments, and diets. Diabetes mellitus and cystic fibrosis are examples. This type of illness may cause physical limitations or may be so subtle that once treatment is begun the parents begin to *doubt the disease or deny that it will result in a shortened life.*

3. *Intermittent, unpredictable chronic illness* may be long-lasting or may go into permanent remission. For example, rheumatoid arthritis, asthma, and epilepsy, because of excellent medical care (or in spite of excellent medical care!), can have exacerbations and remissions. The unpredictability of such a disease is confusing and troublesome to patients, parents, and physicians. Generally the parents appropriately encourage their children to include their medications and diets as part of their regular, everyday life rather than as something special which prevents them from enjoying childhood. When these diseases flare up after a quiescent period, they wonder what went wrong. Is the medical care correct? Is the diet correct? What else can be done? Often the only consistent thing is continuous elevated parental anxiety because of the fear of what is coming next. The child may become overprotected and feel either vulnerable or over-controlled. (See Chapter 16 for more about parent-child control issues in somatic symptoms.) Thus, parent-child conflicts can easily develop into problems as significant as the chronic illness itself.

GENERAL APPROACH TO HELPING PARENTS

The two most valuable commodities for helping parents cope with a child's chronic illness or handicap are time and communication. Time must be given freely yet realistically: time for a comprehensive history and complete physical examination, time for laboratory tests, time for a careful explanation to the parents of the diagnosis and the plan for management. In this communication the parents should feel free to ask each and every question they have. Some parents are afraid to ask questions for fear of sounding stupid or ignorant, even if they have burning questions about such things as the following: the certainty of the diagnosis, the severity of the illness, the proposed methods of treatment and their side effects, and the cause of the illness: Is it inherited; can it occur in another member of the family; was there something the parent could have done to prevent it? The physician needs to help parents feel free to ask such questions by an unhurried attitude and clear communication.

Frequently during the course of a chronic illness parents want another doctor to evaluate their child. Sometimes they are embarrassed to tell the child's physician, but mention it to a nonmedical professional. They should be encouraged to discuss this thought with their child's physician. Understanding their anxieties and concerns, he may be able to explain to their satisfaction when no other opinion is necessary, and direct them to other qualified professionals or medical centers when it seems appropriate. A parent's aggressiveness in finding answers and participating in his child's care should be reinforced.

Unfortunately, some parents waste precious time in beginning treatment or subject their child to unnecessary trauma by searching for a cure when none exists, or for an easy solution to a complex problem. In such cases the physician may wish to refer them to a social worker, clinical psychologist, or psychiatrist for help in understanding the effects of the illness. These mental health professionals can also help parents "pick up the pieces," deal with their anger, despair, and grief, and communicate with each other during the crisis.

SPECIFIC GUIDANCE SUGGESTIONS

A Husband-Wife Contract

The parental pair need to discuss and agree on the following points: 1) which doctor will be the physician responsible for the child's chronic illness; 2) whether this same doctor will care for the child's other health problems such as fevers and sore throats, or whether their family physician or pediatrician will provide this care; 3) which parent will be responsible for the home medical care or special training and for the trips to the hospital, doctor's office, or rehabilitation center. Whenever possible, both parents should share these responsibilities.

Sharing the Parenting

Hospitalizations and treatments are often emotionally stressful; sharing these heavy experiences makes them more tolerable and manageable. To develop an adequate program for the handicapped child, both parents need to understand the disability and its treatment and become involved. They need to share the joys of this child as well as his problems, and to *provide for each other's comfort and support*. Open discussion and some planning will help a husband and wife to work as a unit to meet the crises and continuing demands.

Remember the Other Children

Parents need to tell other children in the family some facts about their sibling's illness or handicap. The amount and type of information shared are dependent upon the age of the siblings. A six-year-old will be satisfied by knowing that his brother has cystic fibrosis, a lung problem which can cause him to have chest colds. The siblings should be reassured that the medicine his brother gets will help his chest cold. Questions should be answered in a short but honest fashion. If the disease is fatal, this fact should be shared, but with very young siblings only when death is imminent.

Parents can talk with their children about ways they can help. Perhaps they will need to assume some additional household chores or help care for younger siblings. Parents need not feel guilty asking children for reasonable help, for they can mature with this family problem.

However, the healthy children's needs should not be forgotten. They need some time with mother and dad when they are not also with the ill child. They need a chance to talk and act as they did before their sibling's illness. It is their right to want to talk about their activities. Sometimes parents are annoyed when their healthy children are loud and happy in their play or conversation. Such a parent can say that he is feeling a bit tired at the moment. "In a while I will feel more like listening to you."

Telling the Truth

Though many parents find it painful to tell a friend or neighbor, even on inquiry, about their child's illness or handicap, they should be encouraged to do so. Friends can be supportive and may help, e.g., by babysitting. This is obviously preferable to the social isolation that results from some families' inward focus on the sick or handicapped child. Furthermore, a parent's ability to tell friends, neighbors, and even curious strangers in a straightforward, formal way will help the child learn to respond to inquiries in the same way.

Reviewing Financial Resources

The care of a child with a chronic illness or physical handicap demands a candid evaluation of a family's finances. Parents need early information about medical costs. They may need help interpreting and reviewing their health insurance: what it will cover, the numbers of hospital days covered, and whether outpatient visits and medications are included. They should be encouraged to inquire about the possibility of care being covered by the State Bureau of Crippled Children's Services. They may need support in admitting that their personal resources are limited. Empathy and tactful candidness can ease their embarrassment and preserve their pride.

Informed, Organized Parents

It is often useful to refer parents to the many local and national organizations for specific diseases designed to inform and to help them. Many of these organizations were founded by parents who struggled to learn about their child's diseases and its treatment. The American Diabetes Association, The National Cystic Fibrosis Research Foundation, Muscular Dystrophy Associations of America, and Alexander Graham Bell Association for the Deaf are examples of national organizations which provide parent information. The local health department or the United States Public Health Service, Department of Health, Education, and Welfare, Public Inquiries Branch, Office of Information, Washington, D.C. can furnish information and the addresses of local groups. Such sources as the United Cerebral Palsy Center, State Services for Crippled Children, Easter Seal Society and Myelomeningeocele Clinics can also provide information for resources. This type of involvement exposes parents to other parents who have experienced and successfully handled similar situations. Informed parents can sort out fact from fiction in newspaper articles and conversation with other people.

Choosing Between a Shut-In or a School Child

When a child has an acute illness, he stays home from school, may stay in bed, and does not play with his friends. Some parents instinctively try to extend this pattern to chronic illness. They need to be reminded of children's need for peer relationships in the neighborhood and at school. Children want to be busy, especially with other children. The challenges of school, with its structure and routine, are important in the development of all children.

Parents who remain overprotective despite these considerations can be apprised that friendship, games, work, and structure are also critical ingredients in the medical management of the physical illness. For example, regular physical activity helps control the diabetic child's sugar metabolism, and physical exercise keeps the muscles and joints of children with muscular dystrophy working longer and better. To restrict activity will actually complicate these conditions. Of course, there may be some risks from attending school, such as acquiring an infectious disease, which should be frankly discussed. The best use of home (or hospital) tutoring is to help the child keep up so he can return to his classroom promptly.

For orthopedically handicapped children there are special educational programs with wheelchairs and adapted furniture. Even physical therapy and occupational therapy may be provided in these programs. In addition to public education, specialized community training programs such as United Cerebral Palsy provide day programs for the special child. Special lift buses are also available for transportation to the schools. When possible, of course, the child should be programmed into a regular school even though he may need some specialized assistance from a resource person.

Promoting Peer Relations

In addition to the peer relation opportunities in school and the community programs, a parent can be encouraged to invite neighbor children in to play with a handicapped child. The relations he has with normal children will help him develop self-confidence in relating to the normal population. Parents may need to plan activities that will be satisfying for both children, such as table games or playing with clay. These periods of play should be time-limited so that the children can leave each other on a good note, having had a mutually enjoyable experience.

Discipline

Like other children, handicapped and chronically ill children need to develop socially acceptable behavior. The manner in which parents teach appropriate behavior to other children may be used for them also. As with normal children, parents must begin early to show approval and encouragement for acceptable actions and disapproval for inappropriate ones. However, in any behavior modification program, it needs to be remembered that physically handicapped children tend to utilize less energy in their daily activities. Therefore they tend towards obesity if treated with unnecessary quantities of food as reinforcers. Other reinforcers should be emphasized, such as smiling, hugging, praising, reading a story, or playing a game.

R & R for the Front-Line Parent

Though beleaguered parents of chronically ill children feel the need to get away a few hours, they may be hesitant or reluctant to do so. They may need permission and encouragement. These can be be given by saying something like:

Even in the armed forces, servicemen who have been on the front lines are given periodic leaves for rest and relaxation. Uncle Sam knows that soldiers can work better when they have had some free time. Mothers and fathers also must make arrangements to have some rest and relaxation time. All parents are better able to handle their work after rest periods. Your child will benefit from seeing the tired look on your face replaced by a look of rest and ease. You owe it to your family regularly to take some free time, perhaps seeing a movie, going to church, or taking a walk.

Homan (1969) summarizes it beautifully: "Their energies and talents are often strained by the demands of raising ordinary children. In the handling of a severely handicapped child, strain the reserves of the community, of the state, of the government—I can't imagine them cracking up. But don't ask the impossible of my mothers and fathers. I can't spare them."

THE SPECIAL CHILD

Each child is special to his parent, but one who is born handicapped or develops a chronic illness becomes truly special. Sometimes the illness provides the opportunity for the child and parent to be unusually close, both physically and socially. Sometimes it may seem to drive parent and child apart, perhaps because of the knowledge that pain and weakness are here and more will come.

Often the course of illness will end with *death* in the forseeable future. Evans (1968) states, "There appear to be two basic differences of approach to the care of a dying child. One emphasizes helping the child to face death and the fears of dying; the other attemps to shield him from death and protect him as much as possible from such fears." Either way can be correct when carefully and effectively handled. The parents and the child's doctor should explicitly discuss what is to be the preferred approach so that all adults can be consistent with the child. Such a discussion should occur when the family, child, and physician have established a relationship of mutual respect and trust. From such a close and communicating relationship will come the best way to care for a dying child. (See Chapter 23 for Elisabeth Kübler Ross' approach to dying.)

Special children can be a treasured part of a parent's life and memories:

> *You were born one pain-filled day.*
> *In love you'd been conceived.*

Despair is in the words we pray;
   God knows we feel bereaved.
The Doctors say you'll never be
   as other children are,
thus shattered were the dreams and hopes
   that you would reach your star.

He hears our prayers; He'll calm our fears,
   He'll lead us by the hand
and gently wipe the healing tears,
   He'll always understand.
They tell us you're a "special child."
   Our love is special too.
We hold you in our arms and know
   That God chose us for you.

—VERA ROBB WHITMER
Marion, Ohio

REFERENCES

EVANS, A. E.: If a child must die. *New England Journal of Medicine,* 278:138-142, 1968.
HOMAN, W. E.: *Child Sense: A Pediatrician's Guide for Today's Families.* New York: Bantam Books, 1969.

Chapter 16

Parents of Psychosomatic Children

Enrique Huerta

Frustrated parents seek professional assistance for a variety of reasons, including hidden agendas frequently unknown to them. They all experience some sort of "pain": dissatisfaction, uncertainty, or helplessness. These feelings may be accentuated by society's expectations and pressures. They often are related to pain or distress that the child experiences or expresses somatically. We will look at children's psychosomatic disorders broadly, including any problem with strongly interdependent organic and emotional components for which attention to either alone does not result in therapeutic success. This definition could include many cases of epilepsy and diabetes, as well as functional asthma, weight problems, peptic ulcer, etc.

"EITHER-OR" SIMPLISM AS A FAMILY CULTURE

Parents frequently come with the question "Is my child's illness physical or emotional?" with the concept that these human elements are

183

mutually exclusive. A more pernicious variant is "Is it real or all in his head?", denying the importance of the child's emotions. A search for the easy alternative, a physical problem that may be "cured" by the doctor (without active patient or family involvement), is usually favored. This hope for a simple answer to complex problems frequently results in further disillusion and frustration. "If only he could get rid of his headache (or control his diabetes or lose or gain weight), everything would be just fine," sounds familiar to professionals who work with such children and their families.

Such families not only use the physical vs. emotional dichotomy but they also have a strong tendency to see all aspects of life in terms of mutually exclusive extremes. They will describe professionals they have previously consulted as extremely good, wise, competent, understanding, helpful, etc. or (more frequently, especially when problems have been chronic) as bad, foolish, incompetent, callous, etc. One immediately suspects that if he cannot induce some significant resolution of the problems, his name will automatically go to the "black list." Though this sounds rather pessimistic, it does not mean that there is no hope of change for these families.

Another example of dichotomous extreme is that the parents may either view the child as totally responsible for both his illness and the family distress or else view and treat him as completely irresponsible, with another family member(s) taking all the responsibility. The child is viewed and treated as either a "victim" or a "victor" within the family context, with the somatic disorder or complaint being used as a highly valued token in personal interactions. Unacceptable or maladaptive behaviors may be exclusively attributed by the parents to the child's being either "bad" or physically sick. The child's described role, whether responsible, irresponsible, victim, victor, bad, or sick, is not static. It may change quite rapidly from minute to minute or week to week, from one extreme to the other. Concomitantly, the roles assumed by the other family members also change.

Bridging the Dichotomies with Complexity

This "shifting simplism" within the family context recapitulates similar happenings throughout the history of mankind. At different stages of history, psychophysiological disorders, as well as other ailments, have been seen as directly resulting from rather oversimplified causes. Examples are punishment, gift, or test from a god; possession by a demon;

aberrant change in cellular structure purely as a result of emotional conflict; or an imbalance of the four basic "humors" that were considered normally present within the body. The latter was an attempt to have a more holistic approach. Even though these explanations can be temporarily reassuring, and one must not underestimate the value of reassurance, their usefulness has been limited. The understanding and utilization of multiple contributing and interdependent factors are yielding more rewarding results.

Reassurance about something that the patient feels we do not understand can only cause more anxiety, disbelief, and alienation. We must not fall into the same simplistic trap as our patients if we are to be useful to them. This by no means implies that we must not show any empathy. We need to acknowledge our patients' concerns as they experience them, which is truly reassuring, thereby allowing them to acknowledge our perceptions. Honest disclosure of the complexities of our own abilities and limitations not only reassures the uncertain and doubting parent but also provides a model for identification. Efficient and effective communication can make a difference between a successful intervention and another failure for the family. Awareness of needs—medical, psychological, recreational, social, educational, religious—allows designing and implementing an interdisciplinary team approach, the ultimate in complexity, to foreclose needless and costly repetitions and omissions.

Problems vs. Positives

Rather than spending a lot of time attempting to understand the problems of a somatizing family, one should actively seek and explore the positives, the basis of what one is going to be working with. Should one not be able to find sufficient positives, it would be more practical to arrange a prompt referral to somebody we know would be willing and able to work with this particular family. This may be a rather difficult decision; a professional may interpret it as a personal failure. However, this kind of "failure" is easier to take than the failure that follows a great investment of time, energy, and money. In order to kick the old habits of dichotomizing, simplifying, and somatizing, the family needs acknowledgment and encouragement to practice their good habits, which will hopefully crowd out the old ones. Successes are even more rewarding when accompanied by the professional's enthusiastic support.

UNDERSTANDING THE CHILD'S BODY

Sophisticated appearing parents and children may easily mislead one into assuming that they have a clear understanding of their bodies and body functions. It pays to review the accuracy of their knowledge about anatomical and physiological facts as well as the attached emotional significance, particularly in regard to the affected organ-system. It is not unusual to find tremendous misunderstandings muddling the overall picture. Consequently, the child may view his body with its functions as "getting out of control." He may perceive diagnostic efforts as intrusions, and treatment, with hospitalization and separations, as an imposition. This leaves him with a frightful sense of losing even more control. He will understandably struggle for some degree of control with his available defenses: oppositional, passive-aggressive, and occasionally submissive, compliant behavior. Clarification of misconceptions may give the parents and child a better understanding of his treatment, promoting in the child an increased sense of mastery over his own body and the way it works and in the parents increased confidence in his psychobiological competence. Clarification of anatomical and physiological developmental changes with their concomitantly changing needs must not be overlooked.

The *impact of body stress* (pathological signs and symptoms) *on physical, psychological and social functions* and their further development should not be neglected; chronic arrests and regressions are more difficultly reversed. An example of this is the adolescent with chronic ulcerative colitis, who is debilitated by the illness, experiences severe physical and emotional pain, and has little control over his bowel movements, with frequent loose, watery, mucous, bloody, foul-smelling stools. His life is disrupted by medical and surgical examinations, hospitalizations, prescriptions, restrictions, and diets. He must refrain from certain foods, physical activities, and "stressing situations" that can affect the course of the illness. Absences from school, restrictions in age-appropriate peer activities, and foul odor interfere with his normal psychosocial development. He feels controlled by his gut and environment. He may either passively comply and lose self-esteem or rebel in every possible way he can, to the extent of complete denial of his illness, eventually realizing that he loses either way. His illness provides a means of satisfaction for his passive-dependent wishes, which are in conflict with his needs to be autonomous and independent. Parents need such explanations, in clear, understandable words and concepts, regarding the child's illness, etiology, precipitating factors, pathophysiology, anatomical changes, and treatment

PARENTS OF PSYCHOSOMATIC CHILDREN

approaches. They need specific education regarding rationale and implementation of treatment methods, particularly when they may be directly involved in specific treatments carried out in the home. They need to be told that the child should not only be allowed but encouraged and supported in assuming realistic responsibilities and some degree of control over his own illness and health.

UNDERSTANDING THE CHILD'S MIND

Children respond differently to body stress depending on their level of cognitive and emotional development as well as their premorbid adaptive capacity. Parents sometimes do not realize the possibility of unevenness in the level of development of different areas. This may be grounds for misinterpretation and may cause serious conflict between parent and child. A child of superior intelligence may be expected to be equally superior in his emotional development; what would be expected as age and stage appropriate may be relatively viewed by parents as "babyish," limiting the satisfaction of needs required for the child to accomplish his developmental tasks. (For more on unevenness of development, see Chapters 14, 18, 19.)

Mental Reactions to Physical Pain

In general, children respond to physically-caused pain in rather different ways from adolescents and adults. Here are two examples:

A couple of hours after a bilateral inguinal hernia repair, a five-year-old boy is constantly crying and seemingly experiencing a great deal of pain. His concerned, anxious mother asks the nurse to give him his pain medication and is surprised to find out that "no pain medications are given postoperatively to children." The boy continues to cry until asked if he needs to empty his bladder. He nods affirmatively and relaxes into a happy state after voiding.

An eight-year-old boy has been crying for about ten minutes after a bicycle accident which resulted in a rather deep but clean thigh laceration. His father examines the wound and tells the boy that he is such a neat boy that he even gets neat wounds. He immediately stops crying, reassured that he is not in danger.

These examples demonstrate the impact parental reactions to the illness have on the child's own response to his illness. Parents play an important role in the development of the child's body image. Understanding of this concept, using the term "body" in the broadest sense, may be useful in providing parental guidance. Distortions and inconsistencies in body image may result in decreased ability to test reality and increased anxiety, further compromising the child's adaptive capabilities. Even though the memory picture of a properly aligned, complete, emotionally invested, intact body is relatively stable, revisions and modifications following alterations in body structure do occur. When the child is assisted in achieving realistic self-esteem and a realistic concept of himself as he is, the sadness associated with loss or change in body structure is experienced without undue anxiety or hostility.

UNDERSTANDING THE FAMILY

The quality of interactions the child has with his family not only strongly affects his growth and development but also alters the course of physical illness in a positive or negative way. Minuchin (1975) describes certain behavioral patterns characteristically present in families of children with psycho-physiological disorders. The constitutionally predisposed child and his illness—signs and symptoms—play an active role in maintaining the family "homeostasis." Not all children with diabetes, asthma, ulcerative colitis, eczema, etc., and their families experience the same degree of difficulties. The extent to which maladaptive transactions are used is also variable. For convenience we will describe families and children with severe illness resistant to conventional intensive treatments, who show four transactional patterns frequently observed to encourage psychosomatic pathology:

1. *Enmeshment* refers to extreme togetherness, intrusiveness, and responsiveness among the family members. Individual privacy is not acknowledged, let alone valued, and individual roles and responsibilities are not clearly defined. Direct communication between two people is overruled by intermediaries. These families have difficulty describing individual members. Even when pressed, they tend to lump all members, providing a group description.

2. These family members show a high degree of *overprotectiveness* for each other, to an extent beyond their ability. A parent may express the wish to go through a painful diagnostic or therapeutic measure for the child. In turn the child may feel a strong responsibility to keep the family together at any cost, his health included.

3. These families adhere to *rigid patterns* and show a great deal of

resistance towards change. Conflict may arise when the growing child's or adolescent's needs for increasing autonomy and independence challenge the carefully maintained status quo.

4. In these families a system is accepted that leaves problems unresolved and *avoids confrontation*. There may be a lot of noise made, but no negotiations.

Identification of these transactional patterns makes it possible to challenge them, give parents permission to foster some independence and autonomy in the family, and support them in risking change and confronting interpersonal problems.

ANOREXIA NERVOSA AS AN EXAMPLE

The anorexic child typically presents with severe self-induced weight loss for which he seems to show no concern, but which has become alarming to the family, school, and even strangers. The parents are further distressed to find that the child has no identifiable organic illness to explain the remarkable weight loss. They watch the child "waste away," experiencing extreme helplessness when their efforts to make the child eat prove unsuccessful. Thus, anorexia nervosa clearly and concretely demonstrates two easily observable and measurable variables: food intake and body weight. These parallel a diabetic child's insulin intake and his sugar and acetone levels, the epileptic child's anticonvulsant intake and seizure frequency, the ulcerative colitic's medication intake and amount of stooling, etc.

These are the things parents tend to focus on, an obvious alarming manifestation of pathology and something that can be put into the child to make him more "normal." This sets the stage for a struggle to control the child's body and its processes, with implications to the child that deep inside he is uncontrollable.

The Control Tower

The anorexic child senses the lack of self-control in regard to his developing and changing body, particularly when he is approaching puberty. This lack of sufficient self-control extends to his emotions and behavior, which were previously "monitored" by the parents. He reacts with a monumental attempt to take over the control all by himself. He focuses all his weaknesses and strengths in one area, that of body weight, hunger, and food. He describes himself as "fat, heavy, and weak." Rather than attributing the feelings of "heaviness" and weakness to fatigue, starvation, or unsatisfied dependency, which he constantly attempts to deny, he attributes the heavy feeling to "fatness," so his "logical" solution is to lose weight and exercise in order to get "stronger!" He derives reassurance and satisfaction in demonstrating to himself and others that he has a *strong will.*

He sees as intolerable failure any compromise in his struggle to have complete control over his feared "uncontrollable" needs (which he identifies as appetite but certainly extends to his dependent, hostile, and sexual feelings). Acknowledging his own needs he sees as accepting vulnerability, "to continue to be controlled by others." No wonder the tension escalates to intolerable levels as a result of the ongoing struggle between such children and their families. It is therefore crucial to help the parents see the problem beyond eating and weight, or beyond insulin and sugar level for the diabetic, or beyond wheezing and bronchodilators, or beyond seizure frequency and anticonvulsants. The developing child needs to gain increasing self-control over his body and body functions as well as his emotions.

APPLIED EDUCATION AND CLEAR COMMUNICATION

The parents may need guidance in order to understand and help their child understand his physiological needs: a safe or unsafe weight, a well-balanced meal, general hygiene measures, the way medications work in alleviating specific symptoms, physiological/anatomical changes during illness and health, etc. This can be accomplished rather successfully when working with intelligent, emotionally intact parents. However, one should not be misled by apparent sophistication and emotional intactness of the family unit or the individuals, either parent or child. The child may be an expert in calorie counting, insulin syringes, insulin units, and glucose levels, but may not have a clear understanding of his body requirements under different circumstances. The parents may use medical terms and psychological jargon showing an apparent level of expertise higher than the general population, but be confused as to how to apply these bits of knowledge. A common pitfall in communicating with parents is to take for granted that the parents understand what we say and that we are understanding what they are saying. Many times this is not the case, and because of fear of admitting ignorance, misinterpretations may snowball.

It is important to explore and understand thoroughly the patterns of family interactions and their impact on the emotional development of the child. For example, when overly close and intrusive family interactions do not allow for any privacy, there would be a great deal of difficulty in allowing a developing child to become gradually more autonomous and independent. An overly rigid family may not have enough ability to "follow the child" to make the necessary changes during different stages of his development. The family may view these changes as dramatic, and therefore a threat. The parents require support in understanding the child's changing needs surrounding the developmental tasks to be mastered. Autonomy, independence, and responsibility for the self (not to be confused with premorbid "pseudo-maturity" or "pseudo-independence") should be judiciously encouraged and supported by the parents. The family will need support in dealing with confrontations efficiently, i.e., by resolution rather than avoidance or accumulation of conflicts.

REFERENCE

MINUCHIN, S., et al.: A conceptual model of psychosomatic illness in children. *Archives of General Psychiatry*, 32:1031-1038, 1975.

Chapter 17

Parents of Hyperactive
and Aggressive Children

L. Eugene Arnold

Behavior disorders of childhood, largely represented by the diagnostic categories of hyperkinetic (hyperactive) reaction and unsocialized aggressive reaction, often have underlying minimal brain dysfunction (MBD). Sometimes there is an associated learning disability, which may be cause or effect of the behavior disorder. To simplify presentation, much of this chapter will assume the presence of MBD and focus on the hyperkinetic child as an example, while admitting that behavior disorders are diverse in etiology and manifestation.

Behavior disorders pose a double stress for parents. Not only do they present all the financial, emotional, and other problems of chronic disorder (see Chapter 15), but they also tax in a special way the parents' time, energy, mental health, and ability to love the child. Though a large proportion of behavior disorders are believed to have been initiated by things beyond the parents' control, such as MBD, temperamental deviation, developmental lag, or partial deprivation because of parental illness or absence, the link between the etiological factor and the full-fledged behavior disorder is not usually obvious. Consequently, such parents fall easy prey to the popular belief of full parental responsibility for children's behavior problems. In many cases this feeds into the pre-existing self-blame that seems to be an occupational hazard for parents of children with chronic disorders. The resulting feelings of inadequacy, doubt, and guilt, sometimes projected onto the child, complicate the parent-child relationship and fuel the hostility already sparked by the child's mischief.

UNDERSTANDING RATHER THAN LABELING

Often the parents are presented with a "catch-22" dilemma. If they assume basic normality in the child, they are forced to conclude—with the encouragement of the community—that they are miserable failures as parents. If they recognize the child's handicap and act logically on it, they may be labeled overprotective or overcontrolling. If they wear out, or if the child breaks away from their control, they may be labeled over-permissive. Before labeling the parent of a behavior-disordered child rejecting, overcontrolling, overprotective, or overpermissive, one should attempt to understand what that parent has been through with the child. Reasons for this are discussed in Chapter 1 under "Appreciating the Parents' Position."

Another important consideration in understanding parents is to recognize that a few of those with MBD children manifest some residual of the same problem from their own childhood, resulting in concreteness, difficulty planning a sustained course of action, and difficulty translating abstract ideas into appropriate action. These impairments have obvious implications for the guidance approach. Many such parents, though incapable of formulating their own specific plans from abstract principles, are quite willing and able to carry out a very concrete, specific plan articulated by the professional. It is advisable in such cases to write out the plan in step-by-step detail if the parent can read. If the parent cannot read, a temporary loan of a cassette recorder with taped instructions may be necessary. The professional needs to beware of falling into the same trap with these parents as many parents and teachers do with behavior disordered children: assuming that they can do the simple task demanded and that their not doing it shows they are resistant, stubborn, or passive-aggressive, when actually they are not able to do it and are ashamed to admit that they cannot. When presented with constructive tasks broken down to their level of ability, such parents and their children can both be surprisingly cooperative.

DISPELLING GUILT AND HOPELESSNESS

Some parents may be defensive about the child's behavior or deny any problems because of feelings of guilt, helplessness, or hopelessness about being able to change his behavior. They will be relieved to learn that they are not being blamed for the child's behavior, do not need to blame themselves, and can do something to help the child. Other parents may frankly admit that the child is having problems and blame or reject the child as hopeless or "rotten." They can have their hopes for the child rekindled.

One of the best antidotes for guilt and blaming is an *explanation of what the problem really is*. In this case, understanding the problem also brings hope, because the prognosis is generally good with appropriate intervention. Therefore, one of the best ways to dispel both paralyzing guilt and hopelessness is adequate attention to appropriate explanation of the child's problems. Furthermore, merely identifying and naming a problem can yield some beginning feeling of mastery over it. Many times a diagnostic label becomes almost personified as an entity that the parent and child can blame instead of blaming each other or the teacher. *Caution:* The professional needs to be alert for parents who wish to label the child in order to blame him.

Naming and Explaining the Problem

The most useful way of naming and explaining a given behavior disorder varies not only with its exact diagnostic category, but also with how much evidence there is for a neurological component, the past history and experience of the family, the family's sophistication, and terms in vogue in the community.

As the first step in naming and explaining, the family should be asked what they think is wrong. Sometimes a family will come suggesting a diagnostic term that they may have read or been told about. In such instances, it is important to find out what the family understands about that particular term. If their understanding of the term and the term itself are both appropriate to the child's condition, this can be confirmed, and attention can then be directed to the implications for proposed management. If the label, but not the family's understanding of it, is accurate, or if the family's description is accurate but not their label, appropriate correction can be made before proceeding to management implications. If neither the term nor the family's understanding of it fits the child's condition, the family can be assured that such is not the problem and can be given the appropriate correct information. It may also be useful in such cases to explore why they thought the child had that particular disorder.

If the family has no term for the problem, the professional then has the luxury of choosing the most useful term for the particular child's situation. In general, I try to avoid the term "brain damage" or "brain injury" because this for many people conjures visions of cerebral Swiss cheese. One exception would be when a child's behavior problem appears to be clearly related to brain damage that the parents are already aware of because of its manifestations in other ways, such as cerebral palsy, epilepsy, or rubella syndrome. In such cases, their awareness of the child's damaged status forms a basis for understanding this additional impairment. Ordinarily, though, there is not such solid evidence for brain damage or injury. The concept of *brain dysfunction* may be useful, but this is often better phrased in terms of a *developmental lag,* or one part of the brain not yet caught up with the other parts in its growth and development.

In many cases the concept of *individual differences of temperament* (Chapter 12) may be the most valid. Explaining that some people are naturally highstrung or nervous like race horses while others are like draft horses can help the parent understand the child's need for supportive firmness. At the same time it implies that the child's trait is not necessarily "bad," since both types of horses are valued for their particular assets. It also implies that the presently troublesome aggression or high energy level can eventually be "harnessed" and put to constructive use.

The concept of a *social learning disability* is often useful. The child's difficulty in learning impulse control and social skills can be analogized to aptitudes or disabilities in learning other skills. One of my favorites is this example: "Some people learn how to swim spontaneously and naturally. You can throw them in the water when they are three years old and they begin paddling around. Other people have to take lessons, and may not learn how to swim until they are considerably older. Some kids spontaneously learn how to control their tempers and sit still. Other kids have to take lessons in learning how to control themselves." This removes blame from both child and parent while at the same time focusing on the hopeful idea of eventual improvement through hard work and practice.

Even in situations where the professional suspects that the main cause of the behavior problem is *faulty training,* the problem can be *stated in a way that avoids blaming* or aggravation of parental guilt. For example, one can say something like, "John is a boy who has a great need for somebody to set very firm limits on his behavior." One does not need to point out that the reason John has such a great need now for someone to set firm limits is that the parents were overpermissive or oversubmissive earlier in his life. Such focusing on the present problem and implications for constructive action models an attitude and approach that one would hope the parents would emulate in their dealing with the child.

Explaining and Retuning the System

The foregoing explanations should help lay a foundation of optimistic expectation of improvement. Such expectation constitutes an important part of modifying the vicious cycle illustrated in Figure 2, Chapter 5, p. 60. Minimal brain dysfunction is shown as an example of an original cause for the cycle, but similar vicious cycles can arise for other reasons. Reference to the figure will confirm that a good deal of pathological parent-child (and teacher-child) interaction results from a psychosocial vicious cycle sustained by expectation, hopeless assumption of the worst, and frustrated blaming of self or others. This cycle may continue to reverberate even after the child "outgrows" the original cause. It can be disrupted by initiating a virtuous cycle: change the expectation of misbehavior to expectation of improved behavior, change parents' frustration and despair into hopeful persistence, change the parents' anger and rejection into acceptance of the challenge of helping the child, and figure out a way for the child to get adult attention without misbehaving. The first step in this retuning of the system for some families might be to explain the actual system.

An important technique in establishing positive expectations and reducing anger and rejection is a *psychological general amnesty.* The assumption should be that the child has always wanted to be good, but was unable to because of his handicap, and the parents had always wanted to do the best for the child, but did not know how. Since the problem is now known and appropriate remedies are available, the stage is set for great change. The parent and child working together with the assistance of professionals will now be able gradually and arduously, but with eventual success, to help the child gain control over himself and behave in the exemplary manner that he always wanted to. The parents, who now understand the problem, will be able more effectively to help him control himself with supportive, firm limits and structure, which can eventually be gradually discontinued. Such expectation of change provides a rationale for parents and child to give up negative attitudes and develop new roles and identities. Instead of seeing themselves as a bad kid and inadequate parents, they can see themselves as a good but slightly handicapped kid and adequate parents struggling to help their child overcome his handicap.

The parents' frustration can be changed to hopeful persistence by providing them tools and techniques to gain control over the situation.

GAINING CONTROL

If there is one issue on which the parents and the professional should be able to reach agreement very early, it is that the child's behavior needs to be brought under control. Surprisingly often the child himself will agree with this goal. Children by and large have a conscious or at least semiconscious desire to have adult support in keeping their behavior under control. Typical comments heard in this regard from children are: 1) From a five-year-old girl, "John's mother must not care about him because she doesn't make him behave." 2) From an unsocialized aggressive, brain-damaged 11-year-old son of divorced parents, "I like to stay with my father better than my mother because he can control me." 3) From 11- and 9-year-old neurotically unruly sisters, "We like to stay with our grandfather because he has a big hand and he whacks us when we do anything wrong, so we don't do anything wrong when we are staying with him." Even where the child does not overtly welcome it, he may be secretly cheering on the professional and his parents in their plans for gaining control of his behavior. Ordinarily, one can assume an alliance with the child as well as with the parents; the child can be a witness (if not a party) to the plans being developed to help him gain control over his behavior, usually via the intermediary step of the parents first gaining control over it.

Before discussing practical ways for parents to help the child gain control of his behavior, we need to mention one thing which *needs to be kept out of the control issue:* the child's medication, if any. When the child is medicated, his parents often tend to see the drugs only as a mechanism of controlling his behavior. Sometimes they welcome this, feeling that it gives them some means of doing something about his behavior; they may even dispense extra pills on "bad days." On the other hand, some parents are grieved by the idea that drugs, rather than they, are controlling the child's behavior. In the latter case the success of medication may merely accentuate their own feelings of helpless loss of control.

Seeing the drugs as a behavior-controlling device constitutes a problem not only for parents, but also for the children. Some children who are willing to cooperate with a plan of psychosocial management to bring behavior under control will balk at using medication when seen as a means of someone else controlling their behavior. This may be because the chemical is such an intrusive way of establishing control that it threatens the child's autonomy. Therefore, one needs to emphasize the role of medication as a stabilizer and normalizer of neurophysiologic status rather than a social control agent, a medical intervention rather than a social intervention. Insofar as the drug has an indirect result of allowing greater control over the child's behavior, this control is by the child over his own behavior, not by the parent. In other words, the *drug should support and promote autonomy*, not impair it, and parents need to be prevented from sabotaging the child's ability to view the drug this way. More about this issue can be found in Chapter 13.

Means of Control

In addition to the *firm, consistent limits* which parents need to provide for most children, they will need to provide even more for the hyperkinetic child. They need to help him compensate for his inability to organize by *planning* for him, *structuring* his days, and *organizing* his activities in ways that would not be necessary and probably not even desirable for normal children. Of course, they need occasionally to reevaluate the necessity of what they are doing so that they do not drift into an overprotective and overcontrolling rut that continues long after the need for it has ceased.

Temporarily, they need to do such things as inviting one or two playmates at a time into the house rather than allowing a large enough group that the child becomes overstimulated. If he shows social clumsiness and disregard of the rights of peers, they may need to teach him social amenities, courtesy, and respect for the rights of others in a more explicit and direct way than is necessary for normal children. Of course, after the child has mastered some social skills with one or two playmates, he should be encouraged to play in gradually larger groups. He may need time, with small incremental steps, to make the same adjustment to large groups that normal children can usually manage spontaneously upon entrance to kindergarten.

For the child with a short attention span or poor organization, parents may need to *break ordinary tasks into small steps.* If he is incapable of putting his toys away with that global direction, they may need first to direct him to put his blocks away, then after he has completed that, tell him to put his puzzle away, then tell him to put his toy cars away, etc. After several successes this way, they can direct him to put his blocks and puzzle away in one instruction and his cars and coloring book in another instruction. After he has mastered this size task, perhaps he is ready to make the step to the global direction to put his toys away.

Appropriate *positive reinforcement* should be inserted after each successful step. For example, an appropriate sequence for teaching a child to put on his shirt (a task spontaneously mastered by many children but which some hyperkinetic children may need to be taught) might go as follows: "Put this hand in this sleeve. Good! Now put the other hand in that sleeve. Good! Put your head in this hole. Good! Now pull it down over your body. Good! You put your own shirt on!"

Mention of positive reinforcement brings us to the very important idea of *behavior modification,* an effective way for parents to gain control that respects the child's autonomy and which the child usually enjoys. Behavior modification is discussed in detail in Chapter 7. However, the application to hyperkinetic children raises some special considerations: 1) Parents need to know that the hyperkinetic child's failure to respond to aversive conditioning (failure to "learn from experience") is part of his handicap, not stubbornness. The normal tendency to respond more effectively to positive reinforcement than to negative is even more marked in the hyperkinetic, who may not respond at all to the negative. 2) Unfortunately, even the responsiveness to positive reinforcement may be somewhat impaired, though not as much as the responsiveness to negative reinforcement. 3) Responsiveness to both positive and aversive conditioning, especially to the latter, tends to be enhanced by successful stimulant treatment. Therefore, parents need to temper the severity of aversive consequences for a medicated child. 4) Social reinforcement (approval, praise, attention) seems preferred by many hyperkinetic children. 5) The axiom "try to catch the child being good" is especially applicable to hyperkinetic children.

Both parents and the relationship between them tend to be stressed by any problem of their children. However, behavior disorders stress the marriage in special ways. The mother may resent the father's absences, leaving her with "the duty," while the father may either blame the mother for not being able to control the child's behavior or else see nothing wrong with the child's behavior and criticize the mother for complaining about it.

Often the father is unable to understand the mother's plight because the child behaves better for him than for the mother. This may be due to: 1) The father, being fresher and not as worn down as the mother, can pursue limit setting more firmly and forcefully. 2) The father is usually physically stronger than the mother. 3) If the father is not around as much as the mother, his directions and limits may carry some novelty value which can better hold the child's attention.

Bringing in Father

When there is a father in the home, he needs to be drawn into more active management of the child, or at least a firm, full commitment to backing up the mother's management. Any complaints the father may have about the mother's management of the child provide a natural opportunity for underscoring the need of the father's involvement. Since most behavior-disordered children are boys, it is easy to argue that a boy needs his father's attention. Since the father was a boy himself, he can better understand the boy's needs and how the boy's mind works, and therefore is in a better position to prevent misbehavior and deal with it in a knowing manner when it occurs.

Sometimes it is necessary to appeal to a father's chauvinistic streak by inviting him to rescue his helpless wife or to demonstrate how a man would manage the child's behavior. A better approach, though, might be to ask him if he still loves his wife, and remind him that the marriage could continue long after the agony of raising this particular child. Try to put the child's present behavior problems in perspective in the larger context of the couple's priorities and plans.

Preserving the Parents' Privacy

One thing which occasionally interferes with parents' "maintenance work" on their marital relationship is the tyrannical interference of some behavior-disordered children with the couple's privacy and social life. If the child's behavior is so bad that the parents cannot find anyone willing to babysit, they may have given up going out together. The expense of the child's treatment may also interfere with their social life financially. At night he may wander around the house, even into their bedroom. Many such parents need permission by a firm directive to reclaim for themselves as a couple a fair share of privacy, time, and financial resources. They should be reassured that any humane means towards that end is justified, including use of locks, occasionally leaving the child overnight or for a weekend in some kind of institutional care, or hiring an adult male sitter who can physically control the child.

What If It Is Too Late to Save the Marriage?

The needs of single parents for privacy, occasional breaks from the child, and support from other persons are no less pressing than those of parents in intact marriages. Such support and backing may be developed from a relative, friend, or neighbor, or in some cases from a professional with a longstanding commitment to the family. Ideally, such a support person would be of the opposite sex from the single parent (e.g., an uncle supporting the efforts of a mother who is raising a boy without a father), but the presence and availability of such a person are usually more important than the sex.

> An absent father was encouraging his son's misbehavior by telling him that he did not have to do what his mother or any other woman told him. The male psychiatrist gave a direct message to the boy that he had to mind his mother, that she was in charge and he would have to do what she said. It was not clear whether the boy's subsequent good behavior resulted because the message came from a male or because the message came from an objective third party with some authority.

BEHAVIOR AS A SYMPTOM OF FAMILY NEUROSIS

The behavior-disordered child's problems are sometimes deeply entangled in a family neurotic process. For example, Barcai (1969) estimates that effective stimulant treatment of MBD children uncovers, in about 20-30%, a family neurotic conflict that had been masked by the child's more florid symptoms, and that interferes with the child's being able to make further or lasting improvement.

Scapegoating

The behavior-disordered child is often the scapegoat for the rest of the family members, who are not about to give up this valuable asset merely because his treatment is making him capable of behaving better. As one "normal" 14-year-old sibling of an identified patient said, "You have to have a bad guy in the family. If you didn't have a bad guy, you wouldn't know that you're a good guy." The scapegoat's resentment of being cast in such a role for the benefit of siblings (and perhaps of parents) can contribute to a degree of acting out that tends to justify the other family members' negative perception of him. Scapegoating warrants family therapy, at least of crisis intervention type. In my experience, explaining the scapegoating phenomenon to the siblings, along with some support in seeing things a little more realistically, is usually enough to nudge them out of the rut.

Excuses and Acting Out

A related but opposite-appearing problem is the condoning of the child's misbehavior by the rest of the family. On more than one occasion a child has informed me in an initial diagnostic contact, while the parent nods approval, that he cannot control his temper because he is hyperkinetic. In some such cases, the child's symptoms are acting out an unconscious feeling or conflict of the parent, who seizes on the child's diagnosis as a convenient excuse for having the child act out. The child is seduced into cooperating with this because it relieves him of the hard work of trying to overcome his problem. This kind of situation calls for a two-step intervention: 1) The child's problem needs to be redefined as something with good prognosis that the child and parent need to continue working on, and 2) the parents' reaction to this news and to the deprivation of a channel of acting out needs to be assessed and dealt with appropriately. Possible interventions indicated may be "treatment of the parent-child relationship" or "theme interference reduction" described in Chapter 1.

Parental Perfectionism Unmasked

Sometimes a perfectionistic parent who has previously enjoyed good grounds for finding the child's behavior and performance inadequate finds his perfectionistic stringency unmasked by the child's objective improvement, with paradoxically deleterious effects on the parent-child relationship. One of my favorite examples of this was a mother who complained that there was no improvement in her son because he was not getting A's in school, even though he had raised his grades from D's to B's and had completely reformed his behavior so that the school was now praising his behavior rather than threatening to expel him. Such parents (and their children) need to hear G. K. Chesterton's admonition that "What's worth doing is worth doing badly." More about helping parents modify pathological expectations and attitudes can be found in Chapters 4, 6, 8, and 18.

GUIDANCE THROUGH BEWILDERING THERAPEUTIC CLAIMS

Both the professional and lay press have been devoting an avalanche of attention to the problem of children with behavior and learning disorders. Any self-styled expert who offers a glimmer of hope for helping such children can get a hearing in the popular press. Consequently, one of the things many parents need help with is guidance through the array of therapeutic claims, some of them contradictory. The confusion is aggravated by the surrounding emotionalism, both positive and negative, and by the fact that practically any treatment will help a few children because of placebo effect. The following information and attitudes are helpful to the professional who needs to discuss those issues with parents.

Be Prepared for Change

A multiplicity of therapy is usually evidence that no one treatment is 100% satisfactory. Therefore, we might hope for improvement, and therapeutic advances may affect the validity of the following points.

Treatments with Documented Efficacy

While no treatment is effective for all children, the following have shown in well-controlled studies or in common clinical experience a significant contribution to the improvement of many behavior-disordered children: 1) *drug treatment,* especially with stimulants, but also with tricyclic antidepressants and major tranquilizers; 2) *behavior modification;* 3) *special education;* 4) *psychological management,* including firm supportive limits, structure, and realistic expectations (the holding described later under "Force-Feeding Affection" might be listed here, but could also be classified under "Treatments Showing Promise"); 5) *supportive psychotherapy;* and 6) certain types of *perceptual remediation.*

Also, reasonable programs to improve coordination (physical education, physical therapy, occupational therapy) are valuable in themselves even if they do not help behavior or learning. While drugs in general boast the best documented efficacy of all the treatments mentioned, there is one currently popular drug that showed dismal results in controlled studies: caffeine. The evidence for perceptual remediation is more erratic and the results not as reproduceable as for drug therapy or behavior modification, but it may offer the most hope for the future because of its preventive potential (Arnold et al., 1977).

Treatments Probably Effective for a Small but Noteworthy Proportion of Children

While not providing an answer for the majority of behavior-disordered children, the following seem, from the limited information available, to benefit some such children: 1) *elimination diets,* restricting intake of colorings, preservatives, flavorings, sucrose, chocolate, cow's milk, and possibly other foods, 2) *deleading* for those with subclinical lead poisoning, 3) *supplemental iron* for those with iron deficiency anemia, and 4) *high protein,* low carbohydrate diet for those with reactive hypoglycemia. Most of these things imply a thorough pediatric evaluation, which is not always done, but could easily be justified.

Treatments Showing Promise But Not Yet Adequately Investigated or Developed

Promising treatments that need further research or development include 1) autohypnosis or relaxation, 2) transcendental meditation, 3) biofeedback, 4) vestibular stimulation, 5) sensory integration, and 6) manipulation of fluorescent light and television radiation exposure.

Treatments of Doubtful Value

Despite the enthusiasm of its advocates, megavitamin treatment has not been demonstrated in any well-controlled study to have any value. At least one well-controlled study found it to be not better than placebo (Arnold et al., in press). Other interventions of undemonstrated value are certain programs of ritualistic exercises, which often coerce parents' full commitment through guilt-provoking dogma. The placebo phenomenon and the benefits of increased parent-child interaction may account for the results which the proponents of these programs attribute to the exercises. Not included in this category are the excellent physical education, occupational therapy, and physical therapy programs that set realistic, moderate goals and cooperate with parents in a mutually respectful manner.

Risks of Treatment

The best publicized risks are those associated with drug treatment, but no treatment is completely without risk. Even therapy which does not seem terribly risky in itself may, if it is inappropriate and ineffective for the given child, carry the risk of delaying effective treatment. Also, the child and parents who have gone through several unsuccessful treatments accumulate discouragement that interferes with optimal cooperation with the next treatment.

HYPERKINESIS AND AFFECTION DEFICIENCY

Hyperkinetic children are as variable in their ability to seek, accept, and enjoy affection as they are in other ways. At one extreme, some of them are extremely clinging and physically affectionate between their periods of misbehavior. At the other extreme are children whose parents complain that they have never enjoyed hugging, cuddling, sitting on the parents' lap, being held, or other normal activities by which parents affectively nourish their infants and children. Both extremes can puzzle well-meaning parents who are not sure how to respond to the child.

The clinging child who demands physical signs of affection may be seen as immature and undeserving of the affection that he seeks. The impulsive, irritable, affectively rejecting child may convince his parents that he is best left alone. The extremely overactive, disorganized child who "cannot hold still" long enough for affectionate interchanges or seems disinterested in them may either convince his parents that he does not need affection or discourage them from pursuing it. The impulsively aggressive child may engender such a hostile relationship that it is difficult for affection to be manifested by either parent or child. This is unfortunate, because the developmental need for affection from a consistent, nurturing parent is often even more urgent for such children than it is for the "easy child" who is as easy to love as he is to manage in other ways.

Even with a normal amount of parental affection, some hyperkinetic children appear to suffer an affection deficiency. Tragically, their behavior problems may effectively reduce the amount of affectionate interaction with their parents, and this deprivation of affection, through its effect on their emotional health, may make their behavior worse, which further reduces the parental affection they receive (another example of a vicious cycle). In very young children, this affection deprivation may be associated with stimulus deprivation, since much of the auditory, vestibular, tactile, and kinesthetic stimulation of very young children occurs in the context of being held, cuddled, rocked, sung to, talked to, read to, etc.

How Can Parents Treat the Affection Deficiency?

With the clinging, demanding type of child and cooperative parents, it is usually fairly easy to recommend a set period of time each day for the parent to initiate affectionate interaction without the child's demanding it. This can be as short as 10-15 minutes and may involve any mutually pleasant activity, such as playing a game or reading a story, as well as just sitting on the parents' lap or alongside the parent. This specified period of affectionate interaction can be supplemented by occasional spontaneous hugs or pats at other times of the day.

A bigger challenge, but also a bigger opportunity for dramatic improvement, is presented by the child who actively resists being held. These children may require a force-feeding of restraint and affection by the parents in the manner advocated by Henderson, Dahlin and their colleagues (1974).

Force-Feeding Affection

In Henderson and Dahlin's technique, the child is held straddling the adult's lap, facing the adult, with his shoes off so that if he kicks he is not likely to hurt the adult. In my experience, the technique also works well with the child sitting on the adult's lap in the usual way, facing away from the adult. The essential thing is to have a comfortable position that can be maintained for a length of time and in which it is easy to prevent either the child or adult from being hurt. The adult holds the child's arms and talks to him. If the child accepts this for a reasonable time, he is cuddled, stroked, and allowed out of the restraint. If he resists or struggles against the restraint, he is held as long as required for him to give up and relax in exhaustion against the adult's body. (Henderson and Dahlin report that the longest time they have found required for this was three hours.) Then he is cuddled, hugged, stroked, verbally soothed, and then released.

After several repetitions of this on different days, the child gradually comes to accept the restraint better and better and even enjoy it. The situation strikes me as analogous to a toddler with iron deficiency anemia who refuses to eat foods containing iron until he is artificially given an initial boost of iron, after which he develops a taste for foods containing iron. I believe there are some hyperkinetic children who have a great need for affection but refuse to accept what they so desperately need until they can be helped to develop a taste for it.

Parents should be given a demonstration of the technique by the professional prior to their attempting it. Even with the demonstration, some parents may not be up to persevering through the first few sessions and overcoming the child's struggle to get out of the restraint. The technique should not be recommended to parents who the professional believes cannot carry through with it; an abortive attempt at this force-feeding would merely be another episode of failure for the parents and another negative interaction between parents and child.

When the parents are able to carry it out, the technique carries several fringe benefits: 1) The parents gain a feeling of doing something concrete, positive, and active to help their child; 2) it provides a *constructive* channel for acting out any "battle of wills" between parent and child; 3) it helps to involve the father. As the physically stronger parent, the father may feel more of an obligation to be involved in this technique than other interventions, and he may take some satisfaction from being able to help his child in a way that may appeal to him as more aggressive than most of the other techniques recommended by professionals.

REFERENCES

ARNOLD, L. E., BARNEBEY, N., McMANUS, J., SMELTZER, D. J., CONRAD, A., WINER, G., & DESGRANGES, L.: Prevention by specific perceptual remediation for vulnerable first-graders: Controlled study and follow-up of lasting effects. *Arch. Gen. Psychiat.,* 1977 (in press).

ARNOLD, L. E., CHRISTOPHER, J., HUESTIS, R. D., & SMELTZER, D. J.: Methylphenidate versus D-amphetamine versus caffeine in MBD: Controlled study by placebo wash-out design with Bayes analysis. *Arch. Gen. Psychiat.,* 1977 (in press).

BARCAI, A.: The emergence of neurotic conflict in some children after successful administration of dextroamphetamine. *J. Child Psychol. Psychiat.,* 10:269-276, 1969.

HENDERSON, A. T., DAHLIN, I., PARTRIDGE, C. R., & ENGELSING, E. L.: A hypothesis on the etiology of hyperactivity, with a pilot study report of related nondrug therapy. *Pediatrics,* 52, 4, 625, October, 1973.

SILVER, L. B.: Acceptable and controversial approaches to treating the child with learning disabilities. *Pediatrics,* 55:406-415, 1975.

Chapter 18

Guiding Parents of "Neurotic" Children in Treatment

Paul L. Adams

A comprehensive program for the family of a neurotic child entails a lot of explaining and explicating—the therapist needs to get his* meanings and intentions across to parents and make *explicit* a lot of things that, for the most sociable or non-therapeutic transactions, we very sanely would prefer to leave inexplicit, hinted at, subtly nuanced, and implicit. There is something very therapeutic—alas, also disenchanting and demystifying—about the operation of making people say what they

---

* I apologize to the reader for an apparent sexist bias (I usually say "he" for either and both genders)—but every other construction (save "co" and "cos" of the radical therapists) seems awkward. I even rejected my daughter's serious suggestion that I should simply write, invariably, "she" as a way of avoiding either the clumsy "he or she" or plain "he" when I mean *she or he*. A final *mea culpa* is owed to my devoted teachers and collaborators—especially social workers—with whom so often I have shared work with families. In this chapter I sound as if it all *has* to be done by one person, but I don't mean that.

think, of leading them to be aware of the full impact and significance of what they have only hinted about heretofore. Psychiatric candor can be upsetting to "let's pretend" parents.

Parents do not come to us with usable, ready-made formulations. Particularly if the family life has been that type which gives nourishment to childhood neurosis, the family has learned to make do, thrashing about in its emotional hothouse, with a deep determination *not* to see, hear or say with candor what they are doing to each other! Ideally, a psychotherapist has completely opposite values. The therapist wants to clarify, elucidate, confront, provoke change, raise consciousness and assist families toward new ways of interacting. The therapist brings not peace but a sword, it seems, and he had better be set to do some explaining.

EXPLAINING A CHILD'S NEUROTIC TROUBLE TO PARENTS

What do we tell parents about the disorder of their moderately or mildly disturbed children in treatment?

> Children do not develop evenly on all fronts and in all their valued capabilities. Smart parents who have had close acquaintance with more than a couple of babies have realized that for themselves. (So all we need to do is to reiterate what parents have observed already.)

> Growth is complex and multi-frontal, and development is so complex that its ins-and-outs (the norms) are still imperfectly understood. Variable developmental rates—for example, if talking and thinking race ahead of motoric gains or "superego ahead of ego or drives"—have been considered by many people to lie at the roots of childhood neuroses.

> A childhood neurosis is like a war-movie that has been internalized, and the theme forgotten—remembered only in a symbolic shorthand which keeps replaying in the child's fears, sadness, loneliness, rages, guilt, shame, sexual desires, and dependency longings. The initial "war scene" fades out but the intrapsychic elaborations of conflicts take over, and while the symptoms are perplexing, not clear at all, they do produce some cognitive strain. Things don't jibe. They don't make sense. The child feels something is wrong inside now. Occasionally, his unnerving emotions and his cognitive tension will be "acted-out" instead of remaining largely inside.

> Neurotic problems indicate unhappiness and unpleasure born of inner conflicts within your child. They are not very likely to gen-

erate a lifelong mental illness that is so severe as to need hospitalization or "Thorazine" in adulthood. But they can be crippling and
incapacitating, producing unhappiness and lack of fulfillment within
the afflicted person and in his immediate interpersonal world. A day
spent unnecessarily suffering from neurotic symptoms is a day of
human wastage, a day of diminished human potential, in the formative years of your child.

Some children develop fear, irritability, restlessness, and lack of
equanimity in very early infancy. We know that these temperamental
differences are inborn. Some of our best psychiatric minds have been
devoted to study of innate temperamental differences among babies.
(See Chapter 12.) Just as it is with temperament—the general
breadth and depth of emotional activities—so it is, within limits,
with a baby's gender, learning abilities, and physique. As a minimum,
we know that any one child is a rich and variegated interplay of
these "biologically pre-programmed" features with the infinitely
more numerous "culturogenic or experiential" traits of personality.
In the neurotic and behavioral problems of children, we are bound
to see all these interacting features, if we look appropriately and
long enough.

CHALLENGING THE DOUBLE TABOO

Life in our present social system being as it is, two of the main conflict zones for "neurotic" children are found in sexual lust and in
anger or aggression. Hence, early in our contacts with the parents it is
well to bring up matters relating to these two topics. Although we may
learn little about the child, such probing may tell us to what degree
the parents can work to advance candor while their child is working
to improve insight. Thus their answers to the following questions act
as a gauge of parental workability: "What kind of sexual life does your
child have? First interest in masturbation? What sexual interests and
questions has your child brought to you? When was the last time your
child went into a rage? What happened? What happens when your
child gets angry at you?"

Parents may be shocked by these direct inquiries into taboo topics in
proportion to the degree that they are unable to work on their child's
problem, preferring illusion and fog. The parents who are not at all
astonished by these questions show the most promise of beneficial work
when their child is in psychotherapy.

Certain parents have learned a popular "cop-out" in acknowledging
their child's genitality—namely, to mean mouth and anus and fingertips,
but not genitals, when they say "sexual" about children. Those parents

will need more intensive help to progress beyond their false conceptions of a fumigated, displaced, and desiccated childhood sexuality.

Some parents cannot bear the sin of a defiant child who has his own feelings, including anger and hatred. These parents feel that unloving children, as Sacred Writ contends, deserve to be put to death if they do not honor and obey their parents (Leviticus 20:9). Work with them tries to promote relinquishing of punitive projections, dropping of demands that children "feed parental egos," and acceptance of a co-existence between parents and children. They need help to accept that all is not sweetness and light for either parents or children, but if all parties are treated as human, with rights, obligations, and mutual respect, the dreary patriarchal no-win game can be replaced by some joyous interchanges.

AFFIRMING THEIR PARENTING OF THEIR TROUBLED CHILD

Parents need to know to what a great degree our work with the child will stand or fall depending on them. We might say that *we do not blame parents for the child's illness, but we do stress their responsibility for future improvement.* Some years ago, therapists were reluctant to say anything to parents, but with many trials (and errors) most psychotherapists have come to the point of being much more direct and outspoken. Research confirms the fruitfulness of educational, didactic procedures when psychotherapy is being undertaken (Hoehn-Saric et al., 1964). If behavior change is your goal, tell people that change is expected.

The parents can (if instructed) take up a less ambiguous role as reinforcers, or dispensers of reinforcers, of the child's behavior. They should realize that they have an important role as an ally of the child's therapist. Under these circumstances, *home visits or family group sessions are clearly a necessity.* I prefer to see the parents and sibs only in the presence of the primary child patient. In this way I can attend to child advocacy within a family context. I might not be trusted if I counsel behind the child's back.

Parental "identifications" with their children need to be teased out. Some parents realize quickly that the child is a projection of their own derogated (or idealized) selves. Some parents know that objectionable traits in the child remind them of the child's other parent or of the other side of the family! Others have different figures from their own past who emerge to awareness when the child behaves badly or well. It helps to elicit these identifications: as parents acknowledge their distorted carry-over from past to present, recognize their own rages and infanticidal longings, and recognize their desire to reverse conscious roles and to receive nurturance from their child, they enjoy an augmented, vivified sense of who they are and what they are up to. In short, projective identification is supplanted by empathy.

The identifications that we regard as most wholesome or promising are those with some favorable perspective. If the parent sees the child as basically made of good protoplasm—to be a good enough "egg"—things are looking up. We should foster such stirrings, whether with a nod, a purr, or a sermonette of celebration.

Hatching as Part of the Life Cycle

Similarly promising is the attitude by parents that the goal of parenthood is to rear one's children to become autonomous and—on their own—to choose (or not) to make parenthood a part of *their* life cycle. Most children know whether they will marry and want to be parents by the time they are in kindergarten (Broderick, 1968). Parents can aid their children in finding parenthood not to be a deadly ordeal. Blessed are the parents who can see an end of childhood and its dependencies and problems, and who can celebrate the zest of closeness and natural relatedness. Of course, those who *overstress* closeness and "love" produce a neurotic hothouse (Green, 1946; Chodoff, 1966). Those who see the goal of family living as a hatching operation from collective to individuality are on track exactly (Rank, 1945). Therapists who can define their roles as assistants to parents in their brooding and hatching of freer souls are also on track. The important point is that parents be enabled to live "abundantly" in parenthood's sector of the life cycle. That alone would enrich family life in ways that would greatly favor neurotically troubled children who are learning the patient role.

One question is whether parents of neurotic children need to be regarded as patients. In general, I think not. However, when neurotic children are in family therapy, it might make as much sense not to call them patients either. We all manifest some anxiety about the term "patient" which we handle in various ways. The euphemism I like best is "young friend," but I also say "patient" without discomfort. Some of my colleagues who are not psychiatrists have consecrated the terms "client," "counselee" or "analysand." I know a health center administrator who feels least anxious when he employs the term "registrant" for anyone served by that health center!

FORMULATING CONTRACT TERMS BETWEEN THERAPIST AND PARENTS

As parents spell out their family problems, their parenting troubles, the child's difficulties, and their separate and idiosyncratic problems as mother and father, some sort of guiding and counseling transaction has already begun. Parents do not unload if there is no hope that they will be aided. What do we at this point need to get the parents to do, wish to do, promise to do, or at least try to do?

They must, as responsible parents, agree to the child's regular and prompt appearance for the therapy sessions. Poor people may not understand this kind of contract at first: "You must understand that a new force now is in your lives, new ghosts in your household, and that practical considerations concerning your child's travel, vacations, and cancellations must be negotiated with the therapist." They also need to understand that the therapist has a life of trips and meetings and vacations about which he (or she) will try to give the parents enough advance warning so that they can make alternative plans.

The parents must understand that the relationship between therapist and parents, like that between therapist and child, is different from what they are used to seeing from doctors. More time, more dialogue, more equality and respect in the interaction characterize the psychotherapeutic undertaking. The patient and parents are needed *collaborators,* not passively recipient "consumers."

Parents derive benefit from being told that time itself is of the essence of therapy. Time is what it takes for people to help make one another crazy or well. It is the medium on which human relatedness is carried, and time is all that the psychotherapist "sells," by and large. Parents learn, therefore, that time is necessarily the costly frame in which psychotherapy transpires. They learn that, in this one added way, psychotherapy is different from other forms of treatment. The pediatrician charges a set fee per visit, the surgeon charges per operation, and the faith healer levies an inexact but conscience-pricking "generous contribution." Fees are set *through some negotiation* by most psychotherapists, and fees are *time-related.* "All this money," parents say sometimes with a knowing twinkle of adult *savoir faire,* "for a guy who pits himself against me on the side of my child, for a guy who wants me to be deeply involved and fully divulging while he stingily may tell me nothing, give me damned little advice, and not even talk to me in a pinch except when I put the kid on an extension phone!"

Therapeutic Double Standard

Parents willingly go to work if we tell them how they need to serve as informants to us, even when we will not be informants to them in return. They also seem, in general, to delight in being told that a child therapist operates on a double standard, as corrupt as that sounds. The parents must show and tell all, from the history and from daily happenings, but the therapist in return will not tell what he may learn from the child. Moreover, the therapist will be free, using some (but not much) editorial discretion, to relay it all to the child. Why? Because the therapist is a child advocate, trying to counterbalance the greater rights and powers that adults possess in our society. He has found that (whether parent or therapist) adults who serve children need to think first and foremost of children, putting the child's well-being in a place of top value. Parents of neurotic children discern that the therapeutic alliance moves doctor and child into a realm where the child's rights will be supported, even if the child's oppression comes from his conventional "protectors"—within juvenile courts, schools, and family. Most parents like the idea of child rights advocacy, despite its radicalism, as soon as they can see that something of worth will accrue.

ELUCIDATING PARENTAL ROLES

Work with parents is not soothing most of the time but the final outcome is doubly rewarding when we *do not cop out on doing a full "course" of parental guidance*. In the full course we delve into 1) roles of each parent within her/his family of origin, 2) their roles within the conjugal pair, 3) their roles within the present family of procreation, and 4) their selves beyond roles.

Parent's Baby Family

The parent's baby family has a lot of relevance for his present life because of the rife transference from that family into the present family. The TA school goes right to the heart of the matter when they ferret out the Parent-Adult-Child in each grownup person (see Chapter 6). In addition to the parent and child within each parent, there are, we know very well, far-reaching networks of invisible loyalties spanning numerous generations. Parents are intrigued by the notion that their children live not only under the shadow of their own parents but also under even fainter influences of ancestors long dead, who exerted a potent force when they were alive and parenting. A parent who has no inkling of how his own baby family shaped him is a parent who will find the parental role confusing and estranging. The therapist must ask: "Describe your family situation when you were at the age of your child. Who lived in your household? What were they like? What did they mean to you?"

Role within the Conjugal Pair

Each parent's role within the conjugal pair should be clarified. Families are still mainly conjugally based, stressing the husband-wife dyad. Ask any child; the heart of the family is in the marital pair. The relations within the conjugal pair are dynamic. "Why did you choose this man, out of all the males you could have chosen?" The attraction, pairing and mating need to be explored. Their answer to the question, "How romantic was the setup at the time of marriage?" tells us how illusory the marriage was at the outset. The rationale for marriage (or not) needs to be stated and checked out again. Who bettered his situation through this marriage? Who came from a more patrician, who from a more plebeian family background? I find that, in some way or other, one partner's family always was held to be superior; whose was it? How so? What was the trade-off for the partner from the higher caste? Many couples have devoted their entire marriage to dirty, underground fighting for an esteem that they have not been getting in the full measure expected. The resentments and shame based on economic class inferiority can plague an otherwise promising marriage. What about the first pregnancy? Did that lay a "marriage trap" or did it follow the marriage? How did each partner react? How were the other pregnancies and deliveries? Was there any way in which the carrying and delivery of the now-a-patient child differed from the others? When did your marriage reach its lowest ebb so that it meant very little to either of you? What stresses and strains have you had to deal with? Have earlier marriages of either one got in the way? How so? Are you orgasmic? lusty? alloerotic? moving toward a more open marriage? toward a divorce? toward unisex? toward equalitarianism? In all of these ways we attempt to get some estimate of how each parent is involved in his conjugal role. One message that we attempt to transmit is that parents do have a right to a happy interaction and to a full sexuality that augments each of them, quite distinct from their roles as heads of household and sources of new life.

Family of Procreation

The *family of procreation* embodies a flowering of the life cycle for parents, for it is in that family system that their own libidinal development comes truly to biologic closure and psychic fruition. In the family where they are the parents, they not only replay some of the formative experiences from their own infancy and youth but also have a chance to transcend and redeem their own past.

BEYOND ROLES

Then, after all the roles of interrelationship are explored—all of our social psychiatry is done—we must turn, with each parent whom we are involving in counseling, to what Otto Rank (1945) called the self beyond roles. This zone of life, which is (as Sullivan said) "immutably private," carries us inward to where our traditional study of interpersonal relations provides a feebler guide. This is the area where we are unmasked, de-roled, disrobed, and derepressed, where some residual *Homo ferus* abides. This is a fertile and creative place; in some ways the hope of the world resides here where human persons tenaciously keep apart a little of their wildness, unsocialized, undomesticated, and unadministered. This is a field for play, for untamed imagination, for eluding the census taker, and for breaking loose, jumping the traces. All of us must have this region of spontaneity lest our parenthood suffer and lest we perish. As Rainer Maria Rilke wrote, there is an "unlived life of which one can die."

Experience shows repeatedly that parents who have time for themselves, in solitude, or with others away from their families, make more empathic spouses and parents and have healthier and happier children. Contrariwise, parents who practice compulsive togetherness, and never break away from the familial nest, are less empathic and spawn more disturbed children. What does it all add up to for parental guidance? Deeper than the roles in original families, in procreative family, and in the marriage—all important grist for the mill—there is the unprogrammed inner life of each parent that needs our attention and reinforcing. Only then is parental role-taking part and parcel of a family-wide growth and healing process.

PARENT GUIDANCE IN PROCESS

Work with the parents needs to be coordinated with the process of their neurotic child's treatment. We can dissect out four distinct waves in this work, each wave ending in a period of shared and mutual evaluation participated in by professional and clients. These times of assessment and reconsideration could be called the *times of intensified consensual validation* that end each phase of the parental guidance process:

> Evaluation (Phase 1) ends with *reconnaissance and planning*. Trial period (Phase 2) ends with *stock-taking*. Hard digging (Phase 3) ends with *termination planning*. Termination (Phase 4) blends with *later life consequences*.

Evaluation Phase

At first, there is a breaking-in, a familiarization, a role induction. During this earliest stage of work the parents are in an evaluation-assessment-diagnosis phase. Everybody is getting acquainted, learning the ground rules and getting started in a new pattern of professional relations. Most of the examples that were given in the foregoing text are things that may occur in the evaluation period. It is a period when we test the parents, and they test us to see how readily we can be manipulated, aroused to sticky countertransference, and drawn into non-professional words and deeds. All their testing of us does not mean that the parents are evil—just human beings trying to get their bearings and make do here in the briar patch.

Evaluation ends when the parents, child, and therapist all get together to reconnoiter and to make plans for the future. Will psychotherapy of a prolonged sort be needed, such as two years or more? Or will briefer and less intensive work be indicated? Under what terms will the parents be included? Will they come once weekly for a family group session? Will they need—or prefer—to be seen by a different person? What if the parents decide to split the family and work with two or three separate therapists—one for the child and one for both parents, or one for each? We can respect their preferences despite our own preference for family group therapy. It is an ancient problem of professionals' craving to dispense what they like rather than what the consumer requests. Sometimes the customer is right (Lazare et al., 1976).

Trial Phase

My own practice has been to set up a six-weeks to three-months trial of the kind of treatment that we have settled on in the planning. During this Trial Period parental roles are elucidated. We wrap up the second phase by *stock-taking*. During the stock-taking we literally ask: How is it going? What has gone awry? What has gone well, and what could improve the progression of the work with the entire family? What problems persist? What new difficulties have come to light?

Hard Digging

During the hard labor of Phase 3 in child treatment and parental guidance, the parents work hardest. Still, it is a relatively easy uphill climb for most parents. Compared to the getting acquainted of Evaluation (Phase 1) it is like child's play. For the child it may not be quite so easy, however, and the parents know this and help out, if all is going well in their own counseling. This is a most salutary turn of events for the entire family because the parents show that they can resume their parenting without requiring too much consultation with the professional. They now have more confidence in their relation to their own child. They are getting ready to "take back" the child who has been on loan to the therapist. Loving identifications have waxed by now.

Termination

At the end of the hard digging, there comes about a brief time of planning for termination of both treatment with the child and guidance with the parents, or of family group therapy interspersing more individualized work. Once more an inventory of gains and losses occurs, a critique of the work, and a naming of what remains to be worked on. Some "testimonials" by the child in the group sessions help to further the work of termination as far as the parents are concerned. Whatever the child may freely say about his abated neurotic conflicts and overt symptoms can only reassure the parents in their dismissal of the child's therapist as their household guest.

The termination process with the parents is not the same soul-gripping experience for their counselor that a child's treatment termination is for the child's therapist. Termination is more matter-of-fact with parents; it is more rational; it is also less sorrowful. For the parents it is also an easier and lighter experience, for guidance does not invite the strength of attachment that one sees in intensive, long-term psychotherapy. Parents seem to say: That's just how it is; we called on you when we needed you and now that we have used your help and services we can do it on our own henceforth. That is the best kind of termination for a guidance transaction with parents of disturbed children.

Upon termination the professional relations come to a halt—in most instances, there is a total cessation of contact. Although sometimes precipitous, it is not traumatic because it is a smooth gear-shifting for the parents. The counselor is of *only professional* help to parents, who move out and away when they no longer feel they are in need of a professional. They can leave the field completely, killing the relationship irrevocably, because they have their real relationships with each other and with their child(ren) to absorb their attention now. They live a better life subsequent to the guidance and therapy. The professional who has done a good job also knows that it has come to an end, a full stop, and the lucky professional has his own beloved "objects" who give meaning and gratification to living.

REFERENCES

BRODERICK, C. B.: Preadolescent sexual behavior. *Med. Aspects of Human Sexuality*, 2:20-29, 1968.
CHODOFF, P.: A critique of Freud's theory of infantile sexuality. *Am. J. Psych.*, 123: 507-518, 1966.
GREEN, A. W.: The middle-class male child and neurosis. *Am. Sociological Rev.*, 2:31-41, 1946.
HOEHN-SARIC, R., FRANK, J. D., IMBER, S. D., NASH, E. H., STONE, A. R., & BATTLE, C. C.: Systematic preparation of patients for psychotherapy—I. Effects on therapy behavior and outcome. *J. Psychiatric Research*, 2:267-281, 1964.
LAZARE, A., EISENTHAL, S., & WASSERMAN, L.: The customer approach to patienthood: Attending to patient requests in a walk-in clinic. *Arch. Gen. Psych.*, 32:553-558, 1975.
Leviticus 20:9.
RANK, O.: *Will Therapy and Truth and Reality*. New York: Alfred A. Knopf., 1945.

Chapter 19

Collaboration with Parents of Psychotic (Autistic) Children

Eric Schopler

Parents of psychotic, especially autistic, children were particularly vulnerable to the disadvantages of traditional psychiatric outpatient treatment (Schopler, 1971), which sought the origins of the child's special needs in parental psychopathology. While childhood autism was once regarded primarily as social withdrawal from difficult parents, it is now recognized as a pervasive developmental disability. These children usually suffer from some form of brain abnormality (Rutter, 1968; DeMyer et al., 1973) resulting in various adaptational handicaps. Like children with other developmental disabilities, these children have needs which place special demands on their families and communities. These include special schooling, individualized behavior management, family counseling, and community and interpersonal support. This chapter is based on our ex-

---

This paper is a shortened and revised version of Chapter 9 in L. Wing (Ed.), *Early Childhood Autism*, 2nd ed. New York: Pergamon, 1976.

perience with developing a statewide program for autistic children in North Carolina (Schopler and Reichler, 1971; Reichler and Schopler, 1976).

CUTTING THE GORDIAN DIAGNOSTIC KNOT

The designation of autism or childhood psychosis conveys less in-information about a child than we like to admit. The overlaps with labels such as symbiotic psychosis, atypical child, and borderline psychosis are well known, as is the lack of professional consensus about the distinguishing features of children with these different labels.

In our program, autism was used in the broad sense as defined by Creak (1964), elaborated by Rutter (1971), and translated into a rating scale described by Reichler and Schopler (1971). *We use autism and psychosis interchangeably* for preadolescent children with the range of severe disturbances mentioned above.

The parents of our children were *not significantly different from "normal" parents*. They represented all levels of social class and education and included the usual range of adaptive difficulties. They usually had other children who were normal. If they showed unusual stress patterns, these were generally in reaction to the peculiarities of their psychotic child. We found with our developmental therapy approach (Schopler & Reichler, 1971) that these parents could be productively engaged as cotherapists. This approach was even effective in a few cases in which one parent was schizophrenic.

COUNSELING AS COLLABORATION

Both research and clinical experience indicate that traditional professional attitudes, regarding parents of autistics as patients, must change. Although parents may need counseling they can be recognized as collaborators for meeting the child's special needs and for helping to organize community services to that end.

General and Specific Problems

General problems are those that cut across different behaviors with the same child: for example, a parent's frustration over the child's picky eating, hand flapping, and lack of verbal responsiveness. Such general problems have often been superficially traced to parental attitudes such as discouragement, disappointment, and anger. They are regarded as

general because they do not necessarily get resolved when scientific behavior modification techniques are used on each of the child's specific
behaviors. Even when such techniques show success, the effects do not
always last nor do they generalize to other situations (Lovaas, Koegel,
Simmons, and Stevens, 1973).

On the other hand, *specific* counseling problems are those relating to
the modification of a child's specific behavior. They are relatively easily
understood by another interested person on the same basis on which
they are experienced. They are the actual individual problems of living
with a psychotic or severely disturbed child, undistorted by excessive
social and emotional pressures.

These two types of problems overlap. They are, however, worth trying
to separate because they tend to respond best to different kinds of intervention. In our experience, the general counseling problems are often
unresponsive to, even aggravated by, specific professional techniques.
They are most elusive to define. Nevertheless, we have been able to
identify three basic (but not all-inclusive) categories of general counseling
problems with parents: 1) *parental confusion*, 2) *erroneous expectations*,
and 3) *conflicting parental and professional roles*.

PARENTAL CONFUSION

When a parent first learns that his child is showing developmental
peculiarities which are later considered autistic, the seeds are already
sown for parental confusion, which can readily grow to hopeless exasperation. Myth-beliefs about child rearing, causes of deviant development, and how to overcome them have all been preestablished in both
popular and professional thinking. They include the idea that a child's
development deviates from the normal range mainly in response to
environmental extremes (Bettelheim, 1967) or in response to improper
conditioning procedures (Ferster, 1961). The parent of a child with pervasive developmental disability is often obliged to discover what sort of
extreme he has supposedly inflicted on his child and whether this
resulted from the parents' personal pathology (Kanner, 1949) or from
faulty communication (Meyers & Goldfarb, 1961) due to marital discord.
The psychoanalytical interpretation of autism as withdrawal from an
unfavorable emotional climate in the family has had widespread clinical
acceptance. Even more destructive has been the belief that long-term
psychoanalytic therapy can invariably resolve the emotional disturbance
and reveal a normal child. The seeds of parental confusion already pres-

ent in the culture before the autistic child's birth are shared by the parents and readily fanned into full flame by some professionals (Schopler, 1971).

How Not to Hide the Truth

Some families have taken their child to several diagnostic centers, only to have their concern and confusion increased with each additional evaluation. When we obtained the results of these evaluations, the records were often stamped "Confidential." This meant *confidential from parents!* There are many possible explanations for this practice. We have been able to identify three probable ones:

1. The *evaluation was written as a psychoanalytic interpretation* of family personalities and how their interactions produced the autistic child. Professionals sense that such interpretations would be "resisted" by the families, or to put it more simply, would be experienced as insulting. There may also be a semiconscious awareness that such an evaluation was focused on inappropriate history information, leading to an inability to answer the main questions parents have regarding their child: What is wrong and what can we do about it?

2. A second reason may be that some *indications of brain damage were found* in the child, based on "soft" signs or other uncertainties. The "confidentiality" is an attempt to protect parents from the shock and discouragement of knowing uncertain and unpleasant possibilities. This kind of "protection" has the predictable effect of increasing parental dread and confusion.

3. A third reason for confidentiality may be to *protect professional status*. For example, IQ scores were often regarded as top secret. It was overlooked that IQ scores are based on test performance. Insofar as the child's test performance actually related to his behavior in other life areas, it was usually no secret from parents anyhow (Schopler & Reichler, 1972).

Ignorance Loves Company

We have found that a frank sharing of both professional knowledge and ignorance was appreciated by most parents. It enabled them to react, think, and feel more rationally about their child.

Confusion reduction is brought about through corrective interaction between parents and professionals. Parents need to persist in requesting frank information and professionals need to stand firm in providing it.

In our program, records and charts are not kept secret from parents. IQ scores are not kept classified. How they are derived, their limits, and their use are briefly explained (more about qualifying IQ scores in Chapter 14). In a similar fashion, the limitations of neurological tests, still largely based on the neurological assessment of adults, are reviewed. The existing absence of diagnostic precision is acknowledged, including the fact that just because a child is considered autistic or psychotic does not mean that he may not also be brain-damaged or retarded. We do not withhold from parents our clinical impressions regarding a child with the kind of language impairment characterizing most autistic children. Even when there are no hard signs of brain abnormality, we admit that we have not yet been able to uncover any clinical evidence that such language impairment is the result of defective child-rearing practices. Our experience has been that parents' shock at unpleasant information and lack of clear knowledge is never as destructive as the confusion resulting from professional attempts to protect them from both.

ERRONEOUS EXPECTATIONS

Confusion is not the only problem that results from uncertainty; erroneous expectations can, too.

In both our clinical and research investigations we have found that parents are quite *accurate at estimating their child's level of functioning.* In one study (Schopler & Reichler, 1972) we asked parents during the initial diagnostic interview, before any psychological testing was done, to estimate their child's developmental levels in the areas of sociability, cognition, language, self-help sufficiency, motor coordination, and overall development. These parental estimates were later found to reach significantly high correlations with test results. Parents were able to differentiate higher and lower levels at which their child was functioning in different areas.

However, we noted that parents had greater *difficulty knowing what to do and what to expect* from this understanding. They were uncertain about its meaning for both the child's short- and long-range future planning—that is, his potential to achieve relative independence in his own life. Too much uncertainty of what to expect from the child in the present is unsettling and crippling to effective interaction with the child. Absence of any meaningful long-range expectations inflicts converging insecurities upon the daily uncertainties.

When parents have erroneously been told that social withdrawal is the cause of their child's autism, their realistic assessment of his difficulties is impaired. Not only does the social withdrawal belief mislead parents about the current knowledge of autism, it also suggests that the condition can be reversed through vague emotional therapeutic experience. Parents become unsure about trying to have the child conform to their style of life. If they try to structure socially desirable behavior, "he may withdraw further into his own shell." This kind of concern usually obscures and misrepresents the child's special educational or vocational-rehabilitative needs.

All sorts of treatment possibilities, at widely ranging costs, from megavitamin therapy to residential treatment, are covered in the press. These are usually held out as effective. They are usually difficult to evaluate, and complicate the formulation of realistic expectations.

When the child's special education needs are obvious, a class is not always available in a particular community. Sometimes a special education program is funded this year, but not next year. It may have an age cutoff that excludes the child. When he reaches adolescence, a needed sheltered workshop may not be available, or the child may not have received the appropriate education and training to make use of the existing facility. Other examples of limited resources can be cited. What they add up to is this: When the special educational resources for an autistic child are missing or unavailable, it is impossible to have clear and rational expectations for the child's future.

Debunking

In our program we have found that we could help parents avoid irrational expectations by sharing with them both the results of their child's intelligence testing and the *probabilities derived from current research*. Rather than hiding assessment attempts behind the mysterious term "untestable," we have found substantial clinical support for Alpern's (1967) finding that even uncooperative autistic children will respond to testing when easier or lower developmental test items are used. If a child responds to an easier item, lack of cooperation or "untestability" can no longer be the main explanation for his poor test performance. We share with parents not only the test results but also the statistical probabilities for improvement (Gittelman & Birch, 1967): Autistic children with an IQ under 50 tend to remain stable, while those with IQ's over 50 tend to be more variable over time, depending upon their education and experience. This kind of information, when elaborated with accurate observation of the child's individual learning peculiarities and rate of learning, forms a basis for realistic and meaningful expectations. Parents can be shown how to observe and record the way their child learns and how many repetitions are needed to insure integration of a new skill or concept.

CONFLICTING SOCIAL ROLES OF PARENT AND PROFESSIONAL

Professionals and experts are sometimes referred to as *authorities,* especially in England. The dictionary definitions of authority refer to the power to make statements, express opinions, and select citations and precedents for a decision. The emphasis is on special information and knowledge, access to the research and information of other authorities. To fulfill this social role it is necessary to have expert knowledge of a field, an exclusiveness sometimes defined by special terminology and jargon. Because of lengthy educational preparation, apprenticeship, and professional certification, it has become part of the professional's social role to consider these preparations both necessary and sufficient for attaining authority status. To have the professional role evaluated or to be held accountable to anyone other than professional peers is usually not part of the authority self-concept. How far an authority must go to protect his social role varies by area of specialization. The professional role seems to work best when it pertains to clearly defined activities such as dentistry. There are other roles with overlapping functions which in time evoke struggles of territoriality and influence. The area of child rearing may well be the foremost example.

The *parent role* is generally defined as meaning *responsibility for child rearing.* Responsibility means to be morally, legally, and mentally accountable. Not too many generations ago the division between parental responsibility and authority was negligible. Today with the increasing division of labor and specialized bureaus, the split between parental authority and responsibility has often reached painful and ludicrous proportions. In the case of autistic children the level of confusion and myth-beliefs of professionals has been high. This has been due to not having better knowledge available when the maintenance of the professional role demanded more special knowledge. The lack of congruity between professional role and parental role and between authority and responsibility appears to be a major source of parental disability in rearing autistic children.

Inadvertent Collusion by Role Needs

Both parents and professionals have contributed to the creation of the incongruity between parental responsibility and professional authority. Parents wanted someone to search for causes or make authoritative causal statements. Professionals wanted to fulfill this role. It is interesting that the causal emphasis with the most sustained support, parental psychopathology and mismanagement, is the least plausible from the viewpoint of empirical clinical research and observation but the most attractive from the viewpoint of social role needs. The social role demands of parental responsibility bond with a natural inclination to help and sustain the child. Parental uncertainty and self-questioning are predictable responses to the child's obscure developmental peculiarities. The professional role, on the other hand, demands authoritative responses to questions of causative probability and treatment choice. When the answers are unknown, the hypothesis of parental guilt with its treatment implications seems to be the best match for sustaining both parental and professional social roles.

A Possible Solution

Rather than dividing the two roles by authority and responsibility, we could define both roles as having authority-responsibility components, but in different circumstances.

Parents have the strongest motivation for rearing their child effectively and within the range of their own life-styles. Furthermore, parents are not hampered in their patience or diligence by the professional's need to find treatment approaches with replicable results. They can feel 100% success as long as an intervention works for their own child, even if he is the only one it works for. Thus, they do not feel the same frustration as the professional with the trial-and-error approach required by the present state of knowledge. In fact, *parents have the greatest potential for being the primary experts on their own child,* understanding his learning levels and forming realistic expectations for his future. In addition to some recognition for their authority over their child, they also are entitled to some sharing of responsibility in his care and treatment. Sharing of social responsibility for care has not in the past been extended to parents of autistic children.

In a similar vein the *professional's social role* needs to be redefined, with priority on sharing parental responsibility by *developing special service programs,* schooling, sheltered workshops, and other environmental supports. His authority should be for the understanding and development of these services and his responsibility ("accountability") should be in terms of reasonable service delivery. Instead of the traditional social role hierarchies, parental and professional authority and responsibility need to be shared. If there is any hierarchy, it is that the professional's role is to provide special support to families with a handicapped child. Since the parent's fees or taxes provide the funds for the professional, his accountability to parents cannot be denied.

Examples of Role Modification

Here are some examples from our developmental therapy program of how these roles can be modified.

> 1. The professional or therapist demonstrates special education approaches and behavior modification techniques to the parent who observes through a one-way mirror. This prevents giving advice on management procedures which cannot be practically carried out.

> 2. Rather than using as therapists specialized professionals who have both expertise and commitment to their special area of expertise, we have used non-specialized therapists. They are free to develop commitment to rational help and support for the family with the handicapped child, rather than to their own special discipline.

> 3. The criteria for successful interventions are not established in a behavioral laboratory. Instead interventions are only judged by how effective they are within the child's family and living context. If a behaviorist publishes "research proof" that a child's tantruming is extinguished by isolating him and if the use of this technique does not work in a given family, we *do not attempt to control the child's environment for scientific conformity with the behavioral lab.* Instead of assuming the parents' home environment to be ineffective, we consider that the "scientific" behavior shaping technique may be ineffective for this child. This admission frees us to search for a method to fit the child within the life-style of his family.

GUIDANCE WITH SPECIFIC PROBLEMS

Even when reasonable social supports and collaboration between parents and professionals are achieved, still remaining will be the special needs and rights of a psychotic child, which require special effort and consideration at home and in the community.

I submit that there are not many scientific problem-solving techniques available at this time for professionals to give parents. Even though there are procedures for managing behavior with systematic rewards and punishments, it is not usually the scientific method that helps the parents of autistic children. Most of them have raised other children successfully, using the intuitive parental operant procedures that long predated the psychologists' discovery of behavioral principles. They have also tried a great many different interventions with the autistic child long before they sought professional guidance. Some of their efforts are ingenious, some seem unsympathetic to the child, and others appear desperate. Usually they have also attempted some "reasonable interventions" (ones we would agree with), but not for very long and not with very much confidence or success. One strategy therefore is to have the parents try the reasonable intervention again and to support them by taking the responsibility with them for repeating the intervention. With this renewed and more confident effort, the outcome is often quite successful.

To maximize the child's adaptation within the family, *individualized solutions offer the best potential.* These solutions can be derived from asking the following kinds of questions: Can the child be taught responses to solve the management issue? Can some changes be made in the child's environment? Can the parents tolerate or accept behavior that cannot readily be modified? The solutions implied by each of these questions have attending costs and risks to be shared between parents and professionals. Individualized solutions are best made in terms of long-range treatment goals.

Treatment Goals and Severity of Impairment

Management crises of autistic children frequently result from poor fit between treatment aims for the child and the severity of his handicap. These crises usually vary according to individual personality differences and situational peculiarities. Examples are school expulsion, requests to medicate, increasing negativism, and self-destructive behavior. Whenever we had such a crisis *it invariably involved conflicting or inappropriate treatment aims* by responsible adults. To some extent, discrepancies between treatment aims and impairment are shaped by the lag between the establishment of new knowledge and its dissemination to professionals and parents.

The importance of balancing treatment aims with severity of impairment is underlined by several follow-up studies of autistic children. DeMyer's (1973) group found that 89% of the autistic children in their follow-up study were severely or moderately retarded, an even higher rate than the 68% found by Mittler et al. (1966). These IQ levels remained stable over the ten-year follow-up period. There is, in fact, no follow-up research to my knowledge that shows evidence of change in this group of children.

Treatment goals for psychotic children share a significant *commonality with those for retarded children.* (For more on the latter, see Chapter 14.) Though treatment aims will differ with every individual, the limits of adaptation can be anticipated according to the child's degree of retardation. When these limits are misjudged by either professionals or parents, the result is increased stress in adults and increased psychotic behavior in the child. Some details of adaptation levels to be anticipated according to the degree of retardation have been projected by Baroff (1974). Psychotic children with severe and profound handicaps need special help to attain the treatment aims possible for their developmental level, just like the children with milder handicaps.

Psychotic children at all developmental levels tend to need structure (Schopler, Brehm, Kinsbourne, and Reichler, 1971) and active teaching impingement in order to maximize their potential. These teaching and treatment aims need to be geared to the developmental limitations of the handicap. Professional collaboration is needed to plan and program the child's learning into specific steps of skill development and also to do so within reasonable long-range expectations. When parents can collaborate with professionals toward defining the child's reasonable long- and short-range educational needs, the interaction between child, parent, and community can proceed without undue stress and without socially exacerbated management problems.

REFERENCES

ALPERN, G.: Measurement of "untestable" autistic children. *J. Abnormal Psychol.,* 12:16-25, 1967.

BETTELHEIM, B.: *The Empty Fortress.* New York: Macmillan, 1967, p. 484.

BAROFF, G.: *Mental Retardation: Nature, Cause, and Management.* Washington, D. C.: Hemisphere Publ. Corp., 1974, pp. 28-33.

CREAK, M.: Schizophrenic syndrome in childhood: Further progress report of a working party. *Devel. Medicine and Child Neurol.,* 6:530-535, 1964.

DeMYER, M. K., BURTON, S., DeMYER, W. E., NORTON, J. A., ALLEN, J., & STEELE, R.: Prognosis in autism: A follow-up study. *J. Autism and Childhood Schizo.,* 3:199-246, 1973.

FERSTER, C. B.: Positive reinforcement and behavioral deficits of autistic children. *Child Development,* 32:437, 1961.

GITTELMAN, M. & BIRCH, J. G.: Childhood schizophrenia: Intellect, neurologic status, perinatal risk, prognosis, and family pathology. *Arch. Gen. Psych.*, 17:16-25, 1967.

KANNER, L.: Problems of nosology and psychodynamics in early infantile autism. *Am. J. Orthopsychiat.*, 19:416-426, 1949.

LOVAAS, I., KOEGEL, R., SIMMONS, J. Q., & STEVENS, J.: Some generalization and follow-up measures on autistic children in behavior therapy. *J. Appl. Behav. Anal.*, 6: 131-166, 1973.

MEYERS, D. I. & GOLDFARB, W.: Studies of perplexity in mothers of schizophrenic children. *Am. J. Orthopsychiat.*, 31:551-564, 1961.

MITTLER, P., GILLIES, S., & JUKES, E.: Prognosis in psychotic children: Report of a follow-up. *J. Ment. Defic. Research*, 10:73-83, 1966.

REICHLER, R. J. & SCHOPLER, E.: Developmental therapy: A program for providing individualized services in the community. In: *Psychopathology and Child Development.* E. Schopler & R. J. Reichler (Eds.). New York: Plenum, 1976.

REICHLER, R. J. & SCHOPLER, E.: Observations on the nature of human relatedness. *J. Autism and Childhood Schizo.*, 1:283-296, 1971.

RUTTER, M.: Concepts of autism: A review of research. *J. Child Psychol. and Psychiat.*, 9:1-25, 1968.

RUTTER, M.: The description and classification of infantile autism. In: D. Churchill, G. Alpern, & M. DeMyer (Eds.), *Infantile Autism.* Springfield: Charles C. Thomas, 1971.

SCHOPLER, E.: Parents of psychotic children as scapegoats. *J. Contemp. Psychother.*, 4:17-22, 1971.

SCHOPLER, E., BREHM, S., KINSBOURNE, M., & REICHLER, R. J.: Effect of treatment structure on development in autistic children. *Arch. Gen. Psych.*, 24:415-421, 1971.

SCHOPLER, E. & REICHLER, R. J.: Developmental therapy by parents with their own autistic child. In: M. Rutter (Ed.), *Infantile Autism: Concepts, Characteristics and Treatment.* London: Churchill Livingstone, 1971, pp. 206-227.

SCHOPLER, E. & REICHLER, R. J.: How well do parents understand their own psychotic child? *J. Autism and Childhood Schizo.*, 2:387-400, 1972.

Chapter 20

Guiding Parents of Children with Habit Symptoms

Daniel J. Safer

In children, habit disorders (special symptoms) include tics, stuttering, bed wetting, obesity, and soiling. They represent persistent, largely involuntary patterns of dyscontrol of motor functions.

The cause of habit symptoms is usually a mixture of intrapsychic conflicts, interpersonal tensions, and biological proclivity. Therefore, treatment is multimodal. A treatment emphasis on intrapsychic conflicts is appropriate for some adolescents, but slow and tedious for younger children. Interpersonal approaches, supporting parents to be therapeutic agents for their deviant offspring, constitute a mainstay in the treatment of habit-disordered children. Symptom-suppressing approaches have lately become popular; these include positive reinforcement, classical and aversive conditioning, and tranquilizing medication. This chapter will emphasize involving parents as collateral therapists in the treatment of their habit-disordered child. It will cover three aspects: strategy, objectives, and symptom-specific considerations.

STRATEGY

Focus on Central Achievable Goals

Because a child is brought for treatment of his habit disorder does not mean that the professional must immediately focus on his presenting symptom. Enuretics often have behavior problems that are far more serious. If the "soiling" child also presents rebelliousness, tantrums, and destructiveness, these misconduct patterns should receive the major early treatment emphasis. Likewise, if a child with secondary enuresis has co-existing nightmares or regressive behavior, home security issues (such as father's drinking) should receive the initial therapy focus.

Habit symptoms can usually wait or be a minor treatment focus in deference to more serious emotional problems because: 1) they generally have a good remission rate over time; 2) by themselves, they seldom *seriously* disrupt emotional, social or school functioning; 3) they may recede if more serious home difficulties lessen. One can, however, focus initially on a habit symptom if it appears to be easily manageable (e.g., by the use of conditioning treatment for nocturnal enuresis), if it indeed appears the sole problem, or if other treatment directions are blocked.

In parent counseling, the directive clinician *focuses on key behaviors* or home patterns which can: 1) when altered, have a positive influence on the child's symptoms; 2) be readily modified by a joint effort of those involved; 3) be successfully changed with modest effort. Two examples of achievable early goals are: decreasing excessive reliance on physical punishment, and increasing the use of time-out procedures in response to misconduct. Two examples of quite difficult treatment goals are: stopping the child's tics, and mediating a legal custody fight.

The emphasis on home management rather than on the concerns of neighbors or school personnel is generally appropriate for habit disorders because: 1) the home climate created by the parents will exert a primary influence on the child's behavior; 2) attemping to influence neighbors, the police, and school officials is not likely to succeed in reducing habit symptoms.

Emphasize the Positive

Most children are brought to a mental health clinic for the purpose of rectifying their undesirable behavior. Although this is appropriate, it reflects an unduly limited parental focus. Consequently, the counselor will have to work to shift a good share of the parents' attention from their child's limitations to his areas of successful potential .

Emphasizing the positive does not mean telling the parents to look the other way when their habit-disordered child violates explicit rules. Rather, it means encouraging parents to make available to the child all the opportunities (cultural, social, academic, athletic, and otherwise) which they and his siblings have had. It also means encouraging them to view their child as a person, stressing his areas of strength and letting him learn from his mistakes.

Whereas a personable attitude and a supportive posture should be unconditional, the parental offering of special privileges and rewards should not be. Positive incentives for change (e.g., extra spending money, increased social freedom) are best offered contingently (see Chapter 7). Thus, in the management of the habit-disordered child, special and attractive rewards should be offered, for example: 1) to the encopretic child —when he places his soiled underwear in the assigned bucket in the laundry room; 2) to the obese child—when he accurately charts his eating pattern; 3) to the stuttering child—when he applies his speech correction training to live situations.

Enlist Family Support and Cooperation

An effort should be made to enlist all concerned and appropriate parties to aid in the psychological management of the habit-disordered child. Even if the child receives a conditioning treatment (such as bell and pad for enuresis), he still needs a parent to set up the apparatus, awaken him if he sleeps through the alarm, and give him social and other reinforcers when he succeeds. Sibs, too, can help. Primarily, they can be encouraged to decrease or cease their teasing for soiling, tics, bed wetting, etc. Furthermore, they can help their anxious brother or sister succeed, compete, or be appropriately assertive.

The professional should direct or engineer family support along certain avenues. If the mother-son relationship unduly limits the boy socially, the father or stepfather can be encouraged to play a more helpful role with his son (see chapter 25 for more on the importance of stepparents taking an active role). Likewise, the mother or older sister can assist a teenage girl.

Adapt to the Resources Available

If the professional cannot get the parents to follow his usual recommendations or he foresees that they would be unlikely to succeed, he will have to make some adjustments to achieve and maintain a therapeutic impact. If the mother of an encopretic boy is a compulsive house-keeper and will not separate herself from her son's symptom, the professional might need to channel the mother's compulsiveness into keeping a running count of the boy's remaining clean underwear. If a parent expresses guilt that he has been repulsed by his son's habit disorder, it might be useful not to assuage this guilt, but rather to shift its direction and relate it to the treatment goals. ("You *should* feel guilty if you persist in this pattern of child rearing.")

In situations where unproductive parent responses remain intense—in spite of repeated professional efforts—a physical distance (or separation) between the parent and the symptomatic child may be advised. Patently simple separation moves include maternal employment, sending the child to an organized recreational program daily, and re-enrollment of the parent in school. One additional benefit of maternal employment is extra money, which can make the purchase of tangible reinforcements easier.

OBJECTIVES

Decrease Parents' Critical Response to the Symptom

Most parents of habit-disordered children repeatedly prod their child about his symptom. They badger him to take less fluids at night so he won't wet, check his underwear often because he soils, attempt to restrict his overeating, or constantly remind him to stop his tics and mannerisms. This directs an unpleasant, pervasively critical focus on the child. When such parental admonitions have resulted in no symptomatic benefits for the child, parents are advised to stop them.

It is not easy, however, for most parents to refrain from critical responses to behavior in their child that bothers them. Consequently, *specific alternative directions* frequently have to be given and reinforced. One method is to encourage the parent to respond to the symptom in a different and less emotional way. A parent can be directed to noncritically and mechanistically chart the child's symptom rate so that he can later reward rate decreases. Rather than constantly reminding the stuttering child to slow his speech rate, the parent can instead slow his own speech rate in all communications in the household. Still another less critical parent response involves the use of temporary exclusion. After a family rule is made that no one can "raid the refrigerator" after supper, the offending (and presumably overweight) child can be quietly but forcefully ejected from the kitchen following his transgression.

A related method of lessening a negative parental response involves the parent being *selectively inattentive* to minor expressions of the symptom, followed by a *response directed to positive elements* in the child's or his sibling's behavior. If this is too difficult (as it often is), the parent can at least say, "You did this well, but could have done better in this respect." [Contrast this with Chapter 30's warning against coupling compliments and complaints.—Ed.] A third method of altering a critical parent response is for the parent to be more selective, to respond to the child's symptom *only in the appropriate locale*. Thus, an encopretic child's smell could evoke a parental response when it is a problem to others in a family setting (e.g., in the kitchen or living room). However, the child's smell in other locations or situations should not evoke a parental response.

Interrupt Home Patterns That Reinforce the Symptom

When stuttering is aggravated by competition to speak, it would be useful to decrease this speech pressure on the child. Likewise, if obesity is supported by the offering of larger quantities of rich food at meals, such a pattern should be altered.

Increase the Child's Responsibility for His Symptom

Children should routinely take responsibility for their own clothes, hygiene, and bedroom—more so with advancing age—whether or not they have habit symptoms. It is not the parents' responsibility to bathe the encopretic child or to make him bathe when he soils. Rather, it is a parental responsibility to exclude him from family situations when he is bothersome (e.g., smelly). If the enuretic child has his own room and the mother can tolerate a wet bed behind his closed door, he can be given a supply of sheets and told to change the bed as often as he sees fit. Likewise, the overeating child can be encouraged to chart and better manage his dietary intake and to weigh himself, with appropriate parental incentives (such as new clothes or allowance adjustments) given following the attainment of a goal.

Family-Related Objectives

1. *Support a Harmonious Parental Response.* Parents naturally respond with distress, guilt, and anger to deviant patterns in their offspring. Behavioral expressions of these feelings include aggression and

protectiveness. Often, when one parent responds in an extreme manner, the other attempts to compensate, leading to a parental polarization on the matter. Therefore, one major treatment goal is to help both parents take a less extreme and a more interrelated course. Such a positive, middle path includes setting some limits, making some demands, and offering some incentives. (See Chapter 4 for more on balance and the middle road.) These naturally should be spelled out. In effect, parents are asked to chart a harmonious response, *not an identical course.*

2. *Help Draw Family Boundary Lines.* It should be stressed that parents cannot directly stop the child's habit disorder symptoms. When the symptoms occur at play or in the school room, parents cannot be there to influence them. They cannot tie their enuretic child's penis at night, plug their encopretic child's rectum, or sew down their ticquer's facial muscles.

Thus, parents should clearly appraise what they cannot successfully achieve and stay clear of it. Moreover, they should consider that they can easily impair their child's adjustment by hostile or disdainful responses to his habit symptoms. On the other hand, they should understand that if they ignore mild habit symptoms of early childhood, the chances are that these will recede in time. Generally, parents should be informed that creation of a helpful, cohesive home atmosphere is a major contribution to the emotional and behavioral adjustment of any child, habit-disordered or not.

3. *Lessen Parent-Child Conflict.* Habit-disordered children tend to develop conflicted parent-child relationships characterized by separation anxiety, seductiveness, dependency induction, or persistently hostile interchanges. Such relationships can reinforce the child's anxiety and regressive patterns of behavior. The successful lessening of such parent-child conflict will decrease home tensions and may also result in an attenuation of the child's habit disorder.

4. *Support Child's Social Achievement.* Because habit-disordered children are sensitive about their symptoms, they frequently need additional support for social activities. When faced with social adversity, the involvement of a relative, an older sib, a respected peer, or a recreation worker can help.

DISCUSSING SPECIFIC SYMPTOMS WITH PARENTS

After a thorough diagnostic evaluation, it is a useful counseling endeavor to clarify the symptom picture, its natural course, its usual consequences, its etiology, and its potential for alteration by treatment. The professional guiding the parents needs to be familiar with the following information:

Enuresis

Enuresis (urinary incontinence past age three or four) is a common age-related problem of childhood. Twelve per cent of children age six to eight wet the bed at least once a week, 5-6% at age 10-12, 3% at age 12-14, and 1-2% in young adulthood (De Jonge, 1973). Each year, 11-16% of nocturnal enuretics have a spontaneous remission.

Usually, nocturnal enuresis is not caused by an emotional disorder. However, the condition is always distressing to parents and embarrassing to children. Most nocturnal enuretics (80%) have primary enuresis, continuous since infancy. The cause of this can best be viewed as an inborn developmental deviation, largely related to inherited tendencies (Bakwin and Bakwin, 1972).

The other 20% of bedwetters have secondary enuresis; they have become continent for at least three months, but return to bedwetting —often after an emotional stress (e.g., birth of a new sib). Obviously, parent counseling is particularly appropriate for these children.

Daytime enuresis (one or more times a month) occurs for only 1-2% of children at ages 6-8. By teenage, it becomes a rarity. More so than for nocturnal enuresis, its presence tends to be *associated with emotional problems* (Rutter et al., 1973).

A medical checkup for enuresis, though a conservative precaution, is usually therapeutically unproductive. However, if the child has both diurnal and nocturnal enuresis, painful urination, or possibly a seizure pattern, a thorough examination is appropriate. Estimates of an organic etiology for enuresis range from 1-10%, with 1% being the more likely figure. Finding and treating a medical problem related to enuresis, such as a mild urinary infection, unfortunately does not usually result in a decline of the symptom.

Usually, parents of nocturnal enuretics have tried a number of methods to train their symptomatic child. These may include shaming him, attempting fluid restrictions after supper, and physically conveying him to the toilet to urinate during sleep. Less commonly used now is having the child change the bed when he awakens and hanging the wet sheets in the yard. The effectiveness of these approaches is minimal at best.

Professional approaches focusing on symptom alleviation have been numerous. Individual psychotherapy has not met with much success (De Leon and Mandell, 1966; Werry and Cohrssen, 1965). Improving day time bladder retention has been reported to reduce nocturnal enuresis (Paschalis et al., 1972), but it has been utilized only infrequently. Diet management is apparently a failure (McKendry et al., 1975). Tricyclic antidepressant drugs (e.g., imipramine) have been found to alleviate bedwetting totally in one-third of enuretics. Unfortunately, when the medication is withdrawn, a relapse is the general rule. The bell and pad conditioning apparatus is the most successful of reported therapies for symptom removal. It succeeds in 60-75% of cases, with a relapse rate of only 25%. Though widely used in England, Australia, and Canada, its use trails that of drug treatment in the United States. Operant conditioning, including "star charts" (see Chapter 7), is highly thought of, especially for preschool enuretics (Azrin and Foxx, 1976), but it has yet to be adequately compared to other treatments.

Parent counseling can cover matters such as where to obtain bell and pad equipment (e.g., a mail order catalogue). Parents should be prepared for a relatively long wait for success with the bell and pad, but a short wait with drug treatment. Discussing relapse in advance is also important. With the bell and pad approach, a relapse should simply lead to another period of treatment.

Encopresis

Encopresis is generally defined as the involuntary evacuation of feces into underclothes (or other unsuitable locations) without apparent physical cause. It occurs in 1.2.-1.5% of children at age 7-8 and declines spontaneously at a rate of 28% per year (Bellman, 1966), virtually disappearing by age 16.

Encopretics have more anxiety, conflict over aggression, enuresis, and a greater family history of soiling than do non-encopretics. One in six shows obstipation and at least one-fourth are regularly constipated. The disorder occurs infrequently during school, but commonly in play after school.

Parents of one-third of preschool encopretics appear indifferent to the problem. For the school-aged encopretic, although the symptom doesn't appear to bother the youngster, it typically infuriates the parent. The parent then pressures the child to conform to conventional bowel hygiene. This characteristically fails to produce positive results; instead, it usually leads the child to hide his soiled underwear in order to avoid punishment. When the hidden underwear is eventually found, the ensuing rebuke perpetuates this conflict pattern.

About half of encopresis is continuous—present since infancy—and half discontinuous. Stresses reported to cause regression in bowel (and bladder) control after satisfactory training are birth of a new sibling, starting school, separation of the parents (see Chapter 24 for prevention of such stress), abrupt departure of the mother, and an unacceptable degree of anger associated with a fear of injury. More so than for enuresis, a physical examination is useful for this disorder. Constipation is not an uncommon complicating factor, and when it is present, it should be treated.

A major symptomatic treatment for persistent encopresis is operant conditioning. Rewards (e.g., ice cream at night, points for a new phonograph record) are first given when frequency charting is accurate and next when a decrease in the frequency of the symptom occurs. The underwear hiding, if not influenced by positive incentives, may need to be handled more forcefully; for example, two pair of underwear not located by washtime can be replaced with money from the child's accumulated savings or allowance. Although uncommonly used, tricyclic antidepressants have been reported of value for discontinuous encopresis.

Because many encopretics have conflicts with their aggressive impulses, it is particularly useful to *help the parents stress both behavioral control and appropriate assertiveness* for their children.

Tics

Tics are recurrent, abrupt, involuntary spasms of specific skeletal muscle groups, the most common type being "eye blinking." They usually develop at ages four to nine with a prevalence at that period of 5%; by age 12, their rate decreases to 1%. *Only 6% of ticquers are said to maintain their patterns into adult life.* Within eight years after psychiatric evaluation, 50-70% of ticquers cease ticquing. Thus, the long-term prognosis is generally favorable, especially when the symptom begins early and is uncomplicated. The prognosis of multiple tics (including vocal ones) is distinctively worse (Bruun et al., 1976).

Obviously, the few cases where tics abruptly develop after a traumatic event should be explored in psychotherapy. Generally, symptomatic treatment of isolated tic patterns has usually been frustrating. Behavioral treatment (massed practice) has not lived up to early reports (Yates, 1975). Of all symptomatic treatments, only haloperidol for multiple tics has been impressive (Bruun et al., 1976). However, even its effectiveness tends to decrease with use.

Therefore, parents of children with simple tics should be advised *not to emphasize attempts to alleviate the symptom.*

Stuttering

The most common age of onset for stuttering is two to four. There is commonly a strong genetic component to the disorder. The prevalence drops from over 4% in preschoolers, to 1-2% in school age children, to less than 1% in adulthood. However, three-fourths of those who stutter at age ten retain this pattern into adulthood.

The remission rate depends on severity. Although 80% of all children who stutter cease by adulthood, only 50% of *severe* childhood stutterers are so fortunate (Sheehan and Martyn, 1970).

In selected cases, active speech correction can lessen the handicap (Van Riper, 1971). In recent years, also, the use of a hidden metronome (Brady, 1971) or of delayed auditory feedback has received favorable mention.

Parents of young stutterers should be urged to *reduce their pressures on their children*—both in speech and in other areas—and to *give them greater acceptance and approval.* Parents are also advised to downplay the teasing which stuttering children so often receive.

Obesity

Obesity, the excessive accumulation of body fat (Dwyer and Mayer, 1968), can be clinically approximated by the criterion of 20% or more above the norm in weight—relative to age, height, and sex. The prevalence of overweight is greater in relation to increasing age, female sex, and low socioeconomic status. It also has a strong familial component; it increases from 7% when neither parent is obese, to 40% with one obese parent, to 80% with both parents obese (Bayer, 1975). Of children grossly overweight at ages 9-13, 83% continued obese as middle-aged adults (Abraham et al., 1971). The heavier the child and the earlier the onset of weight excess, the greater the likelihood of adult obesity.

Four psychological and behavioral patterns characterize the juvenile obese: 1) body image problems—a feeling of loathing about their body; 2) overeating; 3) underactivity; and 4) a tendency to be influenced externally in their eating: the more available the food and the more cues for eating, the more they eat.

Weight control programs produce little or no *long-range* symptomatic benefit. However, behaviorally oriented programs stressing the recording of eating habits and food intake and the reinforcement of "desirable" eating patterns result in more short-range weight loss than do diet-oriented group programs (Stunkard, 1975). The efficacy of these efforts has, unfortunately, not been reported for obese youth.

Common parent responses to their child's overeating include threats, scare tactics, and the restriction of access to food. Such methods are "time honored" by failure. Instead, parents should shift the burden of change to the child. Because of their superior results in the treatment of excess weight in adults, behavioral methods can be tried. The parental effort would be directed to increasing the obese child's motivation to alter his eating pattern by tangibly reinforcing achievement of goals specified in a behavioral contract.

An alternative approach is to alter the eating pattern of all members of the household. This is generally not acceptable, but on occasion a major change in circumstances (e.g., moving to Hawaii and shifting to the native vegetarian diet) can do it. Drug management is not recommended for obese children because it does not produce long-term benefits. Intestinal bypass surgery has not been used to treat obesity in minors.

CONCLUDING COMMENTS

It is too often *insufficient* to focus on the family dynamics of a youngster with secondary enuresis without considering symptomatic treatments. It is too often *inaccurate* to tell a parent to ignore the stuttering of his four-year-old son because the boy "will outgrow it." It is too often *incomplete* to engage a seven-year-old encopretic boy in play therapy and fail to request a complete physical examination. It is too often *callous* to treat a developmental or habit disorder as if the outcome depended upon professional intervention.

Counseling parents of habit-disordered children is not simply an attempt to curtail adverse environmental influences and initiate a growth-inducing home atmopshere. It also entails providing the parents with complete information. This should include details about the disorder, its seriousness, its prevalence, its developmental nature, its usual outcome, its medical aspects, its usual effect on parents, its effect on the child's peer relationships, alternative treatment considerations, and treatment benefits and limitations. The professional, the parents, and the child build on this knowledge to develop a coordinated and comprehensive effort aimed at the successful alleviation of the habit-disordered child's distress.

REFERENCES

ABRAHAM, S., COLLINS, G., & NORDSIECK, M.: Relationship of childhood weight status to morbidity in adults. *HSMHA Health Reports,* 86:273-284, 1971.

AZRIN, N. H. & FOXX, R. M.: *Toilet Training in Less Than a Day.* New York: Pocket Books, 1976.

BAKWIN, H. & BAKWIN, R. M.: *Behavior Disorders in Children,* 4th Edition. Philadelphia: W. B. Saunders, 1972.

BELLMAN, M.: Studies on encopresis. *Acta Paediatrica Scandinavica* Suppl., 170:1-151, 1966.

BRADY, J. P.: Metronome conditioned speech retraining for stuttering. *Behav. Therap.,* 2:129-150, 1971.

BRUUN, R. D., SHAPIRO, E., SWEET, R., WAYNE, H., & SOLOMON, G.: A follow-up of 78 patients with Gilles de la Tourette's syndrome. *Amer. J. Psychiat.,* 133:944-947, 1976.

DE JONGE, G. A.: Epidemiology in enuresis: A survey of the literature. *Clin. Develop. Med.,* 48/49:39-46, 1973.

DE LEON, G. & MANDELL, W.: A comparison of conditioning and psychotherapy in the treatment of functional enuresis. *J. Clin. Psychol.,* 22:326-330, 1966.

DWYER, J. & MAYER, J.: Psychological effects of variation in physical appearance during adolescence. *Adolescence,* 3:353-380, 1968.

MAYER, J.: Obesity during childhood. In: M. Winick (Ed.), *Childhood Obesity.* New York: Wiley and Sons, pp. 73-80, 1975.

PASCHALIS, A. P., KIMMEL, H. D., & KIMMEL, E.: Further study of diurnal instrumental conditioning in the treatment of enuresis nocturna. *J. Behav. Therap. and Exper. Psychiat.,* 3:253-256, 1972.

RUTTER, M., YULE, W., & GRAHAM, P.: Enuresis and behaviour deviance: Some epidemiological considerations. *Clin. Develop. Med.,* 48/49:137-147, 1973.

SHEEHAN, J. G. & MARTYN, M. M.: Stuttering and its disappearance. *J. Speech and Hearing Res.,* 13:279-289, 1970.

STUNKARD, A. J.: From explanation to action in psychosomatic medicine: The case of obesity. *Psychosom. Med.,* 37:195-236, 1975.

VAN RIPER, C. G.: *The Nature of Stuttering.* Englewood Cliffs, N. J.: Prentice-Hall, 1971.

WERRY, J. & COHRSSEN, J.: Enuresis—an etiologic and therapeutic study. *J. Pediat.,* 67:423-431, 1965.

YATES, A.: *Theory and Practice in Behavior Therapy.* New York: Wiley-Interscience, 1975.

Chapter 21

Parents of Delinquents
in Juvenile Court

Richard S. Benedek and

Elissa P. Benedek

We are concerned here with the parents of a youngster who finds himself in juvenile court because of delinquency. (Different considerations apply to matters such as neglect or abuse, discussed in Chapter 22.) Since the child or his family are frequently in the midst of treatment with another agency or practitioner at the time that juvenile court comes into the picture, we will discuss the role of the professional from the outside agency as well as that of the court social worker or "probation officer." If the court professional and outside professional are to work together, as should often be the case, it is important that they understand each other's problems with respect to dealing with the parents.

The unique character of juvenile court has a profound impact upon everyone—parents, children, and professionals—who comes within its province. Therefore, our discussion initially turns to the special nature of this unusual institution.

THE NATURE OF JUVENILE COURT

Juvenile court is something of a *hybrid*, possessing characteristics of both criminal courts and social agencies. Up to the time that it is determined that the minor has committed the offense with which he is charged, the court resembles a *conventional criminal court*. After this, however, the court's *social agency characteristics* become, or should become, more significant.

The function of most criminal courts is essentially twofold: 1) to determine whether the accused is guilty; 2) if so, to punish him—rehabilitation seems rarely considered—or to "give him another chance," i.e., probation, which frequently involves little or no meaningful treatment. The first of the two functions of juvenile court is similar to adult criminal court: to determine whether the minor has committed an offense. The second function also often looks unfortunately similar, amounting to little more than the meting out of punishment or awarding of probation. However, if the juvenile court is to realize its full potential, its objective should differ to include understanding and modifying behavior.

In this respect the court closely resembles social agencies. Unlike such agencies, though, the court has the power to order the treatment it prescribes. Such treatment, sometimes with justification, is often viewed as punishment. Indeed, primarily because of the court's power to mandate a course of action which may interfere with one's personal liberty, the Supreme Court has concluded that minors there possess rights similar to those of adults in criminal courts.

The Hearings

In order to adequately safeguard the minor's rights, juvenile systems typically provide for a hearing at each critical stage. However, particularly where the charge is not contested, these hearings are sometimes combined or dispensed with entirely. Usually, there is an intake procedure (with an interview by a social worker) for the purpose of determining whether the court should entertain the complaint filed by the police officer or other interested party. The minor may next be entitled to a preliminary or probable cause hearing, roughly analogous to an adult's right to indictment. If the case is not dismissed then, a fact hearing or trial, sometimes with the right to a jury, must take place. If the minor is found to have committed the offense, a dispositional hearing follows. This is comparable to the sentencing stage in criminal court, although the hearing at this juncture in juvenile court may be more extensive. During the ensuing treatment phase, there may be a number of review hearings.

Differences from Social Agencies

With respect to treatment, there are fundamental differences between juvenile court and social agencies. Professionals must not only familiarize themselves with such differences but withstand any temptation to ignore or resist them because of their unalterable nature. The more significant of these readily emerge from even a cursory review of the juvenile court process: the existence of *extraordinary rights of the client* which cannot be tampered with by the "agency"; the correlative *extraordinary power* of the "agency" *to order the treatment* it prescribes and *impose punishment* for one's failure to comply; and, perhaps implicit, the fact that the adolescent, the primary object of the "agency's" attention, is almost invariably *present involuntarily* and frequently against the wishes of his parents as well.

The client has not come to the court because of his anxiety, psychic pain, or any form of recognized personal maladjustment. Initially, he is there because he is charged with having committed an offense; subsequently, he is there because he has been found to have done so. Accordingly, children and their parents may view the court as an instrument of punishment rather than help. They may be hostile, angry, suspicious, and not overly interested in entering into a therapeutic alliance.

Implications for the Professional

The fact that the court is often dealing with recalcitrant clients may dictate maintaining a low profile during the initial stage of the court's intervention, when the minor and his parents may be contesting the charges. This is clearly their right. Even if its exercise is ill-advised in a particular case, interfering with this right (or seeming to) may make it considerably more difficult to establish the necessary rapport later.

The behavioral professional may find it difficult to orient or maintain his thinking along lines compatible with the judicial process. Yet, he must learn to maneuver within its framework before he can help the parents to profit from their experience there. This includes recognition and acceptance of the *parties' rights*. The attorney, in particular, should not be viewed as an obstacle to treatment. Rather, if at all possible, his presence should be exploited by the professional to the advantage of his client. Moreover, many behavioral professionals are inclined to rely upon intuition and find it difficult to accept a judge's traditional insistence upon the need for facts. They may also become impatient with a judge's failure to consider psychological motivations or his propensity for dictating meaningless platitudes. To be relevant in this context, the professional must be able not only to influence the court's decisions when it is appropriate to do so, but also to utilize the court's structure to his therapeutic advantage.

ROLE OF THE "OUTSIDE" PROFESSIONAL

There will naturally be times when a minor becomes involved with juvenile court while he or his family are in the midst of treatment with an "outside" agency. Under such trying circumstances it is particularly important to provide continued support. Initially, the outside professional must deal with the anxiety or anger of the family and adequately prepare it for this new experience. However, if he is unable to identify and handle his own feelings, this will prevent him from accomplishing anything productive during the term of the juvenile court's involvement.

Therapists' Reactions

Therapists frequently feel protective towards their clients and responsible for their actions outside of treatment. Truancy, shoplifting, or other deviant behavior is often identified as acting-out in the transference and attributed to events in therapy. Even when this explanation is valid, it is hardly sufficient to guarantee immunity from juvenile court intervention. Once the court becomes involved, the outside professional loses a degree of control over the case. He may consider this situation an indication of treatment failure. Like the parents, he may feel guilty, concluding that better therapy or a more skillful intervention could have prevented the offensive behavior. His therapeutic omniscience and omnipotence may both be threatened. Thus, in order to continue to help the parents, the professional must pay close attention to his own feelings.

It is important that the outside professional refrain from making excuses or vindicating himself. The professional should avoid translating his own feelings of inadequacy into complaints about court personnel. As a projection of his own "failure," it is easy to see the court as mishandling a case. Feelings of anger or guilt inadequately coped with provide a poor model for the parents. The ultimate consequence of his failure to identify and handle his own feelings may well be the sabotaging, consciously or unconsciously, of any treatment efforts by the court. His first task is to ease the family's transfer from one agency to another, although it is entirely possible that he will continue to participate in treatment. Since his ultimate role may initially be somewhat uncertain, he must be careful not to allow this uncertainty to upset the family or interfere with his judgment.

Protecting by Preparing

The outside professional should protect the family against any inappropriate reaction to the juvenile court by preparing them. He should spend some time with a court professional to acquaint himself with local practice and programs. The participants whose roles should be defined for the parents are ordinarily the *judge* or *referee, prosecuting attorney, defense counsel, social workers* (sometimes referred to as *probation officers*), as well as the youngster, his parents, and witnesses. The series of hearings described under "The Nature of Juvenile Court" should be outlined for the parents.

Though sufficiently conversant with juvenile court to discuss it intelligently, the outside professional must still bear in mind that he is not an authority and avoid overpreparing the family. Initially, he will probably have to deal with the family's anxiety. A degree of anxiety may be beneficial and prove therapeutic. Unrealistic or excessive anxiety should be allayed. Parents may be threatened by the possibility of separation, both from the outside agency and, even worse, from their child. Where such fears appear to be totally irrational, they should be assuaged.

On the other hand, it is important to refrain from making promises as to what the court will or will not do. If the professional turns out to be wrong, his credibility will be jeopardized. Moreover, any false promise or other misinformation may induce the family to deal inappropriately with the court and impair its treatment efforts. Misleading the family is also bound to disturb court personnel and this, in turn, may destroy the outside professional's chances for establishing the necessary rapport with them.

The outside professional should encourage the parents to cooperate with their child's attorney and be willing to do so himself. There are instances where the minor's interests are at odds with those of his parents, such as when the parents (perhaps with the concurrence of the professional) feel that proper disposition calls for residential placement, while the minor remains intent upon an entirely different "sentence." In such cases the parents may even wish to retain counsel to represent them, but they should not expect their child's attorney, even if secured by them, to advocate a course likely to be perceived by the minor as betrayal.

Cooperating with the Attorney

It is entirely appropriate for the professional to tell the attorney what he feels to be in the youngster's best interests. Although this is primarily so with respect to the disposition or treatment, it may also apply to whether the charge should be contested. Likewise, it is proper for the attorney, if sold on the wisdom, to attempt to persuade his client. However, if the minor remains adamant, we believe his attorney is bound to articulate his position. The professional should respect this attorney-client relationship and also help the parents to understand it. Once the minor has been found to have committed the offense, the outside professional, unlike the attorney, is entirely free to urge upon the court any disposition that he believes appropriate, irrespective of the minor's wishes.

The outside professional who has been treating the family is often in an excellent position to know its strengths and weaknesses, understand its problems, and have some idea as to which therapeutic techniques are or are not likely to be effective with it. Therefore, it will probably be to the family's advantage to have him share this information with the court, particularly at the dispositional stage. This should be explained to the parents. Once in juvenile court, families sometimes fail to disclose prior contact with other agencies, even in response to inquiries specifically addressed to this point. The professional should ordinarily be willing to share information, and the parents should be encouraged to take the necessary measures to facilitate his doing so.

Taking the Initiative

There may even be occasions when the outside professional feels it would be best for the family if he were to take the initiative and contact the court without even waiting to hear from personnel there. For instance, if he believes that the court, in essence, should refer the case to him for treatment or that he should at least share in the treatment, he is probably wise to communicate these sentiments to the court as early as possible.

The advantages of this course of action should naturally be discussed with the family before securing from it the necessary permission to do so. The juvenile court, of course, will ordinarily play the major role in determining the extent to which he will continue to participate in treatment, and the parents should be made aware of this fact. Particularly where his relationship with the family is intense, the professional should carefully examine his own motivations and feelings before concluding that he should no longer take part in the case or that he should not enter into any discussion with the court. However, even where he concludes that it would be best for the family if his role were to be phased out, he may still wish to give court personnel the benefit of his experience—e.g., relative to the kinds of intervention that are likely to succeed.

THE COURT PROFESSIONAL

Once it has been determined that the minor has committed the offense with which he is charged, the court professional must ordinarily recommend to the judge a suitable disposition. In some cases (the minority) placement will be called for. Although many courts are staffed to provide a variety of treatment, others possess neither sufficient nor adequately trained personnel and, consequently, refer most cases. Sometimes, where the minor or his parents are already in treatment, it is desirable to continue or at least share this treatment, irrespective of the court's own resources. Thus, the emotional state of the family must be evaluated (beginning with the intake stage may be none too soon) in order to deal with its emotions and defenses.

Parental Reactions

Juvenile court involvement, primarily because of its criminal implications, may cause parents to react in ways subject to misinterpretation or inconsistent with treatment goals. Parents frequently exhibit *denial* with respect to their child's problems. For instance, even though advised by school personnel that some form of action will be taken if truancy persists, parents are still often stunned when this eventuates in juvenile court intervention. They may act out in a number of ways, such as absence or tardiness for appointments. Conversely, some parents insist that placing their child is necessary, even though such a course of action is inappropriate. The professional must be able to recognize and make the parents understand their motivations and, perhaps, overreaction, reflecting their own frustration—a sense of being at the end of their rope. Their particular concerns, problems, and anxieties must ordinarily be recognized, acknowledged, and dealt with before they can become productively involved in the court process.

Orientation

Parents are more likely to respond to juvenile court in the most beneficial manner if not preoccupied with their own bewilderment. Court personnel become so familiar with the order and purpose of the several hearings, the roles of the various characters, and the variety of available dispositions that it is easy for them to become contemptuous of the fact that families are often totally ignorant, if not misinformed or even overwhelmed. Even if they have been in treatment with another agency, it is entirely possible that they will have received either no information or misinformation about what will take place. Frequently, orientation is provided both at the intake and dispositional or treatment stages. This policy, though desirable, sometimes results in both the intake worker and the probation officer assuming that the other has the primary orientation responsibility. Consequently, neither adequately informs the parents. Obviously, both should take this task seriously.

It is important that the parents be *educated as to the nature and purpose of the hearings* that are to be held at the various stages of the proceedings, and the roles of the judge, social worker, prosecutor, and attorney for the minor. Included in a discussion of the latter should be some exploration of the possibility of retained counsel, court appointed counsel, and, in some jurisdictions, the public defender. It is also necessary for parents to understand their own right to counsel since their child's attorney should not be expected to advocate their position if adverse to what the minor perceives as his own best interests. The child and his parents must be advised at the intake stage of the nature of the charge and of their rights. While one must be careful to avoid promising what the judge will do, one may at times wish to inform the parents what is likely to occur next, in order to allay their fears. At the proper time, the parents should also be familiarized with the variety of dispositions and forms of treatment that are possible. Where appropriate, their input with respect to this should be solicited. This may enhance their sense of involvement and increase their investment in the course of treatment that is selected.

It is not uncommon for families to expect the court to perform miracles. Perhaps conditioned by television, and caught up in their own fantasies, wishes, and needs, they envision a magical judge making short shrift of problems that may have developed over a period of years. Sometimes parents have heard of success that the court has had with another youngster and anticipate similar results in their case, although the circumstances may be entirely different. There are occasions when parents feel that placement is the only solution and take for granted that the court will be their ally, if not their agent, in bringing about this outcome. It is not nearly sufficient for the court professional to merely spell out the various dispositions and forms of treatment that are available either in the court or as a consequence of its intervention. He must help the parents to discover and limit their expectations and assist them to acquire a realistic perspective with respect to what the court can and cannot do. It is not inappropriate to point out that the court has neither unlimited financial nor therapeutic resources at its disposal, that behavioral science itself has limitations, and that the court's goals may differ from those of the parents.

Parents, Child, and Attorney

An attorney retained by the parents for their child, or even one who is appointed, may also be unfamiliar with juvenile practice, let alone with the court's services or philosophy. He may be inexperienced or uncomfortable with juvenile clients. Under such circumstances he is likely to feel threatened by court professionals and generally behave in a defensive manner. It is, of course, entirely proper for the atttorney's objectives to differ from those of the court professional. Because on occasion he is able to achieve his objectives even in the face of opposition from the court, court professionals often also feel threatened by attorneys. A *divisive tug of war* can develop whereby a wedge may be driven between the court professional and the parents or between the parents and the attorney. Many attorneys do know their way around juvenile court and, while advocating their client's position, are also sophisticated in cooperating with court personnel.

The court professional is actually in an excellent position to assist the attorney: 1) by educating him about the court and his role there, and 2) by aiding him in his communications and dealings with the child and his parents. Indeed, he may be best able to define common goals and coordinate joint efforts. However, tact is necessary in dealing with the attorney to establish a working relationship with him. For instance, if the court professional thinks it desirable therapeutically for the minor not to contest the charge, he should carefully explain his reasons. However, he should realize that attorneys are not behavioral scientists and that a youngster may reasonably oppose "copping-out."

Often the judge is most likely to agree to a disposition that is acceptable to the parents and the minor's attorney as well as to the court professional. Such *consensus* also *enhances the chances for success* in treatment. While it is desirable to spell this out for the parents and, if possible, to work with the attorney toward achieving this end, the professional should respect the right of the adolescent, through his attorney, to try for what he may perceive as a "lighter sentence." This, of course, does not mean that the professional should not continue to press for the disposition that he feels is appropriate. However, he should keep the parents advised of his reasons for doing so. It is important to refrain from acting in a manner likely to be interpreted as contrary to the child's interests; this is bound to make later dealings with the parents unnecessarily difficult.

Countertransference

Although therapists often recognize difficulties in treating clients who fall into specific diagnostic categories (e.g., personality disorders) because of the special countertransference reactions they provoke, much less frequently do they acknowledge problems with clients belonging to distinct age groups, such as adolescent or geriatric. Even when such difficulties are identified, the conscious or unconscious dynamics are seldom examined. These dynamics assume particular significance when treating the entire nuclear family, as is generally the case in juvenile court, since it becomes necessary to work simultaneously with two generations of clients.

The court professional often belongs to the same generation as the adolescent. In fact, the age difference between these two may be relatively insignificant in contrast to the considerable age disparity between either of them and the parents. The professional may still be involved in intrapsychic conflicts much like those of the minor, such as concerns about separation or relationships with authority figures. Their views about sexual freedom or drug use may also be quite similar and in con-

flict with those of the parents. This can result in the *professional identifying with the minor inappropriately* and being perceived by the
parents, sometimes with justification, as an adversary.

Such an atmosphere can make it very difficult for the professional to
provide adequate assistance to the parents, particularly if he interprets as
pathology attitudes which merely reflect a generation gap. (See Chapter
13.) Sometimes, he consciously or unconsciously minimizes contacts with
the parents. It is important for the professional to pay close attention to
his own strengths and weaknesses. If he generally has difficulty relating
to parents vis-à-vis their child, he must work through this problem
and, when necessary, candidly seek supervision or consultation with a
colleague.

Find the Strengths

While the professional may perceive himself primarily in the light
of his strengths, families with delinquents may become quite accustomed to presenting their weaknesses. It is not difficult for professionals
to accept the pictures of gloom and doom that are unfolded before
them. Yet, even the family that is beset with problems is frequently able
to draw upon untapped resources in times of stress. Thus, exploration
should center on family dynamics and on assisting the parents to discover and build upon such positive forces as may be available to them.
While psychological strengths may be most vital and best concealed,
the significance of *financial or familial resources* must not be overlooked
either. Parents are often greatly relieved to learn that placement with a
stable member of the family who has expressed interest in the child may
be a viable alternative to institutionalization.

Included among the family's resources may be an ongoing *treatment
relationship with another agency*. If such a relationship exists, every
effort must be made to determine whether disposition should result in
the case being referred back to that agency or, at least, in treatment
being shared with it to some extent. Irrespective of whether the family
is currently in treatment, the modes of treatment previously employed
and their successes or failures are relevant to the disposition that should
be made by the court. The court professional must be willing to share
information about the family's strengths and weaknesses and treatment
alternatives. Also, he must be prepared to cooperate with an outside
agency.

Practical Dispositions

The court professional must, in this context, recognize and deal with the parents' financial and time limitations as well as with their attitudes toward the outside agency. Insistence upon a great deal of court involvement at the same time as contact with another agency is encouraged or ordered may place an undue burden on the parents, causing them to fail the court, the outside agency, or both. Not only must the professional acquaint himself with the parents' particular financial situation, he should also have some ideas about alternative approaches to funding that may be available. He should acquire an understanding of the commitments of time and money that the family can reasonably be expected to make. He must involve parents in these considerations. Apart from contributing necessary input, such involvement is also likely to make them more receptive to the disposition and responsive to treatment.

In addition to information received from the parents and from an outside professional, the court professional should be thoroughly familiar with the dispositional resources generally available to the court. His awareness and rapport should extend beyond the local community, since in some instances, particularly with respect to placement, it is necessary to look elsewhere. There will be occasions when it becomes necessary to persuade an agency or residential treatment center of the desirability of its participation in a given case. It is naturally easier to accomplish this if the court professional and outside professional have some confidence in one another. Similarly, if the parents indicate a predisposition on their part to cooperate, this is likely to enhance the prospects of a reluctant agency agreeing to intervene. The parents will probably be far more receptive to the prospective disposition or placement if the court professional speaks to them about this from a position of genuine familiarity with the agency that is being considered. This will also ease the transfer of the parents from the court to that agency or treatment center.

Remember the Sibs

Especially where residential placement becomes necessary (although by no means limited to these situations), juvenile court involvement can have a great impact on the minor's siblings. They may feel stigmatized because a member of their family is in court. More significant are the psychological effects of separation and loss. The long-term consequences of such emotional reactions may be easily overlooked by the parents, and it is up to the court professional to explain. He must also be willing to see the siblings, either individually or in family interviews, and he should encourage the parents to make them available as circumstances dictate. He should make certain that the parents appreciate the importance of such contacts and properly prepare the children for them.

Part IV

Guiding Parents Who Have Specific Problems

Chapter 22

Help for

Abusing Parents

Vincent J. Fontana and

Cecilia Schneider

Until recently, few efforts were made to rehabilitate abusive parents. Therapy was rarely offered. Even now, a punitive, anti-parent view is still advocated by many laymen, as well as by a number of professionals. Nevertheless, it has been proven by some existing treatment and prevention programs that rehabilitation is possible in the majority of cases.

It is, of course, not only the identified abused child who should concern us. Abusing parents may already have, or may in the future have, other children who can be mistreated. So, obviously, handling the immediate situation is only one aspect of the professional's responsibility. Under-

---

Dr. Fontana is Chairman of the New York City Mayor's Task Force on Child Abuse and Neglect; founder of Temporary Shelter Rehabilitation Program for Abusing Parents; member of Board of Directors of National Committee on Child Abuse and author of *The Maltreated Child* and *Somewhere a Child Is Crying*. Ms. Schneider cooperated in setting up The New York Foundling Hospital's Temporary Shelter Rehabilitation Program for Abusing Parents.

standing the total pattern of life in that family and instituting necessary remedial measures offer the only real chance for breaking the pattern of child abuse (Irwin, 1974).

Child abuse is by no means a new phenomenon. Any person placed in a social or psychological situation conducive to violent behavior, subjected to marital discord, financial stress, a crying, wailing disobedient child, impersonal urban living, bereft of the helping role of relatives and neighbors, could do the "unthinkable" and turn, in a given moment, upon one's own child (Dankerbring 1971). Under the stress of modern living, in our violence-prone society, child abuse is more prevalent today than ever before.

Abused or neglected children range from the simple undernourished infant reported as "failure to thrive" to the "battered child" who may be dead on arrival. Gradations in between include bruises, abrasions, burns, fractures, dehydration from water deprivation, and acute abdominal trauma. It is not only physical battering that is damaging to a child. Verbal or psychological abuse is equally responsible for future emotional abnormalities. Parents who continuously criticize, demean, reject, or ignore a child, as well as those who sexually exploit a child, inflict psychological injury.

RECOGNIZING THE ABUSIVE PARENT

Our studies of parents who neglect and maltreat their children indicate that some are emotionally immature, some are sadistic, and others are neurotic or psychotic. Some are drug addicts or alcoholics, and others are severe disciplinarians. Many of these parents have a genuine feeling for their children but lack the ego strength to cope with their problematic behavior. It is a fallacy to assume that child abuse is committed only in the slums by people who are mentally ill. Among the middle and upper classes, child neglect and abuse occur secretly behind closed doors and shuttered windows.

Abuse and neglect may be suspected when several of the following factors are in evidence (Fontana 1973):

The parent or parents discourage social contact.

The parent seems to be very much alone and to have no one to call upon when the stresses of parenthood get to be overwhelming.

The parent is unable to open up and share problems with an interested listener and appears to trust nobody.

The parent makes no attempt to explain the child's most obvious injuries or offers absurd, contradictory explanations.

The parent seems to be quite detached from the child's problems.

The parent reveals inappropriate lack of awareness of the seriousness of the child's condition and concentrates on complaining about irrelevant problems.

The parent blames a sibling or third party for the child's injury.

The parent shows signs of lack of control or fear of losing control.

The parent delays in taking the child in for medical care, either in case of injury or illness, or for routine checkups.

The parent appears to be misusing drugs or alcohol.

The parent ignores the child's crying or reacts with extreme impatience.

The parent has unrealistic expectations of the child: that he should be mature beyond his years; that he should "mother" the parent.

The parent indicates in the course of the conversation that he/she was reared in a motherless, unloving atmosphere; that he or she was neglected or abused as a child; that he or she grew up under conditions of harsh discipline and feels that it is right to impose those same conditions on his or her own children.

The parent appears to be of borderline intelligence, psychotic, or psychopathic. (Most laypersons will find it difficult to make a judgment here. It might be better for the observer to note whether the parent exhibits the minimal intellectual equipment to bring up a child; whether the parent is generally rational or irrational in manner; whether the parent is cruel, sadistic, and lacking remorse for hurtful actions.) However, only about 10% of abusing parents are psychotic.

The child seems unduly afraid, especially of his parents.

The child is kept confined, as in a crib or playpen (or cage), for overlong periods of time.

The child shows evidence of repeated skin or other injuries.

The child's injuries are inappropriately treated in terms of bandages and medication.

The child appears undernourished.

The child is given inappropriate food, drink or medicine.

The child is dressed inappropriately for weather conditions.

The child shows evidence of overall poor care.

The child cries often.

The child is described as "different" or "bad" by the parents.

The child does indeed seem deviant physically, emotionally, or behaviorally.

The child takes over the role of parent and tries to be protective or otherwise take care of the parent's needs.

Most states have laws that not only require the reporting of suspected abuse but also grant immunity from liability to *bona fide* reporters. What should one say to a parent he is about to report for suspected child abuse or neglect? One approach might be: "I am obligated by state law to report any injury that is hard to explain in order to get some help for you and the child." Emphasize to the parents that this is a means of securing help for the family and not just a report to the police. They should also be assured that the report will be kept confidential.

UNDERSTANDING AND APPROACHING ABUSING PARENTS

The maltreated child is usually the victim of *emotionally crippled* parents who have had unfortunate circumstances surrounding their own childhood. The abusive parent appears to react to his own child as a result of past personal experiences of loneliness, lack of protection and love. Some of these parents have been raised by a variety of foster parents. Many have experienced intense, continuous demands from their own parents, accompanied by constant parental criticism and rejection. Their parents may have given them a great deal of attention, but of a harsh, demanding, and critical nature. Inevitably the child (parent-to-be) feels rejected, unloved, and unwanted, with his own needs unfulfilled. Such maternal deprivation experienced in early childhood leaves the parent with an inadequate "mothering" imprint. (See Chapter 28 for more about the child-parent relationship as antecedent basis for the parent-child relationship.)

Having experienced a lack of adequate parenting themselves, such parents have very unreal expectations of their children, as well as difficulty in establishing a trusting relationship with other adults. This distrust of others is reinforced by a series of disappointments by one's family, peers, and marital partner. These mothers' marital relationships are based, for the most part, not on love and affection, but rather on a desperate, dependent fear of loneliness. Oftentimes, the mate also expresses violent reactions during crisis situations, inflicting physical abuse upon the mother and/or child. Both may act infantile and explosive, with a low tolerance for frustration and poor impulse control.

Abusive parents have *little or no self-esteem*, a sense of incompetence and a deep lack of basic trust for others. They tend to lead a life of isolation, having no friends, belonging to no community organizations and having little or nothing to do with relatives.

The abusing parent frequently has a *history of having been brutalized* himself as a child and so the pattern of violent behavior perpetuates itself from generation to generation. These parents are unable to distinguish between their own childhood suffering and their vicious reactions toward their children. Their parents were usually immature, narcissistic, egocentric, demanding, impulsive, depressed, and aggressive. They appear unwilling or unable to accept responsibility as parents. They appear to have disorted perception of a particular child at a particular stage in its development. When the child is not able to perform, the parents may be triggered into a reaction leading to abuse.

Role Reversal

The abusive parents show inappropriate expectations of their children, with a *reversal of dependency needs*. The parent deals with the child as if the child were older than the parent. The parent will often turn to the child for reassurance, nurturing, comfort, and protection, and expect a loving response.

Paradoxically, such parents also expect their children to be submissive and to follow orders. They display a sense of righteousness about discipline for their children if they don't obey. The parents may have excessively ambivalent feelings of love and anger toward the child. The mother may hit the child at one moment and embrace the child moments later.

Why Do Parents Abuse?

Divorce, alcoholism, drug addiction, mental retardation, recurring mental illness, unemployment, and financial stress are important factors often present in the family structure of abusing parents. Three components—a potentially abusing parent, a child, and a sudden crisis—are the necessary ingredients for child abuse and battering. Maltreating parents are unable to deal with crises, whether financial, social, or environ-

mental. Even the breakdown of a household appliance may seem overwhelming. At the same time, they are unable to obtain help or comfort
from others because of their social isolation. They may unrealistically
turn to the child for help. The child's inability to provide adequate
comfort or help is interpreted as deliberate withholding, making him an
apparently suitable target for the ensuing volcanic eruption of frustration and anger. In many cases this essentially represents an immature
tantrum by the parent directed toward a child who has been unwittingly
cast in the role of a withholding, depriving parent to the parent.

Accepting a basic premise that the majority of abusive and neglectful
parents have themselves experienced physical or emotional abuse and
violence to some degree in their own early childhood will allow the
therapist to deal effectively with the parents in an empathetic manner
without necessarily condoning their action.

Establishing Rapport

With this understanding, how should the professional attempt to relate
to a referred abusing parent at first contact? One way might be to say:
"It is our hope that we can help you as a parent find answers to many
of your troubles. Through this counseling you will learn how to understand your child, cope with his problems, cope with your own problems,
and find a way of developing a loving, secure relationship with him. The
outcome depends on your cooperation, understanding, patience, and
wisdom. We will work with you to build a more constructive family life
in which parents and children can live together helping each other."

One obstacle to rapport faced by many professionals is a natural
repugnance to the abusing parent. Despite an intellectual understanding
of the foregoing, professionals who care about children may be overwhelmed by anger or hostility at the brutal act of the parent. In extreme
cases, it may be necessary to refer to a colleague who can be more
objective. Often, however, the professional can resolve his negative feelings sufficiently by taking some time out to deal with them before
attempting to help the parent. One technique might be to review the
material above. Ventilation with supportive colleagues or a supervisor
may help. In some cases it may help to displace the anger onto the
grandparents, who deprived the parents of the kind of childhood needed
to become adequate parents. Actually, the blame—if one feels a need to
blame—can often be traced to the great grandparents or great, great
grandparents . . . to Adam and Eve?

How can we obtain adequate parenting for the child in the future? Two major intervention options exist: 1) A permanent substitute parent can be provided through foster home placement (see Chapter 27 for guidance of foster parents); 2) efforts can be made to enable the parent to function more appropriately (rehabilitation or treatment).

There is at present no evidence to indicate that any one approach to the treatment of abusive parents is more effective than another. A variety of innovative crisis intervention programs staffed by various disciplines with different techniques are providing effective models. Expertise and time are required to unravel the causative factors. Social and environmental factors may be found which, though objectively undesirable, are not necessarily responsible for the parent's malfunctioning; the adverse social factors may be the result of the parent's psychological state rather than the cause. If the physician lacks training, time, and interest to ascertain which factors are responsible for the child abuse situation, an evaluation by a social worker, psychologist, or psychiatrist is essential.

Improving the Parent's Functioning

Ideally, each parent should have an intervention plan developed for her or him based upon an assessment of a number of factors which include:

1. The factors responsible for the parent's dysfunction.
2. The severity of the parent's psychopathology.
3. The overall prognosis for achieving adequate mothering.
4. Time estimated to achieve meaningful change in the mother's ability to mother.
5. Whether the parent's dysfunction is confined to this infant or involves all of her children.
6. The extent to which the mother's malfunctioning extends to her roles, i.e., wife, homemaker, housekeeper.
7. The extent to which the parent's overall malfunctioning, if this is the case, is acute or chronic (reflects a lifelong pattern).
8. The extent to which the mother's malfunctioning is confined to infants as opposed to older children. (The incidence of abuse is inverse to the child's age.)
9. The parent's willingness to participate in the intervention plan.
10. The availability of personnel and physical resources to implement the various intervention strategies.
11. The risk of the child's sustaining physical abuse by remaining in the home.

Based on the information thus obtained, several options can be selected to improve the parent's functioning:

1. Eliminate or diminish the social or environmental stresses.
2. Lessen the adverse psychological impact of the social factors on the parent.
3. Reduce the demands on the mother to a level which is within her capacity (this can be achieved through day-care placement of the infant or provision of a housekeeper or baby sitter).
4. Provide emotional support, encouragement, sympathy, stimulation, instruction in maternal care, and aid in learning to plan for, assess, and meet the needs of the infant (supportive casework).
5. Resolve or diminish the inner psychic conflict (psychotherapy).

A MODEL REHABILITATION PROGRAM FOR ABUSING MOTHERS

One child abuse treatment and preventive program in existence since 1972 is located at The New York Foundling Hospital Center for Parent and Child Development in New York City. This program attempts to provide a residential treatment approach so as not to separate the child from the mother, yet allow some distance during the time of crisis. It stresses 1) protection of the child without actual separation and 2) crisis management for the parent.

Paraprofessionals are used in two positions:

1. *Group Mothers*—two per each eight-hour shift who have the following responsibilities: a) To act as role models in assisting the abusing parent in caring for the child; b) To provide instruction to mothers, by example, in how to mother a child. Examples: working with the parent in preparing meals, handling tantrums of children, responding to child's emotional needs as well as physical needs, providing support to the mother in her efforts to care for her child as well as herself.
2. *Social Service Assistants*—modeled after the lay therapist concept, these paraprofessionals have the major responsibility to "mother the mother" in an attempt to fulfill her unmet dependency needs and form a life-line which the parent can utilize in times of stress.

As the mothers are preparing to leave the program, the Social Service Assistants help them to modify their environment by a) Securing better apartments; b) Helping them find jobs or job training; c) Teaching them to use community resources, e.g., day-care centers, hospitals, etc.

Education for Parenting. Several courses are aimed at teaching good mothering in terms of meeting the physical needs of the child:

a. Course on sex education, child development, child's medical needs—by visiting nurse.
b. Child development groups—by psychiatric social worker. Films and discussions are utilized to help mother understand developmental stages.
c. Consumer Education—by the Director of the Home Economics Department of Hunter College. Experience in budgeting, shopping, etc.
d. Arts and crafts course—this is aimed at helping the parent with home furnishings and decoration.

Therapy. Individual and group therapy are provided for the parents, and a therapeutic nursery for the children. The mother stimulates the infant under supervision of a psychologist to learn the best ways of responding to him. The psychologist teaches her the child's needs.

Videotaping. A videotape feedback confrontation technique is used to affect the behavior of the children by enlisting the mothers' help as therapists. With the use of video feedback, the opportunity to record a segment of typical interaction between parent and child can immediately be used to confront the mother with her own pattern of reacting.

Aftercare. This is a very important aspect of the program. The mother with her child remains in the Shelter Residential Program for three months and if it is determined that she is ready to assume the care of her child in the community, she is discharged. However, she is part of the aftercare program for one year. During this year she 1) is visited in her home at least twice a week by her Social Service Assistant, who is continuously on call for an emergency; 2) returns to the agency for individual therapy; 3) returns to the agency weekly for group therapy; 4) is visited once a week at home by a visiting nurse.

Mothering the Mother

The paraprofessional who serves as surrogate-mother to the mother is considered a crucial component of treatment. Through this relationship an abusing mother can relieve her anger, stress ,and anxiety instead of projecting them onto the child. It is therefore imperative that such a relationship evolve between client and surrogate-mother. If, within eight weeks, such a relationship has not developed, the situation is carefully reviewed to determine the inhibiting factors, which may be a personality clash, negative transference, or countertransference. It gives the clinic director and team members the opportunity to decide if the client needs a change of surrogate-mother, or if the surrogate-mother needs to modify her approach, or if it is realistic to expect the client to establish such a relationship in view of her deprived and pathological life experiences.

In weekly contacts the surrogate-mother visits the client in her home. There are daily contacts through the "hot-line" facility, and the client visits at the agency with the surrogate-mother. The surrogate-mother is closely supervised by the psychiatric social worker. She also participates in the weekly case discussion of her client, and this involves the multi-disciplinary team, thus enabling her to understand the client and be able to respond to the latter's needs. (See, also, the technique of self-reparenting in Chapter 6.)

This program has been successful in preventing separation of mother and child in 65% of the cases served. In the remaining cases, separation was necessary to insure safety of the child while continuing therapy for the parent. We believe that the *mothers who respond to treatment* are:

1. The immature, hedonistic, neglectful mother who has a tendency at times to become abusive, but whose primary mode of relating to her children is abandonment of responsibility.
2. The overwhelmed mother whose characteristic mode of relating to her child may not be abusive but who at moments of great tension and crisis will lash out at the child.
3. The non-classical abusive type—those who periodically inflict excessive physical punishment on their children, admit to feelings of strong dislike towards their children, feel guilt and conflict over these feelings, and ask for help.

In general, child abuse preventive and treatment programs should include the following objectives:

1. To prevent separation of parents and child whenever possible.
2. To prevent the placement of children in institutions.
3. To encourage the attainment of self-care status on the part of parents.
4. To stimulate the attainment of self-sufficiency for the family unit.
5. To prevent further abuse or neglect by removing children from families who show an unwillingness or inability to profit from the treatment program.

REFERENCES

DANKERBRING, W. F.: The growing tragedy of battered children. *The Plain Truth*, July, 1971.

FONTANA, V. J.: *Somewhere A Child Is Crying*. New York: Macmillan, 1973.

IRWIN, T.: To combat child abuse and neglect. Theodore Irwin Public Affairs Pamphlet #508, Public Affairs Committee, Inc., 1974.

Chapter 23

Helping Parents Teach
Their Children
about Death and Life

Elisabeth Kubler-Ross

Over the past 75 years a great change has occurred in life/death education of children.

EROS, THANATOS, AND THE FAITH OF OUR FATHERS

In our grandparents' day, life and death issues would never have found their way into a classroom, just as it would have been inconceivable to have classes on sex education. A little girl was instructed by her grandmother, aunts, and mother how to dress, sit, curtsy, and accept a dance invitation, and was chaperoned to her first ball. Teaching sexual behavior was part of normal upbringing at home. An identical approach was taken to preparation for hardship, loss, death, and dying. Children experienced the death of classmates. Infectious diseases, sometimes in epidemics, took the lives of youngsters. Childbirth with pains and risks was anticipated. Funerals became family affairs attended by the oldest and youngest. There was hardly a child who by maturity had not experienced the illness, death, and funeral of at least one beloved person. Life itself was the teacher, the family was the classroom, and the attitudes of those around set the tone and background. Regular church attendance gave the families faith to accept the tragedies of daily life.

Modern Denial and Deprivation

In the mid-seventies, we see a mobile society with little interaction between the generations. Mortality of children has greatly decreased. With the rise of numbers of hospitals and nursing homes, care for the sick and dying has shifted from home to institutions. The majority of today's high school students have never visited a dying person, have not seen or touched a corpse, have often not even attended a funeral. The children of "white upper-middle-class suburbia" have in fact been raised in the most "deprived" fashion in the midst of wealth and affluence. They remind me of flowers raised in a greenhouse, protected and nourished well. Sooner or later they have to be transplanted out into a colder, less protected environment where they quickly wither if they have not been prepared for the shock.

While adults shy away from discussing death with youngsters, morticians prepare the bodies as if the deceased were just asleep and "resting in a slumber room." The face of death is covered with powder and lipstick. Most hospitals make strenuous efforts to bar children from the rooms of the patients; youngsters fall asleep in a waiting room under the sad signs "NO CHILDREN ALLOWED UNDER AGE 14." A mother visiting her critically ill husband feels torn between staying with him and returning to and consoling her waiting children, while the children wonder what could be such a terrible sight that would exclude them from their dad's room. When death occurs, they have been deprived of holding his hand once more, of bringing him a cup of tea, of simply slipping him a little note under his pillow.

Since families are no longer prepared to help their children in the face of unexpected or "premature" death of a young parent, other forms of help have to be forthcoming. Clergy have not filled this gap. Few children are referred for professional counseling before, during, and after a terminal illness of a parent (or sibling). The result is an increasing number of persons who have repressed their early unresolved grief, are fearful of death, and avoid discussion of these issues. Thus the problems of the next generation increase.

Immediately after the death of a parent or during the funeral, children often amaze their kin with unexplained behavior. Some parents complain about a boy's apparent indifference, his request to return to a football game as if nothing had happened. Other children begin to act out, become truant or promiscuous, or perhaps defiant, angry, and provocative at a time when the family is in mourning, preoccupied with a hundred unfamiliar tasks, and unlikely to pay attention.

Suspect the Perfect Child

For children who quietly do their homework, wash dishes, slip into their pajamas at night, and turn into obedient, helpful little adults, no help is forthcoming. Having "grown up overnight," they are showered with compliments for having been such help and support at a time of crisis. Yet young children who suddenly become very good may well need the most help. Children around first grade still believe that their angry wishes have contributed to the death of a parent or sibling. They still view death as a temporary happening and believe that their good deeds can make mommy return and forgive them. Johnny was an example:

> At the time of his mother's death the family was deeply touched by Johnny's helpfulness and amazed by his willingness to pitch in with household chores previously done by his mother. He even started voluntarily going to bed on time, something he had resisted before his mother's death. He was viewed as an ideal child who had adjusted well.
>
> A housecall revealed an adorable first grader, verbal and cooperative. No overt or hidden messages of troubles were elicited. It was on our way out of the house that we discovered a red apple on the windowsill, exposed to the cold early winter weather. We inquired about the purpose of this apple. Johnny blushed, "Mommy always used to love red apples. Maybe she sees it and will come back to me. And then she won't be mad at me anymore."

Thus, parents need help with 1) children who were deprived from sharing the dying process with their parents, and 2) those who apparently show no signs of grief, especially those who behave well and gratify the adults.

HOW TO SURVIVE DEATH

When we look at population groups who face death with equanimity we can distinguish some cues for teaching psychological survival of death.

Farmers and the Life Cycle

People who grew up on a farm in a cluster of family members who attend to the earth are unlikely to face terminal illness and death with great turmoil. They have spent a lifetime watching birth and death in nature, in animals, and often in their fellow man. For them *death is part of life*, part of the cycle of life, and they accept it as they accept the seasons.

Sufferers and Skill from Practice

Poor people or others who have gone through a life of deprivation, losses, letdowns, and tragedies often remain calm and composed at the news of a terminal illness. It is indeed true that there is a blessing in suffering, but not because a reward will come to those in heaven; the reward is here, during life. What we do not appreciate enough is the fact that every tragedy, every blow is in a sense a gift: a lesson to be be learned, a trial to be mastered, and a seed for potential growth. Those who have suffered in early age will have gone through the stages of dying (Kübler-Ross, 1969) many times. They will have faced the need for denial at the first shock, the anger of "why me?" and the bargaining with God, followed by depression and ultimate resolution. Those who have done this repeatedly will face each day with less strain and more preparedness. When death comes, they will know that every ending is a new beginning.

Our "treatment" of people in suffering situations is often wrong. We attempt to soften the pain, rather than focus on the result, which is increased strength and maturity, and lessons learned.

Believers and Their Bastion

Others who are not afraid to die are those with a deep abiding faith. It is not very important what faith they confess; it is the authenticity, the genuineness of their faith that will be questioned at the time of such great crisis. It is something that needs time to be internalized. It is not something that is likely to happen at five minutes to twelve. It needs time to grow, to be tested, to be called into question, so it can prove stronger than the storm.

Lovers and Helpers and Their Vicarious Deaths

Another group of people who can gradually become prepared to face death with equanimity, and are therefore also able to help those in need, are you and I. We can become relevant and meaningful helpers to children and their parents. Yet how can we help when we ourselves have not resolved our own fears? How can we avoid projecting our own feelings of inadequacy and fright when called to see a mother of young children who requests to return home to die? How can we answer the questions of five-year-olds who sit in front of a dying mother and ask if God will take their mommy away?

If we sit with those in crisis and involve ourselves very personally, so that through identification we pass through all the stages with them, then little by little we will find this peace. It is a slow process that requires time, love, pain, and patience. It requires the willingness to get hurt, to become vulnerable, to make mistakes. Through this process we learn that *no pain is unbearable if shared.*

EVERYTHING YOU WANTED TO KNOW ABOUT DYING
AND WERE AFRAID TO ASK

There are few theories and few techniques that have to be learned. Anyhow, they fail sooner or later; often they do not work at all. It will help the beginner to know that most human beings react in certain stages to an impending loss:

The stages of dying are:

1. Initial reaction to the news of a potentially fatal illness is almost always one of *denial,* later replaced by partial denial.

2. If the people in the patient's environment do not need denial themselves, the patient is able gradually to acknowledge his impending death, and then frequently responds with great *anger* and the question, "Why me?"

3. After much displaced anger is expressed to family, physicians, nurses, and chaplains, this expression of dismay is gradually replaced by a temporary truce, a stage of *bargaining.* In this period of time, the patient acknowledges his prognosis but asks for a little more time to finish unfinished business.

4. Next follows a period of *grief,* reactive *depression,* and finally a silent preparatory grief. The patient begins to withdraw and loses interest in external affairs.

5. Finally, many patients find peace and *acceptance* rather than *resignation,* which results almost exclusively if the family and health care staff play "games" to the end.

If you expect every person to pass through these stages, you may cease to listen and may get "out of tune" with the patient. No two people react the same way. Very few patients pass from stage one through five. Dying with dignity does not always mean having been able to work through the stages to reach a final peace and acceptance. *Dying with dignity means to die in character!* It means that at least one percent need denial to the end and would regard it as extremely cruel to have a well-meaning counselor try to break this defense down.

However, a majority of patients who need help will remain in an apparent stage of denial, not because of their own need, but because *they sense the professional's need to deny the grim reality.* They play into the need and expectation of the therapist. Therefore, it is of the utmost importance for every professional to know at all times his own readiness and comfort in this issue. It is often only through years of painfully learning to be at peace that the task becomes easy. Knowledge of the stages of dying only helps as a general outline. It is a preparation for a variety of behaviors. *It should not be used as a rule of behavior.*

It helps to be familiar with the interpretations of drawings by dying children and by those in the process of losing a loved one. We all know that we have to die, and even suspect when. This knowledge can be brought to our awareness through many paths. We can learn to "center," to get in touch with our inner self through various methods of meditation, dream material, or an "out-of-body" technique (Monroe, 1971).

DYING PARENTS AND CHILDREN'S DRAWINGS

Spontaneous drawing is the best and least time consuming method to elicit a child's inner knowledge and concerns. Bach's (1969) paper on drawings of terminally ill children gives an outline of the technique and some understanding of the often symbolic language (Kübler-Ross, 1974).

Since time is limited, I rarely see patients in ongoing therapy. In the majority of cases referred to me, a young parent is close to death and "beyond medical help." Rarely have the children of such a parent been prepared. Rarely have the surviving partners had the option to choose

the place of death. Often the dying parent has not even had the opportunity to speak openly and freely about the knowledge of impending
death.

Case One

A friend of the family calls, asking rather desperately for help. A
mother of two children, 1½ and 5 years old, is dying. She insists on
being allowed to die at home. Medically, nothing else can be done.
Her cancer has spread despite chemotherapy and radiation. Her
husband has spent much time either at work or sitting by her side,
fluctuating from shock and denial to extreme anger. He married her
only three years ago, caring for her little girl from a previous marriage and looking forward to seeing their children grow up. Soon
after her second baby was born, the malignancy was discovered;
they had little "normal time" together. Now he is told to take his
wife home to die! In his rage he blames her for leaving him with
two children, one not even his own.

The patient therefore had serious concerns besides her own pain:
She became increasingly frightened about the probability of having
her two children separated after her death. She was also troubled
by her husband's anger and lack of affection. She felt lonely and
rejected, unable to find consolation and too weak to consider the
possibility of bringing about a change.

Permission was granted to take her home for whatever time she
had left. A special hospital bed was placed under the window in the
living room, easily accessible to the children and visible from the
kitchen. Thus she was at all times observable even when not directly
attended.

A brief interview with her husband, parents, and both children
revealed a close knit family, with great eagerness to help and share
but simply no way of knowing what to expect and what to say.
Within her husband's hearing, an open discussion showed her clear
understanding of the reality of her situation. She expressed her concerns quite directly, namely her husband's need for support and
help, and her fear that he would separate the children after her
death. In the adjacent kitchen the children drew pictures and it
became obvious that the five-year-old realized that mommy would
soon die.

After all members of the family had shared their own concepts,
they ate a brief meal together and then gathered around the young
mother. They listened to music and watched the children pick
flowers in the garden and bring them to mommy, asking all the
questions that were on everybody's mind.

It was the five-year-old who helped with her open and honest
inquiry, "If I go to bed tonight and pray to God that it is OK for
Him to take mommy, is it OK to pray a little later and ask Him to

send my mommy back to me again?" By this time both parents had tears in their eyes. I answered the girl that she could pray for anything she needed, but in heaven there was no time, so she should not be surprised if she would not see her mommy again for quite a while. She seemed satisfied with that, but came up with another question, "If this mommy dies now—soon, does that mean I am going to get a foster mother?" Silence fell, and father uncomfortably shifted in his chair. Mother looked first at her beautifully open daughter, then at her husband. I told the girl that some daddies did get lonesome and look for another mommy, but that, too, would be something we could not know yet. The dying mother then encouraged her husband not to feel guilty should he ever make such a decision. She then added her only concern, that the children should always stay together. Her husband leaned over her bed, kissed her gently, promised that he could never conceive separating the two and hugged his little girl, who had made this last meeting such an incredible sharing.

We dimmed the light, lit a candle, and supplied soft music from a tape player we had brought. We shared the last few moments in silence as the emaciated woman gasped for air. There was no fear, no more barriers, no panic or disguise . . . the children were there, and her parents; her husband felt surrounded by others who would share his grief and responsibility.

It did require a housecall lasting a couple of hours, but one patient died with peace; her parents shared this important moment with their only daughter; her husband will resume life again without guilt; most importantly, two young children received a start early in life and are already far ahead of many adults.

Case Two: Helping When the Parent Is Unavailable

A first-grade teacher called about Mary, a good student who suddenly became very clinging and unwilling to leave the class at the end of the day. An aunt revealed that Mary's mother was dying. Father was spending days and nights in the hospital, and no one had told the two children that their mother was not expected to live more than a day or two. The aunt would appreciate if the teacher could help.

The teacher then brought the five- and six-year-old girls and I explained to them that I was a doctor who looked after many mommies who were very sick, and some of them were dying. I asked for a picture from everyone, including the teacher. Mary drew a stick figure with unusually clumsy, thick, dark red legs. She admitted that this was her mommy. I asked what was the matter with her legs (which according to my information were almost the only parts of her body not affected by her malignancy). Mary stated that she did not know, but looked increasingly sad. I asked her how someone with such legs could ever walk or stand? She looked at me with surprise and said, "You see, my mommy will never again stand up or walk in the park with me." I told her what it was like to die, showing her a picture of a cocoon that opens up and delivers a butterfly who is free and much more mobile than it was inside the cocoon. I told her that our body was like the cocoon and that her mommy—if and when she would die—would become like the beautiful butterfly.

The girls asked permission to see their mother once more. Both children visited with their mother and personally delivered flowers they had picked for her. Mother was already in a coma, but they continued their dialogue nevertheless and seemed satisfied by having seen her once more.

The teacher called the next morning to report through tears that the six-year-old requested to share something with her class the next morning at "show and tell" time. She proudly told all her classmates that her mother was going to die today and that she soon would be like a butterfly. She carefully drew the cocoon and the butterfly on the blackboard and casually mentioned that her mother not only would be able to walk again soon, but she would actually fly. Her mother died the same day.

No textbook, no method or technique can teach us how to become comfortable in the face of death. Terminally ill parents and their children are the best teachers. Through their honesty they teach us genuineness, love and openness. Their gifts to us are lessons in LIVING. Only with such lessons of life can we learn and therefore help dying or widowed parents and their children see that birth and death are all part of life—"the walking is in the lifting of the foot as in the laying down of it" (Tagore).

REFERENCES

BACH, SUSAN: Spontaneous paintings of severely ill patients. *Documenta Geigy Acta Psychosomatica*, No. VIII, 1969.
KÜBLER-ROSS, E.: *On Death and Dying*. New York: Macmillan, 1969.
KÜBLER-ROSS, E.: *Questions and Answers on Death and Dying*. New York: Macmillan, 1974.
KÜBLER-ROSS, E.: *Coping with Death and Dying*. Cassette Teaching Tapes, Ross Medical Associates, S. C., 1825 Sylvan Court, Flossmoor, Illinois 60422.
MONROE, R. A.: *Journeys Out of the Body*. New York: Anchor Press, Doubleday, 1971.

Chapter 24

Guidance for Separated and Divorced Parents

Richard A. Gardner

Children whose parents are divorced or even "merely" separated are more likely to develop psychiatric disorders than those growing up in a relatively stable intact home. This chapter will concentrate on divorce, with the understanding that most of the principles apply also to separation, which is often a prelude to divorce. In either case, the net result for the child is very similar—absence of a living parent (usually the father) from the home.

Two parents can provide the child with far more guidance, sustenance, and protection than one. The boy who grows up without close contact with a father loses an important model for identification (McDermott, 1970) and may develop oedipal problems (Meiss, 1952; Neubauer, 1960). A girl who grows up without a father may develop difficulties relating

Dr. Gardner is author of *The Boys and Girls Book About Divorce*, *The Parents Book About Divorce*, and *Psychotherapy with Children of Divorce*.

to men (Hetherington, 1973) or manifest maladaptive attempts to regain her lost father (Mahler & Rabinovitch, 1956). In addition to these hazards of parental absence, the child is often exposed to psychological trauma prior to divorce (McDermott, 1968) and pathological interaction between the parents following the divorce (Gardner, 1974, 1976). Although divorce may thus increase the child's emotional risk, it does not necessarily condemn him to maladjustment. Probably the most important factors determining whether detrimental reactions will develop is the nature of the child's pre- and post-divorce exposures and interactions with his parents. When the child's reactions are mild and related to parental misguidance and naïvete rather than deep psychopathology, they may often be alleviated or even prevented by the approaches here presented.

PRE-DIVORCE GUIDANCE

Although parents prior to the separation are typically subjective and even irrational regarding many aspects of the forthcoming divorce, I agree with Whitaker and Miller (1969) that pre-divorce counseling is best done jointly with both partners. Joint counseling gives the therapist the best opportunity to hear both spouses' opinions and thereby reduces the chance of a distorted view. In addition, it lessens the likelihood that the therapist will be seduced into taking sides. Such joint counseling, of course, should not preclude individual and family interviews when indicated. The parents typically are struggling with questions such as the following.

"Should We Get Divorced?"

The professional does well when counseling parents contemplating divorce to take a strictly neutral position regarding whether or not the parents should separate. The decision is theirs. It would be grandiose for the professional to believe that he knows better than the parents whether they are better off separating or remaining married. He must appreciate that even in the sickest relationships, both healthy and pathological factors are operating. The traumas associated with separation may be more psychologically detrimental than those of continuing the relationship. Similarly, urging people to stay together may result in a prolongation of pathological interaction. The professional's primary aim should be to help the parents get the clearest picture of their situation so that they can most judiciously make their decision.

"Should We Stay Together for the Sake of the Children?"

Although many studies (e.g., Nye, 1957; Landis, 1960) have dealt with the question of whether children are better off in an intact, unhappy home than in one in which divorce has occurred, there is no conclusive evidence that one is preferable to the other. Both have their disadvantages when compared to the intact, relatively happy home, and it is almost impossible to predict which of the two undesirable alternatives would be least detrimental to a given child. Even if one believes that *on the whole* children are better off in a divorced home than in an intact, unhappy home (as the aforementioned studies suggest), one cannot be certain that this would be true for a particular child. Accordingly, the professional does well to advise parents to take into consideration the possible effects of the separation on their children (both the advantages and the disadvantages) when making their decision. However, the effects on the children should not be their overriding consideration—especially since they cannot be certain that their speculations in this regard will prove valid. In fact, when making their decision, they do well to focus primarily on factors that relate more directly to themselves and hope that their conclusion will also serve the children's best interests.

The professional should appreciate that staying together for the sake of the children can be a rationalization for the maintenance of various kinds of pathological interactions that are being gratified in the marriage. Other factors, as well, may contribute to the rationalization: fear of the financial pressures following the separation, fear of being left alone, and avoidance of the increased responsibilities that divorce usually entails.

"Is There a Critical Age at Which Divorce Can Be Particularly Detrimental to a Child?"

Some believe that during the oedipal period the child is particularly vulnerable to the detrimental effects of a divorce. Not having an opposite-sexed parent in the household makes it very difficult for a child to resolve his or her oedipal conflicts. Others hold that in early adolescence, when the youngster may reexperience oedipal conflicts, the divorce can be particularly harmful. The early-adolescent girl usually needs her mother as a confidante and her father as a healthy model for male relationships. Others (such as this author) hold that the earlier the child is deprived of healthy involvement with a parent, the greater

the chances of developing untoward psychological reactions to the deprivation. In any case, it may be injudicious to recommend that parents
sustain their relationship until a child has passed through a crucial
period. Thus prolonging the parental agony may expose the child unnecessarily to the traumatic effects of the parental discord. The child
might even become the target of parental resentment for prolonging their
agony. In addition, if there are many children in the family, after one
child has gone through the critical period a second may enter it—requiring the parents to stay together even longer. Strictly adhering to such
counsel might result in the parents' staying together many years beyond
what they otherwise would have.

GUIDING PARENTS AROUND THE TIME OF SEPARATION

"How Long in Advance Should the Children Be Told?"

Informing the child long in advance of the anticipated separation provides him or her with the opportunity to work through many early reactions while the departing parent is still in the home (Kliman, 1968). However, the younger the child, the less will be his or her appreciation of
future events; a young child may not start to exhibit reactions until after
there has been concrete evidence of the parent's departure. The parent
who withholds disclosure until the last possible moment, in order to
shorten the child's agony, will probably deprive the child of the opportunity for working through his or her reactions in the optimum way.
Accordingly, the child can be told anywhere from a few days to a few
weeks in advance of the day of separation. The parents should also be
helped to appreciate that some children will have little overt reaction to
the news. They should be helped to recognize that the child's failure to
react with remorse is not generally the result of lack of concern, but rather
a possible manifestation of his or her utilization of the denial mechanism
or the result of the inability to actually appreciate what is going on until
he or she has directly observed the event.

"Who Should Tell the Children and How Much Should Be Revealed?"

I agree with Grollman (1969) that it is preferable that both parents together tell the children about a forthcoming separation. Such an approach
is likely to communicate to the children the fact that *both* parents have
played a role in the marital deterioration (the usual situation) and this
lessens the chances of their viewing one party as solely at fault (a situa-

tion conducive to the formation of inappropriate and maladaptive reactions to the divorce). In addition, when both parents make themselves available for discussion of the separation, the stage is set for such discussions with each of them in the future.

Occasionally, one parent may not wish to participate in such a joint discussion because it may involve the *revelation of facts that would be embarrassing* to him or her; that parent may even request that the parent who alone informs the children of the impending separation not reveal the compromising information. The parent who complies with such a request is doing the children a disservice. For example, if a father asks that his wife not reveal to the children that he has become involved with another woman, he is not only making an inappropriate request, but is asking his wife to comply with a plan that is not in his children's best interests. The children are entitled to learn the basic causes of the separation in order to help them avoid some of the detrimental reactions that they may develop. When such important information is withheld from them, the children sense the parental duplicity. This causes them to lose trust in their parents at a time when they are most in need of a trusting relationship with their parents. In addition, sensing their parents' reluctance to answer such questions makes it less likely that they will ask others, and this deprives them of the opportunity for preoccupation, repetition, and emotional expression vital to the process of working through their reactions to the trauma of the parental separation.

The father in such a situation should be helped to appreciate that his embarrassment is a small price to pay for helping his children adjust optimally to the divorce. It may be easier for him to reveal his extramarital involvement if the mother has to reveal deficiencies of her own that contributed to the marital deterioration (the usual case). If both parents can be helped to appreciate that the father's involvement is neither a sin nor a heinous crime—but rather a common result of marital discord—then it may be easier for the father to sanction the revelation. It may also help for the parents to understand that not every personal detail of their lives need be revealed, only the basic issues. For example, frigidity, impotence, or a lover's identity (the disclosure of which might have unfortunate repercussions) is not the children's business.

A mother may hesitate to tell the children lest she become very upset in front of them, break down and cry. Such a mother should be helped to appreciate that withholding her own emotional reactions to the separation would serve as a poor model for healthy emotional expression by her children. The children's healthy working-through necessitates their venting their feelings; if the parent refrains from ventilation, how can the children do it? Of course, if the mother is prone to uncontrollable outbursts of rage, wild hysterical reactions, or other pathological manifestations, then attempts should be made to help the mother reduce these before discussing the separation with the children.

A closely related problem is the parent who says to a child, "Big boys don't cry," or "See how brave you can be." This encourages suppression of emotional reactions and contributes thereby to the development of psychopathological reactions. The parent should *permit and encourage the child's emotional expression.*

"Should the Teacher Be Told?"

Some parents fear that if the teacher learns of the separation she may indulge the child, dote over him, make him a "privileged character," use him for classroom demonstrations on children's reactions to divorce, or react in other ways that may worsen the child's plight. Although such misguided reactions occasionally occur, their danger does not warrant the child's being deprived of the many benefits to be derived from the teacher's knowing. When the teacher is told about the separation she is in a better position to handle any reactions that the child will exhibit in the classroom and perhaps even prevent them (McDermott, 1968). On the other hand, when she has not been apprised of the situation, she is less likely to be tolerant of behavioral disruptions, may react with strong disciplinary measures, and thereby add to the child's stresses.

The parents should be helped to recognize that the teacher, as one who often has a good relationship with the child, is an excellent person to help him or her during this trying period. She generally spends five to six hours a day with the child and she is in a unique position to provide him with solace and advice. Because the teacher can be a convenient surrogate for the departed parent, it is unfortunate that there are so few males teaching at the elementary level. Because it is the father who leaves the home in the overwhelming majority of cases (recent trends toward the mother's leaving notwithstanding), the availability of such male teachers would be a boon to the ever-increasing number of children whose parents have separated. Fortunately, more men are recently being attracted into such teaching.

In any event, parents need to realize that attempts to withhold such information from the teacher are often futile. If the child does not tell her, other children are likely to. It is best for her to learn it firsthand, when she is in the best position to help the child and when she can be of help at the earliest possible time. Parents telling the teacher themselves lessens the likelihood that she will be given erroneous information that might compromise her ability to be helpful to the child. If the parents fear that the teacher will handle the child inappropriately, they should be advised to talk with her in an attempt to prevent it.

"What Will Happen in Court?"

While the superficial aspects of this question may be best answered by the attorney, the mental health professional may need to help parents understand and clarify the practical and psychological ramifications of custody, visitation, and support payments. These are discussed in Chapter 32 on divorce court.

GUIDANCE IN THE EARLY POST-SEPARATION PERIOD

During this phase, parents (Despert, 1953; Arnstein, 1964; Gardner, 1977) and children (Gardner, 1970) may find it useful to read books designed to help prevent and alleviate some of the more superficial types of psychological problems attendant to the divorce situation. In offering supplementary guidance, professionals may find the following ideas useful.

Working-Through

It is important for the parents to appreciate that a crucial part of the child's healthy handling of the separation trauma is to become desensitized to it by reiteration of his or her reactions to it. Therefore, they should invite the child to ask as many questions as he or she wishes. They should appreciate that the child may need the same questions answered many times over in order to deal effectively with the trauma. More important than answering the questions is the child's reassurance that the parents will be available to answer them. In fact, often the questions merely serve as an excuse for the child's involving himself or herself with a parent and thereby gaining reassurance of the parent's availability. To the degree possible, easy access and an open line of communication with the parent who has left the home should also be established and maintained. The child should visit the departed parent's new living quarters as early as possible, be provided with the telephone number, and be encouraged to call whenever he or she wishes.

The parents must also be helped to realize that emotional release of the child's feelings about the separation—grief work—is crucial if he or she is to adjust properly. They themselves must serve as models for such expression and should attempt to facilitate the child's eomtional expression at every appropriate opportunity. The child needs parental help and permission to grieve over the loss of a parent.

Anger

The child whose parents are divorcing is bound to be angry (except when the separation results in relief from cruel treatment). The child is losing a parent, one of his or her most valuable possessions, who will never live in the same household again. The child's pleas that the parents not separate have been in vain and he or she feels totally impotent to change their decision. Anger is a predictable result of such deep frustration. The separating parents have to be helped to develop greater tolerance of the child's angry expression during this period. Accordingly, they should be advised to relax somewhat (but not completely) their usual disciplinary measures during the early post-separation period.

The child whose parents have separated not only has more reason to feel angry than the child living in an intact, relatively happy home, but also has more reasons to develop inhibitions in the expression of that anger. The child may fear revealing the angry feelings toward the departed parent, lest he or she see even less of him. He or she may fear exhibiting anger to the remaining parent, lest that parent depart as well. As the child views the situation, he or she must be careful not to alienate dear ones. If the parents are excessively inhibited themselves regarding the child's expressing anger toward them, the child is likely to suppress and repress anger even more and the likelihood of symptom formation is further increased.

Time Alone with a Parent

A child's spending periods of time alone with each of the parents is probably the most potent preventative of psychiatric disorder and one of the most effective antidotes to such disturbance. This is especially true during the period following parental separation when the child is most in need of reassurances of parental love and affection. Optimally such experiences should take place every day; they should have the highest priority. Each sibling should have his or her opportunity to be alone with the parent and the other(s) strictly prohibited from involvement (unless specifically requested by all parties concerned). These periods together are most effective when an activity is selected that both parent and child genuinely enjoy. If the parent feigns pleasurable involvement, the child is likely to sense the parent's lack of enthusiasm. During such times alone, the mutual sharings of thoughts and feelings are among the most salutary experiences that a parent and child can enjoy.

LATER GUIDANCE

The last stage of established divorce holds several pitfalls, including some specious but common advice.

"Always Reassure the Child That His Father (Mother) Still Loves Him"

Such advice is valid in *most* divorce situations, even though the child usually questions the affection of the departing parent and considers him- or herself abandoned and unloved (Gardner, G., 1956; Sugar, 1970; Westman et al., 1970). Unfortunately, there are times when the parent who has left the home has no affection for the child, yet the remaining parent will try continually to reassure the child that he or she is still loved. For example, the child of a father who has neither been seen nor heard from in many years may be told that the father still loves him or her but "keeps it inside" or "can't show it." Such a mother generally subscribes to the misguided belief that to tell the child the truth, that the father does not love the child, would be psychologically devastating. She does not realize that her approach is more devastating. She is confusing the child about love by providing him or her with a concept that considers love possible without any communication of it or direct involvement with the loved one. A loving relationship, if it is to be worthy of the name, must involve some reciprocity. When the child gets old enough to appreciate the mother's duplicity, his respect for and trust of her cannot but be compromised. And the confused concept of love so engendered is likely to interfere with the child's developing loving relationships with others.

Such children have to be helped to come to terms with and accept the fact that their father does not love them. It is important to help them appreciate that just because their father does not love them does not mean that they are unlovable or that no one else can love them either. By gaining substitute gratifications from other relationships they can prove to themselves that they are still lovable. They have to be helped to appreciate that the failure of their father to love them is not the result of some defect within themselves; rather, the deficiency lies within the father who does not have the capacity to love his own child. In the less extreme case in which the absent father exhibits occasional involvement or interest, the child has to be helped to come to terms with *that* reality. Such children have to be helped to avoid engaging in the futile attempt to gain more contact and affection than the parent is able or willing to provide. Again, they have to be helped to gain such gratifications elsewhere.

"Never Criticize Your Ex-Spouse to Your Child"

This is among the most common advice given to divorced parents by both professionals and laymen (Despert, 1953; Grollman, 1969). Its rationale is that a parent should not undermine the child's relationship with an ex-spouse, even though the parental relationship has dissolved. The parents, although they have little respect for one another, still appreciate that a child's respectful relationship with both his parents is important for healthy psychological development. This sounds good. However, the child cannot but be *suspicious of a parent who follows such advice.* He or she knows that the parent must have had significant reservations about the other parent—why else would there have been a divorce? Accordingly, the child loses trust in the parent at a time when he can least afford to. The divorce may be viewed by the child as blatant proof of parental distrustfulness. Disbelieving his or her parents can only add to the child's burden of distrust.

Sugar (1970) describes the creatively destructive parent who ostensibly follows this misguided advice but manages to criticize the ex-spouse in the very process of implementing it. Comments such as, "I never criticize your father to you," and "There are many critical things about your mother that I could tell you, but it wouldn't be right of me to tear her down to you," are likely to conjure up in the child's mind far worse deficiencies than the real ones that are not being disclosed.

Children (whether or not their parents are divorced) do best when they clearly recognize each parent's assets and liabilities. If this is accomplished in their formative years they are less likely to grow up with the notion that people are either perfect or totally defective. They will thereby be in a better position to relate realistically to others.

Unfortunately, separated and divorced parents are not famous for their objectivity regarding one another's assets and liabilities. How can the professional expect such parents to impart such information accurately to their children? I generally suggest that parents try to recognize that when such data are communicated *in a state of anger*, there is likely to be *some distortion*. Hopefully as time passes there will be less anger and less distortion. Also their children have to be helped to understand (the older they are, the more capable) that parental criticisms made in a state of rage or resentment must not be fully accepted as valid. Rather, they must try to rely on their own observations to either substantiate or refute what they have been told. Though this approach, of course, may be difficult and imperfect, it is, in my opinion, the best way to handle the difficult situation (Gardner, 1976).

Perpetuation of Parental Hostilities

One of the most common causes of post-separation psychopathology in children of divorced parents is the maintenance of a hostile relationship between the parents. For example, observing the parents to be cruel and brutal to one another may cause (by identification with the parents) superego defects in the child (Despert, 1953; McDermott, 1970). Paradoxically, the hostile involvement provides the child more false hope for parental reconciliation than the situation in which the parents have truly extracted themselves from one another. The child seems to appreciate that the hostile involvement between the parents is not the same as a neutral one, that it is a type of relationship that frequently brings them together. Accordingly, such involvement can perpetuate reconciliation preoccupation. The child may become so frightened by the parental fighting that he or she may become inhibited in expressing anger and this can contribute to the formation of neurotic symptoms such as depression (in which the anger is self-directed) and compulsive behavior (in which the anger is symbolically discharged).

The parents should be warned that the present legal structure, modeled on adversary proceedings as a way of solving many types of marital conflict, is likely to intensify their hostility and thereby can be detrimental to their children (Gardner, 1976). The children may be used as scapegoats. Mother, for example, may release on her child (a safer and more available target) the hostilities she feels toward her former husband. At times children are used as pawns in the parental conflict: "If you don't send me the money, you can't see the children." (See the discussion of support payment and visitation in Benedeks' Chapter 32. Sometimes the children will take advantage of the situation and play one parent against the other. The children may be used as spies, informants, or allies in the parental conflict. It behooves the professional to warn the parents of the consequences of their conflict and to do everything reasonably possible to bring about its discontinuation.

COMMUNITY RESOURCES

A number of community organizations provide services that can be beneficial to divorced parents and their children. Probably the most well known of these is Parents Without Partners, which has chapters in most cities throughout the United States, Canada, and England. In addition to providing parents with gratifying social, recreational, and intellectual experiences (which indirectly are therapeutic to their children), there are many activities for the children. The children gain a sense of camaraderie with other children whose parents are divorced and are thereby helped to feel less different from others. Discussion groups for adolescents can help these youngsters deal with their common problems in constructive ways. Recreational activities (for example, picnics and outings) may provide the children with relationships with adults of the same sex as the departed parent.

Big Brothers of America is an organization that can be useful for boys when they have little contact with their fathers. Men volunteer to spend time with such boys in an attempt to form meaningful relationships with them—relationships that can serve to compensate such youngsters for the deprivations they may have suffered as a result of the absence of their fathers. Big Sisters International provides similar opportunities for girls who do not live with their mothers.

REFERENCES

ARNSTEIN, H. S.: *What to Tell Your Child*. New York: Pocket Books, 1964.

DESPERT, L. J.: *Children of Divorce*. Garden City, New York: Dolphin Books, Doubleday & Co., Inc., 1953.

GARDNER, G. E.: Separation of the parents and the emotional life of the child. *Mental Hygiene*, 40 (1):53-64, 1956.

GARDNER, R. A.: *The Boys and Girls Book about Divorce*. New York: Jason Aronson, Inc., 1970; Bantam Books edition, 1971.

GARDNER, R. A.: Psychological aspects of divorce. In: S. Arieti (Ed.), *American Handbook of Psychiatry*, 2nd Edition. New York: Basic Books, Inc., 1974, pp. 496-512.

GARDNER, R. A.: *Psychotherapy with Children of Divorce*. New York: Jason Aronson, Inc., 1976.

GARDNER, R. A.: *The Parents Book about Divorce*. New York: Doubleday and Co., Inc., 1977.

GROLLMAN, E. A.: *Explaining Divorce to Children*. Boston: Beacon Press, 1969.

HETHERINGTON, E. M.: Girls without fathers. *Psychology Today,* 6 (9):46-52, 1973.

KLIMAN, G.: *Psychological Emergencies of Childhood.* New York: Grune & Stratton, 1968, pp. 95-101.

LANDIS, J. T.: The trauma of children when parents divorce. *Marriage and Family Living,* 22:7-13, 1960.

MAHLER, M. S. & RABINOVITCH, R.: The effects of marital conflict on chlid development. In: V. W. Einstein (Ed.), *Neurotic Interaction in Marriage.* New York: Basic Books, 1956.

McDERMOTT, J. F.: Parental divorce in early childhood. *American Journal of Psychiatry,* 124 (10):1424-1432, 1968.

McDERMOTT, J. F.: Divorce and its psychiatric sequelae in childhood. *Archives of General Psychiatry,* 23 (5):421-427, 1970.

MEISS, M. L.: The oedipal problem of a fatherless child. *The Psychoanalytic Study of the Child,* 7:216-229, 1952.

NEUBAUER, P. B.: The one-parent child and his oedipal development. *Psychoanalytic Study of the Child,* 15:286-309, 1960.

NYE, I. F.: Child adjustment in broken and in unhappy unbroken homes. *Marriage and Family Living,* 19:356-361, 1957.

SUGAR, MAX: Children of divorce. *Pediatrics,* 46:588-595, 1970.

WESTMAN, J. C., CLINE, D. W., et al.: Role of child psychiatry in divorce. *Archives of General Psychiatry,* 23:416-420, 1970.

WHITAKER, C. A. & MILLER, M. H.: A reevaluation of "psychiatric help" when divorce impends. *American Journal of Psychiatry,* 126 (5):611-618, 1969.

Stepparents and
Their Spouses

Irene Fast and Morton Chethik

The focus of this chapter is on difficulties stemming from the anomalous social role of the stepparent. The stepparent is focused on, not because his or her problems are likely to be greater than those of the spouse or stepchild, but because folklore tends to hold the stepparent the villain, and he or she is therefore most in need of sympathetic attention.

In 50 case experiences with such families there were three times as many stepfathers as stepmothers, and a few families with both. Half the previous marrigaes had ended in death, half in divorce.

The material from one family, the G's, will be used in extended form to illustrate ways in which issues may become evident clinically:

Portions of this chapter are reprinted with permission from *American Journal of Orthopsychiatry*, where they first appeared Apr. 1966, 36:485-491.

Mr. and Mrs. G. sought help because of the strained and distant relationship between Mrs. G. and their ten-year-old daughter Ruth. The G's had been married a year. Following the suicide of Ruth's natural mother five years earlier, Mr. G. had for four years maintained the home for Ruth and her older brother with housekeepers.

Mrs. G. felt that though she had extended herself to Ruth in the past year, she had been received coldly, totally avoided, or met with hostility. For example, she and Ruth had gone clothes shopping, and, with some enjoyment, had purchased several outfits. However, Ruth had not worn a single thing they had bought. She also "forgot" to bring home classroom notices of school programs, plays, or parent-teacher meetings. Mrs. G. was embarrassed and angry; she was being made to look neglectful and uncaring before the world. Ruth seemed deaf to all requests by Mrs. G. to "clean up your room," "wash your hair," or "clear the table." Mrs. G. found herself moving from requests to commands, from a reasonable tone to an angry shout. At this point, she and Ruth rarely exchanged a pleasant word. Ruth constantly used the special "we," referring to the pleasures of the past shared with her father, brother, and natural mother. A very special third person "her" referred to Mrs. G., the intrusion who had disturbed the previous idyllic harmony. When Mrs. G. made a special French dinner, Ruth reminisced about the wonderful Jewish dishes her natural mother had made.

Mr. G. often felt that he was "in the middle." While he could understand why Mrs. G. became furious, he also felt that she reacted too fiercely. While he felt at times that she didn't stand up to Ruth as she ought, he couldn't stand it when she "overreacted."

Both parents felt that in the year and a half they had known one another prior to the marriage, they had been very compatible. Both were frightened that the friction was driving them into separate camps and imperiling their marriage. It was decided that they would meet with the therapist as a couple and that Ruth would meet with him individually.

STEP ROLE CONTRADICTIONS

A major structural problem in families with step relationships concerns the role definition of the stepparent. In this society that role is poorly articulated and implies contradictory functions as "parent," "stepparent," and "nonparent." Folk tradition describes the stepmother as wicked and cruel. Even dictionaries define the term stepmother as implying unparent-like behavior, neglect, or deprivation of the stepchildren. Not quite so explicitly, the stepfather is seen as neglectful, cruel, or as finding the child a burdensome appendage to his wife. To enact those traditional roles is socially disapproved. Instead, the stepparent is encouraged to assume the role of parent.

For this role enactment legal support is also offered, in the explication of the rights and duties entailed by the "in loco parentis" relationship. But the stepparent cannot totally assume the role of father or mother; he or she is also nonparent. Some of the most obvious parental role functions are biological, financial, and educational, but a stepparent cannot assume biological parenthood, frequently shares financial obligations with the natural parent, and usually shares the socialization of the child (the child's time may be divided between two homes simultaneously, or at least successively in the course of the two marriages).

In the cases we saw, attempts at resolution of pressures to be parent, nonparent, and stepparent were observed in the behavior of almost all stepparents. In a few cases a single role seemed to be expressed with the overemphasis of caricature: a "real daddy," a tormenting and depriving stepparent, or a nonparent (remaining severely separate from the child or achieving the closeness of friend or pal rather than parent). In most, however, the three roles seemed interwoven.

How Much to Be Parent?

A central unsettled question was, "How much to be parent?" Decisions about some easily identified questions such as the child's place of residence, financial responsibility, the use of a surname, could usually be made. But even these relatively public commitments sometimes failed to remain stable. Some were changed by external pressures, others were inappropriately made the child's responsibility. Still others were precariously dependent on the stepparent's mood, or the shifting fortunes of his intrapsychic or interpersonal struggles. More subtle parental relationships, less easily made explicit and less amenable to conscious decision, were even more difficult to stabilize: the maintenance of an appropriate generation barrier; the assumption of the rights and responsibilities of discipline; mutuality with the child in work or play; the offer of the self as an object for identification.

Uncertainty Complicated by Conflicted Feelings

Intrapsychic and interpersonal difficulties often interacted with stepparents' uncertainties about their appropriate roles as parents. Many stepparents were burdened with their spouses' hypersensitivity to their every act, tonal nuance, look, omission, or suggestion of negative feeling. Such sensitivity often expressed the natural parents' own uneasy feelings 1) that their children were only "part of a package deal" and not really wanted, 2) of guilt toward the spouse for having foisted the children on him or her, or 3) of guilt toward the children for having broken their homes, deprived them of their natural parents, and provided them with "stepparents." The stepparents' own realistic feelings that the children were an encumbrance, an unwanted financial burden, and a continuous unwelcome reminder of their spouses' previous marriages were sometimes strongly fended off as heinous, no matter how strongly balanced by positive feelings. Some stepparents, afraid of being or seeming the traditionally evil stepparent, could not be adequately assertive in discipline. Still others were unable to treat as absurd the stepchild's fantasy-based complaints of overwork, neglect, and deprivation.

Some of these problems did not arise for Mrs. G.: Questions of surname change, financial responsibility or place of residence did not occur. However, more subtle role-related issues did. In matters of discipline, Mrs. G. was indecisive, overwhelmed by the feeling that she was not, after all, Ruth's "real" mother. After she had battled with Ruth, she was appalled. It seemed to her that Ruth's glowering coldness and her husband's silent criticism confirmed her fears that she was the epitome of the stepmother she had no wish to be. Her outrage about the "forgotten" notices from school was intensified by her sense that as a result she was being seen by the world as the neglectful and uncaring stepmother.

Such matters came up clinically only indirectly. On one occasion, for example, Mr. and Mrs. G. expressed concerns about their sexual life. In recent weeks, Mrs. G. seemed less interested and, on occasion, Mr. G. was impotent. It soon became clear that the sexual problem, unusual for them, was an expression of estrangement in other areas of their lives.

Most obvious was a change in Mr. G. He seemed of late to be "pussyfooting around," unable to be "real." When he didn't like the radio news commentator Mrs. G. selected, he did not say so but suffered in silence. Though his job pressures were heavy, he became increasingly helpful around the house. He urged domestic help on Mrs. G., though they could ill afford it. Mrs. G. had become increasingly uneasy. She liked the help but felt Mr. G. was being unnatural, a "goody-two-shoes."

Gradually Mr. G.'s feelings became more clear. He was feeling guilty and frightened. He felt he had tricked Mrs. G. into a bad bargain: He had wanted to marry her because he loved her but he had also been looking for help with the children. Soon, he feared, she would wake up, see how she had been exploited, and leave. At the same time, he felt miserable at silently finding fault with someone who had sacrificed so much: He hated her shouting, thought she overreacted to Ruth, and felt she was too easily threatened by her.

Admission of such complexities of feelings cleared the air enormously. In this instance, Mrs. G. had been acutely aware of Mr. G.'s silent criticism and had understood it in terms of her own fears, as an accusation that she was not a mother, did not care. She had not, in fact, felt tricked: She had thought long and hard about taking on the two children before doing so. They were not an unwanted burden: She was attached to them and by no means ready to give up. She agreed that she did tend to "gc overboard" in her reactions to Ruth, dreaded doing so, and welcomed the stabilizing support of her husband.

RECIPROCAL ROLE RESISTANCE

The stepparent's ability to assume the role of parent does not depend only on his or her own willingness and capacity. The reciprocal acceptance of that role by spouse and child is essential. In Parson's terms, "The success of ego's action is contingent on alter's reaction."

Some *children's repudiation* of the stepparent as parent is extreme: No gift is accepted. Every punishment is treated as an attack. No identification is made with the stepparent's goals, values or personal characteristics. Every forced accommodation to the stepparent is responded to as though he or she were an intruder or occupying army. Sibling groups sometimes treat any member's deviation from total rejection of the stepparent as traitorous to both the displaced parent and to themselves.

The natural parent, *spouse of the stepparent,* usually intensely wishes the stepparent to assume the role of parent. But this wish is not unambivalent. Indirect expressions of the wish to maintain exclusive control might occur in a mother's assumption of more than her share of disciplinary and financial responsibility, or a father's performance of duties more typically the mother's in our society.

It was clear from the beginning that Mrs. G.'s difficulties involved more than uncertainties about the appropriate balance of mother, non-mother, and stepmother in her role. To enact her role required that Ruth accept her in it. And Ruth did not.

Her "deafness" to Mrs. G.'s requests or instructions had less the quality of a child resisting a parent than of a child ignoring a stranger with no right to any authority whatsoever. Mrs. G. was baffled by what she could only call something "unchildlike." When she had confronted Ruth about hanging up her clothes, getting her hands washed or coming to the table, Ruth might turn and stare at her in an indescribable way. It was not the way a child looked at an adult. It was not just as though Mrs. G. were a stranger or even a hated intruder. There was an absoluteness in the way Ruth held herself separate from Mrs. G. that was frightening, almost uncanny.

It gradually became clear that Ruth felt she must vehemently resist any temptation to accept the proffered role relationship, to become "daughter" to Mrs. G. To do so felt like "a slap in the face" to her natural mother. Nevertheless, until Ruth did accept herself as "daughter," Mrs. G. could not be "mother."

SYMPTOMATIC EXPRESSIONS

The uncertainties about appropriate role behavior, related intrapsychic conflicts, and problems due to failures in reciprocal role behavior by other family members find a variety of manifestations. Three seemed particularly prevalent:

1. *Denial of any problems* usually occurs early in any clinical contact. It is the statement that the stepparent treats the child as his or her own, i.e., is completely "parent." This assertion is rigidly, even belligerently, maintained, supported by the spouse during joint interviews, and often stated so persuasively that no further clinical inquiry is attempted despite overwhelming evidence of its falsity.

2. The stepparent often develops an acute *hypersensitivity to every event as "proof"* that he or she is or is not seen as "parent." In addition to the tensions this creates for the stepparent, a particularly heavy burden is placed on the child, whose every act is weighted with such significance that spontaneity and decisive action become difficult.

3. Perhaps most damaging to the stepchild is the parents' united *focus on the child as the source of all marital dissension*, a threat to the marriage itself. It is not difficult to see a basis for this in the child's actual wish to separate parent and stepparent, the fact that the difficult steprelationships would not exist at all were it not for the child, and the negative feelings of both marital partners toward the child as reminder of the natural parent's previous spouse.

Although the G.'s had not focused all the blame on Ruth, one could see fertile ground for such a development in the G.'s own compatibility and wish for their marriage to succeed, their fear that the problems with Ruth threatened their relationship, and Ruth's unreasoning rejection of their efforts.

In Mrs. G.'s preoccupation with her successes and failures in the mother role with Ruth, she tended to perceive any problem as a reflection of her failure. At a parent-teacher conference, Mrs. G. was told that Ruth was increasingly sloppy in her handwriting, had reverted to reading books more appropriate for seven-year-olds, and was asking "stupid" questions in class. Mrs. G. was angry and depressed. She knew Ruth could do much better; Ruth was being stubborn. Fueling her anger at Ruth was her own sense of failure. Her insights from the individual work with Ruth helped. The regression occurred in the context of emerging fears of growing up. Ruth anticipated beginning to menstruate soon and was frightened. Reverting to an innocent seven-year-old was a temporary escape. Knowing this, Mrs. G. was able to be empathic rather than feeling attacked.

At another time, Mrs. G. felt personally responsible and angry at Ruth for "boyish" trends. When she learned of Ruth's fear that to be a girl meant being predestined to suicide like her mother, Mrs. G. was able to be forthrightly empathic with Ruth's actual problems.

EFFECTS OF STEP ROLE ON OTHER ROLES

Whatever the reasons for the stepparent's behavior, his particular pattern of role functioning must affect the role enactment of every other family member. To the extent that the stepparent does not appropriately carry out the role functions of parent, the complementary roles and relationships of the natural parent and of the children will also suffer. Even when he or she does function as parent, his idiosyncratic enactment of that role also forces modifications in all familial relationships. In either case, then, both the dyadic relationships involving the stepparent and all the other relationships among family members will be modified. Insofar as a stepfather behaves as nonparent, an intense mother-son bond, not appropriately tempered by a father-son relationship, prevents the boy's adequate individuation. In one case a boy's highly sexualized tie to a sister was used as replacement for an emotionally distant stepmother. A fiercely female mother-daughter competition occurred for a man whose disparate roles as husband to one and father to the other were not adequately defined. One adolescent girl focused on her mother's role changes from woman-about-town to housewife, and more especially, from mother of herself to wife of the intruding stepfather. Sometimes, too, a painful but healthy separation between natural parent and child becomes evident as each develops his appropriately different relationship to the stepparent.

During the four years between the death of Ruth's first mother and the second marriage, there was no mother to help maintain appropriate role relationships in the family. Ruth's role had assumed some aspects more appropriate to wife and mother than to child. When a new housekeeper was to be hired, Ruth would beg her father to be without one, to let *her* handle things. She had become physically possessive of Mr. G., brushing the dandruff off his shoulders or stroking him in ways not typical of ten-year-old daughters. Reinforced by his interest, she used Yiddish words and expressions that had become almost a private and tender language between them.

Now Mrs. G. asserted her own place with Mr. G. Though the effect on the role relationships between Ruth and her father was salutary, the process for Ruth was difficult.

GHOSTS AND OTHER LIMITS TO ROLE ASSUMPTION

But however strong the stepparent's determination to be parent, however skillful the effort, he or she cannot succeed totally. Furthermore, social norms make it inappropriate to attempt complete assumption of the parent role. They require graceful acceptance to parental rights of another, sharing of residential, educational, and financial decisions regarding the child with a living noncustodial parent, or perhaps acceptance of the moral and religious legacy of a dead one.

Perhaps the most steady reminders that the "stepparent" is also "nonparent" occur in divorce. The activity of the noncustodial parent, the child's visits, the continued relationship to the ex-spouse force awareness. But a deceased natural parent has by no means lost influence as parent. In some families constant unfavorable comparisons between stepparent and the overidealized image of the dead parent occur. One boy's potent identification with his dead father as worthless and destructive prevented a confidence-giving identification with his stepfather. Other children maintain the relationship with the dead parent by firm belief in his or her continued existence as a wandering ghost, a benign helper, or a vengeful and still powerful punisher.

Whether the natural parent is dead or alive, the child maintains a contemporary relationship. In some families bitter competition between the stepparent and the previous parent replaces the sharing of rights and responsibilities. Seemingly endless internal ruminations or acrimonious discussion occur about the child's preference for one over the other, the other parent's spoiling of the child, relative adequacy in living up to financial obligations, relative "goodness" as a parent. In some families, particularly those in which embittering divorce proceedings ended the previous marriage, the couple of the current marriage unite in an uncompromising denunciation of the natural parent. In others a withdrawal occurs from any relationship with him or her. Sometimes the child functions as go-between, makes decisions in relation to the adults, and is burdened with a frightening degree of power.

> The continued unseen presence of Ruth's mother permeated the G.'s household. Actually, the idyllic life Ruth now remembered had never existed. For a long time before her suicide Ruth's mother had been moody and unpredictable. She had come to hate caring for the children and managing a household, wanting professional work instead. Well before her death she had moved out of the home into an apartment. In this situation Ruth had taken refuge in idealization. After her mother's death she developed the habit of a repeated "willed" dream: Her mother called her from heaven. Ruth would float up out of the house, through the clouds, to meet her radiantly glowing mother. They communicated without speaking.
> In Ruth's defensive splitting of loving from angry feelings, her natural mother became the repository for all that was good, her stepmother for all the bad. It was a difficult split to maintain in the face of temptations to respond to Mrs. G.'s overtures. It was her recognition of their shared pleasure in the shopping trip that made her refuse to wear the clothes, the temptation to enjoy Mrs. G.'s special dinner that made her emphasize the superiority of Jewish dishes.

LEARNING DISABILITIES

Roles are learned. In the normal course of the establishment of a family, marriage follows courtship, and the birth of children follows a period of marital adjustment. In a marriage in which one partner has children from the very beginning, a number of role-learning opportunities ordinarily offered the natural parent are not available. Reciprocal marital role relationships between husband and wife are not worked out prior to the assumption of parental roles. Husband and wife cannot *gradually* acquire their parental role functions. There is not opportunity to establish a primary husband-wife bond prior to the birth of children (see, also, Chapter 2 on family developmental tasks). And parents have no time gradually to establish a generation barrier between themselves and their offspring.

The premarital relationship of the stepparent to family members as acquaintance, friend and fiance of the natural parent seems to interfere with his establishing appropriate differential relationships as spouse and parent, and with his function as authority figure. The working out of marital and parental problems simultaneously seems to encourage the inappropriate involvement of the children in marital dissension. The natural parent's prior relationship to the child, often pathologically intensified during and after the dissolution of the previous marriage, makes a primary husband-wife bond more difficult to establish. This difficulty is often increased by a mother's guilt about taking away from her son the status of "man of the house," or by a child's terror of desertion by his only remaining natural parent.

The relationship of Mrs. G. and Ruth before the marriage came to have particular importance in the severe strain between them after it. Ruth had liked Mrs. G.'s cooking and liked going for walks with Mrs. G. When she had gotten a new haircut or dress, Mrs. G.'s opinion was important to her. Now, when there seemed to be nothing but antipathy between them, it was the memory of that earlier time that sustained them in looking for a resolution.

Taboo Dilution

Sexual relations between parent and child are strongly prohibited, but implications for stepparents are less clear: In 1940, 26 states permitted stepfather-daughter marriage. No taboo at all exists for "nonparent." As the stepparent is all three of these, the impact of the taboo is weakened, and the roles dependent on it are diffused.

In our cases the absence of clear sanctions against sexual relations between stepparents and children intensified normal difficulties in channeling sexual impulses of family members. In some cases mothers "saw" potential incest in every intimacy between stepfather and daughter. In others highly sexualized fondling, hugging, and kissing between stepfather and daughter alternated with horrified and embarrassed avoidance of any intimacy. In a few, overt sexual relations occurred. The effects of such confusion were: pressures toward the breakdown of generation barriers, the abrogation of the primary husband-wife bond, and a blurring of the differential relationships of stepfather as husband and father.

SUMMARY OF GUIDANCE IMPLICATIONS*

1. Stepparents and their spouses need to be confronted with the fact that the unnatural attempt to be 100% sweetness and light in order to disprove the popular image of "wicked stepparent" will eventually backfire. It may even confirm the child's suspicions that the stepparent is phony. It needs to be clarified that stepparents, like natural parents, will have both negative and positive feelings about the child.

---

* This section was written by L. Eugene Arnold.

2. By the same token, stepparents need to be reminded that children have both positive and negative feelings to natural parents as well as to stepparents. Therefore, a few negative manifestations by the child do not imply either that the stepparent has failed in his parent role or that the child has necessarily rejected him as parent.

3. Even where the child is obviously rejecting, the stepparent can be apprised that this is still not proof of stepparent failure: It may merely be the child's problem, possibly related to what he has suffered in the past. It can be pointed out that the most vehement rejection may in fact be a noble defense against what the child would see as disloyalty—embracing the stepparent wholeheartedly as parent.

4. It needs to be clarified that the stepparent has indeed intruded into the child's life, and it is understandable for the child to react, but the stepparent is within his rights, even his duty, in these intrusions. Therefore, the stepparent need not feel defensive and the child need not be blamed for realistic adjustment problems.

5. Like adoptive and foster parents (see Chapter 27), stepparents need to admit that their families are different, and learn to live with the child's continuing psychological relationship with his previous parent, whether dead or divorced.

6. Stepparents and their spouses need to be supported with realistic empathy for the stepparents' stressful task of quickly learning the double role of spouse and parent. It is helpful to remind them that learning any new skill or role takes a while, and they can expect improvement with practice.

7. In some cases a frank discussion of "taboo dilution" anxieties can help by a) providing ventilation and subsequent support, b) revealing that both are trying hard to do the right thing for the child, and c) emphasizing that feelings or impulses do not equal action.

8. The stepparent needs to be given permission to take the parent role, especially in discipline. It is important that such permission come from the stepparent's spouse as well as from the professional. This may require that the spouse (natural parent) work through some doubts in his or her own mind. The professional can be supportive and even directive in this regard.

9. The stepparent's spouse may need to be confronted with the necessity for clarifying the reasonable primacy of the husband-wife bond. This may be necessary to disabuse the child of destructive fantasies or hopes that he can get rid of the stepparent and again be first in the natural parent's heart. Many parents find this difficult to do. They feel

that it is not right because the child was there first. They need permission, support, and maybe even direction in making this difficult move. It helps to point out that this move is actually best for the child: it will give him security, certainty, reality, and the opportunity to develop his own life, with later attachments to his own spouse in a real, rather than fantasy, relationship.

REFERENCE

FAST, I. & CAIN, A. C.: The stepparent role: Potential for disturbances in family functioning. *Amer. J. Orthopsychiat.*, 36:485-491, 1966.

Chapter 26

Helping Teenage Mothers

Myrtle L. LeBow

Parenting is a dynamic process starting in childhood and continuing throughout life's developmental phases (see Chapter 2). Gaps in the teenage mother's own parenting become evident when pregnancy activates stresses in her relationship to her own mother. Bibring (1959), Benedek (1970), Deutsch (1945), and others have documented the shifts in familial relationship and its impact on life situations and behavior. Most teen mothers suffer the additional problem of being unwed. To help the teen mother, wed or unwed, one needs to start while she is pregnant, supporting her throughout the pregnancy, delivery, and postpartum period, as well as helping her with the technical parenting of her child.

Many programs seek to handle the medical, educational, social, and

The author wishes to acknowledge the assistance of Joan Albert, M.S. (Psychology), Gayle Nathanson, M.S.W., Vera Bergan, Principal of Lloyde School, and the teachers of Lloyde School.

emotional needs of the pregnant teenager. Some programs are able to help the teen mother after the birth of her child. I do not know whether they see the program (as we do) as enhancing the parenting process for both the mother and her child. The information in this chapter is derived from two sources: 1) a program sponsored by Los Angeles County School District teen mother's program (Lloyde School), and 2) mothers seen in a child guidance clinic with a history of being unwed mothers. Both groups are low income.

LLOYDE SCHOOL TEEN MOTHERS' PROGRAM

Many girls come from broken homes, or homes with remarriages of the parents. Their ages range from 13 to 17 years. Because of the liberal abortion laws in California, these are girls who choose to keep their babies. Over the last seven years, only about 2% have given up their babies for adoption.

The staff is composed of three high school teachers, a teacher's aide and a part-time nurse. The function of the latter is to take a medical and pregnancy history, make home visits, especially if the girl is ill and cannot attend class, and conduct the class on Family Development. This course covers prenatal care, nutrition, obstetrical problems including delivery, and questions of general health for the teen mother and her child. A child development specialist helps the girls with the physical and emotional care of their babies. The psychiatric social worker is both individual and group counselor. She is also coordinator of the program and the contact with outside agencies, arranging for outside speakers, such as public welfare workers, adoption workers, and vocational counselors. I act as psychiatric consultant to both the girls and the staff.

The three classrooms are located on a high school campus, but separate from the other students. One is a loosely organized room with study tables, sewing machines, and kitchen facilities. The second is a nursery and rest area for the girls who may be tired; the third is a conference room.

A girl is referred as soon as her pregnancy is confirmed by a physician. She remains throughout pregnancy and for four to six months postpartum. The Education Code of the State does not allow us to keep the girls longer. We encourage them to *bring their babies to school,* keeping them in the nursery area. This has an advantage not only for the new mothers, but also for the other pregnant girls: They have an opportunity to hold a real baby before their own arrives. This brings the comprehension that a baby isn't an inanimate doll, but a squirming, crying infant.

In this program, as in Webster School and YMED (Howard, 1968; Osofsky et al., 1968), the girls live at home, in contrast to maternity homes such as the Florence Crittenton Homes (Bernstem, 1971). It is my impression that girls choosing a maternity home put their babies up for adoption more frequently than do girls living in their parents' home. Of course, the type of girls going to maternity homes may be different, even though some of the problems are similar.

PSYCHODYNAMICS OF THE TEEN MOTHER

Although each girl has her own unique problems, a persistent theme with all our girls is the feeling that prior to pregnancy there existed a *poor mother-daughter relationship*. The girl felt emotionally on the periphery of her nuclear family. As her adolescence approached, conflicts over emancipation were expressed in struggles around obedience, school, dating restrictions, and truancy. The girl would vacillate between deep *longing for dependency* and abrupt, explosive "independence." Many of the girls incorporated into their own self-image the negative expectations of their parents. Unconsciously they *incorporated the rejecting, unnurturing mother*.

We see two variations of family dynamics: 1) The girl's mother sees the daughter's adolescence, with its sexuality, as a threat to her relationship with her husband and unconsciously *encourages the daughter to act out sexually* with her peers. There is often a nonverbal collusion to break rules set by the father. The daughter acts out to please the seductive father (real or fantasied) and to please the mother by bringing her a gift, the baby. She unconsciously hopes the mother will nurture her baby, thus indirectly nurturing her. 2) The girl may *resent a stepfather*, feeling she has lost her pre-adolescent position to this stranger. Here there is a great deal of overt *competition for mother's love*. Once again, the mother may push her to act out away from the home.

Her *relationship with the putative father* appears related to her own feelings of low self-esteem. He fulfills her desperate wish to be held and nurtured, to be loved by someone, if only for a moment. Most girls have little erotic feelings in their sexual encounter. Many of the boys leave them before the baby is born; by delivery time the girl may be relating to another boy.

The *feelings toward the baby are vague*. The baby represents a companion, a source of unconditioned love, a plaything without any sense of reality, and sometimes the hope of achieving a positive adult status in contrast to the previous negative child status.

The teenage mother needs as much nurturing as her child. Therefore, the parenting process begins as soon as the girl enters the program. By mothering the pregnant teenager in a positive, accepting manner, without encouraging regression, we hope to free her emotionally to be able to parent her own child. (Cf. the surrogate mothers for abusing mothers in Chapter 22, and contrast with the self-reparenting by transactional analysis in Chapter 6.)

GUIDANCE DURING PREGNANCY

Medical

In regard to medical risks of teenage pregnancies, Osofsky et al. (1968) have pointed out that many girls are in triple jeopardy: 1) As adolescents their body is already under metabolic and physiological stress. Therefore they have increased risks of weight gain, anemia, urinary infections, hypertension, toxemia, and Caesarean sections. 2) In general, adolescents have *poor nutritional habits,* which gain greater significanec in pregnancy. 3) A third stress for some girls is the *burden of health problems* frequently seen in lower socioeconomic families: poor nutrition and increased incidence of such illnesses as tuberculosis, diabetes, respiratory problems, and genetic and other physical abnormalities. The infants, too, are in the high-risk category, with prematurity, less than average birth weight, high neonatal death rate, early respiratory infections, and multiple neurological defects.

Emotional problems interfere with prenatal care. Because many girls deny their pregnancy, they do not seek early prenatal care. They see the doctor as another authoritarian figure in their lives. They feel that doctors, like teachers and parents, are critical of them, and they are sometimes right. Many girls are frightened by the changes in their physical appearance; with this may come anger and feelings of lowered self-esteem. Moreover, they are exposed to an incredible number of superstitions and "old wives' " tales, which they believe under the influence of their tremendous anxiety.

Group counseling sessions tend to deal with these anxieties. Since most of our girls are on welfare, we have sought to recommend certain obstetricians who are warm, sympathetic, and patient with the girls' provocative behavior. Our workers keep close contact with the doctors throughout the pregnancy. Many girls eventually develop pride and trust in their doctors, which, if held within bounds, is a valuable asset during the trying period of delivery. The teacher's and counselor's interest in the girl's physical health enhances her feeling that "someone cares."

Classroom discussions and projects center around nutrition and general health for mother and baby. In homemaking projects they make clothes for themselves or the baby. Although many girls had chores at home, few were allowed to experiment and prepare food they deemed enjoyable. They are encouraged as part of group participation to make their lunches at school.

Social and Educational Problems

The attitude of the public and of the schools concerning pregnant teenagers has shifted. By 1969 only 10% of unwed mothers entered maternity homes (Goodman, 1969). Thus 90% remained in the community.

Teen mothers need to be *guided through the social agencies* that can help them. We assist them with the complicated paperwork necessary to obtain public assistance. We try to protect them from the hostility and moralizing of the unskilled workers in some agencies. At group meetings a social worker from public welfare talks to them about their legal rights.

Many of the girls have poor school records, so an attempt is made to devise an *educational program that meets the need of each girl*. Since productivity will vary with the physical and emotional health of the individual girl, a program has evolved whereby each girl is expected to complete a specific number of assignments or "contracts" per semester in order to receive school credit. Many girls for the first time have experienced success in school work, enhancing their self-esteem at a crucial period in their lives. This success apparently results from these facts: 1) Each program is individualized; 2) reading material is consciously chosen to be relevant to adolescents and teen mothers; 3) although many girls have initially tested the teachers with provocative behavior, they soon develop a personal relationship with them. For the first time, they are able to ask questions when confused. Peers encourage this relationship. The *teachers accept their role as encouraging, nurturing persons.* The nurse and teachers try to coordinate the subject matter. Creative writing encourages the girls to express their anxieties and other feelings. An English composition or a casual conversation between student and teacher can serve as clues to potential emotional conflicts. The teacher may suggest that the girl speak with the social worker or psychiatrist. If she refuses, at least the entire staff is alerted to emotional crisis.

Emotional Problems

There are always crises in the girl's lives that demand immediate intervention: an altercation with the boyfriend, a fight with parent resulting in temporarily leaving home; a severe depression precipitated by physical illness and resulting absence from the program. For all such problems crisis intervention attempts immediate resolution. In addition, a more continuing support is needed for some problems. Pregnancy of the teenager awakens not only her own earlier unresolved conflicts but also those of the parents. There is a shift in the entire family's dynamics that must be treated.

Since many girls seek to deny the pregnancy, they also deny potential family conflicts. Indeed, during pregnancy many of the overt confrontations between a girl and her parents actually do decrease. She receives a great deal of emotional support from the program, decreasing her provocative behavior at home. Sometimes her mother's concern about her physical status relieves her of her normal household chores. Frequently her parents begin treating her on an adult level, exchanging adult sexual jokes and discussing personal problems. Conflicts about social activities and late hours abate because she is content to stay home. She has attained the position she had secretly desired, to be nurtured by mother and to be accepted into the family structure. She needs to realize that this sand castle may be abruptly washed away by the inevitable tide of delivery.

Using an Unexpected Crisis to Enhance Emotional Growth

On one occasion, one of the girls started going into labor during school hours. Unable to contact her mother or relatives, the nurse and one of the teachers took her to the hospital. This incident stimulated great anxiety among the girls. Until then many of them were never confronted with the anxiety associated with going to the hospital. An emergency counseling session dealt with their fears of being left alone when their labor would start. This led to more specific expressions of earlier fears of abandonment by their mothers. They were able to express anger toward their mothers who they felt were never available, either physically or emotionally. To make the group session more meaningful and concrete, the teachers suggested as an English assignment that the girls write what alternate plans they could suggest if their mothers were not available. In this way we further decreased their anxiety and had available an alternate plan for each girl.

We have learned to use each similar crisis as a possible growth experience. We have dealt with miscarriage, stillbirth, hospitalization for toxemia, hospitalization of a newborn infant, and severe postpartum depression, including one psychiatric hospitalization.

Denial

Most frustrating to the counselor is the inability of the teenager to face the reality of her pregnancy, delivery, and responsibility for raising a child. The denial by both girl and mother is often so great that she reaches the fourth or fifth month before entering the program. Her reason for her change in appearance is, "I thought I was just getting fat." Morning sickness is described as, "I thought I had the flu." Often the girl's mother raises the possibility of pregnancy only after she has noticed for months that the girl has not menstruated.

Older married women often fantasize while pregnant what sex the baby will be, what its physical appearance will be, whether it will be physically normal, or whether she herself will be able to function as an adequate mother. By contrast, our teen mother's fantasies, if expressed, are vague. Sometimes we hear them say: "This baby is the one thing that is really mine," or "My baby will love me forever." An awareness of the baby having a separate personality is rare.

We show the girls films on pregnancy and delivery and take them on field trips to the hospital, labor and delivery rooms, and nursery. It is our impression that the impact is not great. A greater impact has resulted from including in our discussion group both pregnant girls and mothers who have recently delivered. Their personal description of the delivery and their feelings about it are far more meaningful. It is a shared experience. Anxieties focus on fears of pain, body mutilation, abandonment, and loss of control verbalized in such statements as, "I'll scream like a baby."

None of our girls has considered natural childbirth. We do, as part of the physical education requirement, teach the Lamaze exercises. We encourage the girls to use them during labor to feel some control in the delivery. Their relationship with their physician helps decrease the sense of abandonment. Many girls suppress the details of the delivery.

GUIDANCE DURING THE POSTPARTUM PERIOD

The two to three days postpartum in the hospital are described as a period of maximum enjoyment. The teen mother is completely cared for and receives maximum attention from friends and family.

Weathering the Withdrawal of Support

This makes the first few weeks after delivery crucial. After two to three days of total narcissistic gratification, she abruptly finds the *attention turned toward the new baby*. Gradually she builds up deep resentment toward "that creep who everybody thinks is cute."

These feelings are not unique to teenage unwed mothers. They occur whenever there is a new baby. Since most hospital stays are only two to three days, the woman has not had time to recoup from the physical exhaustion of the delivery. Postpartum hormonal changes add to the mild, transient depression seen in many women. With a mature couple, the husband can compensate by increasing his personal affection toward his wife. The wife is able to gain gratification and encouragement in her sense of mothering. Often another person is available to help in the care of the baby and the household duties.

The unwed teen mother has none of these advantages. Her parents, except for the one day of excitement when she and baby return home, go about their normal routine. She is given the total responsibility of the infant, often with constant pressure that she "keep that kid quiet." We believe that two important sources of the postpartum depressions in our girls are the continued feeling of alienation and the awareness that pregnancy has *failed to achieve the unconscious goal of acceptance by mother*. The new mother may turn toward her baby for her source of love, but the baby fails her. This adds to her frustration. She often verbalizes her *longing to return to the period of her pregnancy* when "everybody took care of me. Now it's all gone." This dynamic plays a role in repeat pregnancies despite contraceptive information.

Usually one of our staff makes a home visit within the first week postpartum. Correctly interpreting this act as our concern for them, many girls return to the program as early as two to three weeks after delivery. Most of the group discussions concern the teen mother's relationship with her own mother. We interpret how fruitless and self-destructive it is to expect and demand dependency gratification from her mother. We focus on the girl's normal needs as an adolescent, encouraging her moves for independence. Living at home presents many practical problems. She is expected to be an adult with her baby, but an adolescent in her social life. Some individual crises are handled in group discussions while others are treated individually, including the girl's parents or boyfriend (husband if she has one) in the discussions.

Practical Problems

The new mother must face some practical concerns. She is usually deeply troubled about her physical appearance. She resents the striae on her abdomen and breasts. As part of the physical education class, we encourage her to do the exercises recommended by her physician. Her narcissism usually helps her lose weight and strengthen her muscular tone. Nevertheless she feels different, not like the other teenagers. This is a constant theme—that this experience has made her different from her girlfriends. One can only deal with this reality in a supportive manner.

Another area of practical concern is the health and physical care of the baby. Many of the babies are slow in development and smaller than average. Chronic respiratory infections and dermatitis are common. The girls tend to ignore many symptoms as part of their denial of the mother role, but they also lack experience. There may be an amazing lack of common sense information in spite of coming from a large family. Apparently the girls' mothers have never taken the time to explain practical household tasks and child rearing. This problem, of course, may not be unique with teen mothers. However, one must constantly encourage the girls to ask questions, so they do not need to "fake it." Our child development specialist often finds at the first home visit that the girl is afraid to bathe the baby and cannot make a formula. Concrete suggestions relieve her anxiety and again she feels someone cares about her.

In spite of the value of breast feeding medically and emotionally, we have discovered that most of the teen mothers have a strong aversion to it. Perhaps it reawakens their own dependent wishes. The girls associate breasts to sexuality, openly stating it is "too embarrassing" to feed the baby this way.

Problems Nurturing

Even when a bottle is used, the feeding process is difficult for them. If not encouraged to hold their baby, most teen mothers would prop the bottle. We have rocking chairs in the nursery, encouraging them to relax, sing, and talk to their baby. Almost all of the girls use pacifiers. The reason given is "I can't stand his yelling. He must be mad at me." They have not learned how to distinguish the different cries of their baby. They also constantly *misinterpret his actions*. The following vignette is an example:

> The child development specialist was encouraging a mother to push against her baby's feet to strengthen his muscles. The mother's re-

sponse was one of annoyance: "He's pushing me away. He doesn't like me." When it was suggested she look at his face, she saw that he was laughing. Only then did she realize they were playing a game and that the baby was having fun with her.

Only with such realization can a mutually gratifying relationship between mother and child develop.

Another crucial period occurs when the baby becomes mobile (9-12 months) and begins to assert his individuality. The significance of this period is described by Margaret Mahler and her coworkers (1975) in their work on symbiosis and individuation. Our teen mothers have shifted their dependency tie from their own mother to the boyfriend to the baby, always hoping to be loved. As the baby asserts its own identity, symbolized by the "no" response, the symbiotic relationship is threatened. Not appreciating or understanding her child's nonverbal communication, the young mother becomes frustrated and angry. She sees this stage of normal development as a rejection of her and her love. Sometimes she becomes punitive, expecting the child to have adult responses. We see this as a time for potential child abuse (see Chapter 22).

Teenage Fathers and Marriages

Our girls' relationship with the putative fathers is fleeting and based on a storybook fantasy of marriage, with the hope that the father will be an all-giving, nurturing person. Most of the fathers are peers. They are concerned about the girl's health but do not intend to marry her, and few do.

Of the teenage marriages that do occur, few have been successful. Many of the mothers did not marry the putative father but someone else. The reason repeatedly given for marriage failure is, "We were too young. We didn't know what marriage was like." The consistent complaint from the wife is, "He just wants to stay with the boys and have fun." The young husband feels his wife's demands on his time are overwhelming. Gradually he resents being a husband and mother to both his wife and child. We handle each case individually, referring the couple to an outside agency if necessary. We found we can be supportive on practical problems such as housing, budget, vocational training, but it is more difficult to involve them in discussing their emotional needs.

FOLLOW-UP

We lose contact with our girls after 8-9 months. Many other programs have the same difficulty. The program does represent a sense of security—

a good parent. After the girls have left the program, they still call at times of personal crisis. They informally will drop by to talk to other girls or to show us, with a mother's pride, the child.

The reality problems of returning to regular school, seeking economic and emotional independence and returning to a social life with peers are tremendous. Many girls never return to school because they have no one to care for their children. If a girl leaves home, her life is lonely and isolated. If she works, she can only afford an inadequate babysitter. If she remains at home, she has constant battles with her own mother for the baby's attention and love.

We have long felt that the most meaningful way to help the wed or unwed teen mother would be the establishment of *infant day-care centers,* preferably close to the girl's school. Medically and psychologically these babies are high-risk, needing expert care. Therefore, such a program should include trained personnel and a child development specialist. The young mothers could be offered guidance whenever they came to pick up their babies. This way we could continue to cultivate the parenting process for the young mother and her child.

BIBLIOGRAPHY

BENEDEK, T.: The psychobiology of pregnancy. In: E. J. Ánthony & T. Benedek (Eds.), *Parenthood.* Boston: Little, Brown, 1970.

BERNSTEM, R.: *Helping Unmarried Mothers.* New York: Association Press, 1971.

BIBRING, G.: Some considerations of the psychological processes in pregnancy. *Psychoanalytic Study of the Child.* Vol. XIV. New York: International Universities Press, 1959, pp. 113-121.

DEUTSCH, H.: *The Psychology of Women.* Vols. 1 & 2. New York: Grune & Stratton, 1945.

GOODMAN, E.: Providing uninterrupted education and supportive services for adolescent expectant mothers. *Excep. Child.,* May, 1969, pp. 713-719.

HOWARD, M.: *Multiservice Programs for Pregnant School Girls.* Washington, D. C.: U.S. Department of Health, Education & Welfare. Children's Bureau, 1968 (a).

HOWARD, M.: *The Webster School—a District of Columbia Program for Pregnant Girls.* Washington, D. C.: U.S.G.P.O., 1968 (b).

McDONALD, T. F.: Teenage pregnancy. *J.A.M.A.,* 236:598-599, 1976.

MAHLER, M., PINE, F., & BERGMAN, A.: *The Psychological Birth of the Normal Infant.* New York: Basic Books, 1975.

OSOFSKY, H., HAGEN, J., & WOOD, P.: A program for pregnant girls. *Amer. J. Ob. & Gyn,* 100:1020-1027, 1968.

Chapter 27

Adoptive and
Foster Parents

Kenneth W. Watson

The difficult task of parenting is made more complex if the child is not one's own "natural-born." In addition to the concerns common to all parents and those particular problems generated in any specific instance by individual or family dynamics, there are also certain problems that arise from the foster or adoptive situation.

The terms "foster care" and "adoption" both describe families in which the child-parent relationship has been socially constructed rather than biologically determined; therefore the two situations share some problems. Other problems occur according to the particular kind of foster or adoptive plan. For instance, parents who have adopted an infant must decide how and when to tell the child about the adoption, while foster

Dr. Watson is a member of Adoption Committee, Child Care Association of Illinois; Committee to Review Standards on Adoption, Child Welfare League of America; Illinois Adoption Advisory Committee.

parents providing indefinite care must commit themselves fully to a child knowing that he might be reclaimed by his natural family at any moment. However, both must deal with questions from the children about why they are not living with the parents of birth.

ADOPTION-FOSTER CARE CONTINUUM

All adoptive plans are distinguished from all foster care plans by the legal action which confers upon the adoptive parent substantially the same rights and responsibilities that exist in a natural child-parent relationship. Further distinctions among the various possible plans in each category are based on the purpose or intent of the plan, the commitment to permanence, and the degree of family autonomy provided.

Using these factors, we can construct a continuum. Foster home plans can be arranged on one side and adoptive plans on the other with formal legal action as the midpoint. On the far end of the adoptive side would be the traditional infant adoption in which a couple who cannot have children biologically adopts a baby whose natural family is unrelated and unknown to them. This couple intends to assume full parenting responsibility for the child on a permanent basis. At the far end of the foster care side of the continuum would be a family who accepts a child on a temporary or indefinite basis because the child needs shelter. These parents expect that most of the legal and financial responsibility for the child will remain vested with the natural family, a social agency, or the court, and that the child will be with them only a short time. Between these two end points, all other foster care and adoptive plans can be accommodated.

Some kinds of foster care (for instance, a long-term plan in which the foster parents assume guardianship and financial responsibility for the child) approach adoption, and some kinds of adoption (for instance, the adoption of an older child who has special needs and whose placement is supported by some continuing financial subsidy) are very near foster care.

Common Areas of Concern

All foster and adoptive parents experience varying degrees of difficulty in: 1) accepting that their family is different; 2) explaining to the child the circumstances around his being a member of their family; 3) recognizing that the child is a shared child—that he has another set of parents; 4) determining the boundaries of their parental role and accepting the appropriate constraints and sanctions around that role; and 5) recognizing the needs within themselves that the child is to fulfill and assessing the appropriateness of their expectations in that area. The rest of the chapter will discuss these five concerns more fully.

ACCEPTING DIFFERENCES

The moment one acts on a wish to become an adoptive or foster parent, one creates a set of conditions which distinguishes one from parents who beget their own children. An acceptance of these conditions and the ability to work within their framework is essential to success in the parental role. Being a foster or adoptive parent is *not* the same as being a biological parent. Understanding and dealing with the differences are the first tasks these parents face.

Differences in Adoptive Families

The childless couple who seek adoption in order to experience parenthood usually do so only when it becomes clear to them that they cannot have a child biologically. They try to recreate through the adoptive situation circumstances similar to those of the biological parenthood which they have been denied. Thus they seek a healthy child as young as possible who resembles the fantasied child to whom they would have given birth. They *wish to deny,* rather than recognize, the differences that adoption makes. This denial may reflect the parents' inability to come to grips with their own *problem of infertility.*

Such a denial impedes their talking with the child about his adoption or his "other" family to help him deal with concerns about his origins and identity. It also complicates the adoptive parents' acceptance of the child for what he really is. All parents have expectations for their children and may be disappointed when the child develops in ways contrary to these expectations. If the adoptive parents wish to perceive the adopted child as conforming to their own "family traits," they may fail to notice or support desirable characteristics which are different.

Differences in Foster Families

Denial of the differences that foster care makes is usually less pronounced because it is not as easy. Usually the foster child comes to the

foster family at a later age, has memories of an earlier family, and often has involvement with that other family, a social agency, or a court. These realities make it difficult for the foster family to ignore the fact that it is different. Yet the attempt persists. Often the foster family suggests that the child use its family name. If the parents also have biological children, it may be hard for them to accept that they should *not* treat the foster child the same as their own.

The foster parents' inclination to deny the intrinsic differences in their families may reflect a wish to simplify their own role. If they recognize that a foster parent is significantly different from a biological parent, they must examine the differences and learn how to parent in a way that meets the special needs of the foster child. It is easier to believe that the kind of love and family interaction they already have is really all that is necessary. While many foster children have suffered a lack of love in their past, few are those for whom that can be remedied by placement in a loving family alone. A loving family is only the beginning point of successful foster care.

Foster parents may also wish to deny the reality of the foster placement to ease their feelings of discomfort within their community. They may be seen as contributing to neighborhood or school problems by bringing "problem children" into the community. They may even be perceived as odd because of their willingness to undertake foster parenting. They feel the less attention paid to the foster care situation, the better.

A third source of foster parents' wish to deny the differences is their wish to protect the foster child. They know that he may feel stigmatized and unworthy as a result of his placement. However, they need to realize that they only add to his burden if they encourage a denial of the foster care status; this gives the implicit message that it is bad to be a foster child.

COMMUNICATION WITH THE CHILD AROUND HIS SITUATION

Only when parents understand and accept the different kind of family that they have, and resolve the issues discussed in the preceding section, will they be able to communicate well to the child the reason he is in their home.

Communicating Adoption

Perhaps the most frequent problem that faces parents who have adopted infants or very young children is *when and how to tell the child that he is adopted.*

One possibility, of course, is to *not tell him at all*. This brings three problems: 1) It is difficult to keep such an event a genuine secret, and in many instances the adoptive parents, other family, or friends let slip the information; 2) the sense of trust between parent and child, which is the basis of the child's development of a capacity to trust, is jeopardized by the lie about the child's origins and closest relationships; and 3) the implication is that adoption is such a terrible event that neither adoptive parents nor child have the capacity to face up to it and its consequences.

A second possibility, which *acknowledges the adoption but denies the child his natural family,* is to tell him that his other parents were both killed in some accident. Again the issue of trust between parent and child arises. Also, the adoptive parents may be perceived by the child as either rescuing him or being burdened by him as a result of the accident.

The third possibility accepts that a *child's awareness about his adoption should be a natural part of his growing up.* Information is shared at each stage of his development in response to his questions or his capacity to understand. This approach, though sound, can only succeed if the adoptive parents are comfortable with their decision to adopt and in their role as adoptive parents.

Adoption and Sex

This approach is analogous to sensible sex education. A simple recitation of the general facts about adoption, either in response to a child's questions or introduced in the normal discussions about family relationships, will provide a background for the child to raise concerns that he may have. It will also make it clear to the child that it is acceptable for him to raise those concerns. The facts themselves are relatively simple; the problems usually come when they are embroidered with statements intended to make them easier for the child to comprehend or assimilate but which usually only becloud the situation.

Adoption can be explained in three direct statements: 1) some people give birth to children but do not wish or are not able to parent them; 2) some other people would like to be parents but are unable to give birth to children; 3) adoption is a process which allows children to grow up with parents who do wish them and who feel able to parent them, even though those children were born to different parents.

Obviously each of these statements can lead to questions from the child that will guide the adoptive parents to the child's concerns. Parents feeling uneasy in their role tend to romanticize the adoptive process. They may attempt to justify the natural parents' decision by telling the child how thoughtful they were in working out an adoption plan for the child's care. They need to justify their own role as adoptive parents by telling how much love they had and how much they wanted a child to whom to give this love, or by putting themselves in the role of rescuers. They may try to help the child feel more wanted by telling him about how they chose him above all of the other children whom they might have adopted. While none of these will necessarily damage the child, they all tend to clutter the process of sharing adoption with the child. They block the child's opportunity to raise his own questions, fantasies, and concerns.

One problem for adoptive parents is that the opportunities to discuss adoption frequently come as responses to the child's questions about the origins of human life. In addition to possible uneasiness around dealing with sexual questions, the adoptive parents may feel particular discomfort in this area because of their infertility. Sexual adequacy is often equated with procreation, and any questions about why they did not have children biologically may be threatening. To add to the complications, the adopted infant was likely the product of a relationship without marriage. Feelings about this or feelings about the unfair ease with which some people can have children in contrast to themselves may intrude on the adoptive parents' attempts to discuss adoption in an open and natural way.

Adoptive Parenting and the Child's Identity

The child usually has questions about his natural family. He may wish to pursue a search for further information or for the family itself. Adoptive parents frequently react defensively, feeling that the child's questions or search are somehow a repudiation of the parent-child relationship established by the adoption. They can be helped to realize that a piece of the child's identity is lodged with the family who gave birth to him, and that no adoption nor any amount of "good parenting" by the adoptive parents can replace that missing piece. *The test of the quality of the adoption lies not in whether these questions come, but in the response of the adoptive parents to the questions.*

If the adoptive parents can perceive the naturalness of this sort of inquiry and are secure that they are indeed the child's "real" parents, they can respond to the child's questions with information that they may have and frankly admit ignorance when they do not know. They can also try to assess the importance to the child and decide whether the search should be pursued. *The adoptive parent must ally himself with the child's attempts to establish his identity*—confident that the core of that identity is the child's feeling of value and worth which develops from his experiences in the adoptive family.

Communicating with a Foster Child

The issue for foster parents is generally not the wish to hide the fostering situation from the child, but the *wish to protect the child* from the painful question of *why his natural family has discarded him*. Frequently foster parents discourage a child from talking about his earlier experiences and the circumstances leading to his placement. This only supports the child's fantasy that foster care is something so bad that one should not discuss it.

In some instances the circumstances that lead to a child's placement are unknown to the foster parents. In such cases it is best for them simply to say that. When they do know the facts, these should be shared with the child in a simple, direct way which makes clear to the child that his *placement is the result of his parent's inability to take care of him*. It is inevitable that the foster child will feel some responsibility for his placement (and with older children it may be appropriate), but he needs to be helped to see that he is not responsible for his natural parents' decisions nor for their limitations as parents.

When a child asks why he became a foster child, he may be seeking reassurance of his own value more than factual information. This reassurance comes from the foster parents' acceptance of his foster care status and their continuing respect and affection for him.

Often foster parents are uncomfortable sharing negative information about a child's parents with him—such as alcoholism, mental illness, or criminal conviction. Not sharing such information increases its possible destructive impact. For if the foster parents cannot talk about it, the child perceives it as too terrible for even adults to confront. It may be hard for the foster parents to accept that the *child has the right to the facts* about his natural family *and to the pain* which this information may cause him. They cannot protect him, and attempts to do so only add to his burden. The support he needs comes not from attempts to hide the facts but from efforts to help him understand and cope.

Of course, the foster parents' capacity to share openly with the child information about his placement is dependent upon their own acceptance of it and their ability to deal with their own negative feelings about the natural parents. This may not be easy for them. People who have decided to become foster parents usually place a high value on the parent role. It is hard for them to respect parents who have failed or abdicated that role. In addition, they may feel in competition with the natural parents for the child's affection. Therefore, they may rightly fear conveying to the child some disrespect for the natural parents, and, implicitly, for the very foster care plan in which they are participating.

SHARING THE CHILD

Whatever differences various kinds of foster and adoptive parents may experience, they all have one thing in common: *The child they are parenting also has another set of parents.* The child is always shared with those parents who exist as a *psychological shadow* even if not as a physical presence.

Sharing in Adoption

However early a child is adopted and however well he is assimilated into his adoptive family, his *genes and ancestors* come from his "other" family. The fact that one's genes or ancestors cannot be changed does not render them unimportant in one's *self-perception*. If the adopted child is to integrate these threads into his identity, the adoptive parents must recognize their significance and not be threatened by the importance the child attaches to them. The child's questions and interest can be handled in the natural way described under "Communication with the Child" in the preceding pages.

Sharing in Foster Care

Sharing the child is a much more immediate and continuing problem for foster parents. Often both of the child's families are a part of his ongoing experience; frequently they are in conflict with each other in matters of values or procedures. Even when they are in basic agreement, some tension seems inevitable. The child's *placement suggests some failure of the natural family* to fully meet the child's needs; to the extent that the foster parents are successful in doing so, they are competing with the child's natural family!

Most foster parents wish to provide for the foster child that which will *make up for any deprivation* prior to coming into their home. Most children come into foster care following a period of time with their natural families. Unlike newborn infants, they bring into the new family memories of their life thus far, often including scars of prior experiences. Foster families generally feel that they possess a restorative capacity to make up for previous problems. To some extent this may be a realistic expectation (indeed, it is one of the reasons the community sanctions foster care), but it colors the way the foster parents relate to the child and may cause many concerns for foster parents.

If the foster child is currently in contact with the natural family, perhaps even spending some time with that family, there may be problems with *conflicting value messages* to the child from the two families. If the foster and natural parents are allied around the major issues, this presents a problem of limited size; if they are openly in opposition, the problem is severe for both child and foster parents.

Frequently the foster parents feel their task of parenting would be easier if the natural family would just abandon the child to their care. Then they could integrate the child into their family and not have to deal with these value conflicts. When that does happen, the foster parents must deal with a new problem: helping the child come to grips with abandonment. This is different from the situation with which the infant-adoptive family has to deal, because in that instance the child's tie to the natural family is not based on shared family experience nor is the loss of of the natural parent experienced so directly.

Another difference from adoption is that foster parents have to *share the child legally*—perhaps with a social agency or court. Legal authority for the child's long-range planning generally lies outside of the foster home. Although foster parents provide day-to-day care, natural families and/or social agencies are usually responsible for decisions about the child's future. This paradox can lead to tragic situations, which can be best avoided if foster parents keep the legal realities in mind.

SANCTIONS AND CONSTRAINTS

Nature and society sanction most parents in their parent role as a result of the child's birth. Within rather broad limits, *giving birth establishes one's rights to rear the child* with minimal interference from outsiders and with a generally recognized sense of "ownership." If the family moves, the child will, of course, go along. The parents are reasonably free to instruct and discipline the child, to guide him in moral and spiritual matters, to make major decisions for him until he is able to make them himself, and to assume responsibility for his behavior. The issues with foster and adoptive parents are less clear. *The particular plan dictates the particular sanctions and constraints;* these in turn shape the particular problems which the parents experience.

Adoptive Sanctions and Constraints

At the adoptive end of the continuum, the courts have bestowed upon the parents society's legal sanction. They have, in effect, said that the adopted parents "own" the child as much as any parent owns his child; the parents are free to act as birth parents would. To be effective, however, this external sanction *must be accompanied by an internal sanction.* The adoptive parents must *feel* as if they have the same kind of sanction as the birth parents. Reservations about this often result in a holding back in some areas of the parenting role. Discipline is one example.

Even with court sanction, the adoptive parents may not feel the same kind of permission to discipline that a natural parent does. This may relate to concerns that the adoptive child will be resentful and turn against his adoption; or the adoptive parent may feel that he has been entrusted with something that really belongs to someone else. This goes back to the earlier discussion about the adoptive parents' comfort with the idea of adoption and with the differences that it makes. Ironically, *it is only their comfort with the differences that allows adoptive parents to function day-to-day the same as natural parents.*

Foster Sanctions and Constraints

Sanctions and constraints are far more problematic for foster parents because their role is always limited and conditional. They have neither legal nor social sanction to act fully as the child's parent. In most instances the boundaries of the foster parent role are poorly defined. The sanction for placement may be the informal request of the parent, the quasi-formal arrangement of a social agency, or the formal plan of the court. In each case constraints limit the foster parent in the parental role.

Perhaps the foremost constraint is time. Foster care is generally begun on a temporary or short-term basis. While the plan may continue over the child's life span, the original intent in most cases is for the child to live again with his natural family or to be adopted elsewhere. The *ambiguity about the length of time* that the foster parents will be serving as parents puts the foster family in the difficult position of trying to parent the child as if he were going to be raised within that family, while at the same time preparing for the fact that the plan could end the next day.

The problem this creates for the foster parents, of course, is whether to invest fully and seek full investment from the child, or to hold back. Experience suggests that when there is a holding back, both the child and the foster parent are frustrated and the placement is undermined. It is the difficult task of the foster parents to commit themselves to the child in a full parental way—and then to deal with the frustrations that arise from the lack of authority to act in the child's best interest.

Like adoptive parents, foster parents may experience special difficulties in discipline. The child they have is "borrowed." They may feel that they have no right to discipline. Indeed, the involvement of the natural family or the social agency may introduce *restrictions around the way the family can discipline.* Underlying all discipline with a foster child is the knowledge that if the situation becomes too difficult, the *foster parents can bring it to an end by demanding the child's removal.* When the boundaries of foster care are clear, and the commitment of the foster parents firm within those boundaries, discipline problems tend to fall into the normal range.

PARENTAL NEEDS AND EXPECTATIONS

In any family situation children meet certain needs of their parents. For instance, they allow their parents to experience the full measure of the adult role, they provide a focus for communication and shared experience between the parents, they represent the future and allow the parent to feel that a part of him will continue in this world beyond his life, and they provide an opportunity for parents to re-work some of the unfinished business of their own lives. Thus, when a child comes into a family there are certain expectations.

For an adopted or foster child, the expectations are different, related to the motivations for seeking a child in this way. The parents' unconscious motivations and hidden expectations for the foster or adopted child may cause problems for the family.

Parental Needs in Adoption

If an infertile couple adopts an infant, he falls heir to all of the expectations the couple had for the biological child that they were denied. In addition, since he represents a partial solution to the infertility problem, he may unwittingly play a role in that area of parental communication and feeling.

Adoption is frequently pursued as a means of reducing tension between a couple who are experiencing childlessness. If no physiological cause of childlessness has been determined, the adoption may be undertaken in hopes that a pregnancy will follow when the couple is not trying so hard to conceive. If a couple also has children biologically, the motivation for adoption needs to be explored to ascertain the special role the adopted child plays within the family and the particular expectations for him.

Parental Needs in Foster Care

Since foster parents, unlike most adoptive parents, are not attempting to duplicate a community norm by taking a child into their family, it is even more important to understand their reasons for taking a foster child. Generalizations about foster parent motivation are dangerous, but a few may suggest areas worth further exploration in a given situation.

For some reason it is important to the family that they have foster children. If they have children born to them, then the motivation to take foster children must relate to the expectation that foster children or the fostering situation will meet some needs different from those met by natural children. If they do not have children, then the question must be raised as to *why they would seek foster care rather than adoption.* For some families, the presence of the child's other family or a social agency is important. They feel a sense of support in caring for the child and do not feel as overwhelmed by parental responsibility.

It is also possible that the family is working on some *unfinished business* for which the presence of a foster child is important. Perhaps they are trying to *prove their competence* because of real or fantasized failure in the past. Perhaps the wish is to demonstrate parental competence beyond that of either the child's family or the family in which the foster parent was raised. Sometimes foster parents have been foster children themselves or have experienced deprivation as a child.

The importance of understanding the motivation of foster parents is not to pass judgment on it, but to see in what ways it may be affecting their expectations.

SUMMARY

Adoptive and foster parents should be helped to recognize and accept the fact that their families are different and to communicate those differences as simply and directly as possible to the children. One of the major differences, of course, is that the child derives his identity from two families. Whether the biological parents are involved with the child from day to day or not, the child must come to terms psychologically with that family, and the foster or adoptive family must accept the existence of that family and share the child with it. Adoptive families should be supported in accepting the full parenting role and performing it, while foster parents need help in locating the boundaries of their role and living with the frustrations that those boundaries impose. Finally, each family places upon the child a burden of living up to its expectations and meeting certain needs of the parents. If the parents can become aware of these needs and decide whether or not it is appropriate to expect that their adopted or foster children meet them, they may be able to focus more on the child's needs and potential and be more comfortably adequate in the parental role.

Chapter 28

Counseling Very Disturbed Parents

E. James Anthony and

Manon McGinnis

Parents with serious psychiatric disorders (psychosis, borderline personality, and severe character pathology) are not only disturbed themselves but are also disturbing for their spouses and children. (Anthony, 1970a, 1970b, 1972, 1975). In our studies of such parents we became increasingly aware of the actual and potential damage that they could inflict on the children. Work with them needs to have two goals: 1) diminishing their psychotic impingements on the daily lives of the children, and 2) helping them to act and feel more competent as parents. However much the disturbing impact and the child-rearing ineptness are denied, the inner parental concept is liable to deteriorate at moments of crisis.

THE INTERMITTENT PARENT

The more pervasive the parental psychopathology is, the more invasive are its effects on the personalities and psychobiological functioning of the children. Yet, we have shown (Anthony, 1972, 1975) that outside the acute episode, the psychotic process, even in the relatively chronic case, tends to function intermittently, so that the child's exposure to abnormal reactions and interactions is not constant. The "psychological day" of the psychotic parent tends to be erratic and unpredictable. Trivial upsets within the family are likely to build up to catastrophic proportions and reverberate longer than for normal parents. Outside such crises, the "psychological day" may be relatively uneventful.

The whole period of development has a similar tendency to intermittence. At certain developmental phases and transitions, especially during development of autonomy and differentiation, parental functioning may deteriorate, or become rigid. There is a proclivity toward greater difficulty over time. Though a disturbed parent can often care adequately for an infant, trouble increasingly ensues as the psychological demands of the mother-child relationship become more complex and psychologically exacting. The range of emotions and interactions accompanying adolescence overtaxes psychological resources that are as limited in dealing with interpersonal as with intrapersonal demands. Normal developmental tendencies toward disillusionment can be grossly exaggerated in these cases; these vulnerable parents are subjected to hostile and ruthless criticisms of themselves both as people and parents. These reinforce their own self-doubts and frequently drive them to "try too hard." Then they often become overprotective, overcontrolling and overanxious, precipitating the very disorders in their children that they are seeking to avoid. The self-absorption of the disturbed parent may also interfere with the exercise of empathy so that their interventions into the lives of their children are characteristically ill-considered, ill-suited, and ill-timed.

Bringing up Father (and Mother)

Normal parents develop along with their children, not only in terms of external qualities of parenting but also in the internal representations of themselves as parents. Thus, as time progresses, they not only deal with their children more efficiently and with greater understanding but they think of themselves as parents. Such external capacities and inner convictions are by no means born with the first child: They have been in the making for many years prior and they may still remain undeveloped after several children.

The preparation for parenthood has a prolonged childhood phase during which the little girl and little boy need to develop elements of motherliness and fatherliness through a growing identification with good and giving parents. The wish to be like a parent imperceptibly gives place to the wish to be a parent and realize the ideals of nurturance, responsibility, and dependability. The passive stance of "being given to" switches to the more active one of "giving," the stance of "being looked after" becomes one of "taking charge." A normal child-parent relationship gradually generates a normal parent-child relationship. When the child-parent relationship of the parent has been unsatisfying or disturbing, the parent-child relationship that follows may become equally problematical.

Under normal conditions, the parental function grows and develops along with the children. The parents take pleasure in their increasing competence as parents and in the increasing competence of the developing child. (See Chapter 2 for more on normal development of parenting.)

The Very Disturbed Person as Parent

All these normal transitions from child to parent and from child-parent relationships to parent-child relationships can undergo distortions. Preparations for parenthood go awry: Motherliness and fatherliness fail to develop adequately; active attitudes of "giving" and "looking after" fail to emerge; the empathic capacity is stunted. The mutual identifications of child with parent and parent with child, based on the presence of admired models, are lacking; consequently, the inner representations of parenthood are as faulty as the outer behaviors.

Pregnancy affords a searching evaluation of "parentability." During pregnancy the very disturbed parent can become even more disturbed and therefore even less prepared for actual parenting. This is particularly true when the mother's own dependency needs are unmet or when the father experiences his wife's final trimester introversion. His narcissism may intensify with his wife's disinclination for sexual relations (interpreted as rejection of him), her demands for more attention, and her increased disposition to anxiety, depression, and fear about her less appealing bodily configuration. Prepsychotic individuals or psychotic individuals in remission are vulnerable to decompensation during the prenatal period.

With the birth of the baby, many disturbed parents find the additional adjustments and pressures too much to cope with. The more that they fail to adapt to the baby, the more the baby fails to adapt; a *mutual maladaptation syndrome* develops in which the parents feel more and more helpless and the infant more and more upset. (See Chapter 5 for more on vicious cycles.) The baby appears to lose (or fail to develop) confidence in the parents, and the parents lose confidence in themselves. This sets the stage for a battering response.

During the toddler phase, both mother and child normally learn to separate from each other: The mother becomes less intrusive and the child more autonomous. In a disturbed situation, both parties find separation fraught with a great degree of ambivalence. A severe *rapprochement* crisis (Mahler, 1975) may follow and the toddler may become tyrannically clinging, demanding, and aggressive.

With the next step in development, the disturbed parent may further impede the growth of the child's independence, reality testing, and wish to achieve, both at school and on the playground. As a result, he may withdraw from outer contact and immerse himself in the unrealistic and often irrational home environment. The child's capacity to overcome these regressive and isolating tendencies depends not only on innate, genetically-transmitted forces but also on the *strengths provided by his other parent*.

Role of the "Well" Parent.

The "well" parent is frequently a misnomer. Due to the general tendency toward homogamous mating, the spouse selected by a mentally sick person is not uncommonly as sick as the index parent. As a result, disturbing provocations are doubled and there is no one close that the child can turn to during crises of insecurity. The "well" parent, besides being preoccupied with personal problems and difficulties with the sick spouse, may also have an equally deficient parenting capacity. One of our studies (Anthony, 1970a) showed a correlation between the degree of a child's disturbance and the "well" parent's rating on an avoiding-attacking continuum. The less helpful and more noxious the parent seemed to be, the more disturbed was the child. It is therefore important to include the "well" spouse in counseling; otherwise he may undo whatever good is accomplished with the "sick" parent.

THE COUNSELING SITUATION WITH VERY DISTURBED PARENTS

Characteristics of Parent

Very disturbed people are as varied as others; generalizations and categorizations have only heuristic value and are not meant to be rigidly applied to every case. Even chronically psychotic parents differ from one another in their thinking and feeling as parents, their child-rearing practices, their moral understanding of what is right and wrong in children's behavior, their degree of family feeling and family loyalty, and their hopes for their offspring. However bizarre their personal behavior might be, their social attitudes and philosophies may be highly conventional. It is not unusual for a psychotic parent to be uncontrolled himself and yet expect good ego control in his children. (Cf. the abusing parent in Chapter 22.)

The early history of the disturbed parent may reveal instances of loss, discontinuity, and even fragmentation during important phases of development, with corresponding gaps in their own evolution as parents. Their present lives are often sterile, routinized, repetitious, and rigidly forced into channels of conduct from which they seem unable to deviate. Emotional paradoxes abound. They want closeness but reject it; they seethe with aggression but want no show of it; they love their children but also seem to hate them; they want to come for help but often fail appointments. It has been said that the thermostat regulating their emotions is faulty so that the affective temperature is never even. Their future orientation is also faulty; what they plan ahead may never come to fruition. The boundaries between them and their world are neither defined nor fixed so that no clear picture of themselves is available to guide them. They are intolerant of frustration, ambiguous in their feelings, and disorderly in all their activities. They appear to have no continuous frame of reference extending from the past, to the present, and into the future to make good sense of their lives. In general, their experience has not been happy or satisfying and they have no proclivity to like or be liked. They enter the counseling situation suspicious of human relationships, trailing a large number of broken relationships behind them.

These disturbed people test the maturity of those who are working with them since it is hard not to react to the myriad inconsistencies without anger and resentment. Those lacking in resilience and tolerance may find ways of dropping themselves out of treatment even before the patient breaks off.

Need for Relationship

Before working with the very disturbed parent around problems with the children, one must form a viable relationship that can withstand the periodic crises of confidence and trust that are inevitable with such cases. The relationship must be based primarily on respect since borderline and psychotic individuals are often oppressed by a sense of unworthiness and poor self-esteem. It has to be, quintessentially, a human and not an institutionalized contact. The individual is seen as a person and treated as a person before he is seen as a parent or patient.

To further this type of approach, a more thorough understanding of the parent is required than is usual. A full diagnostic workup that focuses on the child-parent relationship of childhood and on the parent-child relationship of adulthood forms a necessary foundation upon which to begin. One should also know the extent to which a marital relationship affects the parental functioning and the extent of the supportive community network.

The counseling relationship is a prerequisite for continuous and consistent use by the parents of the usual community mental health measures (e.g., visiting housekeepers, recreational outlets for the children). The parents come to look upon the counselor's office as a safe and trustworthy place to visit where help is always available when needed and crises are dealt with as they arise. The counselor is available almost on demand, creating an image of constancy, reliability, concern, and deep involvement in the welfare of the family and its everyday problems. The degree of investment necessary to maintain the contact over time varies with the adaptive and supportive capacities inherent in the family.

Being Prepared and Patient

It is also essential to know and anticipate the emotional responses likely in such people lest one be taken aback and rendered helpless by the emergence of unexpected reactions. The counselor must learn to live expectantly with the unexpected; this is basic to the whole relationship. This understanding can mitigate the feeling of therapeutic helplessness that often besets those who work with psychotic and borderline people. Too vigorous or indelicate a therapeutic thrust may open Pandora's box and let out far more disturbance of all kinds than can be handled. In work with such people, it is well to remember that *gradualism and patience* are essential. Nowhere is the adage of "more haste, less speed" more appropriate. The tolerance for counseling is an important variant that requires frequent reassessment. It is important at all times to work within the tolerance level of the patient. [This principle seems to apply also in a less stringent way to work with other parents, as suggested by James, Chapter 6.—Ed.]

The Past Is Present

The meaningful background history involving the child-parent relationship of the past is gathered slowly and unsystematically through working in the "here and now" rather than through a faithful history taking in the first meeting. The material gathered through the reactions of the parents to the behavior of their children seems far more relevant than the data obtained by formal inquiry. The early extraction of detailed past histories often makes the parents apprehensive and wary. Furthermore, using their past to inculcate understanding and insight into the present reactions of their children has more cognitive than emotional significance. It may even create defenses against genuine understanding of the present.

The therapeutic process observed with neurotic patients is not characteristic of work with these severely disturbed ones, at least in the counseling situation where we have made use of the developmental material to bring into greater awareness the parenting of the parent and his own growth as a parent. Since the *counselor assumes the role of a benign parent* (see also Chapter 22), all these parental data from past and present can be channeled very naturally into the counseling situation without any need to bring unconscious feelings into consciousness. Although we use our therapeutic experience to understand the cases better, the focus is mainly on present realities, present needs, and pressing problems. The real life experiences are used to keep the patient closely bound to reality and prevent the counselor's becoming a delusional transference figure.

This emphasis on the "here and now," the real, the rational, and the predictable is often undermined by the patient's disturbance. The counselor needs to note the tendency to regression, the equally dangerous mechanism of withdrawal that constantly threatens to shut him out, and the fluffy ego boundaries that seem to dissolve so easily in the ever-present symbiotic tendency, facilitated by the occasionally overwhelming need to be taken care of. These primitive defenses threaten to take over whenever the stresses of everyday living become intolerable.

Protection Incorporated

In neurotic cases, the identification of the parent with the counselor can often allow the parent to deal with his children therapeutically in the manner of the counselor. With our more disturbed cases, the counselor may be *incorporated* by the parent so that he becomes the counselor; by so doing he leaves enough of his own anxiety to keep it from infecting his children. The counselor's lack of manifest anxiety under stress can help to diminish anxiety "better than a tranquilizer," as one parent put it. The reliability and consistency of his reactions also make him an excellent sounding board for trying out new ideas. His steady reality orientation constantly informs the parent whether what he is doing is consistent with normal behavior. The sick parent will soon come to regard him as being "on his side" against all the destructive and persecutory forces. In this role, the counselor acts as a mediator between the disturbance and the environment, and as a buffer between the disturbance and the children. As one parent put it, "Nothing bad can happen to the children as long as you are there." By "bad," she meant the disordered thoughts and feelings that she sometimes directed negatively against her children.

COUNSELING ABOUT THE CHILDREN

It is imperative to remain neutral and nonjudgmental while at the same time *taking a "child's eye view" of the parent's disturbance*. Any hint of criticism may reinforce the bad parental image that is always lurking in the parent's mind. The "child's eye view" allows the counselor to assess the possible harmfulness latent in the parent's pathology. Since he has the best interests of the children in mind, he must at times look beyond the interests of the parents. Often, though, the interests will coincide. For example, recommending a temporary separation of parent and child may help both.

The counselor must bear in mind both the impact of various types of serious disturbance on children and the degree of vulnerability of the children. A withdrawn, apathetic, and remote parent affects children differently from an attacking, threatening parent. In the former instance, the children frequently suffer a sense of loss, whereas in the latter, they are often alienated (Anthony, 1973). A depressed, immature, dependent parent may drive the children into high states of excitement, while a chaotic and inconsistent one may generate intense insecurity.

It is important to know what influence the prevailing disturbance in the parent has on the different children—to what extent they feel uncertain and insecure, confused and mystified, guilty and ashamed, angry and resentful, or tearful and apprehensive. He must also know to what extent the well parent helps or harms the situation for the children. In seriously disturbed families, the parents are often in perpetual conflict with each other; the children may be used as spies for rival camps. Older children may have special problems: They may be used as surrogate parents or as surrogate spouse in an incestuous or near-incestuous way, or they may lead family movements to exclude the sick parent. One has also to bear in mind children's age and sex since each developmental phase has its own vulnerabilities, with differences for boys and girls, depending on the sex of the sick parent.

Mountains out of Molehills

Severely disturbed parents are often at a loss to deal with quite ordinary problems, especially when these have overtones that resonate somewhere in the past (Cf. the reaction of abusing parents, Chapter 23). Loss in any form appears to stir up great helplessness and apprehension within such families, and vulnerable children are particularly affected.

> A manic-depressive mother was herself brought up in an atmosphere suffused with the constant hushed threat of her mother dying from a severe cardiac ailment. Whenever the condition worsened, she and the other children were taken out on trips, as if to distract them. In her present family life she shows no ability to deal with impending loss. When a much loved family dog was accidentally killed in the children's presence, she immediately bundled them all into a car and took them to an amusement park for joyrides until two o'clock in the morning. In the counseling, the mother was allowed to describe in great detail the story of the dog's death, to which the counselor listened with much sympathy. No attempt was made to link it to her own childhood experience, her sense of helplessness then as related to her sense of helplessness now. Instead the counselor suggested that it often helped children to talk about such matters and to bring out related fears, such as fears of the parents dying, that made them feel helpless. The counseling is kept to the "here and now" and focused on the children.

The children of very disturbed parents develop some implicit understanding that counseling deflects some of the parent's morbid attention away from them. They sense that it is more helpful for the parent to work through current difficulties with the counselor rather than with them. They seem to appreciate this relief even more when they themselves have been in treatment. When the children's emotional load is thus lightened, they respond with a spurt in their own growth and development.

The Drug Dilemma and Depression

Blunting of parents' affect by medication may have devastating repercussions on the daily lives of the children. Even younger ones may
recognize dimly the "double-binding" imposed by the pill: It reduces the
parent's chaotic behavior and all the anguish associated with this, but
at the same time it removes her emotionally from them and brings on
feelings of loneliness, helplessness, and lack of support. At times they
almost seem to prefer the uncontrolled, overexcited interaction with a
decompensated parent to the eerie, zombie-like reactions with medication.

Depression removes the parent even more effectively than neuroleptic
drugs from the direct sphere of activity of the children (Anthony &
Rizzo, 1971). When the psychotic process is circular, as in manic-depres-
sion, the children are stimulated (often over-stimulated) by the excitement phase, showing at this time a vitality of their own, in contrast to
the despondency appearing during the depressive part of the cycle. The
counselor may find it necessary to prescribe a program of activities for
children having to cope with parental depression.

Family Shame

The children of very disturbed parents are often torn by loyalty to the
parent in the face of their own internal criticisms, shame, and resentment, and external criticisms from relatives and outsiders. The counselor
should be especially sensitive to this predicament, which is the common-
est confronted in such children. By working with both parents when
possible, he should try and make it possible for the children to deal
with their embarrassment in some way other than withdrawing from
outside activities. The latter "solution" often accentuates so that the
household becomes embittered and quarrelsome. Quite a few children
seek to deal with this problem by massive *denial:*

> A mother, on returning from mental hospitalization, resumed
> her schedule in a car pool. She wandered around in a confused
> fashion so that the children were late for school. The other parents,
> who knew about her illness, refused to allow their children to ride
> with her again. Even though her son knew exactly what had hap-
> pened, he steadfastly denied that his mother had diverted from the
> main route. In a conjoint counseling session the boy brought out
> very hostile criticisms of his mother, even accusing her of incestuous
> attacks upon him. The counselor pointed out that family difficulties
> and tensions sometimes made for very erratic behavior and that it

was important for the boy to recognize the realities of his situation. It was also understandable that he should want to keep these family affairs private, even though he could still recognize what had really occurred.

Symbiotic Paranoia

The symbiotic relationship that often develops may make the "loyalty" work from the other side. The parent, regarding the child as an extension of himself, may find it extremely hard to tolerate any criticism of the child and may deny it by displacement or projection. So sensitive are such parents that the critic is at once transformed into an ogre who must be destroyed before he destroys the child:

> A very bright boy had reacted to his teacher (as we had often seen him react to his mother) by belittling and teasing her. The teacher had reacted punitively to the torment. The mother was about to charge into the situation angrily and thus probably compound the problem for him. The counselor listened to the mother's detailed recital quietly and patiently without attempting to reassure her, support her in her attitudes, or oppose her intentions in any way. Instead, she looked at the reality of the situation alongside this very disturbed mother in an attempt to understand them together. At one point, she wondered aloud whether the teacher was not perhaps someone brought up in an old-fashioned tradition when it was considered impertinent for a child to be outspoken to an adult. The mother was immediately captivated by this idea and reminisced from her own teaching days when a boy had so tormented her that she had almost decided to give up the profession. Without any real insight into her own particular situation, the mother was able to understand and tolerate the "old-fashioned" teacher's position a little better. She attempted to stop the boy's baiting the teacher—being "old-fashioned," she might react negatively to the extent that he might lose his position as class leader—a matter of importance to both of them.

Many of these *ad hoc* strategies, of course, are reminiscent of Redl's real "life space" interviews that take place when the occasion arises and are tailored to the situation.

Separation

As long as parent and child seem undifferentiated within a symbiosis, it is necessary to treat the child as part of the counseling situation even though he may not be physically present. As they begin to separate from each other, the child can begin to build a more favorable environment for himself. One of the major tasks of the counselor, therefore, is to help undo the symbiotic relationship and release the child from the internal environment of the parent. As the separation-individuation struggle grows, the child's behavior at school may fluctuate dramatically. Teachers must be alerted to expect these sudden and puzzling alterations in scholastic and social performance.

A profound separation anxiety is often a nuclear problem for this type of child. It may infect every child in the family in turn as he reaches adolescence and the prospect of leaving home. In such circumstances, the parent can be counseled to offer the children opportunities for brief trial separations from the family group. This may not be at all easy for the parents since they are often firmly convinced that leaving home is tantamount to being a traitor. A step-by-step approach allows the parent to adjust gradually to the final separation. The children are often ready for the process long before their parents, even though they have been indoctrinated since early life to equate separation with the destruction of family life. Follow-up studies have shown that of the children who later become psychotic themselves, those fared best who had experienced periods of separation from the family during childhood. [This does not necessarily prove that childhood separations are beneficial. An alternate explanation could be that the latter group would not have become psychotic at all without the trauma of early separation, and had more constitutional strength and resilience than those who were so vulnerable that they became psychotic even without such trauma.— Ed.]

SUMMARY

Counseling the very disturbed (borderline or psychotic) parent requires experience and resilience from the counselor and the capacity for endless patience that can put up with interminable recitals of petty resentments, trivial preoccupations, obsessive questioning, repeated recriminations, the breaking of appointments without warning, prolonged telephone calls, unexpected disappearances from the therapeutic scene, and clamorous demands for help at all times of day and night. Such parents have a poor parental concept of themselves and are beset with fears that they have harmed their children who will be taken away from them as a safeguard. Thus, they will resist any attempt on the part of the counselor to "help with the children" as this would at once imply that the children were in need of help and that this was the result of the care they were receiving. Before one can establish a counseling liaison in relation to the children, one must have already developed a firm alliance with the parent. To do this, there needs to be a sense of continuity.

Counseling should be as continuous as the parent will tolerate. In practice, this turns out to be intermittent; such parents appear and disappear in accordance with some mysterious chronology of their own, although crises bearing on spouse or children will often dictate the reappearance. They often seem to know when they have "had enough"; disappearances can be determined by resistances to excessive psychological probing. The good counselor will regard the intermittence as a necessary concomitant to work with such individuals and will make himself available on demand. He will not insist (as he does with the ordinary run of neurotic parents) on such therapeutic niceties as continuity, regularity, punctuality, and reporting cancellations well in advance so as not to interfere with the schedule. His patience with the erratic behavior of his patients will tie them to the counseling situation more effectively than any specific therapeutic skills and strategies. His concern with the total life experience of the disturbed parent gradually draws spouses, grandparents and children into his loosely cast therapeutic net. The spouse will often push his way in since, in accordance with the principle of "homogamous mating," he will have many disturbances in his own right.

All this presupposes flexibility in therapeutic management, sincerity in dealing with the patient as a person, equanimity, incorruptibility under manipulation, and friendliness. One of our patients, who also attended a psychiatrist, recently remarked that he was her doctor but "you are my friend." She could have added "my husband's friend and my children's friend," which would have indicated the usual dimensions of the counseling situation with the very disturbed parent.

Certain psychotic parents, especially mothers, become more stable and realistic as they age and the children have grown up. This tends to have a beneficial effect upon the children as well; they do not have to abandon all ties to her in order to free themselves, but can develop a more congenial relationship while living their own independent existence. A sharp break with the sick parent would leave a residue of unfinished business.

REFERENCES

ANTHONY, E. J.: The impact of mental and physical illness on family life. *Amer. J. Psychiat.*, 127:2, 138-146, 1970 (a).

ANTHONY, E. J.: The mutative impact of serious mental and physical illness in a parent on family life. In: E. J. Anthony and C. Koupernik (Eds.), *The Child in His Family*, Vol. I. New York: John Wiley, 1970, pp. 131-163 (b)

ANTHONY, E. J. & BENEDEK, T. (Eds.): *Parenthood: Its Psychology and Psychopathology*. Boston: Little, Brown, 1970.

ANTHONY, E. J. & RIZZO, A.: The effect of drug treatment on the patient's family. In: C. Shagass (Ed.), *The Role of Drugs in Community Psychiatry. Modern Problems in Pharmacopsychiatry*, Vol. VI. Philadelphia: Karger, Basel, 1971, pp. 95-109.

ANTHONY, E. J.: The contagious subculture of psychosis. In: C. Sager and H. Kaplan (Eds.), *Progress in Group and Family Therapy*. New York: Brunner/Mazel, 1972.

ANTHONY, E. J.: Mourning and psychic loss of the parent. In: E. J. Anthony and C. Koupernik (Eds.), *The Child in His Family: The Impact of Disease and Death*, Vol. II. New York: John Wiley, 1973, pp. 255-264.

ANTHONY, E. J.: Naturalistic studies of disturbed families. In: E. J. Anthony (Ed.), *Explorations in Child Psychiatry*. New York: Plenum Press, 1975, pp. 341-378.

MAHLER, M.: *Psychological Birth of the Human Infant*. New York: Basic Books, 1975.

Part V

Guidance by Professionals Outside the Mental Health Field

Chapter 29

Guidance by Physicians and Nurses: A Developmental Approach

Dane G. Prugh and Lloyd O. Eckhardt

Korsch (1971) states that, "There is a need for physicians and other health workers to attempt to speak the patient's language and, if not to accept, then at least to understand the patient's value system." Szasz describes three basic models of the physician-patient relationship:

1. The active-passive model in which something is done to a patient, as in coma, delirium, or anesthesia (the protoypic model parent-infant).
2. The guidance-cooperation model in which the physician tells the patient what to do and the patient cooperates, as in treatment of an acute infection (prototype parent-child). This approach is sometimes necessary with parents for their children's health.
3. The mutual-participation model in which the physician helps

* Part of this work was supported by training grant MH07740-14 from the National Institute of Mental Health.

the patient to help himself (prototype adult-adult). This is the ideal model for helping parents promote their children's health.

The pediatrician, family practitioner, nurse, and pediatric associate can provide preventive or anticipatory guidance and initial counseling around physical and emotional illness. The opportunity to initiate preventive measures begins at the "conception" of parenthood, that is, at the diagnosis of pregnancy.

PREGNANCY, DELIVERY, AND THE POSTPARTUM PERIOD

Psychological adjustments of both mother and father begin during the pregnancy with the first child and are based on the parental capacities for individual identity, intimacy, and mutuality. The expectant mother commonly exhibits alterations in her dominant mood, emotional lability, greater narcissism, introversion, passivity, and dependence, and changes in sexual desire and performance. A husband may react to the perceived changes in his wife, her enhanced need for emotional support and consideration, added responsibilities for home care, and conflicts over sexual activity and upcoming increased financial obligations.

Preparing

Obstetricians and nurses can offer the prospective parents an opportunity to express their anxieties, fears, or misconceptions. Some family practitioners have arranged for regular group discussions to deal with these problems. Pediatricians and pediatric associates can meet with prospective parents for a prenatal pediatric visit a month or so prior to delivery. At such a meeting, the preparations for the care of the new baby, breast feeding or other feeding issues, skin care, sleep and other physiologic rhythms, and availability of support from the extended family, pediatrician, nurse, or pediatric associate may be discussed. The likelihood of a time-lag in the inrush of maternal feelings should be explained to prevent feelings of guilt or confusion.

High risk mothers include women with: unusual difficulty in developing an active emotional attachment with the fetus; periods of intense anxiety, markedly irrational fears or conflicts; or chronic personality disorder or latent psychosis. Unwed mothers, teen-age mothers, and mothers with a history of early parent loss, deprivation, or abuse during childhood are also at higher risk. Direct discussion without deep probing can be of some help. Referral for more formal psychotherapy may be indicated.

During labor and delivery, mothers may experience *fears of death* and *loss of control* of their feelings under sedation. Natural childbirth and rooming-in have recently been employed to minimize anxiety, encourage family support, and enhance the mother's confidence.

After discharge, enhanced *support from the father* and other relatives is necessary even for an experienced mother, especially to help her deal with the predictable initial regressive responses of the other young children.

Early Bonding

Klaus and Kennell (1970) and others have demonstrated that the early mother-infant interaction is vital both to the mother and the baby. When this early bonding is interrupted because of illness, prematurity, congenital anomalies, or physical or emotional complications in the mother's postpartum course, a high-risk period occurs. Mothers of premature or sick infants should be encouraged to come to the nurseries to see them, to feed them if possible, and to touch them in the incubator. In the case of a congenital anomaly, the mother should ordinarily be permitted to see the baby, and, if possible, handle it soon after birth. Most mothers and fathers are less disturbed by seeing the anomalous baby than by being kept anxiously waiting, often under mysterious circumstances. If the mother's postpartum condition makes it impossible for her to stimulate her baby, this should be provided by a temporary "foster" parent.

Kaplan and Mason (1960) have shown that simple counting of the mother's visits to the premature nursery predicts early home adjustment. If visits fall off during the last two weeks of the infant's hospital stay, problems in the mother-infant relationship are likely. In these high-risk situations, preventive home visits (e.g., by a public health nurse) regularly for several weeks are indicated. The home visitor can begin to discuss feeding or other details, and then offer emotional support and counseling for the parents' anxiety, guilt, and misconceptions which may have crescendoed as the discharge date neared. An appointment can be set for both parents at the physician's office or clinic.

THE FIRST THREE MONTHS: THE UNDIFFERENTIATED PHASE

Parents should be encouraged to make routine visits for health supervision a joint project. This strengthens both the mother-father mutual support bond and the relationship of both to health professionals.

In reacting to the infant's needs and in judging the effectiveness of her maternal care, the mother at first depends upon physiological cues from the infant: apparent feeding satisfaction, relaxation after apparent discomfort, and sleeping patterns. The mother who requires strong evidence of feeding satisfaction, relaxed behavior, and prompt dropping off into sleep from her infant to prove to herself her adequacy as a mother will have difficulty with a very active, easily overstimulated, wriggly infant who fusses frequently and has trouble falling asleep. The mother who expects an alert baby who can pursue and attend to stimuli will have problems with a quiet, drowsy baby who fusses little and sleeps most of the time. (More about the "goodness of fit" between the needs of the infant and of his parents can be found in Chapter 12.)

Feeding the Infant's Body and Soul

The paradigm of early mother-infant transactions is the feeding situation, whether breast or bottle. The concept of a "nursing couple" is helpful. As the infant nurses he comes to associate the mother's physical vitality and emotional state, the configuration of her face, the sound of her voice, her smell, and the tactile sensations offered by her reflex stroking with the appeasement of hunger and the satisfaction of sucking. The physician, nurse, or pediatric associate should encourage both the mother and father to express their preferences, attitudes, fantasies, and fears concerning this crucial initial "family" encounter. Although breast feeding is encouraged because of this naturalness, ease of preparation, lack of allergic potential, and the pleasure which the mother can derive, many women would feel tied down by breast feeding, and some must return to work. Mothers persuaded to breast feed against their preference often fail beyond a few weeks due to either lack of motivation or the effect of psychological conflict on the psychophysiological mechanisms related to lactation. Whether breast or bottle feeding is instituted, the physician, nurse, or pediatric associate can offer anticipatory guidance and be available for immediate counseling if problems arise.

A flexible feeding schedule geared to the *infant's biological rhythms* can bring the parent and the infant together when the infant is in his most receptive state. However, some *parental rhythms* cannot be geared to this "demand" type schedule. For parents who need a more predictable routine, a four-hour schedule with flexibility for periods of over- or under-sleeping or other competing activities can be suggested.

Parents should be apprised of the neurophysiological fact that most infants cannot voluntarily swallow a bolus of solid food until around three months. The neonate who is not ready developmentally to swallow may suck the bolus or extrude it by tongue protrusion (retrusive reflex). Urging of solids prior to three months may lead to feeding avoidance—turning the head away. The parent who strongly needs a positive feeding response may misinterpret feeding avoidance as a rejection of the parent. Such parents may withdraw from their infant or may attempt to prove their parental adequacy by forcing their infant to eat. At this point, the initial feeding avoidance may become a more active feeding refusal, to the point of refusing the bottle, psychophysiological vomiting, diarrhea, or even failure to thrive.

Early identification of food avoidance, with appropriate feeding suggestions, can prevent complications. However, if failure to thrive eventuates, hospitalization can be used to evaluate the family interactions. A temporary surrogate parent (one nurse, attendant, or foster grandmother) can be assigned the painstaking and slow process of helping the neonate begin or reestablish healthy patterns of feeding while the parents get help to deal with their anxiety and guilt and to resolve the conflicts that led to the disturbance.

Crying and Colic

Crying is initially an unlearned adaptive response, with individual differences regarding amount, loudness, and intensity. As the parents learn to respond selectively to such sounds, conditioning begins. Within the first several weeks, crying assumes a cyclic, paroxysmal fussing character at certain periods of the day. With "heavy fussers," the paroxysms may build up to a crescendo, accompanied by leg movements and relieved by passage of flatus. This picture ordinarily disappears by 10 to 12 weeks, hence the name developmental (or three months) colic. Prolonged and severe colic, often persisting through the first year, occurs most commonly in infants who are overactive and tense from birth.

Anticipatory guidance to avoid overstimulation of the more active infant may minimize crying and developmental colic. Knowledge that a certain amount of unsatisfiable crying will occur and may be necessary can be reassuring to new parents. The knowledge that such fussiness ordinarily disappears by three months is also helpful (unless the infant is already older than three months). A pacifier can be soothing, and should not cause problems unless used to avoid any crying whatsoever or as a substitute for tactile, rhythmic, or other forms of necessary stimulation. Allowing parents to think out loud with a nonjudgmental physician, nurse, or pediatric associate can help resolve superficial family tension created by living arrangements, schedules, overstimulation of the infant by the father on his evening return home, arguments over handling the infant, or criticism by in-laws.

Sleep Disturbances

The neonate sleeps about 20 hours daily in short periods. Activity during sleep and responsivity to sounds or other stimuli increase as hunger increases. Satisfaction of hunger ordinarily induces sleep in the neonate, with little effect of conditioning stimuli. In the older infant, diminution of light and other stimuli and the effects of familiar sounds and rhythmic experiences facilitate the release into sleep.

Anticipatory guidance and emotional support for the mother regarding the need for most infants to cry or fuss before dropping off to sleep will help to avoid overstimulation by frequent visits to the bedroom. Rocking the infant gently by moving the bassinet slightly, while humming a lullaby, will often help the easily overstimulated infant drop off to sleep without taking the chance of increasing the stimulation by by holding him. Parents can be advised to check once for discomfort or other problems and then to let the baby fuss for five to 20 minutes. Most infants will fall asleep during this time and worried young parents will have a framework within which to operate.

THREE MONTHS TO ONE YEAR: DIFFERENTIATION AND DEPENDENCE

By the fifth or sixth month, subjective awareness is firmly established. The smile has become a voluntary response and the infant seems to show a need for social interactions.

In a healthy mother-infant relationship, both satisfying and frustrating elements are involved. The primary psychosocial task of this stage is the development by the infant, with the mother's help, of a basic sense of trust: trust in the adequacy of the parental environment to meet his needs and trust in his own capacity to deal with the environment. The infant can now make more active contributions to the transactional feedback relationship. This, in conjunction with rapid brain growth, leads to increasing ability to form a mental image of himself as an entity separate or differentiated from his mother. The baby's homeostatic equipment is now more able to regulate his internal environment, and he can begin to indicate his needs for food, water, or warmth. His drive toward mastery and learning shows itself in his relentless exploration of his environment.

Fathers and Other Strangers

An important part of the differentiation process is the appearance of stranger anxiety at about the eighth (seventh to ninth) month. When elicited by the father's face and voice, it may result in confusion and concern if it has not previously been explained to the parents. It disappears by two years.

Weaning

The pleasure associated with sucking, feeding, and use of the mouth for exploration becomes important during this phase. Therefore, weaning becomes an important issue. Adverse reactions may be encountered if weaning is too early or too abrupt. Many infants can be weaned gradually to a cup around the end of the first year. Some infants will even invite it by resisting the bottle. However, other infants will want a night bottle well into the second year. Infants nursed longer may show greater resistance to weaning.

The emotional climate of the mother-infant relationship and the family is more significant in the response to weaning than the age. Sometimes the mother has difficulty in giving emotionally to her infant or has a strong need to push the infant unrealistically toward early independence. The infant may respond by angrily refusing the cup or even the bottle, as if going on a "hunger strike."

Where the mother is psychologically unavailable because of depression or apathy, some infants may cling to the bottle for substitute gratification and resist solid food. Treatment of the mother's disorder is the obvious intervention.

Distinguishing Normal Adaptation

At the end of the first year the infant begins to deal with separation ("emotional weaning") from the mother. This is often facilitated by choosing some object (a teddy bear, a piece of soft cloth, or a "security blanket") which appears to act as a partial substitute for the mother. Some parents need to be reassured that such *transitional objects* are a normal adaptive mechanism up to four years of age, and actually promote ultimate independence.

Parents also need to be warned of the normal physiological anorexia associated with the slower growth rate and greater activity at the end of the first year. Mothers unaware of this phenomenon may attempt to "force feed."

Advance knowledge of the normality and transitoriness of headrolling, headbanging, and body rocking during this phase of development, combined with the awareness of the infant's need for adequate rhythmic satisfactions and other types of modulated stimulation, can be of great value to parents. If the infant fails to move through this developmental stage, the physician, nurse, or pediatric associate should evaluate with the parents the possible underlying causes. Prolonged or severe headrolling, headbanging, and body rocking represent intensification of the normal patterns of rhythmic posturing in an attempt to provide substitute gratification for insufficient stimulation. In infants who have been overstimulated, they may represent avenues of tension discharge.

Rumination (mouthing deliberately regurgitated food) may begin at around six months of age in infants who have experienced a lack of stimulation or discontinuous or insufficient mothering. When the underlying problems seem to involve a more serious psychiatric or social issue, the health professional may want to enlist mental health services.

THE SECOND YEAR: THE TODDLER STAGE—DEVELOPING MASTERY AND INDIVIDUALITY

The central psychosocial task for parents and child during this stage is the establishment of autonomy and mastery over the environment (Erickson, 1968).

In his effort to achieve mastery, the child often shows demanding and at times manipulative or openly aggressive behavior. The child frequently employs the word "no" or resists control by his parents. The parents need to employ firm but tolerant limits to control his behavior, granting him age-appropriate independence while still meeting his continued (often conflicting) needs for dependence. Then he can commence to build in controls over his own impulses and master them himself.

In his early attempts to become independent, the toddler may discover that he has gone beyond his mother's visual range and he will often respond with separation anxiety. The physician or nurse can suggest practice sessions in which brief separations can be experienced with the aid of a close relative or well selected babysitter.

Toilet Training

Myelinization of the spinal nerves involved in bowel control does not become complete until sometime between 12 and 20 months of age. If a 12-month child can walk to the bathroom, sit alone on the "potty chair," and communicate, at least in a nonverbal way, his wish to produce a stool, toilet training can be initiated. However, if these communication efforts are not present until 15 months, it may be best to wait until after 22 months to begin toilet training. The span from 15 to 22 months is the peak of normal negativistic period. Coercive toilet training attempts during these months or too early attempts may lead to withholding of stool, constipation, or soiling.

Many children develop a definite rhythm to their bowel movement patterns and this can be used as a guide for the most likely time of results on the potty chair. A potty chair is probably better than the seats fitting onto an adult toilet because many children may be afraid of the height or the flush of the toilet. If the child does not have a consistent rhythm, the gastrocolic reflex can be used. Seating him on the potty chair 10 to 15 minutes after a meal, usually breakfast, can begin a regular routine. It is best not to seat him for more than three to five minutes, regardless of production, because constant activity and resistance to enforced restraint are so characteristic of this developmental period.

Parents should be warned that avoidance of a pitched battle is vital, that not every child needs to have a bowel movement every day, and that suppositories, enemas, or other stimulation should not be employed. If "early" training is accomplished, the parents need to know that many children may show a breakdown in control around a stressful situation, such as the birth of a new sib, a move, a physical illness, or other types of stress.

Bladder training is best initiated after bowel training has been completed. Daytime control may be started around two-and-a-half years of age. To some extent, an association between bladder and bowel training occurs when the infant voids in the potty chair at the time of defecation. Therefore, many children achieve daytime bowel and bladder control at the same time. Once the urge to urinate is well associated with the experience of "going to the potty," training pants rather than diapers may encourage dryness. Nighttime control is usually not considered a problem until four to five years. Very early or strongly coercive bladder training is sometimes associated with nocturnal enuresis. Clarifying a positive family history of delayed nighttime control may help the family maintain a patient and understanding attitude toward this problem (see Chapter 20 for more on guidance for enuresis).

Other Problems

Anticipatory guidance regarding the increased motor activity, limited impulse controls, and normal negativism characteristic of the toddler stage is helpful. Appropriate toys can meet the child's needs for large-muscle activities and tension-discharge through activity. This, combined with consistent discipline, limit setting, and the avoidance of overstimulation, will usually help to reduce the normal developmental hyperactivity. Where there is a severe disturbance in the child-parent relationship, one should consider referring the family to an appropriate mental health resource.

To prevent repeated accidents or poisonings, parents should be advised to remove toxic household cleaning and other materials from the child's reach, to lock the medicine cabinet, and to place breakable or expensive objects in safe corners. Such precautions not only can prevent accidents or poisonings, but can also minimize the parents' anxiety around the necessary constant supervision.

To prevent sleep problems based on chronic resistance to sleep, continued separation anxiety, or battles over naps, quiet, nonstimulating routines at night are important. Planning the day so that the active 18-month-old who gives up his nap can go to bed earlier in the evening may help.

THE PRESCHOOL PERIOD: FACT VS. FANTASY

Many parents experience a sense of relief and pleasure in facing the relatively sunny threes. Consequently they forget the tendency toward fluctuation in development and feel puzzled, resentful, or guilty when a temporary regression occurs.

The child's burgeoning sense of initiative is underwritten by the flowering of speech, intellectual capacities, motor skills, and social interactions. It is important that the parents support the child's maturational need to move out in all these directions while still setting constructive limits upon his behavior.

Sex Education

The child's need to recognize, express, and later gain control of his sexual impulses is a major developmental task during this period. The prevention of sexual problems can often be accomplished by helping parents become aware in advance of the normal and natural tendencies of the preschool child to manifest considerable curiosity in regard to sex differences, the origins of babies, and sexual or loving behavior between parents.

Sex education is most wisely carried out in response to spontaneous questions of the child. Information should be geared to the child's level of understanding. A simple, partial answer to a seemingly complex question usually satisfies the child until he is ready to return for more.

In addition to asking questions, it is age-appropriate for preschoolers to satisfy their curiosity by peeping, brief exploratory sex play with other children, and exploring and manipulating their own bodies. Peeping behavior can often be reduced if parents and sibs avoid provocative dress or behavior. When a child of four or five engages in sex play or exploration with another child, the parents can indicate that this type of behavior may upset some parents, and ask the child if he has any particular questions. Occasional nighttime masturbation is best ignored. If the child masturbates publicly, it may help to let him know that it is all right for him to do this in his own room or in the bathroom, but not in public. Some parents may need to be told that it is unwise to let children of this age sleep with them, since this type of experience is often overstimulating.

When excessive sexual behavior or total lack of curiosity occurs, the physician or nurse should inquire into the sexual attitudes and disciplinary practices within the home. Some situations may represent parental overconcern about normal behavior. Others may involve precocious or delayed developmental deviations in psychosexual behavior without serious pathological significance. Still others may reflect the child's reaction to serious marital problems or other types of family crises. Compulsive masturbation, excessive peeping, or sadistic sex play usually indicate more serious disturbances and a referral for psychotherapy is ordinarily necessary.

Sibling Rivalry

The preschooler can be encouraged to participate in planning and preparation for an expected birth. If at all possible he should be allowed to visit his mother in the hospital. At the very least he should be able to see her through a window or talk to her on the telephone.

Once the mother and baby return home, the parents should let the child talk freely about the new arrival. This should include verbal expressions of jealousy and resentment if they arise. Such feelings should not be inhibited or suppressed, and the child should not be made to feel guilty about them. If regressive behavior appears, the parent should be prepared temporarily to let the child become more dependent.

One caution for knowledgeable and concerned parents is the danger of overconcentrating upon the negative feelings of the older child and of striving too hard to cushion the impact. Some parents have tried so hard to protect the emotional security of the older child with extra attention and many gifts that the interests of the new baby may be almost neglected. The older child may actually feel so guilty in such a situation that he cannot express his normal jealousy and resentment. A more positive approach is to allow the older child to participate to some extent, if he wishes, in the infant's care, even to the point of helping to hold the baby. This should be done, of course, without giving him a chance to drop it and become guilty.

The parents may need to arrange a special time with the older sib away from the immediate presence of the baby. The regularity and predictability of such an arrangement are more important than the actual amount of time involved.

Preschool Sleep Problems

Parents can be 1) advised to avoid overstimulating experiences around bedtime, 2) apprised of the developmental occurrence of nightmares, and 3) encouraged to give the child a night light to help him overcome his fears of the dark.

The child is fully awake following a nightmare and can ordinarily recall parts of it but may be afraid to talk about it for fear that it may come true. The preschooler often comes into his parents' bedroom after a nightmare and wishes to be taken into their bed to receive comfort and reassurance. A brief discussion of the child's fears with reassurance that he can return to his own room and go back to sleep will prevent his making it a habit or struggling to sleep with the parents.

Night terrors are less frequent than nightmares and follow a different pattern. The child does not become fully awake after a night terror and does not remember it. Therefore, the parents cannot discuss the night terror in a meaningful way and cannot provide the child with satisfactory reassurance. The parents themselves, however, can be reassured that night terrors are usually transitory. They can be advised to hold the child comfortingly until he goes back to sleep. If nightmares, night terrors, or other sleeping problems become marked and persistent, the physician or nurse should investigate the possibility of deeper, unresolved family tensions or conflicts.

Death

Five- and six-year-olds still believe that death involves primarily a going away, a separation, or a sleep and a forgetting, all temporary and reversible. In dealing with the preschooler's fear of death, parents can help their child grasp the idea that death is something that comes to everyone and every animal at some time. Death should not be compared to a long sleep; the child may become confused and fear going to sleep. The child should be given an opportunity to mourn freely and to ask questions at his level of understanding. The concept that death is no one's fault must be stressed so that the child will not blame himself for his previous angry or ambivalent feelings about the deceased. (See, also, Chapter 23.)

Accidents

Accidents are the most common cause of death in childhood. Some can be prevented by recommending the use of a homemaker service if a parent is ill, making arrangements for sitters for child supervision during family moves or other preoccupying events, or by referring to mental health services for severe marital problems or disorganized families.

Hospitalization

It should be the responsibility of the physician, nurse, or pediatric associate to prepare the child and his parents for hospitalization; it should not be assumed that someone else will do so. In this age group preparation for elective admissions should not be carried out more than a few days before. Though time should be allowed for the child to bring out his fears and misconceptions, too much time will lead to an undue buildup of anxiety. The preschool child, with his limited intellectual development and capacity for judging time, should be told simple, concrete details about what he will see and feel. Illustrated booklets about hospital experiences may help. However, they are no substitute for an open discussion. A drive to the hospital and a visit to the ward may help acquaint the child with the hospital. The child may also be encouraged to play out his feelings with dolls and doctors' or nurses' kits to promote mastery over his anxiety and to encourage questions. The child should be reassured that the parents will visit daily and stay overnight—if provisions for such a stay are available.

During the posthospitalization period, the parents can be advised that their child's regression is normal and no one's fault. They can be encouraged to give the child temporarily greater emotional gratification. The child can then gradually be weaned back to his previous level of behavior.

THE SCHOOL-AGE PERIOD—CONSOLIDATION AND CONSTRUCTIVENESS

In contrast to the previous periods, the school-age period, from approximately six years to the onset of the prepubertal growth spurt, is steadier and more even in both physical and psychological growth. However, unevenness still occurs. Bits of exceedingly mature behavior alternate with babyish mannerisms, demanding behavior, or even temper tantrums. By age eight or nine the more mature trends seem to become firmer.

During this stage, the parents must help the child develop his tools and skills, teach him the work principles and the pleasures of work completion, and help him adjust to the laws and rules of the world outside of the family. They must help him develop his conscience and maintain his ideals, while understanding the values held by others. It is at this stage that the example provided by the actual behavior of the parents, as opposed to their stated values, becomes of central importance. They cannot turn over the further socialization of the child to the school or church. An important mechanism is identification, first appearing in the preschool phase. The child of eight or nine has expanded his range of temporary identifications to include teachers, mechanics, doctors, and nurses.

Anticipatory guidance can help parents understand the behavior patterns of the school-age child and set appropriate limits. Many children are ready to undertake anything from piano lessons to cub scouts. The wise parent may give the child a choice between two different activities rather than allowing him to move into a number of tempting activities all at once. Instead of buying a French horn for the youngster who passionately begs for one, the parent can rent one, thus allowing for the fact that his interests may shift within a short time.

Lying and Stealing

The tendency to experiment with dishonesty by taking money and telling fibs is frequently seen during the early school-age period. Although limits, reproval, or mild punishment are necessary, parents should use these techniques judiciously at this stage. They should be helped to understand that the child, with his growing sense of right and wrong and his still limited sense of conscience, employs harsh internal standards which may lead to excessive guilt or a heightened sensitivity to criticism.

Sex Remains

In spite of a reduced tendency toward masturbation, peeping, and exploratory sex play, questions recur, at a higher intellectual level, about the origin of babies, the process of birth, the sex organs and their functions, and marriage. Parents need to know that by 10 or 11, if adequate information is not forthcoming from them, their children will likely turn to friends or books. Although a book may be helpful, it is no substitute for answering individual questions. Ideally, sex education should take place between the child and his parent. If the parents are too embarrassed or inhibited, the physician, nurse, or pediatric associate may fill in.

School Phobia

A special type of "inability" to attend school involves an irrational fear of some aspect of school, such as a particular teacher, another pupil, or taking showers in the gym. It is generally seen in overdependent, shy, anxious children who have been handled in an oversolicitous or overcontrolling fashion. Somatic complaints (abdominal pain, nausea, vomiting, headaches, feelings of weakness, or low grade fever) may be present, usually appearing on school days and often disappearing on weekends or if the child remains home. The basic fear is not of going to school, but of leaving home. The parents may become overinvested in the child's fear of school. Consequently, a vicious cycle is set up, with the child clinging to his parents who feel helpless, and both become increasingly frustrated and impotently angry.

The physician should first do a thorough physical examination to rule out any actual disease process. If the examination is normal, he or she can reassure the parents that no physical abnormalities are present. It may then be indicated, in a noncritical, nonjudgmental way, that during this period anxiety about new experiences is very common. At this point, the parents will often recognize, without excessive defensiveness or guilt, that they have kept their child too close to them and may then be able to cooperate in the immediate goal of returning the child to school. The professional should inform the school of the child's problem

and suggest to the mother or father that they take the child back to
school. The parents may remain briefly with the child in his classroom
before returning to work or home. If the parents cannot return the child
to school, the professional can arrange to do this himself or he can
enlist the help of school staff to pick the child up and take him back
to school.

Once in the classroom, the younger school-age child usually settles in.
However, it may be necessary to arrange the initial return on a part-
time basis or to excuse the child from gym.

Certain children may be unable to remain in the classroom because of
abdominal pain or other symptoms. In such cases, the teacher can send
the child to the school nurse, who can let him lie down briefly and then
return him with reassurance and encouragement to the classroom. No
matter how worried the parents may seem, the physician *should not
give a medical certificate for home teaching* in cases of school phobia;
this may lead to psychological invalidism.

Even if early return to school is achieved, the involved professional may
want to consider a referral for psychotherapy to help work out the underlying conflicts and prevent the return of the symptoms.

Illness and Accidents

Problems during convalescence from some acute and chronic illness
may arise when the physician and parents join to form overcautious
approaches to the recovery period. Certain parents, out of anxiety and
guilt, may restrict the child's activity to the point of psychological invalidism. School personnel may even be persuaded to provide a home-
bound teacher. Active prevention of such limitations becomes the task of
the physician or nurse.

Family tension may result in the child's becoming more reckless, impulsive, and disorganized, therefore having an accident. Repeated accidents should alert the physician, nurse, or pediatric associate to investigate underlying family problems. A referral may then be indicated to a
social agency, public health nurse, or psychiatrist.

ADOLESCENCE: IDENTITY AND INDEPENDENCE

Adolescence is a developmental rather than chronological phenomenon.
It is a time of increased instinctual pressure, fantasies, and fears, accompanied by a growing estrangement from the family. The adolescent must
develop a new picture or definition of himself in relation to the expecta-

tions of his parents, his peer group, and society. In this search for a satisfying concept of himself, the adolescent may need temporarily to devalue his parents, see their faults more clearly, and find himself through relationships with adult models outside of his family. Nevertheless, the healthy adolescent appears to make his bid for independence gradually, rather than all at once, and his requests generally meet reasonable consideration from his parents who accept, more or less gracefully, his need to grow.

Although the physician or nurse may have developed an important supportive relationship with the school-age child and his parents, this relationship becomes even more important during adolescence. When the child reaches adolescence, he or she may no longer want to share sensitive material in front of parents. Under ordinary circumstances with a new family, the physician or nurse might see the parents first to take a history, and then see the adolescent alone. This procedure may have to be reversed if there is a serious struggle going on between the adolescent and his parents. Some experts would recommend routinely seeing the adolescent first, and in some cases, especially with older adolescents, it may be appropriate to see *only* the adolescent.

Depression and Suicide

Suicide threats are common in children, often occurring as attempts to punish the parents or in retaliation against the parents. They may also result from a need for self-punishment. Suicide attempts rise rapidly after 14 years of age, and are the third most frequent cause of death in the 15-19 age group. A sudden or threatened loss of a key relationship or self-esteem (as with a broken love affair or a bitter fight with a parent), school failure, an unwanted pregnancy, depression over a chronic illness, dejection or guilt over parental illness, or even the acting out of an unconscious wish of a parent or an identification with a parent or friend who has committed suicide may trigger a suicidal attempt. Parents must be cautioned to take adolescent suicide threats seriously.

In adolescent suicidal attempts, the wish to die may be real, but usually also contains an element of a cry for help, indicating how much the young person is really hurting. Hospitalization can buy a moratorium, during which parents can be helped to recognize the seriousness of their child's plea for help and to avoid the tendency toward sealing over the conflicts. Follow-up should be carefully planned to insure that recommended intervention is being carried out.

"Acting Out"

With adolescents, *lying* often represents a type of compensation for real or fantasied inadequacy or lack of emotional satisfaction. It may also be a type of retaliation against overstrict or overly preoccupied parents. When defensive or socially compensatory lying occurs, parents can be helped to recognize the adolescent's need for understanding rather than accusations or punishment.

Stealing may be used by adolescents to bribe affection from friends, as a substitution for loss of love, as retaliation against parents who they feel do not understand them, or as an unconscious neurotic symptom of a compulsive nature. Parents should be helped to identify the causal conflict.

Adolescents who *run away* may do so to seek excitement, as a response to sudden loss of self-esteem, to express rebellion, to deal with depressed feelings, or to "find" themselves or to be found. Repetitive running away can be a response to conflicts in the parent-child relationship or a signal of impending difficulty. New community resources have offered the runaway a temporary sanctuary where frank discussions of problems and feelings can take place and future planning organized. The physician or nurse can often act as a liaison between such programs and the parents, provide further counseling, or refer to a mental health resource if indicated.

The physician, nurse, or pediatric associate can help to identify drug problems and to act as a liaison between community treatment programs and parents. Mixed group discussions with adolescents and parents have proven effective in some cases. (See Chapter 13 for a discussion of parents and drug abuse.)

REFERENCES

ERIKSON, E. H.: *Identity Youth and Crisis*. New York: W. W. Norton & Company, Inc., 1968.

KAPLAN, D., & MASON, E.: Maternal reactions to premature birth viewed as an acute emotional disorder. *Am. J. Orthopsychiat.*, 30:539-552, 1960.

KLAUS, M. H., & KENNELL, J. H.: Mothers separated from their infants. *Pediatric Clinics of North America*, 17:1015-1037, 1970.

KORSCH, B. M., FREEMON, B., & NEGRETE: Practical implications of doctor-patient interaction analysis for pediatric practice. *Am. J. Dis. Child*, 121:110-114, 1971.

SZASZ, T. S., & HOLLANDER, M. H.: A contribution to the philosophy of medicine. *A.M.A. Arch. of Internal Medicine*, 97:585-592, 1956.

Chapter 30

Teachers, Principals, and Parents: Guidance by Educators

William Hetznecker,
L. Eugene Arnold and
Arlene Phillips

This chapter will focus mainly on how a teacher can help a parent form a productive working alliance for the benefit of the child, but the principles, tactics, and techniques explained can be utilized as well by principals, counselors, visiting teachers (attendance officers) and other school personnel who deal with parents.

SOURCE OF FEELINGS

Whenever a relationship between two important social groups or institutions deals with individuals or processes in which there resides great cultural value and emotional investment, that relationship is subject to stress and conflict. Parents and school personnel are highly invested in

---

Dr. Hetznecker and Dr. Arnold are members of the American Psychiatric Association Task Force on School Consultation.

children as individuals and in education as a process. Bonds of blood, affection, nurture, responsibility, mutual gratification and a lifelong involvement bind children and parents. Commitment to children, nurture of their development, the challenge of teaching, and investment in professional goals bind teachers to education and children.

The traditional relationship between school personnel and parents of *in loco parentis* has recently changed. Mass migration, especially into urban and suburban areas, has created family and community instability. As a result of Sputnik, education was caught up in the cold war. This added pressure to school staff, parents, and children. Family distress, rise in divorce rates, and change in the nature of parental authority have increased the burden of socialization responsibilities placed on the schools.

In the sixties, the nature of authority in society—the rules, rulers, and rulemaking procedures—was questioned. Institutions of all sorts became the objects of skepticism and disaffection. Schools were criticized as being agents of oppression and/or being responsible for the rebellious and revolutionizing ideas of the young.

Innovations in education, such as the open classroom or open school, team teaching, programmed instruction, individualization, resource rooms, special language and reading approaches, affective curriculum, and mainstreaming of special education children, have created new pressures. In some cases, confusion, uncertainty, and open conflict have developed among school staff and between school staff and parents.

Educators find themselves in a psychological squeeze. They are required to be more "accountable" for the effectiveness of programs; they are subject to pressures by local communities and by state and federal attempts to establish standards of quality and equality. At the same time, they find themselves increasingly burdened with responsibility for basic socialization of children, and experience frustration, discouragement, and anger over what they view as an abdication of responsibility by parents.

The situation described above requires a new cooperative partnership between parents and educators. In this relationship, both would recognize their differing roles, responsibilities, and expertise. This would promote the education of the child and encourage parents' reasonable participation in various aspects of school life.

GENERAL PRINCIPLES

The following six assumptions can help school personnel develop the most *productive attitude*:

1. Assume that the parent is the expert on his or her child. The parent has been responsible and will be responsible for the child long after the teacher (or principal, counselor) has completed his term of responsibility.

2. Assume that the parent is as well-intentioned as you are.

3. Assume that parents are as consistent in applying their principles as you are.

4. Assume that the parent has a great emotional investment in the child and that the child's success or failure academically or behaviorally affects the parent's self-esteem as a parent. A corollary is that the parent has more to "lose" emotionally and socially by a child's academic or behavioral difficulties than an educator does.

5. Assume that the purpose of the parents' and school personnel's working together is to help the child have the space he needs to be what he is and can be.

6. Assume that you and the parent can find a way to establish a working alliance.

A *working alliance* is characterized by a cooperative relationship focused on an issue which engages the mutual interest of both parties. It depends upon the competencies and strengths of both parties. Their respective roles are different enough so that each contributes significantly to the successful accomplishment of the task. The focus of the alliance is not usually on the relationship itself. However, such an alliance can be facilitated if both parties establish explicitly the nature of their contract or relationship.

A parent-teacher alliance may be formed in as global and implicit a way as this understanding: "I'll be the best teacher I can be . . ." "We'll try to work together for the good of Sally." On the other hand the working alliance can be specific and explicit:

Teacher: "I will try to help Sally be more effective in paying attention to verbally presented material. I plan to use the following methods. . . ."

Parent: "I'll cooperate with you; when I'm talking to Sally I'll use the following approach to help improve listening skills. . . ."

Defining Roles

One of the first issues that faces a teacher when considering a working alliance (whether with students or parents) is the question of role definition. This can be broad and flexible or narrow and rigid. In the same school different teachers can have widely varying role expectations for students and their parents. The following questions can help teachers and other school personnel examine the roles of teacher, students and parent:

What are my expectations of my students academically and behaviorally?

Have I made these clear to myself and my students?

How do my expectations jibe with those of the school organization as a whole?

What are my expectations of parents as they relate to their children as students in my class (school)?

Have I clearly communicated these expectations to parents?

Have I elicited what parents expect of their children?

What do parents expect of me as a teacher (principal, counselor, etc.)?

How do their expectations and mine fit or conflict?

Have I clearly separated out my expectations of parents in relation to their child as a student in my class (school) and my expectation of how good parents in general behave with respect to their child?

Lessons, Liaison, and Listening

A working alliance often begins at a *parent-teacher conference.* A good parent-teacher meeting has some of the same qualities as a good lesson plan: clarity of purpose, limited goal, and careful attention to method. But there are also differences. Both parent and teacher in their respective roles vis-à-vis the child are accustomed to talking more than listening. Advice, correction, admonishment, persuasion, information giving, and questioning are the adult techniques both parent and teacher direct at children. When relating to parents, a teacher needs to shift to a more receptive, attentive mode which emphasizes listening.

If a teacher has a chance to *practice this in a simulated situation,* the actual conference may go more smoothly. In fact, an important part of staff development is the chance to practice ways of relating to parents. Role-playing with teachers who are skillful and experienced may help the less experienced teachers become more comfortable and secure before a difficult conference. Peer support is very helpful in promoting good parent-teacher relationships.

Clearing the Hearing Channels

The formation of a working alliance is infinitely easier if it begins with parents and teachers feeling relatively secure and positive rather than anxious, defensive or accusatory. This underscores the value of teachers' taking the initiative early in the school year to invite parents to a get-acquainted meeting. It can be done at first parents' night or report card conference but it is even better to plan for 10-15 minute periods in the first six weeks of school when parent couples could be scheduled. This may seem costly in terms of time and planning, but the payoff to the relationship bank is significant. If we begin a relationship on a positive, relatively equal footing, then if negative issues have to be dealt with, we are in better shape to hear them. If the messenger is trusted, the message can be heard clearly.

Parents and teachers may experience different "truths" about a particular child. Neither of those opinions may fit what the child is now or what he can become. Expectations of parents and teachers for a particular child may be so different that change which will benefit the child cannot occur unless both sides are heard and respected. Often the ritualized contacts do not allow for carefully constructed compromise, even with the best of intentions. A clever child can manipulate this lack of parent-school communication and compound the problem. When a parent who is unhappy about what is happening at school complains to or in front of the child instead of going to the school, the child may win a battle by playing "Let's you and them fight," but he loses the war. The same is true when school personnel express subtle and often nonverbal disapproval of the home situation instead of having a conference with the parents.

Positive Parent Participation

Situations in which a parent initiates and the school responds are quite often positive contacts. Sometimes a parent has a specific complaint which is easily resolved. If the complaint is more general, the parents may have excellent suggestions for change, and if encouraged by school personnel, may help to make the suggestions work. Where school personnel do not pretend a paternalistic omniscience and are willing to listen and learn, a potentially critical encounter can turn into an opportuity to improve the school program.

In schools in which parents are invited to become a part of mini-courses or special programs, this type of constructive suggestion is more often offered and accepted. More communication takes place if parents are invited to form committees to beg, borrow or steal rugs, rockers, and record players to make the school environment more inviting and comfortable. These things are not "frills" when parents are contributing directly instead of just through taxes. Mutual gratitudes and gripes can be exchanged more easily in this cooperative atmosphere. By contrast, if parents feel shut out of school, unable to participate in things which concern their children, they feel put down by "professionals." This naturally breeds resentment.

Parents want to hear good things about their children but often fail to reciprocate with what they appreciate about the school personnel. Teachers and principals also need positive reinforcement; this is natural. In transactional-analytic terms, everyone needs "strokes" (see Chapter 6). In their absence, it is easy to begin resenting those who could be giving them. School personnel need to understand this phenomenon to keep it from aborting a useful parent-school relationship. If teachers initiate keeping lines of communication open, parents usually respond in kind.

ABC'S OF A SUCCESSFUL PARENT CONFERENCE

A. *Time*—The minimum is 15 minutes. For a conference that is to deal with distressing issues, allow at least 30 minutes to one hour. At the onset make explicit to the parent how much time is available for the conference. Stick to your time limit.

B. *Place*—Insure privacy. The usual line of parents waiting at the teacher's desk on parent's night is the least felicitous method of insuring any significant exchange. See the parents alone in the classroom after the children are gone or use the nurse's room, the counselor's office, a reading or speech room, etc.

C. *Relationship: General*—The teacher (or principal, counselor) is host(ess) for any conference. The conferences are almost always held at school. This tends to make the formal aspect of the relationship *asymmetrical* in favor of the teacher. If, in addition, the purpose of the conference is to deal with negative material regarding the child, the balance is shifted even more. Thus the general task of the teacher is to attempt to decrease the *"one down" position of the parent* and shift the balance of the relationship into a more symmetrical one of a partnership. There are specific tactics which a teacher can employ to bring about this symmetrical relationship that promotes development of the working alliance:

1. Adopt an attitude of receptive listening rather than a feeling or urgency to get a message across.

2. State as clearly as possible the purpose of the meeting as you see it and define the boundaries of time, etc.

3. Elicit from the parents their views of the purpose of the meeting and what they wish to accomplish.

4. Listen for feelings behind the words, especially guilt, resentment, or feelings of ineffectiveness with the child.

5. Don't personalize. One who is busy defending himself will find it much harder to pay attention to the other person.

D. *Relationship: Specific*—Under this heading a teacher might consider all the facts she knows about a particular child and his family relationship. Some teachers also find it helpful to be informed as to how these parents have typically structured their relationship with teachers in previous years. Other teachers may prefer to draw their own conclusions "unprejudiced."

If, for example, Jimmie's parents in previous years have very actively asserted the deficiencies of the school, Jimmie's teacher need not be surprised or take it personally if they begin their relationship that way. Knowing this, she can begin by eliciting the parents' criticism and objections and respond directly and not apologetically or defensively. The next step is to define the teacher's role and method for this class at this time, and place Jimmie in that context. Then it is time to ask the Smiths how they respond to the teacher's concepts and method and how they feel they can help Jimmie function within that framework.

E. *Style*—Style is the *how* of someone's behavior. Each person does the same task differently. One of the central tasks of professional development is the integration or blending of personal style and professional role. Style should not be taken to mean a charismatic, flamboyant showmanship. That may be one kind of style. But style includes the greatest possible range of variation. The teacher who has a good grasp of her own style knows what works best for her, whether it be in teaching math or talking with parents. Style develops slowly out of knowledge, experience, successes, and mistakes. When a teacher senses she has just presented a lesson well and students have learned, she needs to examine the components that contributed to the success. The more specifically she can identify these, the more likely she can incorporate them into a similar future task. Likewise, when a teacher senses she did a poor job, she should attempt to identify the particular errors that contributed.

F. *Script*—Script refers to the actual way of stating things—the words and intonations. Script is as important when giving parents information or judgments that are critical of the child's performance or adjustment as it is when criticizing or correcting the child directly.

Some culturally imbedded *stock expressions,* often used as overtones or entries into corrections or criticism, tend to evoke negative emotions in the hearer and thus interfere with the effectiveness of communication. Here are examples:

1. "Why?" or "Why did you do that?"

"Why" is a very confronting statement that essentially asks a person to justify himself. There may be times that confrontation of this sort is necessary, but these times should be chosen consciously with an intent to produce a certain result. Generally, "Why?" generates defensiveness and emphasizes status and power differences. Alternatives might be: "What did you have in mind when you said or did that?" "I don't understand what you had in mind when you did that. Could you explain?"

2. "Why don't you . . ."

This really means "I want you to. . . ." If that's what a teacher wants to say, then she should say it in that direct manner. An alternative is: "What are some other ways you could do that?"

3. "If I were you, I'd . . ."

This is similar to number two. In addition, it denies the individuality and personal responsibility of the other person. One alternative is: "When I tried that, this way worked pretty well for me. Do you think it could work for you?"

4. "That's okay but . . ." or "That's nice but . . ."

These introductions mean "that" isn't good enough; therefore, it really *isn't* okay. We all learn to tune out the first part of the phrase and listen only to what comes after the "but." Try not to join positive or complimentary statements with negative or critical statements. We do this to soften the criticism, but it doesn't work. Say positive things at one time and negative or critical things at another. Ask for feedback from parents to be sure they heard both the positive and negative correctly as you meant them. One way to elicit feedback would be to say: "I'd like to be sure I got my message across clearly. Could you tell me what you heard me say about John? I'd like you to tell me both the positive things you heard me say and the negative or critical things."

5. "Perhaps you don't realize (understand) . . ."

This is a veiled way of saying "You must be stupid or ignorant." Implicitly such a statement impugns the intelligence, knowledge or good faith of the hearer. This violates mutual respect. Alternatives might be: "I'd like to explain some of the reasons I have for saying (doing) what I did." "Maybe if I make my reasons clearer you can offer alternatives."

These stock expressions can elicit negative response because of the implicit critical connotation. It would be useful for teachers to examine their own habitually used stock expressions and attempt to find alternatives that are more positive, clearer, or both. A good way to do this is to tape-record a class or parent conference and criticize it afterwards, identifying with the children or parents.

PARENTS, CHILDREN AND CRITICISM

Whenever a conference between teacher and parent is concerned with difficulties in academic performance or behavioral adjustment, the parent enters the situation in a one-down position. The teacher needs to remember that powerful emotions, feelings and responses are involved when dealing with parent-child relationships. This is particularly true when the child is criticized by a person from outside the family. Parents' genes influence their children's biological make-up. Parents' psychosocial behavior influences their child's psychosocial development. Thus, when a child is judged to be "deficient," "bad," "poorly adjusted," "hyperactive," "not motivated," "uncooperative," or "slow learner" by the school, the parent reacts to such judgments at a gut level as an attack on both the child and himself.

When a person is one-down he is more prone to react with anxiety, anger, guilt, shame, fear, resentment, futility, depression, hopelessness, and helplessness. Being one-down is a threat to self-esteem, to feelings of competence and mastery; anxiety is generated and the person's typical defense mechanisms automatically come into play. If the parent reacts too defensively and primarily on the basis of feeling, he will be unable to form a working alliance with the teacher and will be unable to use his cognitive strengths to consider the negative statements about his child. Even though the teacher is the immediate source of the distress by reason of his critical or negative statement, he is still in the best position to help the parent cope adequately with the distressing feelings. This is a necessary prelude to dealing with the substance of the critical information.

The Blaming Game

In a conference that deals with criticism of the child, a major temptation to be avoided is the assumption that if something is wrong, someone must be blamed: If a child isn't learning or behaving the way he should, it must be someone's fault—the child's, the parent's, the teacher's, society's. Teachers and parents need to remember that sometimes *things can go wrong even when nobody is at fault*. A child's earning bad grades does not make the teacher a bad teacher or the parent a bad parent any more than it makes the child a bad child. A major criterion of successful teacher-parent interaction is the degree to which blaming is avoided and some responsibility is voluntarily assumed by all parties involved.

A positive outcome can occur when the purpose is to inform parents of some academic or behavioral difficulty. A team conference held before the parent conference can plan to avoid provoking one-down behavior and blame-placing. Reminders can be given that the purpose of the conference is to find ways to help the child be more comfortable in school and to like himself better, rather than to resolve ego problems of parents and/or teacher. If parents and teacher do not see the problem in the same way, it often helps to involve a neutral person (e.g., school psychologist or counselor) who might listen to each side and suggest alternatives.

Discretion, Valor, and Goodness of Fit

If the agenda becomes, "I do not want my kid in your class" or "Get this monster out of my class," then an immediate change may save time and later problems. Some parents are better informed about special problems than are some of the teachers, and all parents have the right to obtain the best education available for their child. Sometimes, of course, it may be of most benefit to the child to learn to cope with the situation. However, many changes are not made because "we don't do things that way." The teacher may resist when the child's transfer is seen as an admission of failure or fault. Teachers, principals, and parents need to realize that children and teachers differ in learning and teaching styles as well as personality. A teacher who is good for one child may not be good for another, and this does not impugn the teacher's competence. The goal should be to find a good "fit" between the child and teacher (see Chapter 12 on constitutional temperament). In any situation, the task is to find alternatives to benefit the child without blaming.

Too often teachers and parents reach decisions without bothering to consult the central figure—the child. The child may have a better solution figured out than anyone else. He needs to be allowed to express it, and perhaps try it out and discover if it works. Many children with "special problems" have spoken with some humor of the ways they found to get along with "my teacher who has a problem" or "my parent who really has a hang-up about good grades."

Psychology of Criticism

Criticism is always difficult to hear. In addition to the usual semantic problems of communication, it reminds us of our earlier experience as children when we were corrected and admonished by parents, teachers, and other adults whose approval we desired and whose disapproval we feared (see Chapter 6). Criticism recalls and provokes anger and resentment that as children we had to stifle, deny, or displace because of our fear of retaliation. Understandably, most people's initial reaction to criticism is defensive, usually in one of four common ways:

1. *A parent can challenge the factual basis* upon which the criticism is based *or* the *interpretation* of the child's behavior. For instance, the teacher may interpret John's repeatedly jumping up from his desk as evidence of defying classroom rules while the parent may interpret this behavior as a sign of John's curiosity, energy, and enthusiasm. One way of dealing with this type of response is to avoid challenging motivation or intent of the child. Instead, concentrate on how the child's behavior affects his own or other children's learning or adjustment.

2. Parents who are knowledgeable in child psychology and educational theory may *react at the intellectual level of opinion* and understanding. For example, the teacher might be concerned about the child's failure to finish tasks. The parent judges that the child's learning is enhanced not by sheer persistence but by pursuing those things of interest to him. The parent may even declare that it is the teacher's responsibility to stimulate and maintain the child's interest rather than requiring completion of tasks.

In such instances a teacher need not be defensive or apologetic or engage in a duel of citing experts. The teacher can clearly articulate her own pedagogical philosophy and style, emphasizing the common ground that she shares with the parents. Further, she can reassure them that children learn in a variety of ways, settings, and situations, and that she adapts her approach to new knowledge and to the needs of a given child. But she also has to be true to her own style, and the better she is able to do this the more effective she'll be with children. She needs to clarify, at least implicitly, that she is not challenging their theory of child development or the methods by which they raise their child. She is merely pointing out academic or behavioral problems whose solution requires the parents' cooperation and help.

3. At the *personal, emotional level,* the parent may react in a way that says, "What you say about my child hurts me and makes me feel incompetent."

One way to deal with this type of reaction is to identify with the parents' feelings. "I know how much you care about John and how much you want him to do well. I know it is difficult to hear that he isn't doing well. I (as a teacher) feel discouraged when any of the children I teach don't do well. I feel as if somehow I'm failing them. But I realize I'm doing the best I can just as I know you're doing what's best for John. And John is probably trying the best he can at the moment. Our job is to figure out how we can help him and how he can help himself. As we figure out some practical approaches we won't feel so helpless."

4. A more ominous way of reacting is to *impugn the motive of the teacher:* "You don't like my child." "You're out to get him." This response sets teacher and parent as adversaries, a fundamental impediment to a working alliance. It may come from a parent whose child has repeatedly been in trouble or failed. The parent's guilt, anger and helplessness, compounded by whatever realism there is in the segregating and blaming of the child, produces this antagonistic posture.

Working with such a parent requires patience, effort, persistence, and the ability to deal with the *pain* beneath the anger and hostility. The teacher need not feel defensive or intimidated. She can explicitly recognize the parent's feelings and verbalize how difficult it is for parents and child to have school be such an unhappy experience. She can explain clearly the expectations that she has for all children, and state that the child will be treated as any other. She can say that because of the unhappy history they have had with school she knows it will take some time for a relationship to develop in which all of them are able to work together to promote the child's learning and adjustment.

It may take several conferences for the distrust, hostility and defensiveness to diminish. The teacher can have a few brief meetings for the purpose of updating the child's progress, with emphasis on building a more positive relationship. By demonstrating her calm, positive objectivity in facing the parents' hostile attitude, she can help them become more positive. When negative feelings or attitudes exist, lack of contact generally enhances the negative feelings. Distance and lack of face-to-face contact leave people to depend on fantasies arising from their pre-existing attitudes or feelings. If the latter are negative, they will be enhanced by deviation-amplifying feedback (see Chapter 5). However, *increased contact* allows each party in the relationship to get modifying input. All but the most obdurate negativism will usually be modified by the willingness of one party to risk taking the initiative and demonstrating interest and concern.

SOME PITFALLS

One pitfall for teachers and parents is to *take responsibility* for things which the child could work out better without their "help." In schools where high importance is given to competition, kids are often impaled by parents' and teachers' projected ambitions. Sometimes we think we can "make" kids become or want to become good students. Some kids need more pushing than others, but some respond to pushing with an equal and opposite reaction. School is the child's work. If the parents and teacher provide support, encouragement, and any special help that is needed, it is then up to the child to do that work without making home a miserable place for everyone. Frequently the child knows that he can get the most attention from his busy parents by making his schoolwork a big issue every night. Why should he do well when he gets so much more attention by doing poorly? Besides, it is his parents who want the A's, not him. The teacher also may need the A's to make him/her feel like a good teacher. These things often come out of a good parent conference, after which everybody can agree to give the responsibility and feeling of competence back to the child. Contracts between the teacher and child, parent and child, teacher and parent, or a combination of all three often help.

Another pitfall is the game of *"label, classify, and discard."* A label of "learning disability" can be used as an excuse for poor teaching. A teacher needs an alarm in his head when he begins to tell a parent what a child *is* rather than what he *does*. Many parents are intimidated by such labels, accept them at face value, or react with blame. School personnel can help by providing specific information about what the

child *does*. The teacher can provide either concrete suggestions of ways
the parent can help, or can refer the parent and child to someone who
can work with the parents to try to understand the child's behavior or
performance.

Another pitfall for the teacher is practicing medicine without a
license, perhaps telling a parent, "Your child needs Ritalin," maybe even
before adequate evaluation. Such approaches can scare parents away from
getting the help that is needed.

SUMMARY AND RECIPE

The social context influences parent-school staff relationships. Changes
in the social and cultural situation in this country have affected families
and schools. This has brought about changes in the nature of parent-
teacher relationships as well as parent-child relationships and teacher-
student relationships.

The teacher needs to examine her own expectations of her role as a
teacher, of the role of students in her class, and of her expectation of
parents in relation to her students. Situations in which parents and
teachers have an opportunity for building relationships include the usual
parent night, parent-teacher conference around report card, and parent-
teacher conference about a child's difficulty in either the academic or
behavioral area.

The goal of any parent-teacher contact is to promote a working alliance. One approach to development of this working alliance is the use
of an *elicitation model,* outlined below in:

A Teacher's Recipe for Approaching Parents

1. Assume that the parent has as much good faith and good
   intention as you do.
2. Assume that the parent acts with as much consistency in his
   role as you do in yours.
3. Adopt a listening attitude rather than teaching, telling, or
   advising.
4. Assume that there are many experiences of the truth. The experience and expression of that truth depend on the focus one
   chooses.
5. Elicit the parents' views, particularly their views of the child
   and their experience with the child.
6. Restrain the impulse to criticize the parental handling of the

child at home. Also refrain from suggestions for home management unless requested.

7. After you listen to what the child does at home and what the parent wants him/her to do, show some positive thing the child does at school. Then show some other things he does and what you would like the child to be able to do.

8. Do not say what the child is. Describe what the child does or is unable to do.

9. Focus on developing a working alliance through which you and the parent can find ways to help the child be more comfortable at school, like himself better, and feel capable.

10. Note things we expect the child to do. Elicit from the parent ideas of ways this could be accomplished.

11. Say what you as teacher will try to do at school to help the situation.

12. Tell the parents when you will report on how the plan has worked and ask the parents to share with you at that time how their efforts have worked.

13. If the parent asks for suggestions on how to help at home, be specific. Say what learning tasks to help with and how to go about it.

14. If a child is using school work to get attention at home, suggest that you or someone else help him with the homework. Suggest that the parents save their time with the child for mutually enjoyable activities.

15. As things improve at school, let the parents know what a good job the child is doing. Congratulate them for the effort they have put out, and their success in your joint venture. (Tell the child the same good news and label his successes for him. It's helpful to point out to the child the specific ways in which he achieved improvement.)

16. If things do not improve, don't complain. Arrange another conference. Better yet, at the end of each conference plan for the next one at some predictable time in the future. The object is to maintain the working alliance and to find new ways to help the child and to encourage him to help himself.

17. Try to find ways to help the parent feel comfortable, competent and helpful in the situation. If the parent feels better, so will the child. If the child feels better, so will the teacher.

18. Be sure that the child has responsibility for himself and experiences the consequences of his behavior. Prevent him from

carrying last week's mistakes into this week. Depending on the child's age and readiness, it might be well to include the child in the parent-teacher conference at an appropriate time. Be sure that such an inclusion does not result in a barrage of criticism or blaming of the child by either parent or teacher.

19. Be comfortable with your own natural human need for positive feedback, whether from child, parent, other teachers, or principal. Remember that if parents fail to give this feedback, it doesn't mean that they are malicious or that you don't deserve it.

Chapter 31

Parent Guidance
by Pastors

L. Eugene Arnold, Joseph Pacheco

and Robert M. Russell

Religion has long been recognized as a major behavior-regulating force, along with the mental health, social welfare, legal-correctional, and educational systems. Religion can underpin mental health by providing a meaning for life (see Chapters 13 and 23) and by promoting healthy moral development, an essential element of mental health. On the other hand, religion can be used as an instrument or excuse for unhealthy child-raising practices, or can even, in distorted application, provoke unnecessary guilt or anxiety or shackle creativity. Therefore, it is important for designated religious leaders to be attuned to the interaction among mental health, morality, religious values, and parenting practices and attitudes. This chapter will use the role of the Christian pastor as an example of how religious leaders can help parents help their children, without implying any exclusion of Jewish, Muslim, or other religious leaders.

Communication between a pastor and parents may be regular and growth-oriented or casual and problem-oriented. In the former case parents may ask, "How do we best instill moral values in our children?" In the latter case parents may ask, "Where did we go wrong?"

PARENTS AS TEACHERS OF MORALITY

Parenting involves provision for the child's physical, mental, emotional, and religious needs. The moral aspect is closely allied with the religious, but also with the emotional and mental (cognitive). The pastor must get across to parents that the deepest and most lasting moral values are communicated by parents. Children absorb their parents' attitudes, often unconsciously communicated. Parents teach their children right or wrong, social values, and prejudices more effectively by what they themselves do. The parent who brings home pencils and stamps from the office might as well stop telling his child, "Thou shalt not steal." The parent who delights in telling jokes that rely on racial or ethnic slurs for their humor or who avoids any commitment to community improvement might as well forget telling his child, "Love thy neighbor as thyself." Parents, therefore, need to define their own moral values and strive to live according to them.

It is useful for pastors to educate parents in the manner in which religious and moral development takes place. Religious development occurs in three phases: I—primitive, no real concept of God (preschool); II—conformity, imitation of authority (elementary school age); III—personal acceptance (adolescence). Moral development roughly parallels religious development.

Stages of Moral Development

Kohlberg's research (1963) delineated three levels of moral development: preconventional, conventional or conformist, and autonomous. Each level has two stages, making a total of six stages:

Stage 1 finds the preschool child *deferring to superior power*. He is concerned with *physical consequences* of an action regardless of human meaning or value. He obeys rules to avoid punishment. He confuses the value of a human life with the value of the person's possessions, status, or physical attributes. Most U.S. children graduate from this stage by age ten, but in every culture studied, some adults retain this as their habitual moral thinking.

Stage 2, while still emphasizing physical consequences and power, takes a more *pragmatic, instrumental view*. The child at this stage sees things as good that satisfy his own needs, sometimes the needs of others. Fairness, reciprocity, and sharing begin to appear, but in a pragmatic way: "You scratch my back and I'll scratch yours." At this stage the individual obeys to obtain rewards. He values a human life as instrumental to its possessor or others.

Stage 3, commonly found in late elementary school, begins the conventional or *conformist level*. The child is interested in being "good" and in *pleasing others or winning approval from them*. He may try to be "nice," often by conformity to stereotypes. He may judge behavior by intention, rather than actual consequences. At this stage the child would recognize that it is worse to break a small item deliberately out of spite than to break a much more valuable item accidentally. He obeys rules to avoid disapproval or dislike. He bases the value of a human life on the affection the person's family feels for that person.

Stage 4 emphasizes *"law and order."* The child is oriented towards fixed rules, duty, and maintaining the social order for its own sake. Authority is respected, not because of its superior power, but because it is right to respect it. Rules are obeyed to avoid guilt or censure. Human life is considered sacred in a categorical order of rights and duties. In some tightly structured, authoritarian societies, this stage is considered the optimum level of moral development. A significant proportion of adults never progress beyond this stage.

Stage 5 ushers in a more *abstract, autonomous morality*, and is ordinarily not manifested before puberty because of its dependence on certain cognitive abilities not usually found earlier. This stage is oriented towards the *social contract*, usually legalistic and utilitarian. Procedural rules, consensus, and agreed-upon standards are emphasized. In contrast to the "tablets of stone" attitude of stage 4, there is a willingness to change laws for rational considerations. One obeys rules to maintain the respect of a hypothetical impartial observer who judges what is best for the whole community. Human life is valued as a universal right and for what it can contribute to the community. Since this is the official morality of the United States Constitution and Declaration of Independence, it should not be surprising that it is the single most common stage of moral development manifested by Americans over the age of 16.

Stage 6 appeals to *ethical principles* based on logic, universality, and consistency, and emphasizes *decisions of conscience.* Justice, reciprocity, equality, and respect for individual human dignity are emphasized. One obeys rules to avoid self-condemnation. One reveres human life because of respect for the individual. There is some doubt as to whether stage 6 is really more mature than stage 5, or whether these last two stages merely represent alternate choices of mature morality.

Promoting Moral Development

Kohlberg (1963) noted that children at any given stage of moral development are able to comprehend all the stages below their own and usually one stage above it. More importantly, when their attention was drawn to it, they tended to prefer that next higher stage! This presents possibilities for parents to promote children's moral development. Children can be stimulated to think about moral issues, thus noticing the next higher stage of moral development, which they would usually find more attractive than the stage they are in. One way to do this is by presenting moral dilemmas in anecdotal form. The anecdote should be removed enough from the child's own situation so that it does not arouse anxiety, but should be realistic enough so that the child can identify with the protagonist. The following example is adapted from Kohlberg (1963) and Brown (1965):

> In a village in a distant land there lived a pharmacist who invented a new cure for cancer. Even though it cost little to make he was able to charge $2,000 a dose for it because only one dose would cure any cancer. One day a poor villager came seeking the cure for his dying wife. By mortgaging his house and all his belongings, the villager had been able to raise $500, which he offered the pharmacist. However, the pharmacist said that his price was $2,000. The villager then went around to all his friends and collected what money he could and begged in the village square. He was able to get another $500 this way. He took the $1000 to the pharmacist and offered to pay the rest when he could get the money. The pharmacist said, "I told you the price was $2,000. I invented this and I have a right to get my price for it. Save up until you can bring me $2,000; then I'll sell it to you." The villager went back to his house and found his wife very ill, looking as if she could not last another day. That night he broke into the pharmacy and stole the cure for his wife. Do you think the villager did right or wrong by stealing the cure? Why? How about the pharmacist?

A simpler example, à la Piaget (1948), would be: "Jane was helping her mother dry the dishes and accidentally dropped her mother's best china punch bowl and broke it to pieces. In the house next door, Linda got angry at her mother and deliberately stomped on a cheap bowl and broke it. Which girl do you think did the worse thing?" Other examples can be found in Piaget's and Kohlberg's writings.

Along with such intellectual stimulation of moral development, parents can share the affective experience of dealing with life's moral and social dilemmas. Examples are the agonies of deciding to lie for a good reason or deciding to report a friend who is doing something harmful to the community or otherwise deciding on the lesser of two evils. Taking the child to see a slum or migrant labor camp can be an effective lesson in social morality.

The parents need to be cautious not to impose their own moral judgments on the child, especially if they are several levels removed from the child's ability. Rather, they need to discuss these interesting anecdotes and actual situations with the child in a manner that respects each person's opinion, and in particular respects the child's fledgling conscience.

Freedom of Conscience

As parents witness their children's progress through the stages of moral development, they must give them more and more responsibility. The pastor has a responsibility to show parents the limits of their authority in the area of conscience. Even a child has a right to freedom of conscience, and that freedom is to be granted progressively more generously as the child grows older. It includes the freedom to make his own choices, even to do evil, to deviate from the faith of his parents and go his own way. While parents may regret the outcome, the wise parents will let go and accept the child's choice as something he, and not they, will have to live with. It is still basic theology that we should reject the sin but not the sinner.

Learning with Children

Parents can function as both teachers and learners of morality with their children. Part of the humility of parenthood is learning an appreciation for the "words of wisdom from the mouths of babes" (Prov. 13:24). Adolescents can be especially instructive. Pastors can help parents avoid the defensiveness that would interfere with such mutual learning.

PARENTAL GUILT

Pastors are in an especially favorable position to help parents resolve their feelings of guilt, whether those feelings have a realistic basis or not.

When parents realistically feel guilty because of something they did wrong, the pastoral function of *forgiveness* becomes important. Unfortunately, some parents resist forgiveness. They find it easier to remain guilty than to accept forgiveness, become responsible, and have the situation or relationship renewed. They need to be confronted with their "wallowing" attitude and apprised that they are addicted to guilt as an escape from constructive planning. The pastor may need to be aggressive in offering the message of forgiveness and exposing the irresponsibility of guilt.

Often parents feel unrealistically guilty for things over which they have no control, such as "honest mistakes" or feelings. Here the pastor's function of *moral clarification and participant teaching* becomes importatn. Parents who have made mistakes in child-rearing because of ignorance, misinformation or confusion may find comfort in the clarification that actual guilt requires knowledge and willful intent. Inadequacies or inabilities do not make one morally bad; problems in being a "good parent" do not make one a bad person.

More importantly, such parents can be reassured that a few parental mistakes do not irreparably ruin the child. They can be successful parents without following every single directive of the child-rearing "experts." Even if we assume that deviance from official expertise is a mistake, most children are resilient enough to tolerate a modicum of mismanagement as long as they feel secure that the mismanager loves them. In fact, St. Augustine's admonition, "Love, and then do what you will," is not a bad axiom for parents. (*Caution:* See the definition of love later in this chapter.)

Amorality of Feelings

It is not only mistakes of action for which parents feel unwarranted guilt. They can also feel guilty for having negative or unworthy feelings towards their children, even though they do not act out those feelings. Pastors need to clarify that feelings, of themselves, are amoral: They are morally neutral, neither good nor bad.

As sensate beings, we are constantly being stimulated, internally and externally, by "messages" over which we may have little or no control. These messages are stored in our conscious and unconscious memory and are sorted out, compared with past experiences, and synthesized into new ones. The mind gives (or fails to give) meaning to the new complex of experiences, and there is a response. We grasp the new situation as good or bad, pleasant or unpleasant, and we tend to be most strongly affected by the need to avoid the unpleasant and seek the pleasant. Accompanying this complex mental-emotional-instinctual pattern is a physiological response of varying intensity. This process is basically automatic, one over which we have little control. Without control, there is no responsibility. And without responsibility, there is no morality. Feelings, then, cannot be morally bad.

Therefore, the parent who has feelings of anger, hatred, rejection, or sexual attraction towards his child need not feel that he is a bad person for having such feelings. He need not even consider himself a bad (inadequate) parent; it is quite possible to be a good (competent) parent while having some negative feelings about the child.

Competence issues aside, morality is determined by decisions and the actions stemming from decisions, not by feelings. Knowing that there is no sin associated with feelings can make it easier for parents to cope with them.

PASTORS AS GUARDIANS OF BASIC TRUST

Erikson (1950) describes religion as institutionalizing basic trust. Basic trust, developed during infancy, is the sense of security and confidence that 1) one's needs will be met, 2) the world is consistent and predictable, 3) the people with whom one has intimate contact will care and love, and 4) those with whom one has casual contact can be trusted. The parent who has not developed basic trust himself, perhaps because of inadequate parenting in his own infancy, is not able to foster its development in his child. Chapters 6, 22, and 28 discuss this point in more detail. Even parents who have had adequate parenting and have developed basic trust often feel a need for reinforcing in themselves this cornerstone of mental health and parenting ability. Many parents thus turn for help to religion, the institutionalized form of basic trust, and to the pastor as an instrument of that heritage.

The Pastor As Parent Surrogate

The pastor has been culturally assigned many characteristics of a parental role. Pastors tend to share the mantle of God's fatherhood. The Catholic pastor is even called "Father." Regardless of denomination, the pastor is commonly assigned the following parental roles:

1. *Nurture,* as symbolized by the act of feeding, characterizes both the parental and pastoral roles. Even the name "pastor" springs

from the injunction to "feed my sheep; feed my lambs" (John 21:16). Most religions have some sort of food ceremony, ritual, or prohibition. In many Christian denominations the pastor even ceremonially feeds the congregation a sign of Christ's presence. The pastor who can be truly nurturing in the fullest psychological sense provides the parents a better model with which to identify as well as giving them needed support and succor.

2. *Limit setting and conscience formation* are also functions of both pastor and parent. The parent teaches the child right and wrong and rebukes the child when he does something wrong. What the parent does in the microcosm of the family, the pastor does in the macrocosm of the congregation. He helps clarify moral issues and, if necessary, rebukes the congregation for such things as hypocrisy in areas of social justice. The pastor is in a good position to empathize with the plight of parents as they face the task of morally guiding their children.

3. *Promoting moral growth* implies that both pastors and parents cannot be satisfied with mere limit setting. Both, to do their job well, must cultivate in their charges courage, imagination, empathy, the capacity to care, and the courage to be.

4. *Forgiveness* or "making it well" is a pastoral function that may not at first seem as obviously shared by parents. However, if we think of a *healing* function, we can more readily see the similarity between a child bringing a smashed finger to a parent to be kissed and made well, and a member of the flock who has stumbled coming to the pastor for absolution or counseling.

With so much overlap between the parental and pastoral roles, it is not surprising that some parents not only see the pastor as an expert on parenting, but also look to him for parenting for themselves. Parents who consult a pastor about some problem they are having with their child may be asking more than advice and information; they may be bringing their smashed pride to be healed. Some attention to the parents' bruised feelings before proceeding with information, advice, or planning can help them restore their sense of basic trust and provides a model of nurturant parenting for them to identify with.

To Be Parent or Not to Be?

Some pastors may feel it presumptuous to assume a parental role. Others may relish the role and attempt to assume it with everyone. The pastor needs to be familiar with the role and sensitive to the various situations requiring it so that he can accept that role when it is needed but not push it when it would be unwelcome. If he feels uncomfortable in taking a nurturant role even when it is clearly called for, he should consider seeking consultation and support either from a fellow pastor or from a mental health professional. One who is called to be "all things to all men" needs to develop a repertoire of roles and behaviors to meet the varying needs of the congregation. One of those needs for some people is sometimes for him to execute and model adequate parenting, whether nurturing, limit setting, growth promoting, or healing.

Basic Trust to Tolerate Ambiguity, Ambivalence, and Tension

There will be many problems in parent-child relations with no clear-cut answer or resolution. Such uncertainty leads to ambivalence and tension. Of course, some tension is healthy: It keeps the Golden Gate Bridge standing; it makes it possible for us to walk; it stimulates creative effort. In fact, the "blessing of uncertainty" opens the road to "life's hurts and life's healings." But even the most optimistic would not claim that all tension or uncertainty is good. Some just has to be tolerated if it cannot be resolved. While we may prefer that it were otherwise, we can't resolve all problems; we can't get clear-cut answers to all questions. Pastors are in a good position to help parents substitute the security of religion for the certainty they are futilely seeking in other matters.

LIFE, LOVE, GROWTH, AND SUFFERING

Life, growth, and love are what parenthood is all about. The parent brings life to the child, witnesses his growth, and loves him. The parents' love keeps the child alive and promotes his growth. The child's growth confirms the parents' life and reciprocates their love. Such concepts can help parents derive the most from their experience of parenting. But what about suffering? Parents need a lot of help and support in seeing how growth includes vulnerability to suffering and how suffering can contribute to growth. Learning to walk involves stumbling. The first day of school may bring painful anxiety but eventual growth through mastery. There are many such "growing pains."

Pastors can help parents to be an instrument of God's love through redemptive suffering. Redemptive suffering can be defined as the willingness to suffer. The parent who is willing to suffer for the sake of his child redeems or "saves" his child through love. He gives the child value through his love. The child has value because he is loved. The parent who withholds love and approval from the child until the child proves his worth needs to be apprised that he can make the child worthy by loving him. The child cannot pull himself up by his bootstraps, but is given value by the love the parent invests before seeing the proof of worth. Parents need to be reminded that love is not just a warm feeling; *love is a decision,* and more. Since feelings do not have a moral value, it is only as a decision that love has moral value.

Growth implies continuity and discontinuity. The past is never dead; it lives on in the one who is growing and who has his roots in the past. Pastors, because of their familiarity with the ancient wisdom of scripture, can share the feeling of continuity with parents and prepare them for the paradox of discontinuity that growth also brings. At various points in the growth process, choices are made as to the direction of development. Choice implies freedom, and parents need to understand the implications of that freedom for themselves and their children. The children are free to leave the parents, and this separation brings suffering, the fulfillment of growth, and hope for new life and love.

Death, Parents, and Pastors

The ultimate suffering of separation is death of a loved one. Death is part of the life cycle. It is the ultimate discontinuity of growth. Love makes separation painful, but loving faith makes it bearable and meaningful. Pastors are the natural instruments of the faith that Elisabeth Kübler-Ross (Chapter 23) describes as giving meaning to death and grief. The "compleat" pastor should be familiar with the concepts in Chapter 23 to be most helpful to parents and their children before, during, and after death in the family.

Resentment, Suffering, and the Death of Love

Nothing kills love faster or separates persons faster than resentment. No suffering seems more futile than silently endured resentment. One of the greatest services the pastor can render is the clear message that "If you are offering your gift at the altar, and there remember that your brother has something against you, leave your gift at the altar and go; first be reconciled to your brother, and then come and offer your gift" (Matt. 5:23). Some parents need help to feel free to ventilate their resentment against the child or to let the child ventilate his resentment against them.

PITFALLS FOR PASTORS

In attempting to help parents, pastors need to beware of several pitfalls of their special role.

1. *Transference* problems arise from the parental role culturally attributed to the pastor. When a pastor finds a parent angry, resentful, blaming, seductive, or defensive for no apparent realistic reason, it may well be that the parent is merely manifesting feelings toward the pastor that he really feels for his own parents. The pastor who takes such feelings personally would be doing a disservice to both himself and the parent. Instead, he can empathize, try to understand, clarify, and attempt to help the parent formulate a reasonable plan of action.

2. Seductions to *feelings of omnipotence and omniscience* can arise from the tendency of some people to look to the pastor with childlike confidence for all answers and solutions. The call to be "all things to all men" can become a temptation to usurp God's role. It is with God, not the pastor, that the buck stops, and God has many instruments besides the pastor. The pastor needs to define carefully his own limits and abilities and set an example of humility that parents can follow in dealing with their children.

3. *Inability to say "no"* can be related to the two preceding pitfalls and is an occupational hazard of those in nurturing, helping roles. The pastor needs to define what he is able and willing to do. Otherwise, not wishing to disappoint, he may become more involved with meeting expectations than with meeting needs. If he agrees to more than he can deliver, he has done the parent, himself, and God a disservice. He can set an example of basic trust by his honesty and comfort with his own limitations.

4. *Failure to make referrals* can result from a desire to handle the problem alone to prove one's omnipotence, from fear that the referral would be resented by the parent, from ignorance of resources, or from failure to recognize the need for referral. Sometimes the best service the pastor can render is to recognize the problem and make a referral to an appropriate resource rather than attempting to handle it by himself. For example, when a pastor has not had training in psychotherapy, he needs to recognize when the seriousness of an emotional problem or mental illness requires referral to a mental health professional. Some pastors, of course, have had such training and may feel comfortable in undertaking

this themselves. When they do, they need to remember in cases where there is not significant progress within a reasonable length of time that some emotional and mental disorders require medical attention. In doubtful cases, they can ask for *consultation*. Discussion of the referral process can be found in Chapter 1.

5. *Theological interpretation of natural events* may be a problem for some pastors. There is a tendency for any professional to conceptualize a given problem in terms of his own background and knowledge. However, the pastor who interprets a child's schizophrenic or toxic hallucinations to the parent as divine revelations or possession of the devil is doing both the child and the parents a disservice. The pastor needs to have enough familiarity with such phenomena to recognize whether a given individual is manifesting something of special theological significance or merely the common human vulnerability to disease. In doubt, consultation is indicated.

6. *Moralizing* when succor is needed may result from a pastor's sense of duty to uphold moral standards. The pastor who takes this duty seriously may find it easy to forget Jesus' example with Mary Magdalene or the parable of the prodigal son. By emulating Jesus' forgiving, nurturing attitude, the pastor models an appropriate attitude and behavior for the parents to emulate in dealing with a pregnant daughter or a son who needs help to get off drugs.

REFERENCES

BROWN, R.: *Social Psychology*. New York: Free Press, 1965.

ERIKSON, ERIK H.: *Childhood and Society*. New York: Norton, 1950.

KOHLBERG, L.: The development of children's orientations toward a moral order: 1. Sequence in the development of moral thought. *Vita hum.*, Basel, 1963.

KOHLBERG, L.: The child as a moral philosopher. *Psychology Today*, September, 1968, pp. 25-30.

PIAGET, J.: *The Moral Judgment of the Child*. New York: Free Press, 1948.

Chapter 32

Parents and the
Divorce Court Worker

Richard S. Benedek and

Elissa P. Benedek

While legally terminating the marriage can solve a number of problems for parents who are already emotionally divorced, it also has the potential for creating a variety of others. The court social worker or other court personnel—hereafter sometimes called "the professional"—may be able to help the parents deal with these in a reasonable manner or even to avoid them entirely.

Some divorce courts have virtually no affiliated professional support. Others limit their professionals to the task of establishing income potential and the ability to pay child support. More elaborate programs involve the evaluation of parents and children for the purpose of making recommendations as to custody. The most sophisticated court-connected programs further employ their professionals to participate in the resolution of visitation controversy and similar areas of conflict surrounding divorce. The professional from an outside agency (i.e., not court-con-

391

nected) may also have an opportunity to assist the family in these areas, as may the court professional who is affiliated with one of the more restricted programs.

The primary objective of the professional who is affiliated with the divorce court must naturally be to fulfill the role that is expected of him there. But this does not preclude him from performing services for the parents exceeding those required by his position. Similarly, the professional who is not court-connected, but who is treating a family or child at the time of divorce, may also find that he can ease their way through the court even though that is not directly related to the course of treatment. What are the critical considerations with respect to establishing appropriate goals and explaining these to the parents?

1. The goal must be *realistic*. However well intending, the court professional should resist the temptation of setting a goal that is out of reach because of time limitations, lack of administrative support, or other constraints. A goal doomed to failure is a guarantee of the professional's inability to fulfill anyone's expectations.

2. Conversely, the professional should seize upon the opportunity to *provide maximum assistance* to the parents commensurate with his training, skills, and opportunities. Unduly restricting the goals (e.g., merely furnishing financial data to the court) may waste a golden opportunity to prevent or minimize considerable conflict both during and after the divorce.

3. Once the professional has mapped out the part he intends to play, he must carefully *explain it to the parents*. No matter how articulately he does this, many families, because of their own internal conflicts, will distort or challenge the role he details. However, the professional who feels secure in the knowledge of his tasks and limitations should, during the course of the interviews, be able to clarify his objectives or confront the parents with their distortions or misperceptions.

4. Whatever limits the professional may place upon his role, it is important that he realize, and make it clear to the parents, that he is neither judge nor referee. His task is not to evaluate the marriage, assign blame, take sides, or offer in-depth therapy directed toward changing the parties' personalities. His goal is to *help the parents do what is best for their children*.

5. The professional should always be on the lookout for circumstances suggestive of the *desirability of referring* the parents to another agency for additional help. In this respect, as well as with respect to making information available to the court or even testifying, he must inform the parents of any limitations upon the confidentiality of the interview.

DEALING WITH FEELINGS

Parents going through the divorce process may present with any number of significant feelings and emotions, either separately or in combination. Those most commonly found are the following:

1. *Depression.* Besides intensely feeling the loss of a mate, the children, security, the home, a dream, and the marriage itself, it is not uncommon for parents to sense a loss of dignity and self-esteem.

2. *Anger.* Sometimes as a result of frustration from the loss, parents are unduly hostile toward their spouses. (See Chapter 24 for more about this and the consequent denigration of ex-spouses in front of the children.)

3. *Guilt.* Anger may also be accompanied by guilt. Parents frequently feel responsible for the damage they believe the divorce is likely to cause, such as the separation of the child from one of his parents.

4. *Confusion.* Even an undesirable status quo is a known quantity. The divorce tends to shatter this. Faced with uncertainty, parents may be shocked and bewildered.

In addition to helping parents honestly explore some of their feelings, the professional needs to help them understand, that being overwhelmed with feelings and concerns about the future, their judgment at this time of crisis is likely to be impaired. He can assist them to sort out the irrational emotions and reactions that tend to distort their perception of reality and interfere with their ability to act effectively for the interests of their children.

INDIVIDUAL, CONJOINT, AND FAMILY CONFERENCES

Every family going through the process of divorce is, to some extent, unique in its constellation, dynamics, and problems. Therefore, the professional should be as flexible as possible both with respect to the people that he sees and when and how he sees them. He needs also to consider time and financial resources of the parents and those of the court or agency, as well as departmental policies, the primary purpose of the professional's intervention, and the techniques with which he feels most comfortable. Some options are:

1. *Individual Conferences.* People are often most comfortable when they can talk to the professional privately. This can facilitate the establishment of rapport and openness. Where the parties are unduly hostile toward one another, the individual conference may have the advantage of denying them the opportunity to waste time by arguing or vying for the support of the professional. Also, where the professional expects to make a recommendation to the court, such an interview may be his best means of securing necessary data.

2. *Conjoint Conferences.* The conjoint conference has the advantage of enabling the professional to confront the parents with the manner in which they interact with one another. Also, where parents in good faith are unable to reach agreement on specific issues, such as visitation, the professional may find that by sitting down together with both of them he can help them to work these through. (See also Gardner's argument in Chapter 24 for seeing both parents together.)

3. *Family Conferences.* There may also be occasions where the professional will want to discuss matters with, or observe interaction between, members of the family in various combinations.

4. *Conferences with the Child.* If a professional is called upon to make a recommendation to the court as to custody, he will want to speak to the child to glean his preference. To encourage candor and avoid embarrassment, this naturally should be done privately. A frank discussion with the child whereby his feelings and concerns can be explored may assuage his guilt or fears.

Essentials for All Approaches

Irrespective of the type(s) of conference employed, the following considerations should be borne in mind.

1. It is essential that the professional *see both parents*. In fact, it is often desirable that he see all of the children as well. Even parties acting in the best of faith ordinarily perceive the same set of circumstances very differently. Thus, it is impossible to obtain a true picture of the marriage merely by speaking to one parent. Likewise, the professional

should not assume that, irrespective of their good intentions, the essence of a discussion with one of the parents or with one of the children will be conveyed accurately to the other parent or to the siblings.

2. If at all possible, parents should be seen *both before and after* the divorce because different issues may predominate at different stages. For instance, the question of custody may be paramount before the divorce; afterward, child support may be the primary problem. Moreover, some conflict may be avoided or minimized by discussing potential problem areas at both times.

3. The *issues surrounding the divorce,* particularly those having the most direct impact upon the child˙ (typically, custody, support, and visitation) should be thoroughly explored with the parents. It is a grave error to assume that their attorneys will or should assume the role of behavioral scientists, even though not infrequently parents leave the divorce "entirely in the hands" of their lawyers. In addition to the personal help, the professional may also wish to provide the parents with written material such as Gardner's (see Chapter 24) that can alert them to some of the issues with which children are frequently concerned, and assist them in dealing with these. However, the professional must *avoid the temptation to simply give or recommend reading matter.* Practical discussion can be stimulated by asking the parents such questions as how they have explained the divorce to their children.

EXPLAINING THE NEED FOR A COURT

Where issues such as custody, support, or visitation are in controversy, need for a court to resolve them may be sufficiently obvious. Where parents are in agreement, however, they sometimes feel the requirement of going through a judicial proceeding is an imposition—even though under these circumstances the process is generally becoming less cumbersome. (Conversely, professionals are occasionally unduly critical of courts for being too quick to "rubber stamp" such accords as are reached by the parties.) Parents' hostility directed toward the "system" is often a complicating and counterproductive factor that the professional should seek to minimize. This task has become more difficult not only because questioning institutions has become more commonplace, but also because of such recent ideas as obtaining lay rather than legal advice, short-form divorces, and do-it-yourself divorce kits, not generally practical where children are involved.

Parents often have difficulty accepting the proposition that society has an interest where children are involved and that it is *through the courts that the children's interests are protected*. Parents, sometimes preoccupied with stress, fantasies, or their own trauma, or simply exercising poor judgment, may enter into agreements that are contrary to their child's best interests. Indeed, such agreements may reflect conscious or unconscious attempts to promote interests of their own. The professional should be on the lookout for situations involving agreements not in harmony with the child's interests. The following examples of what could happen without court involvement may help him to do this, and may also be of value in explaining the necessity of court to the parents.

1. Father agrees not to seek custody or disclose mother's alleged, and perhaps irrelevant, misconduct in return for mother's accepting nominal child support. Such an agreement virtually guarantees that the child will receive insufficient support—and perhaps that custody will be awarded to the wrong parent.

2. Father seeks a divorce because of mother's alleged failure as a wife; mother, possibly with his encouragement, concludes that she is also deficient as a parent and concedes custody to father. Even if she did in fact fall short as a spouse, mother may still be the parent to whom custody should be awarded.

3. Father and mother, unaware of such matters as appropriate child support or visitation, in good faith enter into an agreement that is unworkable or not advantageous to the child.

4. Parents agree on issues involving the children (e.g., visitation) but are subjected to outside pressures from relatives, friends, or even professionals, to act inappropriately. A court order, with implicit court support, can provide them with the face-saving device necessary to implement their good intentions.

Thus, courts play a vital role, not only in resolving disputes as to basic issues (e.g., custody, support, and visitation) but in scrutinizing accords that have been reached and in assisting parties to come to terms that are realistically in the best interests of their children.

EXPLAINING WHO IS INVOLVED

For most parents, divorce is a novel experience. Since preconceptions, perhaps garnered from the movies, newspapers, or television, may influence interactions between the parents or among parents, their respective attorneys, and court personnel, it is incumbent upon the professional to explain the roles of those who are involved in the divorce process.

1. The *behavioral professional.* Court social workers or other court professionals may make recommendations to the court, assist parents in the prevention and resolution of conflict, or both. The professional should not only carefully detail his function, but understand and be able to explain the function of other professionals who are likely to become involved. This means that if there is a court-connected program, professionals from other agencies should take the time to familiarize themselves with it so that they will not convey confusing misinformation to their clients.

2. The *judge* (or *referee*). The judge is ultimately responsible for all of the decisions, particularly those affecting the children. Generally, judges will adopt agreements arrived upon by the parties unless these appear to be contrary to the interests of the children. Judges are limited by the law, by the quality of their professional support, and by the information that is brought before them. While judges are human, with varying degrees of acumen, most can be expected to at least try to do what is right. However, they are neither behavioral scientists nor magicians, and they cannot guarantee that their orders will be carried out or easily enforced.

3. The *attorney.* Parents and professionals alike are often confused by the role of the parents' attorneys. The lawyer's primary duty is to *advocate the cause of his client.* This often requires him to support a position (e.g., with respect to custody) that is fundamentally opposed to the best interests of the children as these may be perceived by the behavioral professional. Nonetheless, the latter should understand and respect the attorney-client relationship and not be threatened or offended by it. Where either the attorney or the professional feels threatened by the other, the relationship between the parent and his lawyer or between the parent and the professional may be damaged. While the attorney is not a behavioral scientist, he is, in addition to being an advocate, also a counselor. Therefore, the professional who is able to establish rapport with the attorney may convince him of the merit of a particular position and the attorney, in turn, may be able to prevail upon his client to accept this.

Both parents sometimes refer to the same attorney as "their" lawyer. One of them may have had no contact with the attorney, accounting for this misconception. The professional should explain that while both parents may not necessarily have attorneys, a particular lawyer can represent only one parent, since the parents' interests are potentially adverse. In many instances, advising one of the parties to obtain legal counsel is providing an excellent service.

Only if the parents understand the roles of the personnel who will participate in the divorce can they translate these for the children. The professional should suggest to the parents areas of concern about which children may be reluctant to inquire: for instance, whether court personnel will realize that they are not the cause of the divorce. Also, parents should be advised to reassure their children that the court will not compel them to choose the parent with whom they are to live.

COPING WITH CUSTODY

Frequently, the most difficult and emotional issue in the divorce proceedings is the question of custody. *Motives for seeking custody* may be conscious or unconscious, mixed, vague, even irrational. A parent may seek custody because his child wants him to, because he doesn't want to be separated from his children, because he is convinced this would be best for his children, because of outside pressures, or because he feels this gives him bargaining leverage—even sufficient to prevent the divorce. He may seek it to vindicate himself, or to emerge as a "winner," or to make his spouse out as the "bad guy." Sometimes to assuage their feelings of guilt, parents contemplate essentially unrealistic custody arrangements such as changing custody at some future date. There are times when a parent will feel that custody should be awarded to him for reasons that are entirely irrelevant to the child's welfare or when a parent who is totally ill-equipped to handle custody will ask for it. Often both parents seek custody for the right reasons; sometimes neither parent does.

Since parents generally *have not experienced being a single parent,* they often have difficulty understanding the intellectual and emotional implications. Also, they are going through a period of stress whereby their judgment may be impaired. The professional must explain that custody means not only physical possession, but almost total responsibility for the raising of the child, and that custody must be decided on a realistic basis from the standpoint of the children's best interests.

The professional should have some familiarity with the law that is applicable in his state. For instance, Michigan's excellent child custody law designates a number of socio-psychological factors including love, affection, and emotional ties existing between parent and child, as well as the child's preference, to be considered in establishing custody.

In some cases, it will be clear to the professional which parent is the logical choice as custodian. Then it is ordinarily incumbent upon him to help both parents recognize that. This may prevent an unnecessary custody contest that would be emotionally taxing to parents and children and likely to leave a bitter aftertaste.

Moreover, unresolved custody ordinarily has an unsettling effect on the child. Consequently, the sooner this issue is decided, the less damage is likely to occur. The parents are then in a better position to prepare their child for the divorce. This, naturally, includes telling him who will be custodian, and usually why (so as to dispel any doubts about the other parent's interest) and assuring him that his relationship with the noncustodial parent will be preserved. Once the custody question is out of the way, other problems likely to be faced by both custodial and noncustodial parents (e.g., support and visitation) can more easily be concentrated upon.

Since parents inexperienced with the single parent situation are apt to fantasy with respect to it, assistance is sometimes best provided by dealing with hypothetical, but typical, situations. For example, one might ask the custodial parent what he would do if he became ill and needed someone to care for the child or if the child were to say he no longer wanted to live with him.

Of course, there will be instances where both parents, sometimes with considerable justification, are determined to seek custody. Frequently, a custody hearing properly handled by a judge or referee will be the most appropriate means of resolving the issue in these cases, both from the standpoint of reaching the right result and with respect to the feelings of both of the parents and the children. Here the child should be told that *both parents want him* and that the court will be deciding who gets custody. Particularly in these situations it is important to help the parents realize that once custody has been determined, they must *regroup* to work together *for the children's welfare*. A residue of bitterness following a custody contest is always possible, but by no means inevitable.

COPING WITH THE SUPPORT ISSUE

The economic problem is often the most troublesome and frustrating one engendered by the divorce. Focusing upon benefits to be derived from terminating the marriage, and upon issues that must be decided prior to judgment, parents frequently fail to face up to the *economic realities* of the situation confronting them. The noncustodial parent is generally required to make specified child support payments to the custodial parent on a regular basis. Whatever formula is employed for determining the amount of these payments, sooner or later custodial parents often find this inadequate, and noncustodial parents, with comparable frequency, find it excessive. From their respective vantage points, there may be some justification for both positions.

Generally, irrespective of whether one or both parents had been working, the family had pooled its income during the marriage and lived at a level commensurate with its earnings. No matter how it is divided, that same income supporting two households will almost invariably result in a *lower level of living for both* of the parents and for the children. This in itself is a bitter enough pill to swallow, but, furthermore, the need to deny a child material things in addition to denying him one of his parents can induce or rekindle feelings of guilt and hostility. Often, to even approach a comparable level of living it is necessary for the parent who has not been working to start.

After the divorce, noncustodial parents who remarry sometimes feel that their second family should come first, or that the remarriage of their former spouse should exonerate them from the support obligation, laws to the contrary notwithstanding.

Facing up to these realities ahead of time will not change the arithmetic, but denying them is likely to cause the parties to plan unrealistically or otherwise act in an inappropriate manner. Sometimes, the custodial parent contemplates remaining in a residence that the parties could barely afford when they were living together. The parents need to understand the economic realities, deal with them reasonably and intelligently, and discuss the subject candidly with their children. Adolescents may have a distorted view of the reasons for their family's financial situation anyway, and if, accordingly, they assign blame to either parent, this is not likely to help anyone.

While rationalizations for doing so are innumerable, nonpayment of child support is ordinarily grossly *unfair to the child* and likely to impair the noncustodial parent's relationship with him as well. Perhaps the most common excuse offered for not paying is denial of access to the child by the custodial parent. Often this is nothing more than a self-serving pretext. In any event, noncustodial parents should realize that since the child is entitled to both visitation and support, denial of one cannot possibly justify depriving him of both. By like token, custodial parents should be reminded that irrespective of the fact that visitation and support are entirely separate issues, encouraging a close relationship between the child and his noncustodial parent is likely to enhance their prospects of continuing to receive child support payments in timely manner.

COPING WITH THE VISITATION ISSUE

Considerations with respect to visitation frequently receive inadequate attention during the divorce proceedings. Parents often perceive this as merely a right of the noncustodial parent. Thus, it is essential for the professional to make them realize that *visitation is vitally important to and, essentially, the right of the child.* Particularly today, both parents often participate to a considerable extent in the raising of their children and develop close ties to them at an early age. The detrimental effects of separation through divorce may be significantly minimized if the child is able to maintain a meaningful relationship with both parents. This means that the professional should encourage the noncustodial parent to continue to see his child on a regular basis after the divorce, and also encourage the custodial parent to facilitate these visits.

To the child, continued contact with the noncustodial parent may be proof of his continued love. (See Chapter 24 for more about the importance of both parents.) Moreover, visitation minimizes the likelihood of the child's creating fantasized images of his absent parent or becoming obsessed with an unwholesome desire to search him out. While visitation must be considered primarily from the standpoint of the child's welfare, it may also be important to the noncustodial parent, minimizing his own sense of loss, as well as to the custodial parent, in that this enables the noncustodial parent to share in the very difficult child-raising process.

At the time of the divorce, the professional is in an excellent position to discuss with the parents both the importance of visitation and *potential problems* surrounding it. Parents should be reminded that even the most wholesome visitation will entail some inconvenience, involving adjustment of schedules to accommodate both parents and the children. (For this reason, the visitation provision in the divorce judgment should ordinarily be couched in general terms.) Parents frequently see visitation as an opportunity to quiz their child with respect to each other's activities, or to compete with one another for the child's affection. Relatives and friends may exert pressure on the custodial parent to terminate visitation. Noncustodial parents may fail to show up for visitation, with devastating consequences for the child. Sometimes custodial parents either deny or subtly discourage visitation.

Visitation also creates some difficulty for the child, involving separation from both his custodial and noncustodial parents. Parents should be advised that acting out does not necessarily mean that a visit was unsuccessful; this may be a reaction to the loss of the noncustodial parent. In any event, parents should be encouraged to discuss visitation with their children, both during and after the divorce. This may help the children to understand that both parents are sympathetic to their feelings and willing to assist them in regard to a difficult situation.

It may be helpful to pose hypothetical problems to both parents pertaining to visitation (e.g., scheduled visitation conflicts with a commitment of parent or child) and discuss with them how these might be handled. Also, in some instances parents will welcome assistance in developing an initial visitation schedule.

HELPING PARENTS DEAL WITH OTHER PROBLEMS

1. In arriving upon the decision to obtain a divorce, parents are bound to focus upon the benefits to be derived from terminating the marriage and, correspondingly, direct *insufficient attention* to the fact that *new problems* are likely to emerge. This is not to suggest either that the divorce was inappropriate or that the new problems will necessarily be as difficult to cope with as the old. However, parents should be cautioned not to expect the divorce to be a panacea.

2. The professional should help the parents to recognize that merely severing their legal ties will not result in automatic dissolution of emotional ties. They must deal with one another not only with respect to routine matters such as support and visitation, but also regarding eventual crises in the children's lives and significant changes in their own. Parents should be cautioned that particularly during transitional periods they are vulnerable to conflict and, ironically, that it is during just such periods that the children need conflict minimized. Accordingly, crises in the children's lives, or changes in their own, should not be seized upon as opportunities for blame or recrimination. (See Chapter 24 for more about criticism of ex-spouses.) During such periods (just as in the case of married parents) it is particularly important that the parties pull

together to do what is best for their children, even if they need to seek professional assistance to do it.

3. Along these lines, the court worker should be prepared to refer to such community resources as a Child Guidance Clinic or Family Service Agency. Sometimes when immediate referral is not called for, parents should be advised of the existence of those agencies that they can turn to should the need arise. Sometimes parents are so emotionally drained by the divorce that they may neither recognize the need for treatment nor possess the capacity to seek it out. The professional should be in a position to ease the referral and establish a liaison with the other agency. However, to take maximum advantage of community resources, he should be more than casually familiar with their staffing and programs.

4. Implicit in the foregoing is the fact that, at the time of the divorce, it is often very *difficult for parents to recognize*, let alone deal appropriately with, the *feelings of their children*. Especially if parents suggest that the children have said nothing about the divorce or incidents related to it, this is a strong indication that the chlidren's feelings are not being dealt with. (Detailed suggestions for helping parents deal with the children's feelings are found in Chapter 24 by Gardner.)

Index

405